ULTIMATE KEYBOARD CHORD BOOK

2 How to Use This book

3 Chord Construction

6 Extensions and Alterations

8 Other Chord Types

9 Introduction to Chord Voicing

12 Chord Chart

14 C Chords

26 C#/D♭ Chords

38 D Chords

50 E♭ Chords

62 E Chords

74 F Chords

86 F#/G♭ Chords

98 G Chords

110 A♭ Chords

122 A Chords

134 B♭ Chords

146 B /C♭ Chords

ISBN 978-0-7935-5144-6

7777 W. Bluemound Rd. P.O. Box 13819 Milwaukee, WI 53213

HOW TO USE THIS BOOK

In the early part of this century, the average popular pianist had relatively few chords to worry about. Things have changed a great deal since then. Today, pianists must know how to construct an astounding assortment of chords. The Ultimate Keyboard Chord Book is a valuable resource that will help in a number of ways:

- **as a chord dictionary**

  If you find a chord you are not familiar with, look it up in this book. If you compose music and create chords, this book will also help you to determine proper chord spelling.

- **as an introductory chord voicing guide**

  Learning the notes of the chords is only "half the battle." Learning how to *voice* chords is also essential to effectively use them. This book provides many helpful suggestions on ways to voice chords.

- **as a resource for improvisers and non-pianists**

  A working knowledge of chords is essential to becoming an effective improviser. This book will help you to visualize possible note choices when improvising. Non-pianists may want to practice outlining the chords in the book as a way to better understand and conceptualize chords and harmony.

CHORD CONSTRUCTION

Learning about intervals is a key element in learning how to construct chords. An interval describes the distance between two notes. The distance from the note C to the note D is a second. The distance from C to E is a third, and so on. The real difficulty with intervals is determining whether an interval is major, minor, perfect, augmented or diminished. The reason intervals are so helpful is that, once you are comfortable visualizing intervals, it will be easy to construct any type of chord in any key. It is important to understand that all similar chords contain similar intervals. For example, a C major triad contains a root, major third, and perfect fifth. Therefore, any major triad will contain a root, major third, and perfect fifth. Look at the example in figure one. You will notice that, in a C major scale (or any other major scale), some intervals are *perfect* and some intervals are *major*. The reason for this is beyond the scope of this book. Suffice it to say that the intervals presented in this chapter are the result of many centuries of theory development. Just remember that fourths, fifths, octaves, and elevenths are perfect, and all other intervals in a major scale are major.

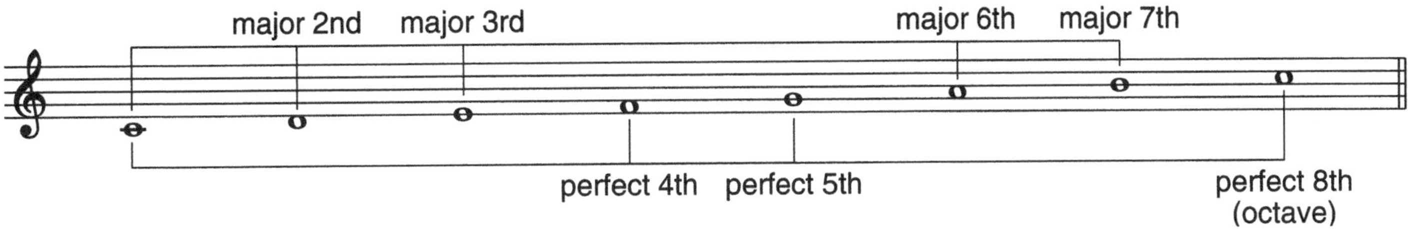

Fig. 1

A critical point to consider when learning about intervals is what happens when we alter an interval such as a perfect fifth. Consider the perfect fifth from the note C to G. What happens if we make the G a G sharp? In this case the interval becomes an *augmented* fifth. In other words, the space (or *interval*) between notes has been augmented. In this example, if the note G were a G flat, the interval would still be a fifth (C to G is always a fifth), but in this instance, the interval would be a *diminished* fifth. In other words, the interval between notes has been diminished. The following example shows the terminology for altering major and perfect intervals. Note that the only difference between the two types of intervals is that when you make a major interval smaller, it becomes *minor*. When you make a perfect interval smaller, it becomes *diminished*. Other than this one distinction, the terminology for major and perfect intervals is the same. Note that the minor interval becomes diminished when made smaller.

Fig. 2

Understanding the theory behind intervals is one thing, being able to utilize intervals in your playing is another. You may find it helpful to use some tricks to be able to comfortably visualize intervals. Begin by learning perfect fifths and major thirds. All other intervals can easily be related to these primary intervals. Regarding perfect fifths: with only two exceptions, both notes in a perfect fifth will share the same accidental. In the following example, you can see that the only fifths that don't follow this rule are B♭ to F and B to F♯.

Fig. 3

Major thirds are also easy to find. To find a major third, count up two whole steps from any note. The following example illustrates common major thirds:

Fig. 4

The following is a list of tricks to find common intervals:

- Major second: Count up one whole step from any note.
- Minor third: Lower the top note of any major third by one half step.
- Perfect fourth: Count down one whole step from the top note of any perfect fifth.
- Major sixth: Count up one whole step from any perfect fifth interval.
- Minor seventh: A whole step "shy" of an octave.
- Major seventh: A half step "shy" of an octave.
- Major ninth: Same note as a major second but an octave higher.
- Perfect eleventh: Same note as a perfect fourth but one octave higher.
- Major thirteenth: Same as a sixth but an octave higher.

As you can see, intervals are relatively easy to learn. The next step is to learn to construct chords using intervals.

Triads are chords consisting of three notes. The primary triads are major, minor, diminished, and augmented. Major and minor triads are most prevalent in music today. Note that in figure five, both the major and minor triads contain a perfect fifth interval. The only difference is the interval of a third: major triads contain a major third, minor triads contain a minor third. As you can see, a diminished triad contains a minor third and a diminished fifth. The augmented triad contains a major third and an augmented fifth.

Fig. 5

In the previous example, the root of each triad was the note C. This brings up an important point regarding construction of chords: Is the root always the lowest note? Unlike figured bass chord construction in traditional theory, the root may not always be the lowest note in popular music chord nomenclature. The root is always the lowest note in terms of chord construction (building a chord using intervals), but the root may not always be placed as the lowest note of the chord. Play the following chords:

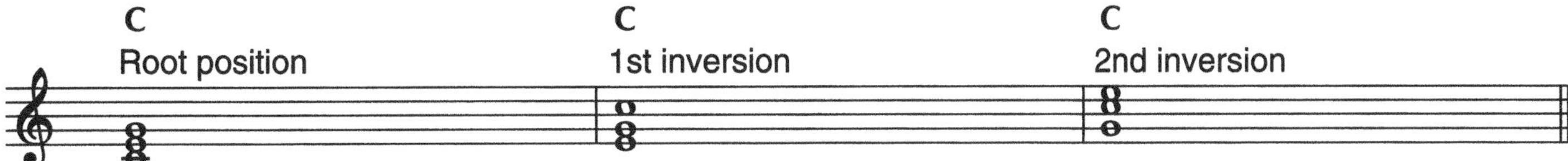

Fig. 6

In this example, the order of notes in the original C major triad has changed, but the chords still sound like the original C major chord. These new varieties of C major triads are called *inversions.* In the previous example, the triads may be described as *root position, first inversion,* and *second inversion.* **To invert any chord, raise the bottom note one octave or lower the top note one octave**. Generally, triads and seventh chords are the only chords that may be practically inverted. More complex chord inversions may be easily handled by adding notes to a simple triad or seventh chord inversion. As you will see, it is also common to omit some notes when inverting more complex chords.

There may be occasions where you would like to hear a chord with a tone other than the root in the bass register. In these cases, notate the name of the chord and use a slash to signify the bass note. C/G would be interpreted as a C major triad over the bass note G. Incidentally, notes other than chord tones may also be used. The chord F/G, for example, is common in popular music today. When inverting chords, be aware that the quality of chord may change if a note other than the root occurs in the bass register. A first inversion C major chord may sound different if placed below middle C on the piano. In this case, the lowest note (E) may start to sound like a root. The best way to determine the difference between a simple inversion and an actual change of chord type is through experimentation. Play chords and inversions in the lower register of the piano. You will start to get a sense of how range can alter the quality of a chord.

Seventh chords are common in many styles of music. The term "seventh chord" refers to triads that also contain an interval of a seventh. If you can construct basic triads, seventh chords are relatively easy to spell. Figure seven lists some common seventh chords.

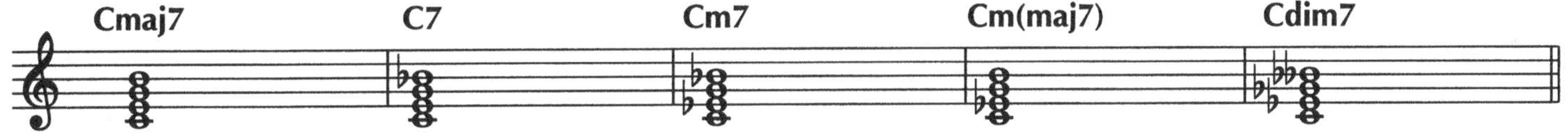

Fig. 7

Some tricks to remember:

- Major 7 chord: major triad and major seventh interval (Remember: a major seventh is a half step shy of an octave)
- Minor 7 chord: minor triad and minor seventh
- Major/minor 7: minor triad with major seventh
- 7 chord: major triad with minor seventh interval
- Diminished 7: diminished triad with diminished seventh interval (chord is constructed entirely from minor third intervals)

To this point, we have considered a variety of triads and seventh chords. Students would be advised to study construction of these chord types as well as inversions for the basic triads and seventh chords. Inversions for these chords may be found in the dictionary portion of the The Ultimate Keyboard Chord Book. In the next few pages we will look at concepts relating to *extensions* and *alterations.*

EXTENSIONS AND ALTERATIONS

An extension refers to an interval greater than a seventh that is added to a chord. Examples of extensions are ninths, elevenths, and thirteenths. The term alteration refers to a chord where one of the primary intervals has been altered. We have already seen examples of altered chords. In the preceding section, a major triad had been altered to include an augmented (altered) fifth. The resulting chord was a C augmented (+) triad.

Questions often arise around the concept of extensions. An interval of a ninth is the same as a major second plus one octave. Why is it that ninth chords are not notated as "2nd" chords? The answer lies in the fact that our chord system is built around a concept of *tertian* harmony — chords built in thirds. A triad may contain a root, third, and fifth. A seventh chord contains a root, third, fifth, and seventh. A ninth chord contains a root, third, fifth, seventh, and ninth, and so on. Although there are a few exceptions, the basic rule is as follows: the higher the extension number, the more potential chord tones may be included in a voicing. To better understand this concept, visualize the difference between a C6 chord and a C13 chord. Although these chords might seem similar, the C6 chord is a simple major triad with an interval of a major sixth added. The C13 chord contains a minor seventh and major ninth interval in addition to a major triad. In the following example, note that no eleventh is present in the C13 chord. In the strictest technical sense the eleventh could be used. In this case the reason for excluding it is simple — it sounds bad.

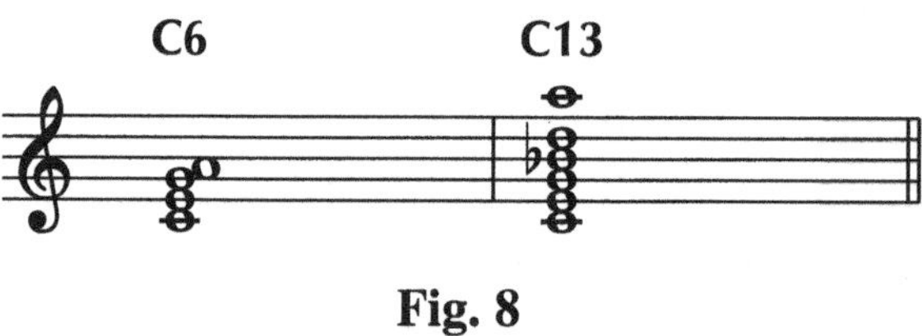

Fig. 8

Ninth chords are chords that contain an interval of a ninth. In most cases, these chords are four-note seventh chords that contain an interval of a major ninth. An important concept to remember when dealing with ninth chords is the following: major ninths are always added to chords unless otherwise specified. In the following example, notice how all of the example chords use the same major ninth interval — a D in this case.

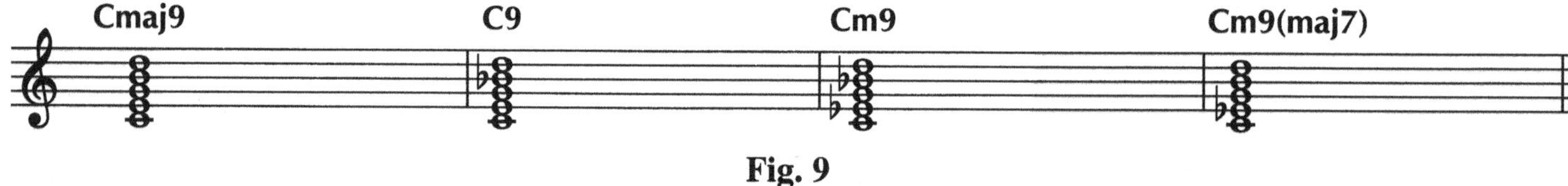

Fig. 9

There will be occasions where a minor or augmented ninth will be used, but this will always be specified with a qualifier such as + or # 9, - or flat 9. Ninth chords can often be a point of confusion for students. With a chord such as a Cm9, you might expect that the ninth of this chord would be a minor ninth. In this case, the ninth is still a major ninth. Just remember that ninths are always major unless otherwise specified. An easy way to tell the type of underlying chord quality for any ninth chord is to replace 9 with 7. For example, an Fm9 is really an Fm7 with a major ninth added. A B9 is really a B7 with a major ninth added.

Eleventh chords are not as common as ninth chords. An easy way to find a perfect eleventh is to count down one whole step from the top note of a perfect fifth interval. An eleventh is the same as a perfect fourth plus an octave. It is interesting to note that the interval of an eleventh is typically altered. In common practice, the only time a perfect eleventh is added is over a minor seventh or minor ninth chord. A Cm11 chord contains a Cm7 chord, major ninth and a perfect eleventh.

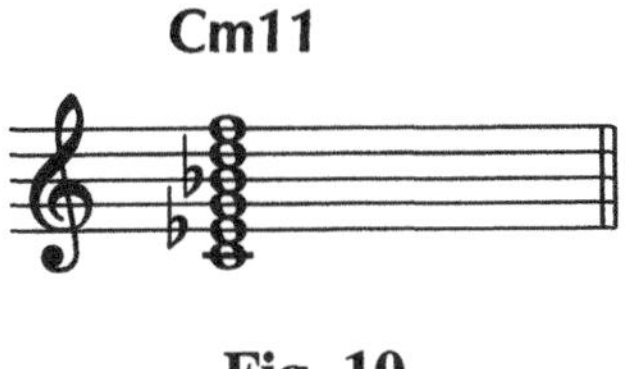

Fig. 10

An augmented eleventh may also be found. This interval is often used in conjunction with major ninth chords and dominant ninth chords. Although the interval of an augmented eleventh is an enharmonic equivalent to a diminished fifth, in the following example you can see that both a perfect fifth and augmented eleventh are used.

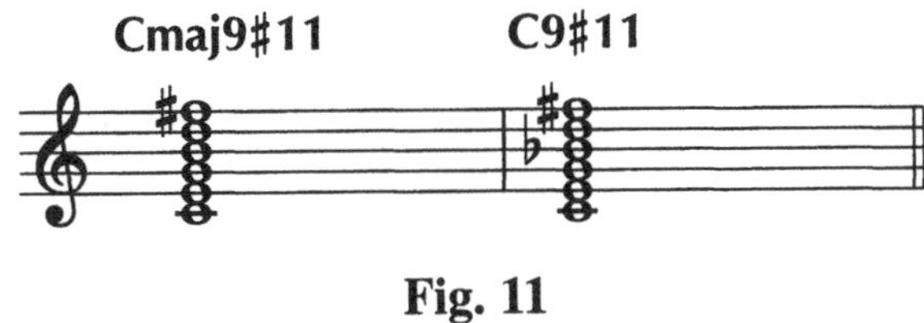

Fig. 11

There is one other variety of eleventh chord that may cause some confusion. A C11 chord looks as if it may have evolved from a C7 or C9 chord. This is true, but unlike other examples to this point, the third is always omitted for this type of chord. A better way to describe this type of chord would be Gm7/C or C9sus.

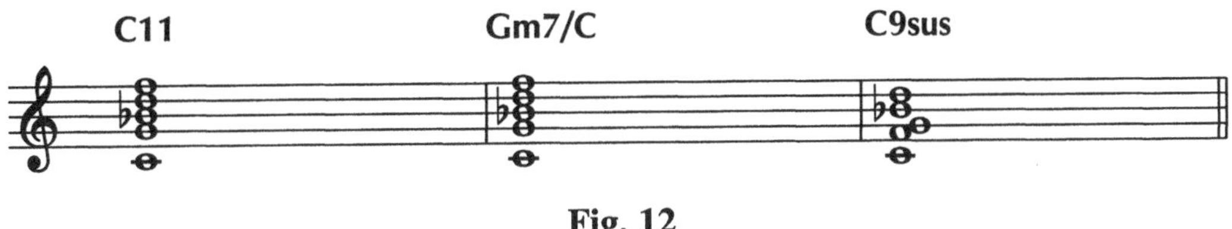

Fig. 12

The last type of extension chord we will look at are thirteenth chords. Like ninth chords, the interval of a thirteenth will always be a major thirteenth unless otherwise noted. The most common thirteenth chord is the "dominant thirteenth." A major thirteenth chord is also fairly common.

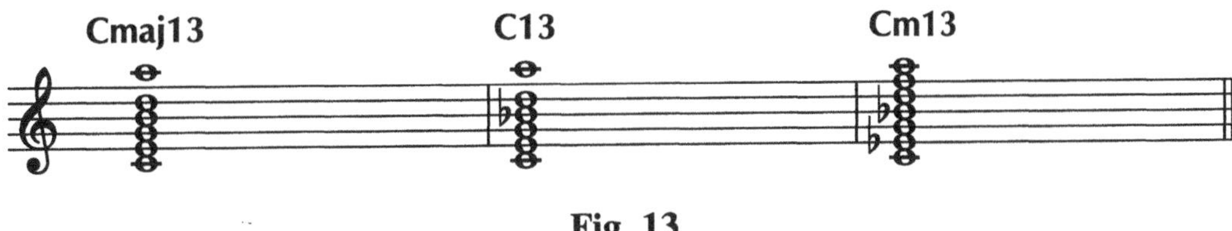

Fig. 13

Notice the absence of an eleventh in these chords. It is customary to omit the eleventh on dominant or major thirteenth chords because the eleventh conflicts with the third.

OTHER CHORD TYPES

There are a great many chords that don't fit nicely into a major or minor category. Unlike major and minor triads and seventh chords, many of these chords may not be built in thirds. Sus4 and sus2 chords are two such examples. The sus4 chord has its roots in Renaissance harmony. At that point in time, *suspensions* were a common device. In a 4-3 suspension, an interval of a perfect fourth resolves to an interval of a third. In our modern equivalent, a perfect fourth is used instead of a major or minor third. The sus2 chord is similar. Here, a major second is used instead of a major or minor third.

Fig. 14

Intervals are sometimes added to a simple triad. In a C(add9) chord for example, an interval of a major ninth is added to a simple major triad. This chord is similar to a Csus2 with the exception that a C(add9) chord contains a major third.

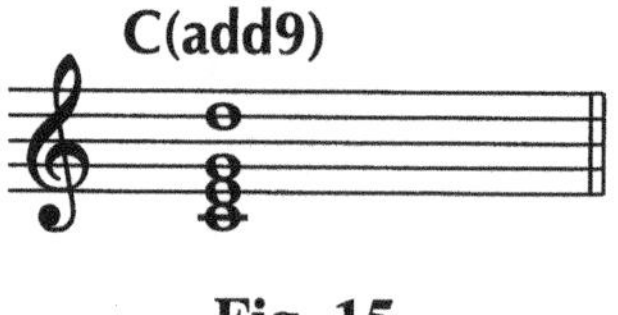

Fig. 15

The interval of a sixth is another common interval that may be added to triads. This is so common that the "add6" qualifier is not needed. A C6 may be interpreted as a C major triad with a major sixth added. A Cm6 would be a C minor triad with a major sixth added. A major ninth may also be added. Note that in all of the following chords, sixths and ninths are added to basic major or minor triads — no seventh is used.

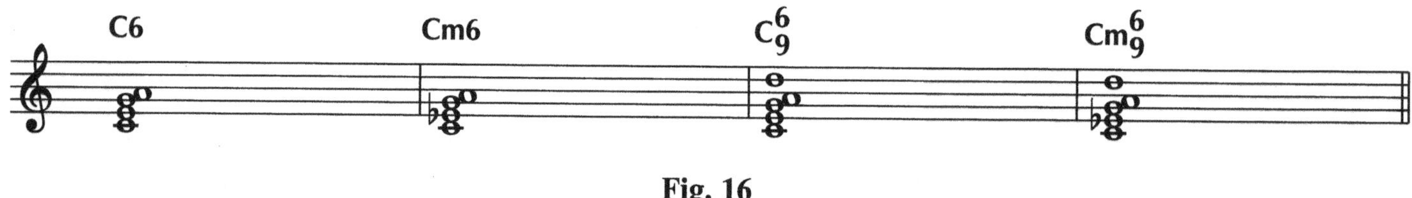

Fig. 16

There is one other chord variety that should be mentioned in this section on chord construction. In some styles of popular music, it is customary to use "power chords" — chords that are not major or minor. In these cases, only a root and perfect fifth are used. A C5 chord, for example, would contain only the notes C and G.

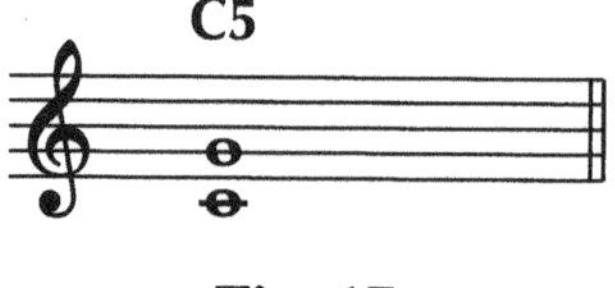

Fig. 17

To conclude this portion of the text, let's review some of the important concepts.

- Intervals are key to learning proper chord construction.
- Perfect fifths and major thirds are two helpful intervals — most other intervals can be found by counting up or down whole and half steps from these intervals.
- Triads are three-note chords.
- The most common triads are major, minor, diminished, and augmented.
- Seventh chords extend basic triads by adding the interval of a seventh. There are a great variety of seventh chords, but the most helpful to learn are: major7, minor7, 7, and diminished 7.
- Extensions may be added to seventh chords. Possible extension notes are the ninth, eleventh, and thirteenth.
- Chord tones may be altered. Augmented and diminished fifths are two examples of altered chord tones.

INTRODUCTION TO CHORD VOICING

Learning the notes of chords is only one facet of actually using chords effectively. Deciding how to "voice" or organize the notes of a given chord can be a daunting task. Many variables must be considered — range, spacing, complexity, and context. This section will provide some suggestions on common voicing techniques.

An important concept to understand when voicing chords is the fact that no specific order of notes is implied. A C9 chord does contain the note D (the ninth). The D may not actually be placed a ninth higher than the root. In some cases it might be next to the root. The key here is to understand that a chord name describes the construction (in root position) of the chord. It does not imply a specific order of notes.

Close or "tight" voicings generally work fine in the mid and upper range of the piano, but as you move to the lower register the voicings will need to "open up." Figure 18 demonstrates a few common left hand structures. Notice how the interval between notes is fairly large in these examples.

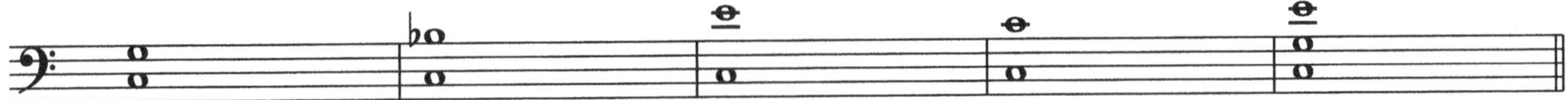

Fig. 18

In the next example, the right hand is voiced using "close" harmony. This works well because the right hand is in the middle register of the piano.

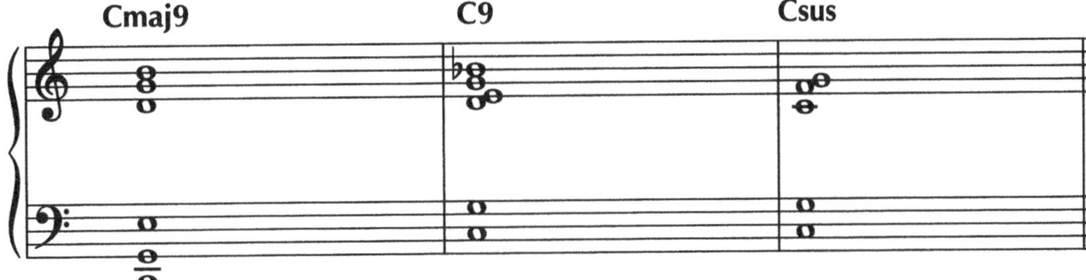

Fig. 19

It is important to avoid changing the quality of chord by placing notes other than the root in the bass register. In the following example, the first chord will sound like an Am7, not a C6. The reason for this is that the note A sounds like a root because of its position in the chord.

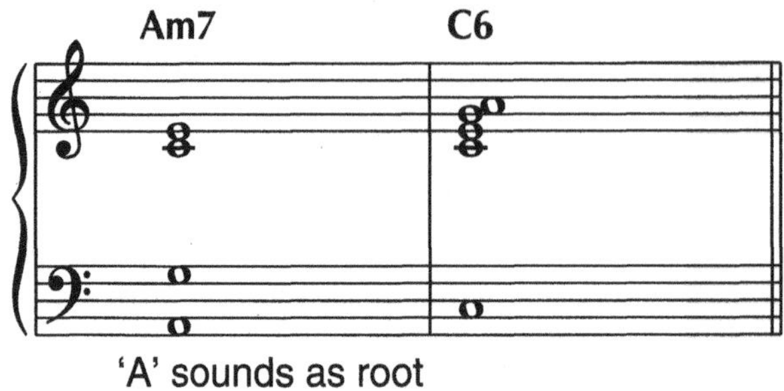

Fig. 20

One of the best ways to learn about voicing chords is to work with four-note seventh chords. The Ultimate Keyboard Chord Book lists inversions for the primary seventh chords. Learn these inversions and you will find it is easy to voice more complex chords by adding tones to these primary inversions. The next few suggestions will apply to four-note voicings in the right hand. These suggestions are also applicable to mid-range left hand voicings as well.

- To add a ninth, drop the root.
- To add a thirteenth, drop the fifth.
- To add a #11, drop the fifth

The term "drop" can mean two different things. You can drop the note to the left hand or you may even omit the note. The next example demonstrates this concept. Notice how each of the chords derives from a more basic seventh chord inversion.

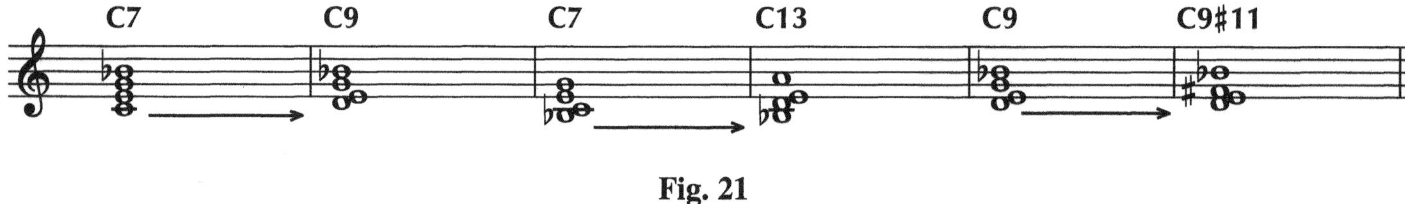

Fig. 21

The following demonstrates some possible voicings using a variety of notes in both the left and right hand. In these voicings, "dropped" notes are placed in the left hand.

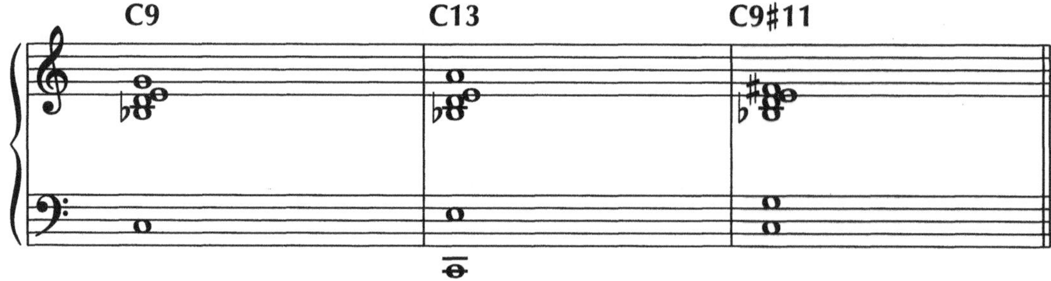

Fig. 22

When trying to voice a complex chord such as a ninth, eleventh, or thirteenth, there are some tricks that may be helpful. For these type of chords, use the third, fifth, seventh, and ninth in the right hand. This is always a good starting point. Extensions and alterations may be applied to this basic structure.

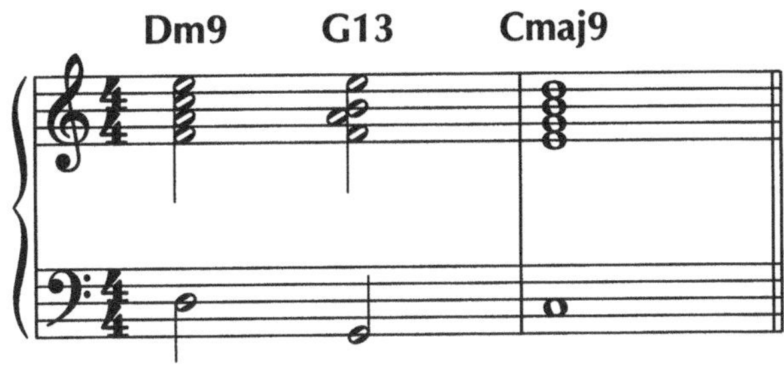

Fig. 23

Another common structure are "drop 2" voicings. To make a drop 2, lower the second note from the top of any close position voicing one octave. Two inversions are particularly helpful: 3-7-9-5 and 7-3-5-9.

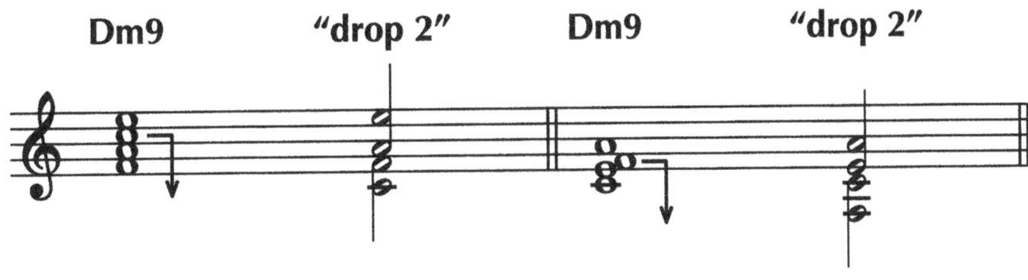

Fig. 24

As you can see, learning to construct and voice chords is not an easy task. The Ultimate Keyboard Chord Book will be a valuable reference for learning chords. You will find an extensive listing of chords and inversions of primary triads and seventh chords. Learn the inversions, and it will be relatively easy to construct and voice even the most complex chord.

m = minor interval d = diminished interval a = augmented interval
All other intervals are major or perfect

Chord Chart

Chord	Alternate Names	Spelling
C	CM, Cmaj., CΔ, Cmajor	1,3,5
Cm	Cmi., Cmin., C-	1,m3,5
C+	Caug., C+5, C(#5)	1,3,#5
Cdim	C°, C diminished	1,m3,d5
Csus	Csus4	1,4,5
C(♭5)	C(-5)	1,3,d5
Csus2	C2	1,2,5
C6	Cmaj.6, Cadd6	1,3,5,6
C(add2)	C(add9)	1,2,3,5
Cmaj7	CΔ7, CM7, Cma7	1,3,5,7
Cmaj7♭5	CΔ7♭5, CM7(-5), Cma7(♭5)	1,3,d5,7
Cmaj7#5	CΔ7#5, CM7(+5), Cma7(#5)	1,3,a5,7
C7	none	1,3,5,m7
C7♭5	C7-5	1,3,d5,m7
C7#5	C+7, C7+, C7+5	1,3,a5,m7
C7sus	C7sus4	1,4,5,m7
Cm(add2)	Cm2, C-2	1,2,m3,5
Cm6	Cm(add6), C-6	1,m3,5,6
Cm7	C-7, Cmi7, Cmin7	1,m3,5,m7
Cm(maj7)	C-(Δ7), Cmi(ma7)	1,m3,5,7
Cm7♭5	Cø7, Cm7-5	1,m3,d5,m7
Cdim7	C°7	1,m3,d5,d7
Cdim(maj7)	C°(maj7)	1,m3,d5,7
C5	C(no 3rd)	1,5
C6,9	C6/9, C6(add9)	1,3,5,6,9
Cmaj6,9	CΔ9(add6)	1,3,5,6,7,9
Cmaj7#11	CΔ7(#11)	1,3,5,7,a11
Cmaj9	CΔ9, CM9, Cma9	1,3,5,7,9
Cmaj9♭5	CΔ9♭5, Cma9(-5)	1,3,d5,7,9
Cmaj9#5	CΔ9#5, Cma9(+5)	1,3,a5,7,9
Cmaj9#11	CΔ9#11, Cma9(+11)	1,3,5,7,9,a11
Cmaj13	CΔ13, Cma13	1,3,5,7,9,13
Cmaj13♭5	CΔ13♭5, Cma13(-5)	1,3,d5,7,9,13
Cmaj13#11	CΔ13#11, Cma13(+11)	1,3,5,7,9,a11,13
C7♭9	C7(-9)	1,3,5,m7,m9
C7#9	C7(+9)	1,3,5,m7,a9
C7#11	C7(+11)	1,3,5,m7,a11
C7♭5(♭9)	C7(-5,-9)	1,3,d5,m7,m9
C7♭5(#9)	C7(-5,+9)	1,3,d5,m7,a9
C7#5(♭9)	C7(+5,-9)	1,3,a5,m7,m9
C7#5(#9)	C7(+5,+9)	1,3,a5,m7,a9
C7♭9(#9)	C7(-9,+9)	1,3,5,m7,m9,a9
C7(add13)	C13(no 9)	1,3,5,m7,13
C7♭13	C7(-13)	1,3,5,m7,m13
C7♭9(#11)	C7(-9,+11)	1,3,5,m7,m9,a11
C7#9(#11)	C7(+9,+11)	1,3,5,m7,a9,a11

C7♭9(♭13)	C7(-9,-13)	1,3,5,m7,m9,m13
C7#9(♭13)	C7(+9,-13)	1,3,5,m7,a9,m13
C7#11(♭13)	C7(+11,-13)	1,3,5,m7,a11,m13
C7♭9(#9,#11)	C7(-9,+9,+11)	1,3,5,m7,m9,a9,a11
C9	none	1,3,5,m7,9
C9(♭5)	C9(-5)	1,3,d5,m7,9
C9#5	C9+, C+9	1,3,a5,m7,9
C9#11	C9(+11)	1,3,5,m7,9,a11
C9♭13	C9(-13)	1,3,5,m7,9,m13
C9#11(♭13)	C9(+11,-13)	1,3,5,m7,9,a11,m13
C11	C9sus4, Gm7/C	1,5,m7,9,11
C13	none	1,3,5,m7,9,13
C13♭5	C13(-5)	1,3,d5,m7,9,13
C13♭9	C13(-9)	1,3,5,m7,m9,13
C13#9	C13(+9)	1,3,5,m7,a9,13
C13#11	C13(+11)	1,3,5,m7,9,a11,13
C13(sus4)	C13sus	1,4,5,m7,9,13
Cm(#5)	Cm+5	1,m3,a5
Cm69	Cmi6(add9)	1,m3,5,6,9
Cm7(add4)	Cm7(add11)	1,m3,5,m7,11
Cm7♭5(♭9)	Cø7(-9)	1,m3,d5,m7,m9
Cm9	C-9, Cmin9	1,m3,5,m7,9
Cm9(maj7)	C-(Δ7), Cmi(ma7)	1,m3,5,7
Cm9(♭5)	Cø9, C-7(-5)	1,m3,d5,m7,9
Cm11	Cmin11, C-11	1,m3,5,m7,9,11
Cm13	C-13, Cmin13	1,m3,5,m7,9,11,13
Cdim7(add9)	C°7(add9)	1,m3,d5,d7,9
Cm11♭5	Cø11, C-11(♭5)	1,m3,d5,m7,9,11
Cm11(maj7)	C-11(maj7), C-11(D7)	1,m3,5,7,9,11
C7alt.	C7altered	1,3,5,m7,m9,a9,a11,m13

C CHORDS

C

Root Position

1st Inversion

2nd Inversion

Cm

Root Position

1st Inversion

2nd Inversion

C+

Root Position

1st Inversion

2nd Inversion

Cdim

Root Position

1st Inversion

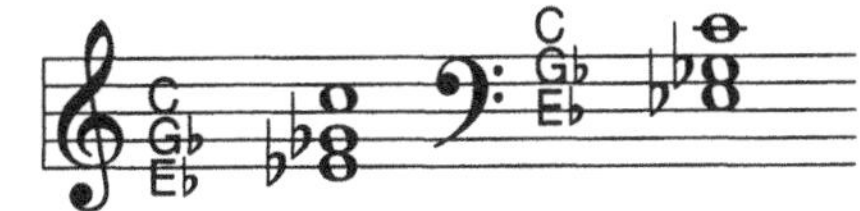

2nd Inversion

Csus

Root Position

1st Inversion

2nd Inversion

C(♭5)

Root Position

1st Inversion

2nd Inversion

Csus2

Root Position

1st Inversion

2nd Inversion

C6

Root Position

1st Inversion

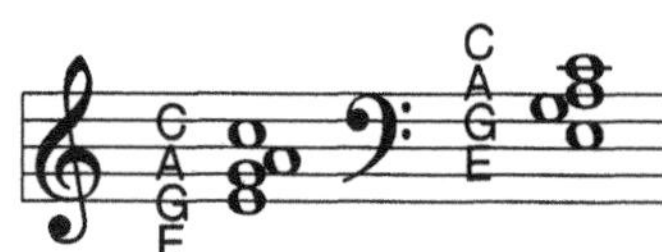

2nd Inversion

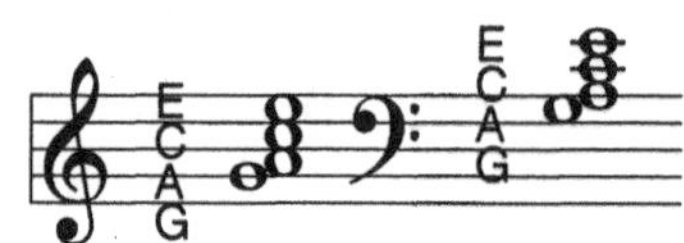

3rd Inversion

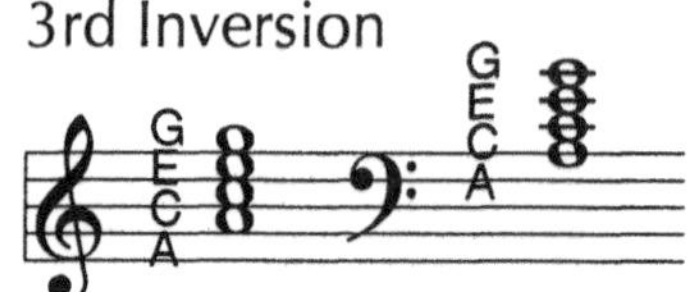

C(add2), C(add9)

Root Position

1st Inversion

2nd Inversion

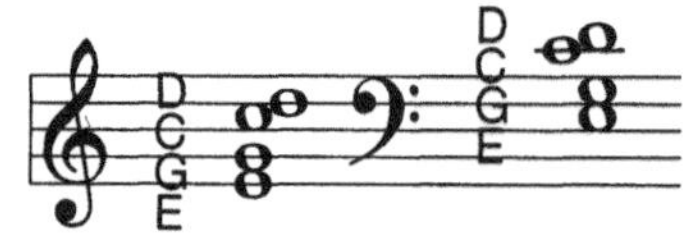

3rd Inversion

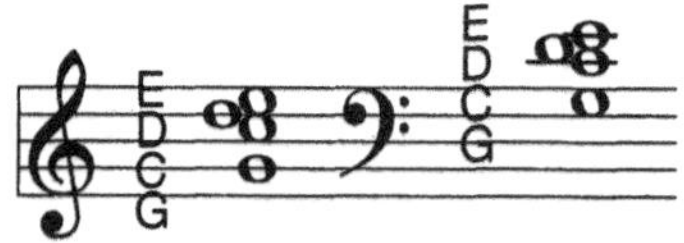

Cmaj7

Root Position

1st Inversion

2nd Inversion

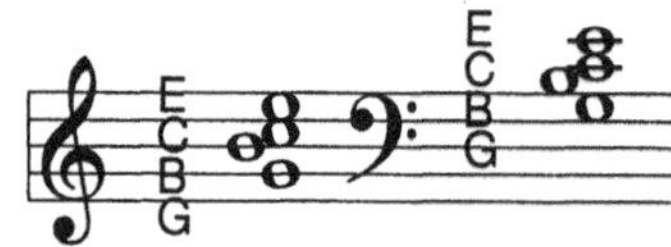

3rd Inversion

Cmaj7♭5

Root Position

1st Inversion

2nd Inversion

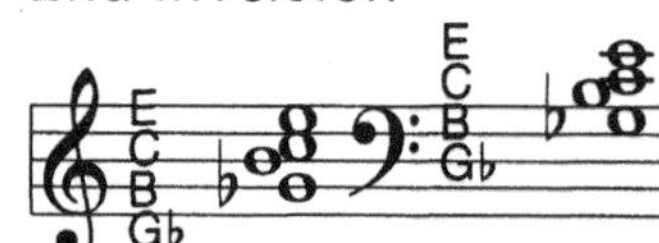

3rd Inversion

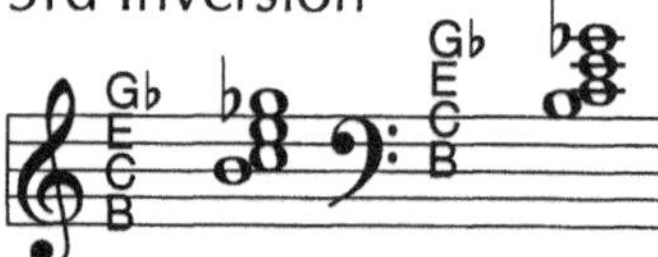

Cmaj7♯5

Root Position

1st Inversion

2nd Inversion

3rd Inversion

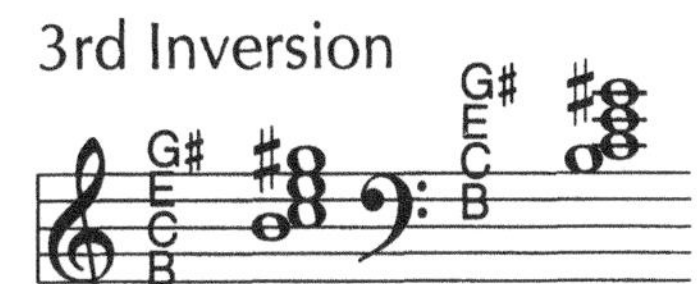

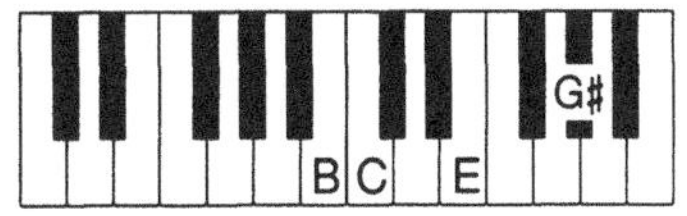

C7

Root Position

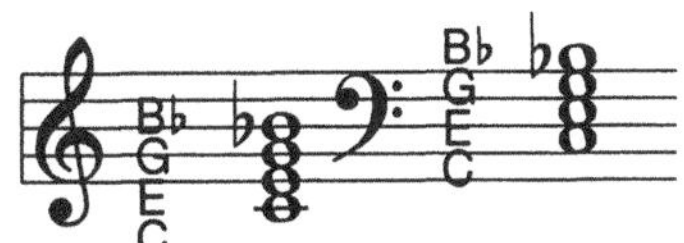

1st Inversion

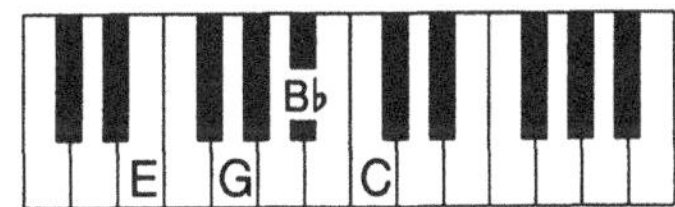

2nd Inversion

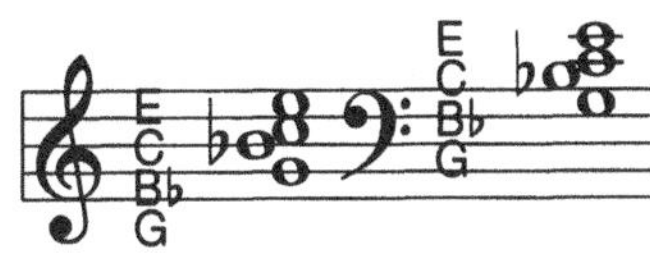

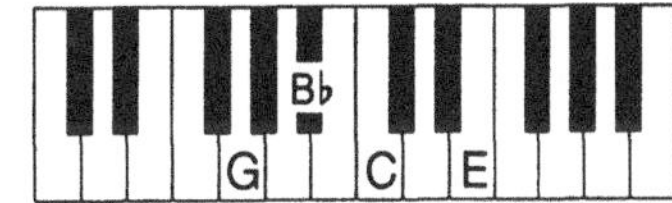

3rd Inversion

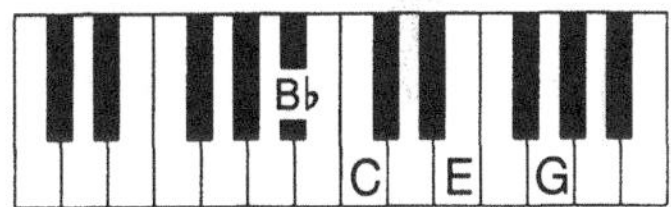

C7♭5

Root Position

1st Inversion

2nd Inversion

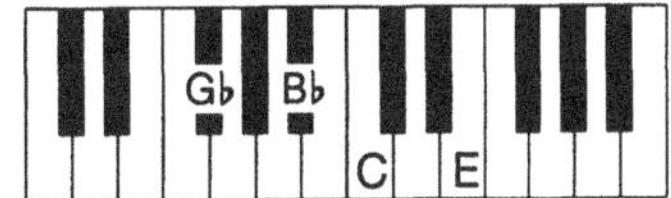

3rd Inversion

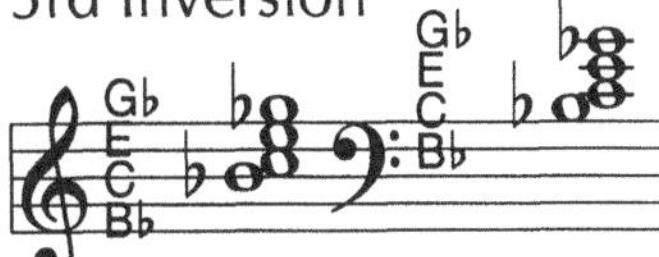

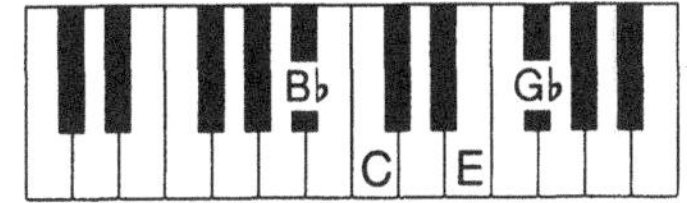

C7♯5

Root Position

1st Inversion

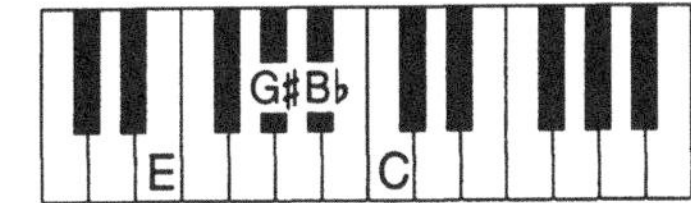

2nd Inversion

3rd Inversion

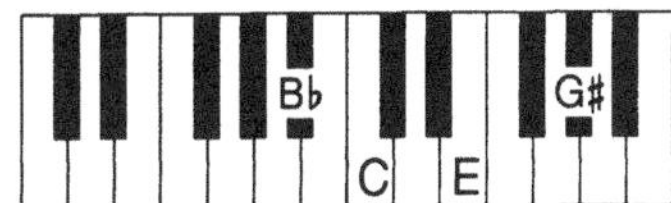

C7sus

Root Position

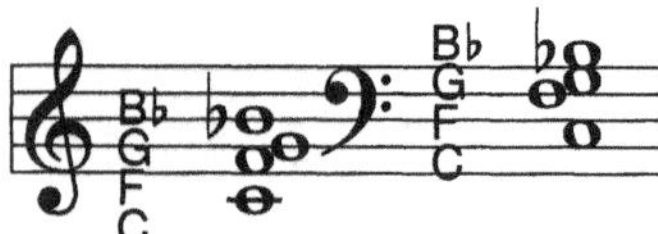

1st Inversion

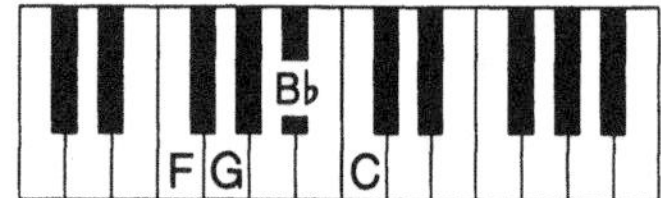

2nd Inversion

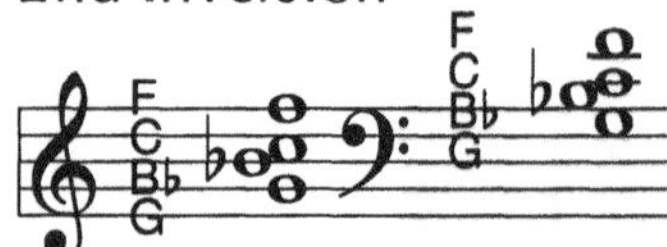

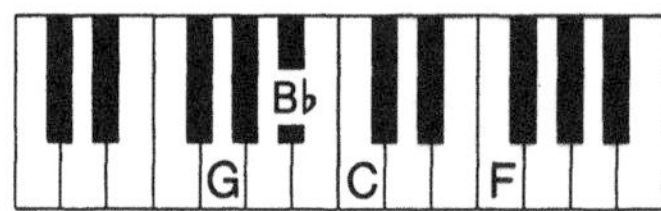

3rd Inversion

Cm(add2), Cm(add9)

Root Position

1st Inversion

2nd Inversion

3rd Inversion

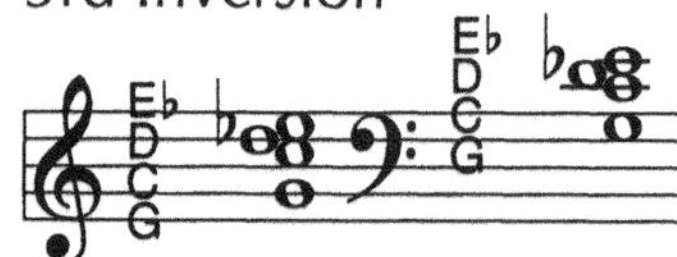

Cm6

Root Position

1st Inversion

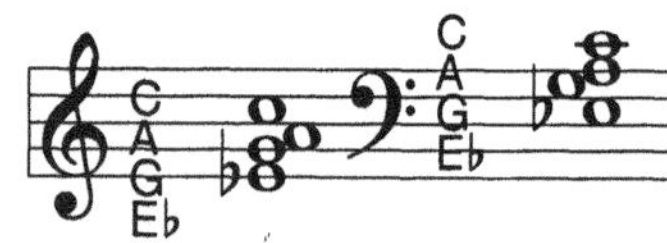

2nd Inversion

3rd Inversion

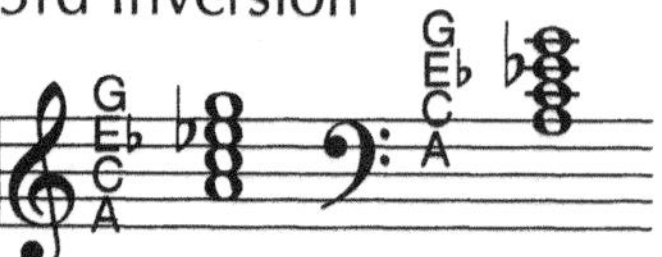

Cm7

Root Position

1st Inversion

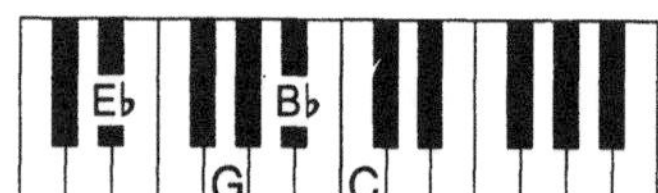

2nd Inversion

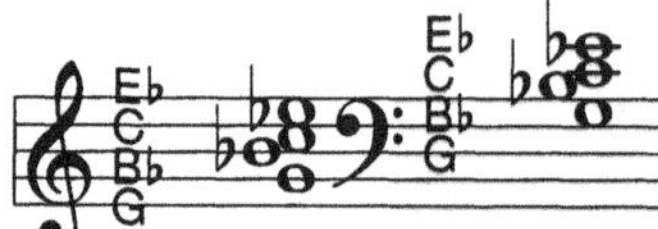

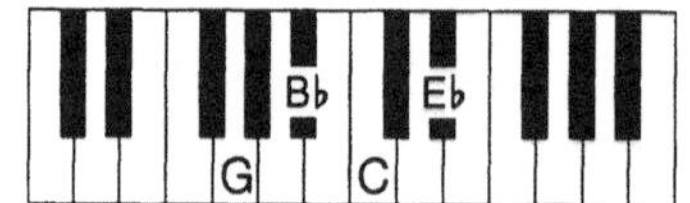

3rd Inversion

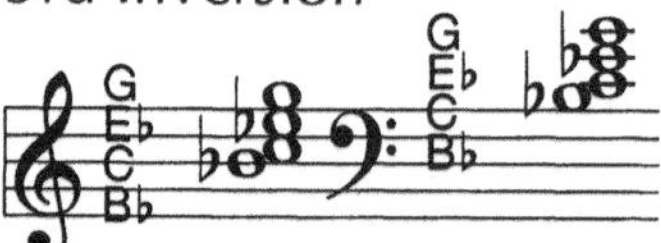

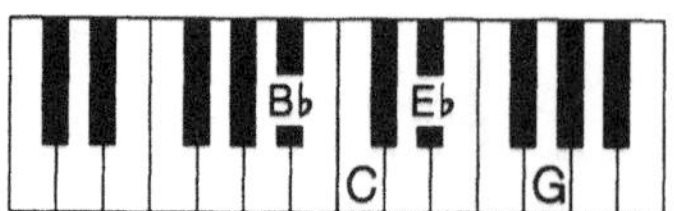

Cm(maj7)

Root Position

1st Inversion

2nd Inversion

3rd Inversion

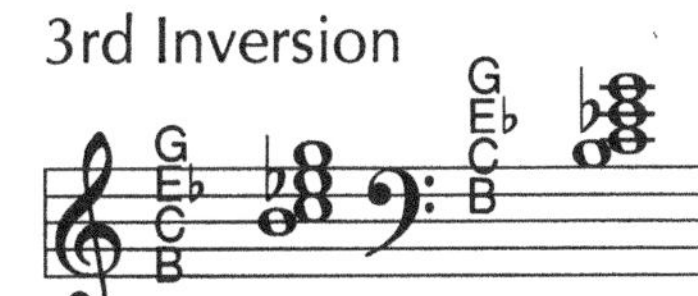

Cm7♭5

Root Position

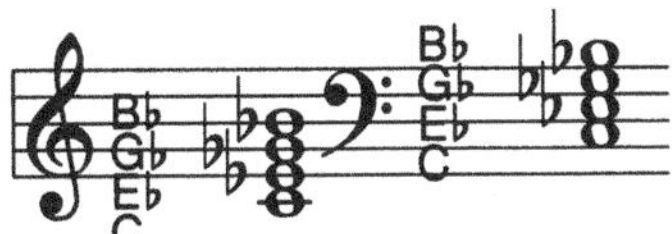

1st Inversion

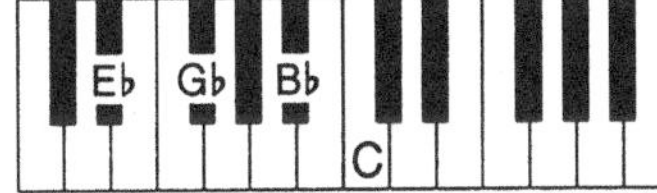

2nd Inversion

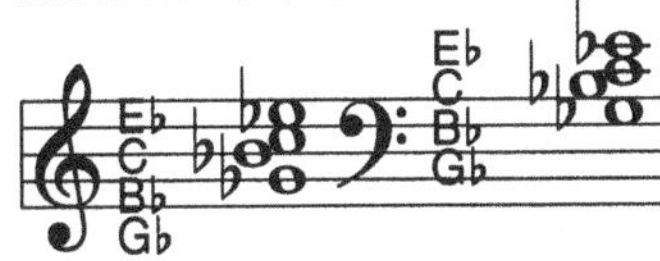

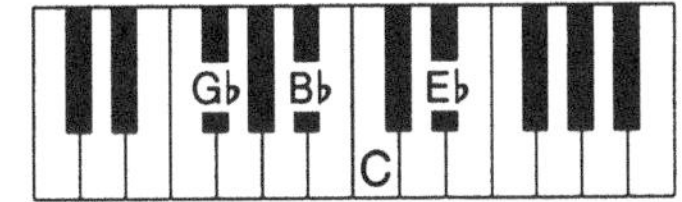

3rd Inversion

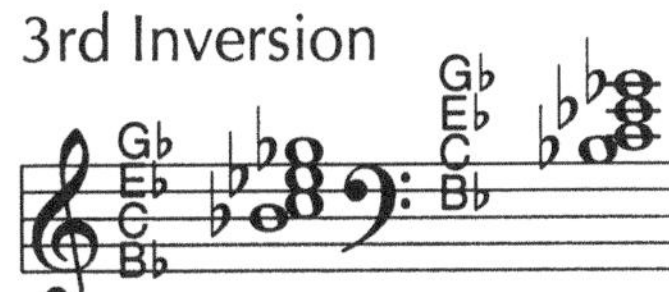

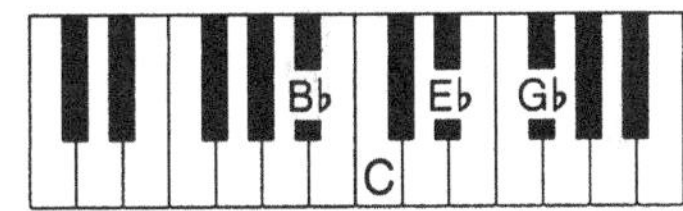

Cdim7

Root Position

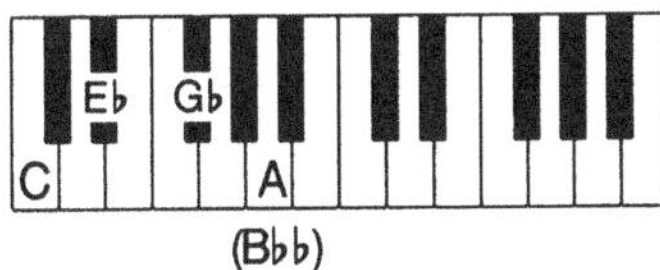

1st Inversion

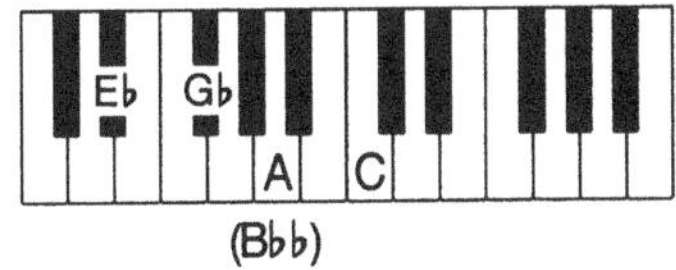

2nd Inversion

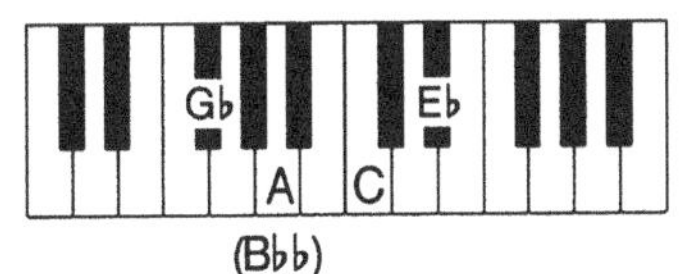

3rd Inversion

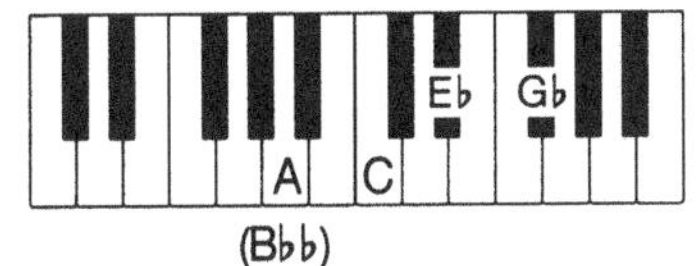

Cdim(maj7)

Root Position

1st Inversion

2nd Inversion

3rd Inversion

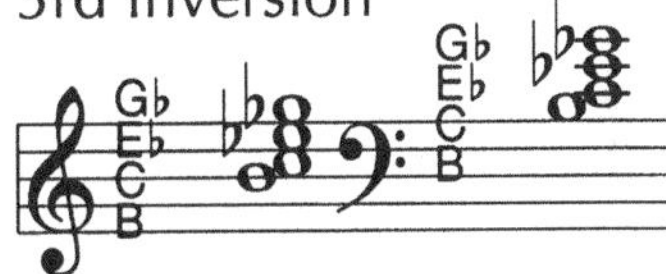

ADDITIONAL C CHORDS

C5

C$^{6}_{9}$

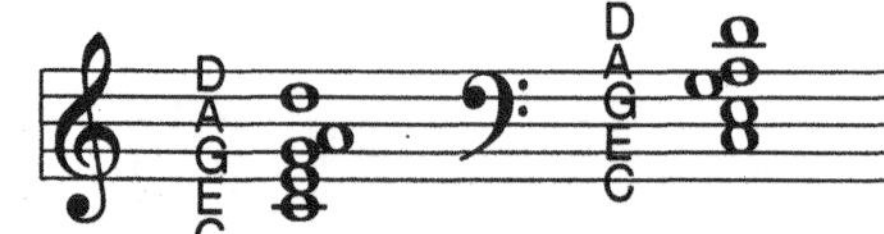

Cmaj$^{6}_{9}$

Cmaj7♯11

Cmaj9

Cmaj9♭5

Cmaj9♯5

Cmaj9♯11

Cmaj13

Cmaj13♭5

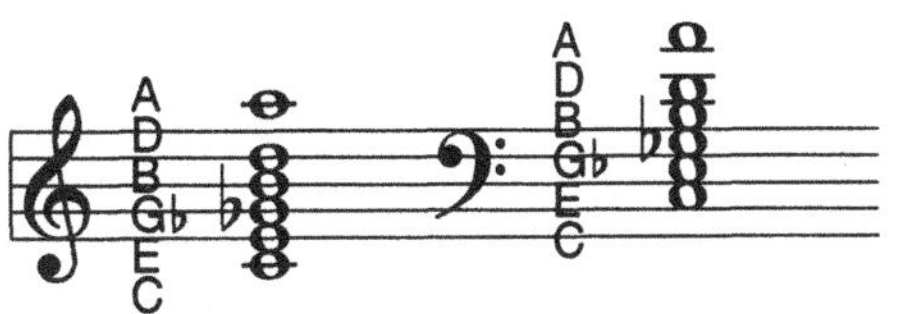

Cmaj13♯11

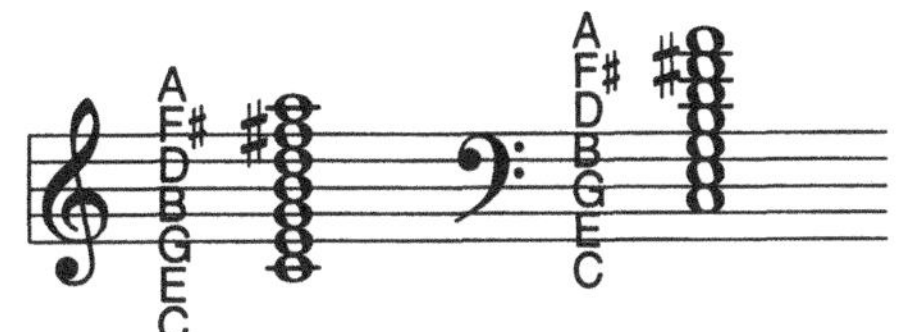

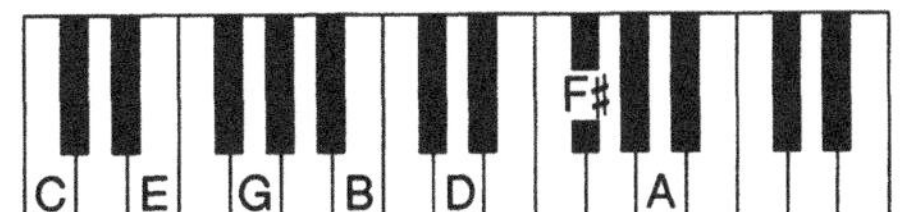

C7♭9

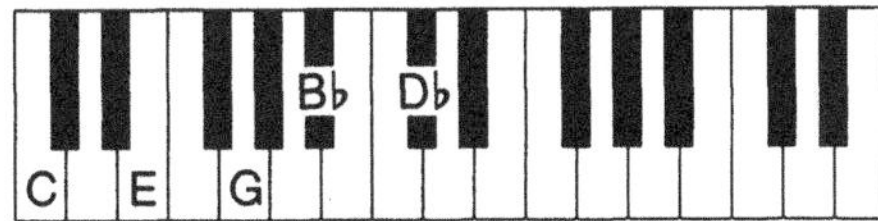

C7♯9

C7♯11

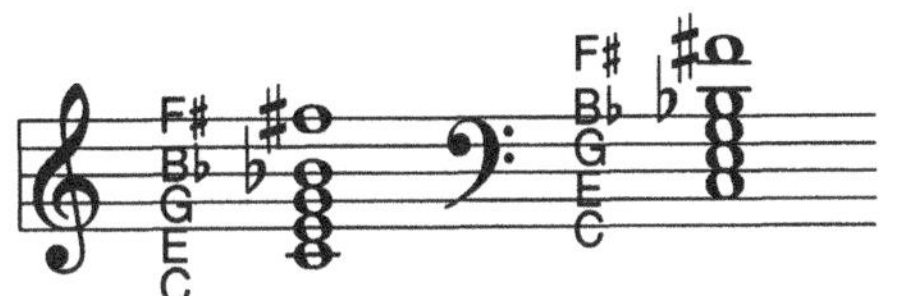

C7♭5(♭9)

C7♭5(♯9)

C7♯5(♭9)

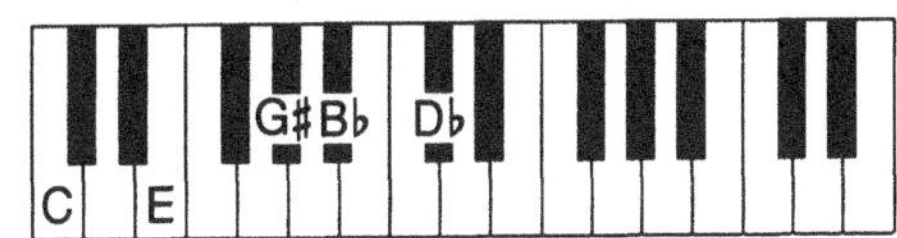

C7♯5(♯9)

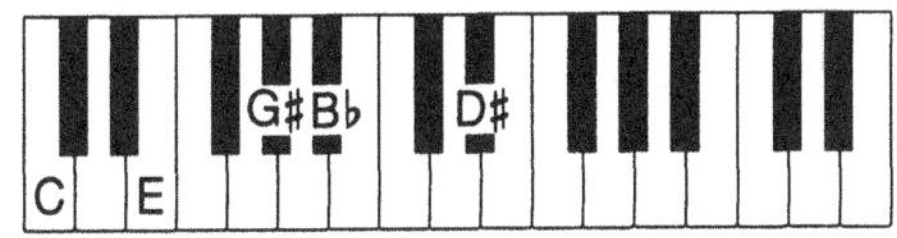

C7♭9(♯9)

C7(add13)

C7♭13

C7♭9(♯11)

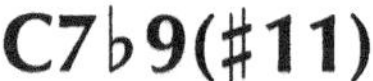

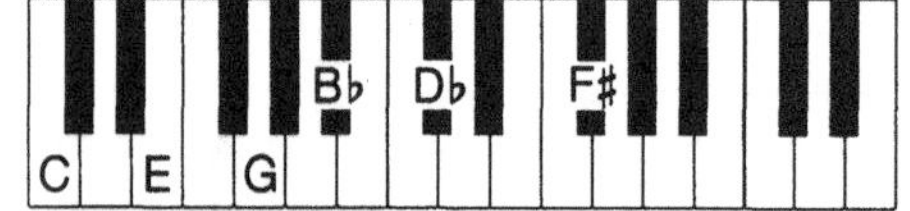

C7♯9(♯11)

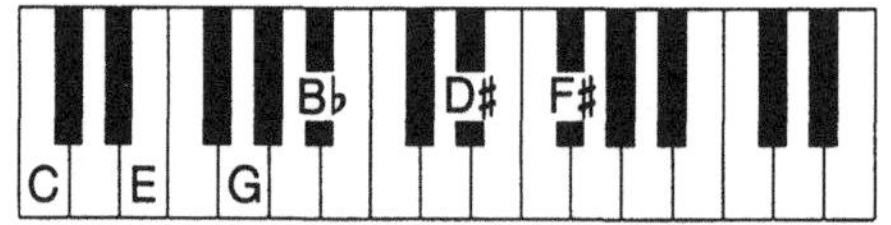

C7♭9(♭13)

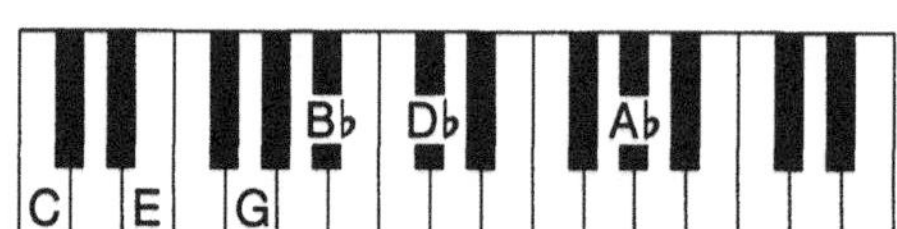

C7♯9(♭13)

C7♯11(♭13)

C7♭9(♯9,♯11)

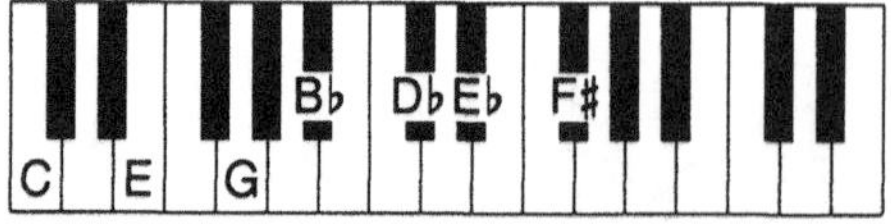

C9

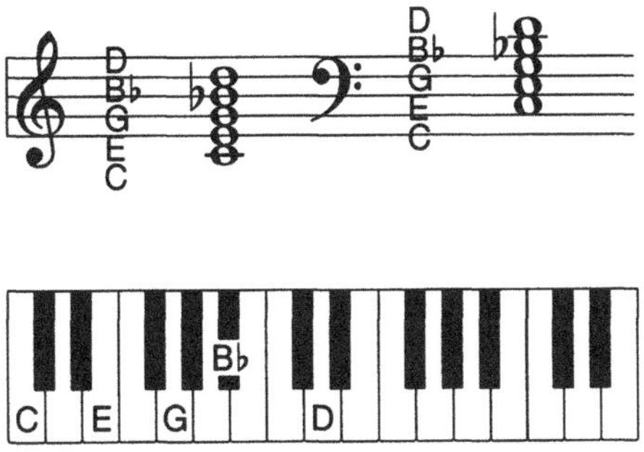

D Bb G E C
D Bb G E C
C E G Bb D

C9(♭5)

D Bb Gb E C
D Bb Gb E C
C E Gb Bb D

C9♯5

D Bb G# E C
D Bb G# E C
C E G# Bb D

C9♯11

F# D Bb G E C
F# D Bb G C
C E G Bb D F#

C9♭13

Ab D Bb G E C
Ab D Bb G E C
C E G Bb D Ab

C9♯11(♭13)

Ab F# D Bb G E C
Ab F# D Bb G E C
C E G Bb D F# Ab

C11, C9sus4

F D Bb G C
F D Bb G C
C G Bb D F

C13

A D Bb G E C
A D Bb G E C
C E G Bb D A

C13♭5

A D Bb Gb E C
A D Bb Gb E C
C E Gb Bb D A

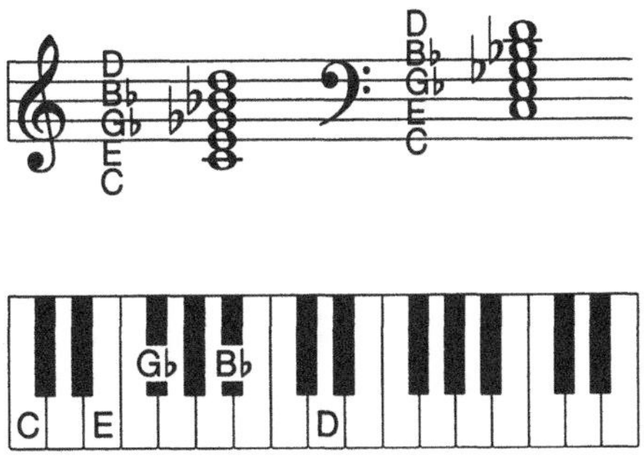

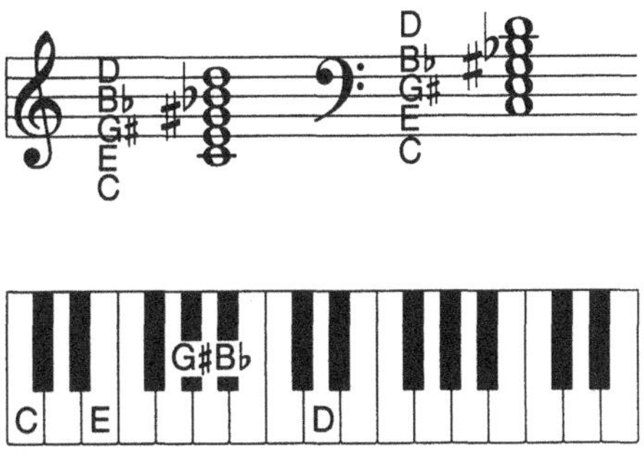

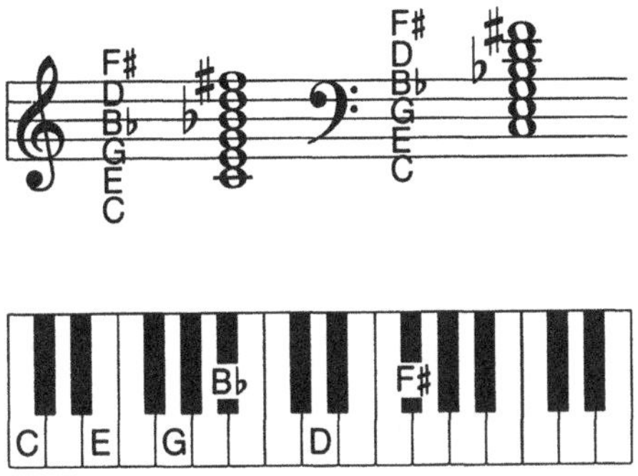

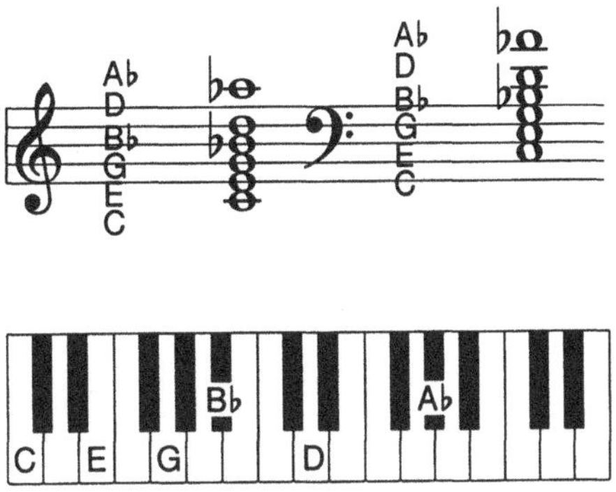

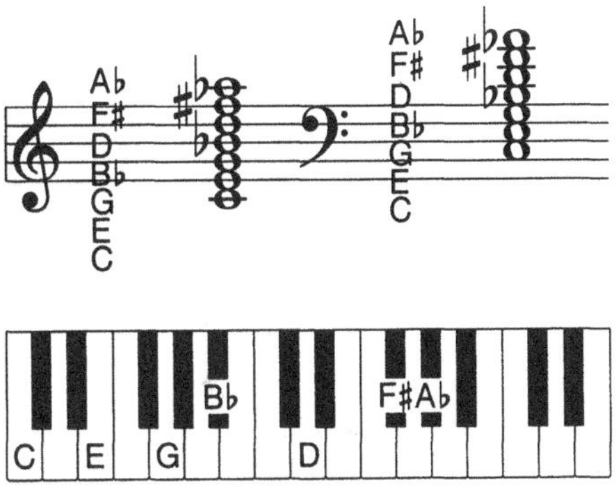

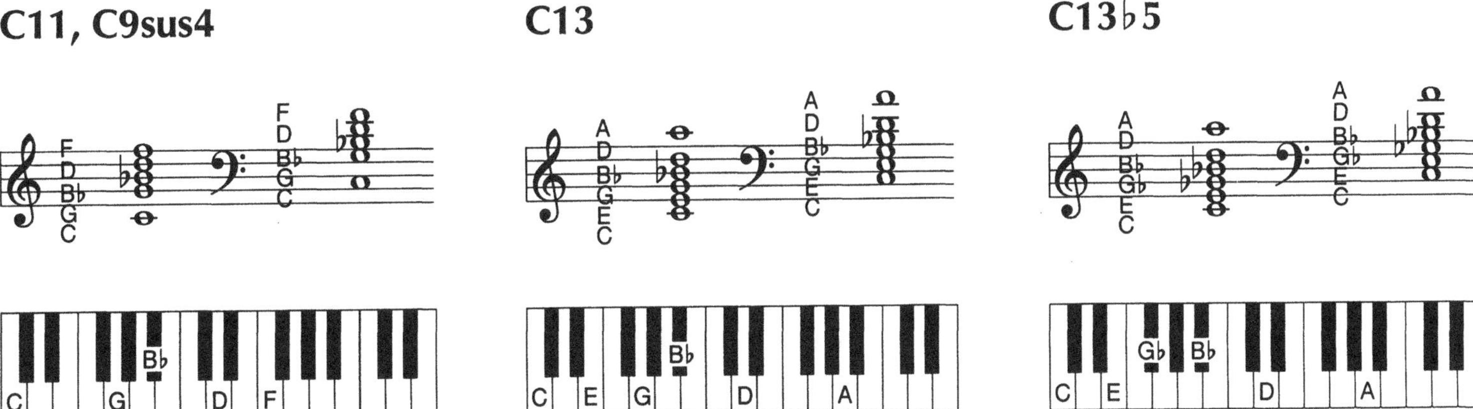

C13♭9

C13♯9

C13♯11

C13(sus4)

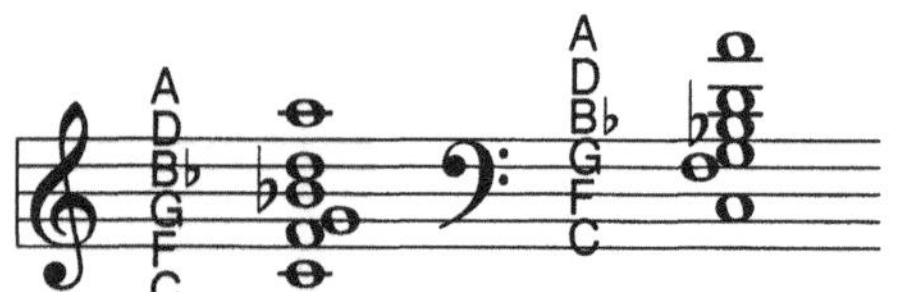

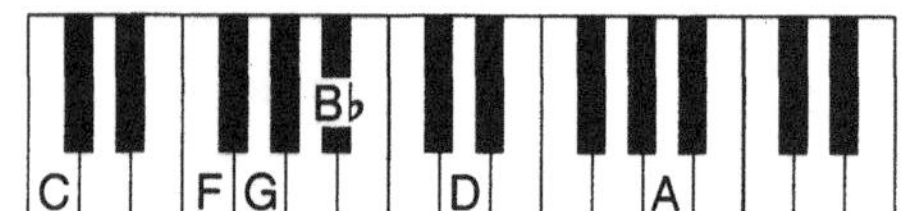

Cm(♯5)

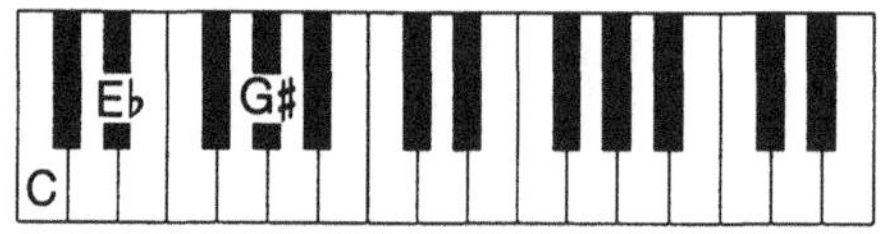

Cm$^{6}_{9}$

Cm7(add4)

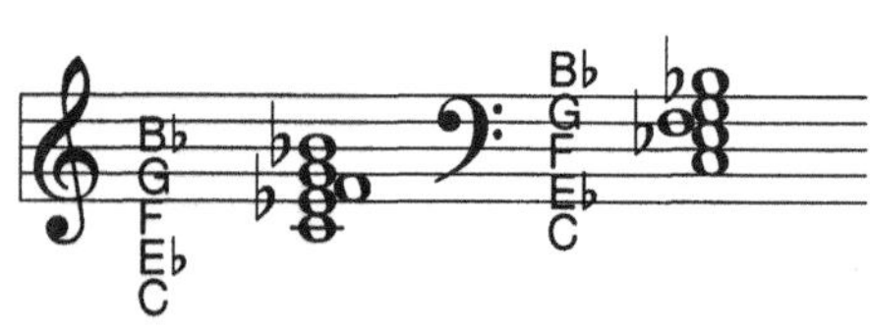

Cm7(add11)

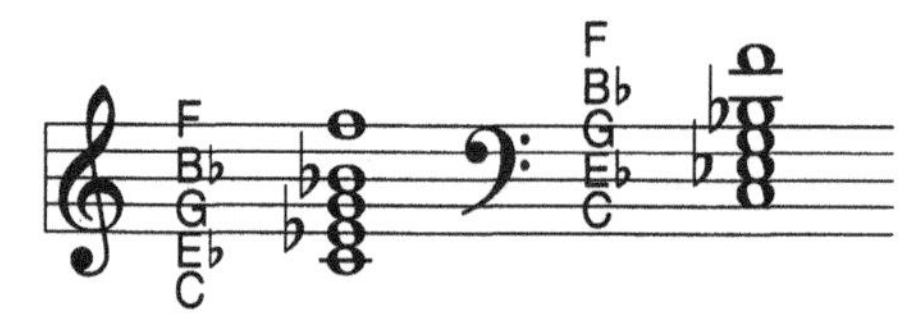

Cm7♭5(♭9)

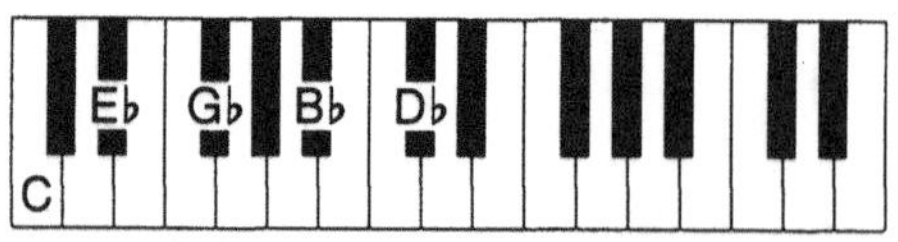

Cm9

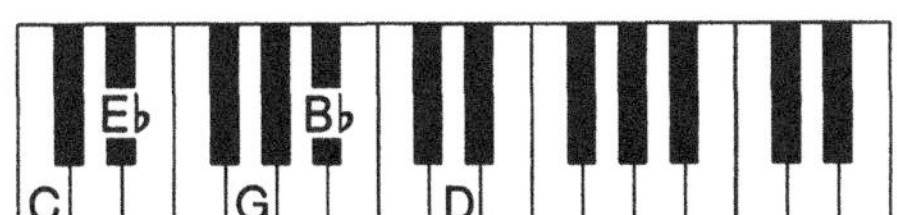

Cm9(maj7)

Cm9♭5

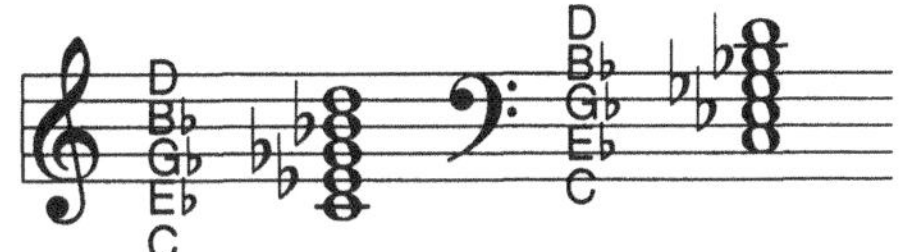

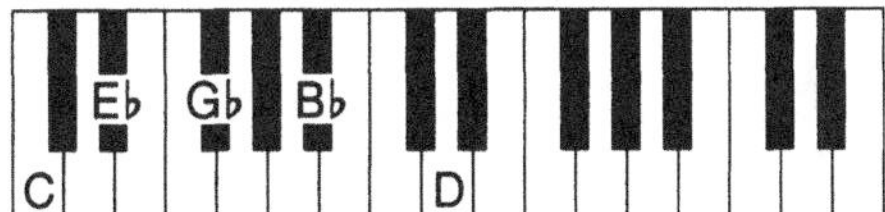

Cm11

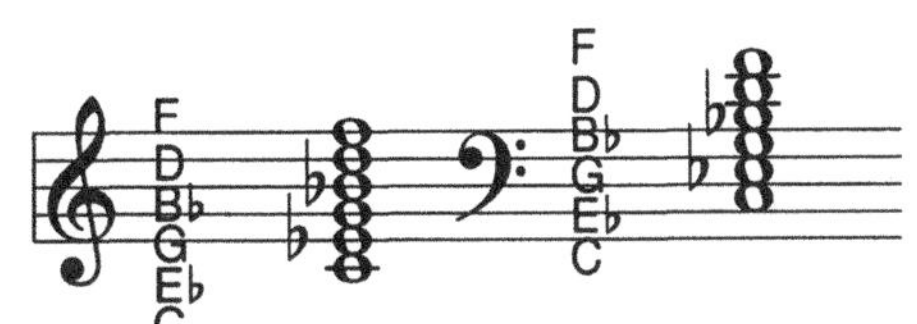

Cm13

Cdim7(add9)

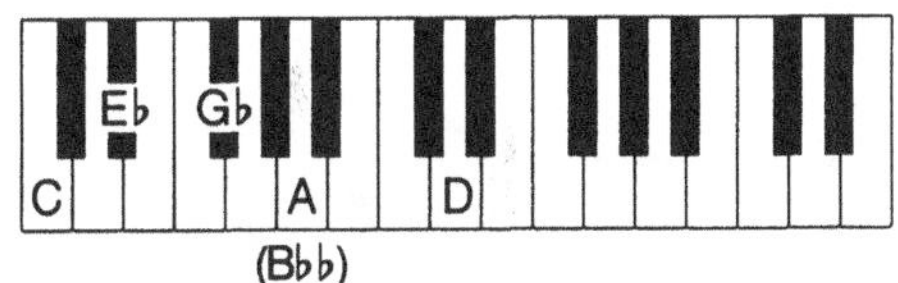

Cm11♭5

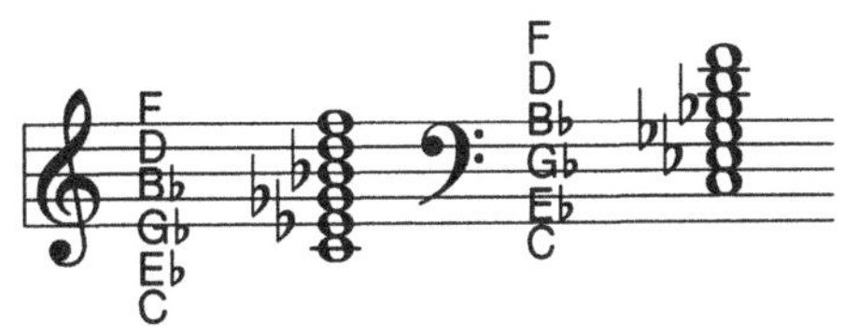

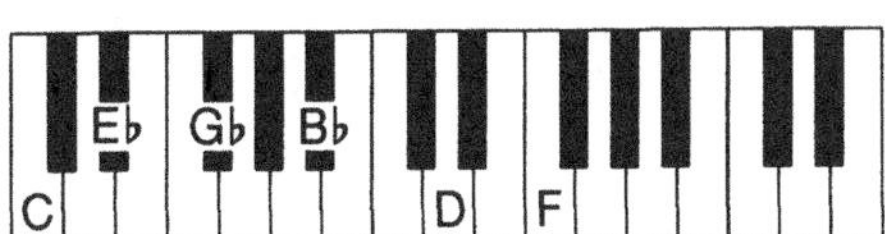

Cm11(maj7)

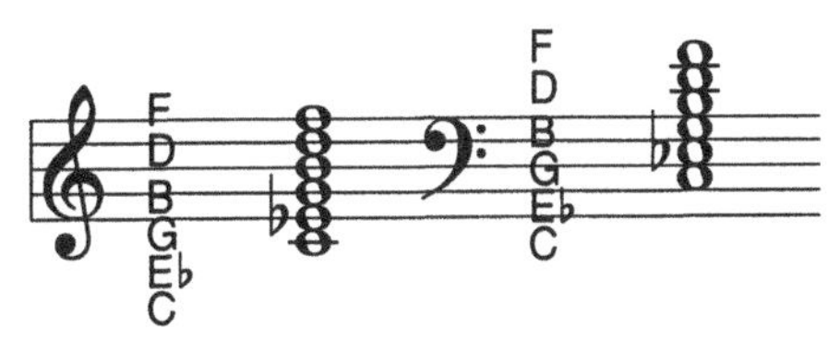

C7alt.

C♯/D♭ CHORDS

C♯

Root Position

1st Inversion

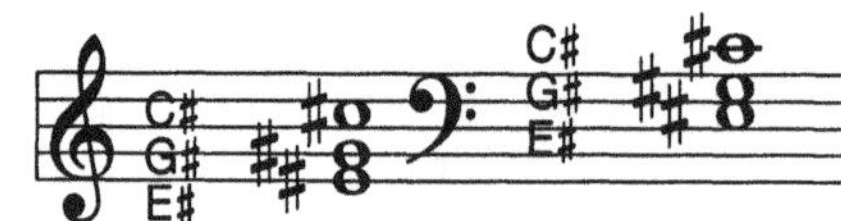

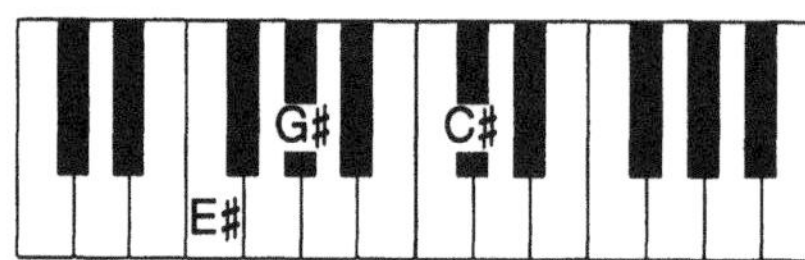

2nd Inversion

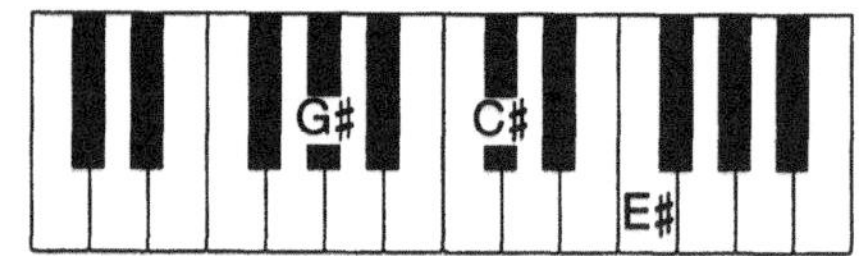

C♯m

Root Position

1st Inversion

2nd Inversion

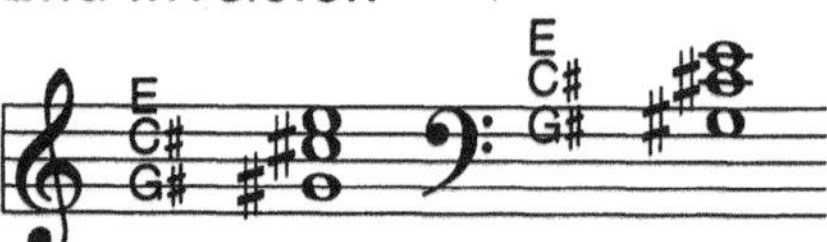

C♯+

Root Position

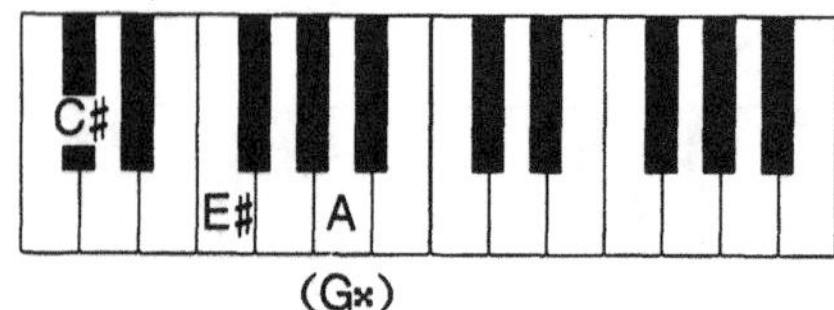

1st Inversion

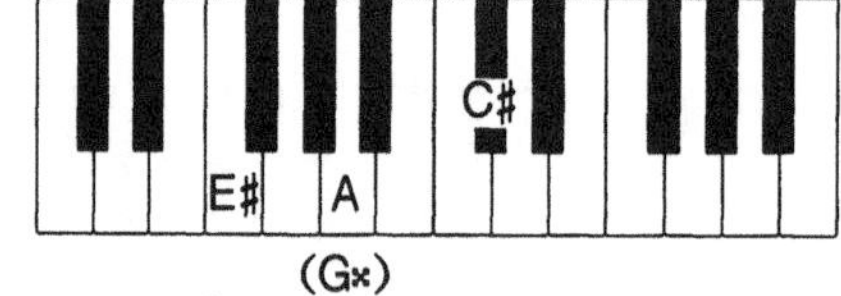

2nd Inversion

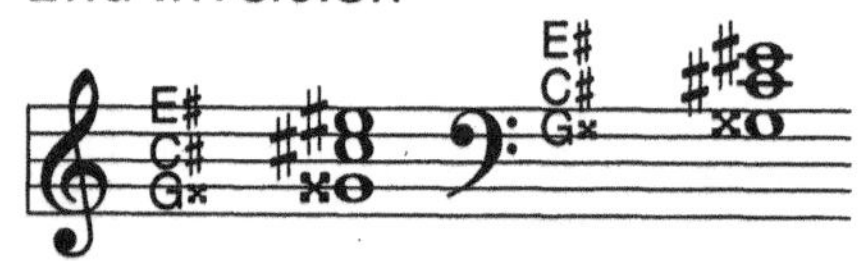

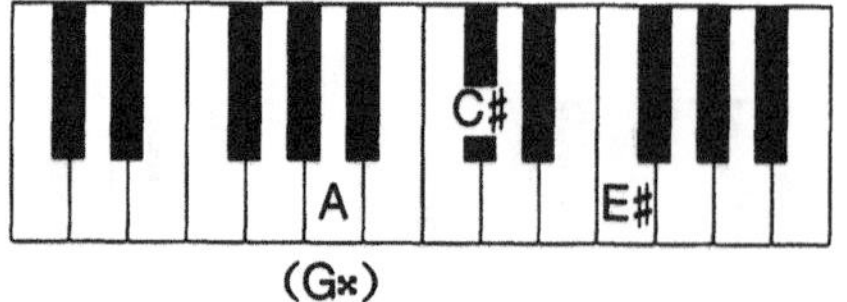

C♯dim

1st Inversion

2nd Inversion

C♯sus

Root Position

1st Inversion

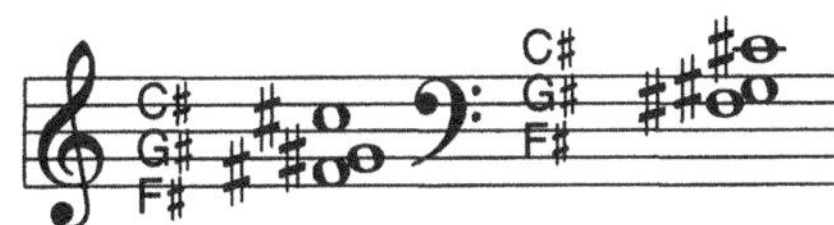

2nd Inversion

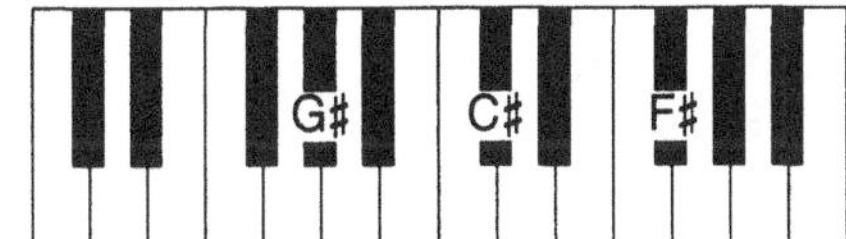

C♯(♭5)

Root Position

1st Inversion

2nd Inversion

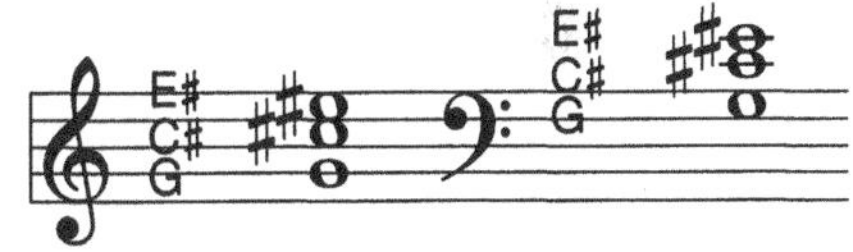

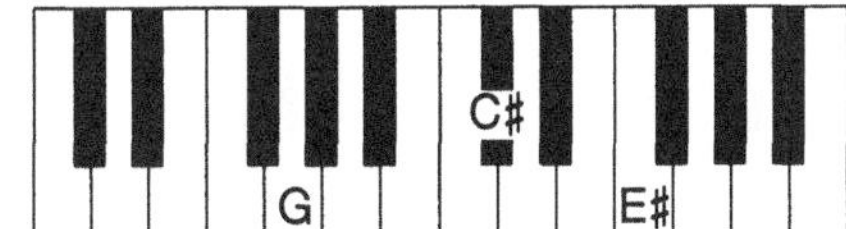

C♯sus2

Root Position

1st Inversion

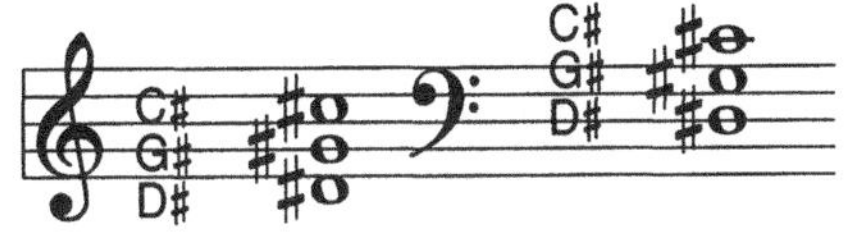

2nd Inversion

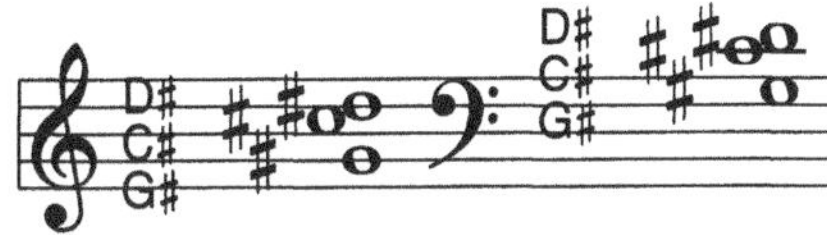

C♯6

Root Position

1st Inversion

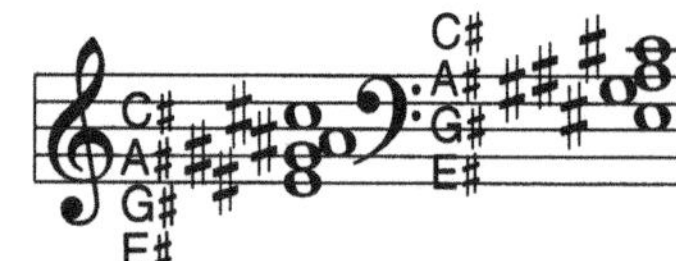

2nd Inversion

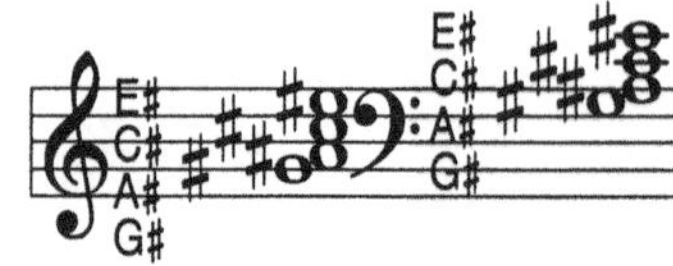

3rd Inversion

C♯(add2), C♯(add9)

Root Position

1st Inversion

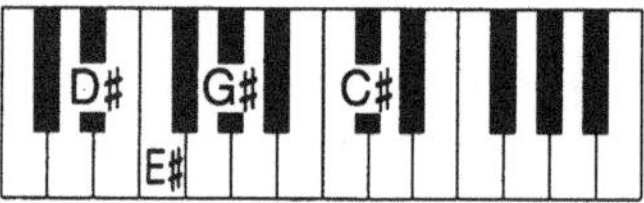

2nd Inversion

3rd Inversion

C♯maj7

Root Position

1st Inversion

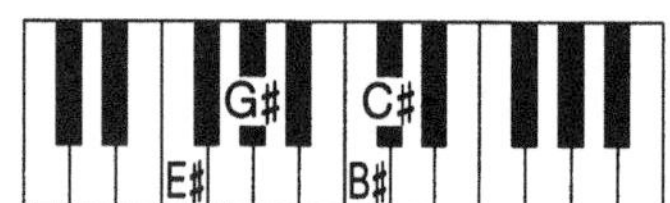

2nd Inversion

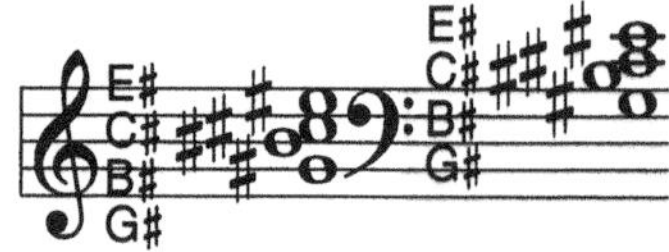

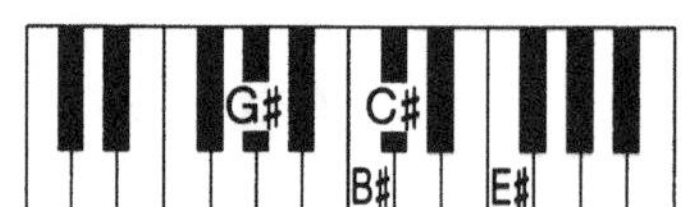

3rd Inversion

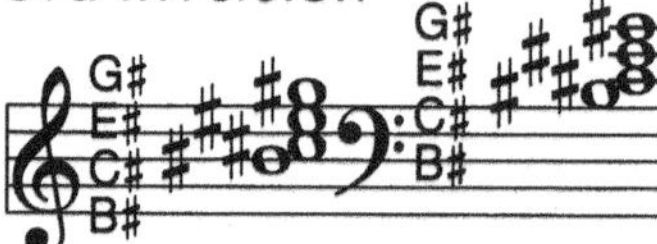

C♯maj7♭5

Root Position

1st Inversion

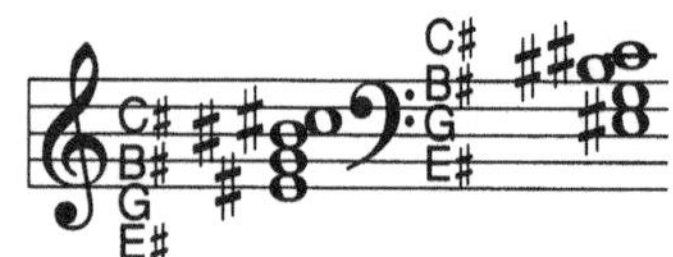

2nd Inversion

3rd Inversion

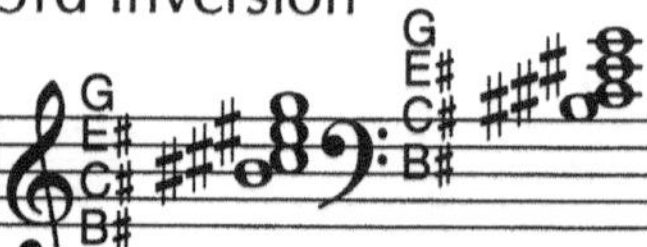

C♯maj7♯5

Root Position

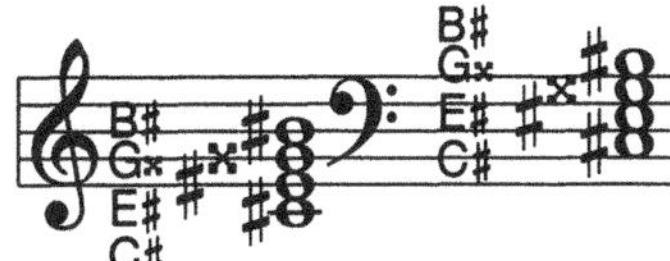

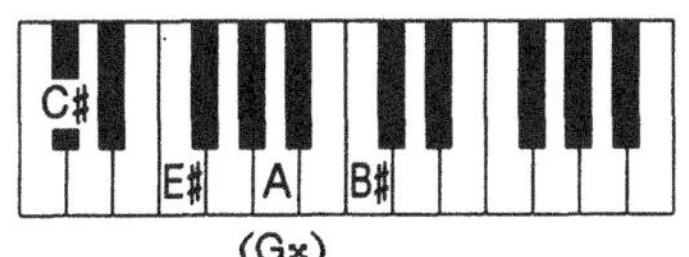

1st Inversion

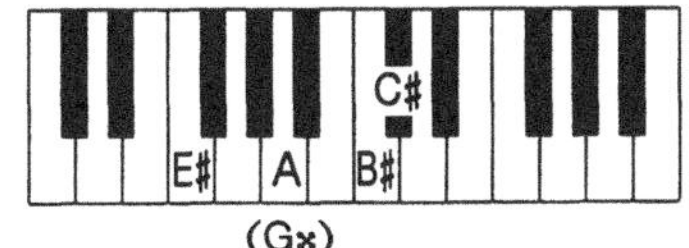

2nd Inversion

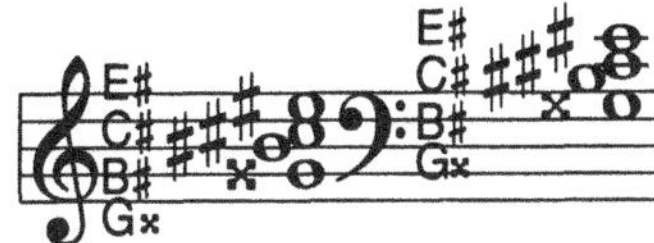

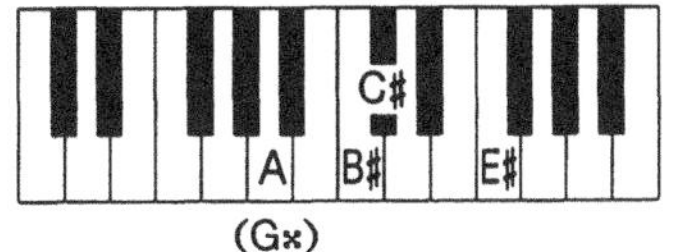

3rd Inversion

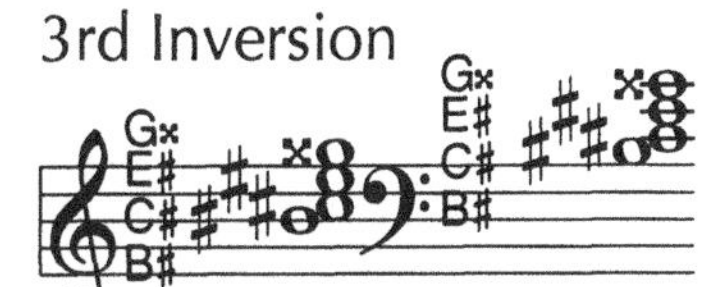

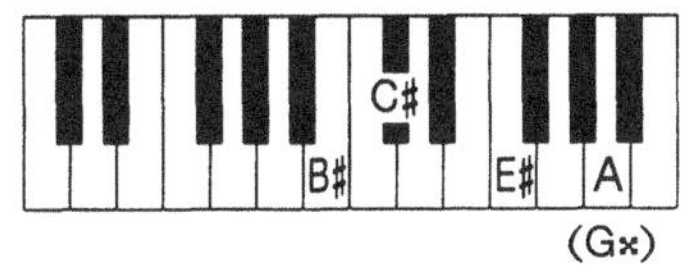

C♯7

Root Position

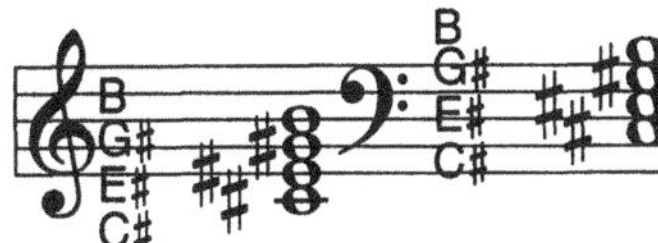

1st Inversion

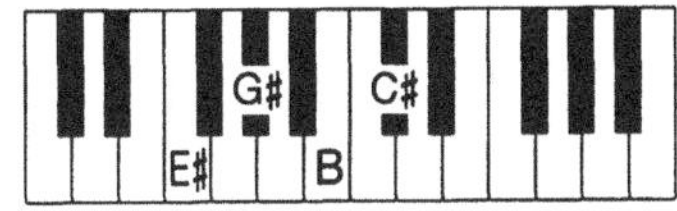

2nd Inversion

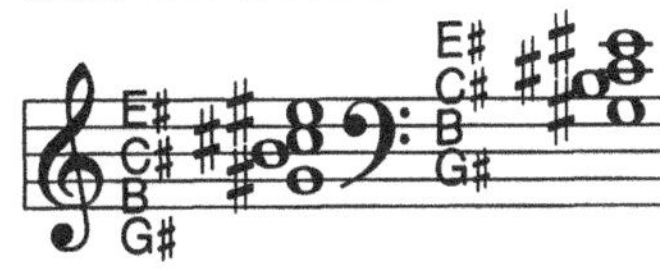

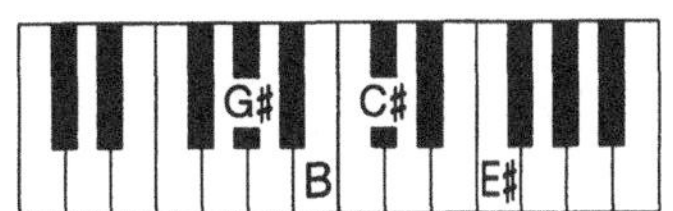

3rd Inversion

G♯
E♯
C♯
B
G♯
E♯
C♯
B

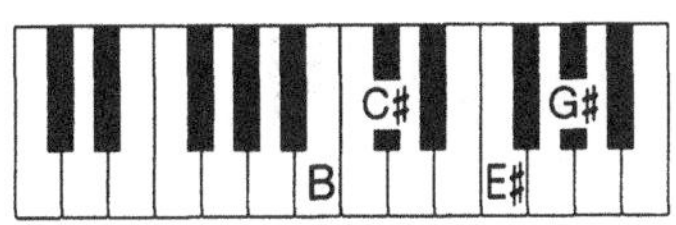

C♯7♭5

Root Position

1st Inversion

2nd Inversion

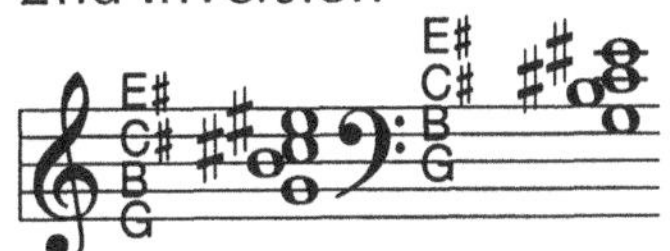

3rd Inversion

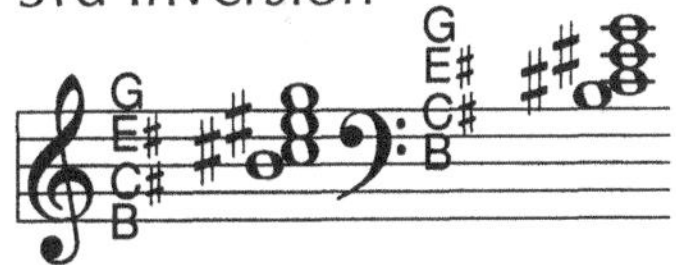

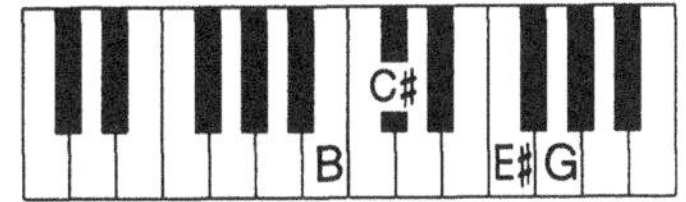

C♯7♯5

Root Position

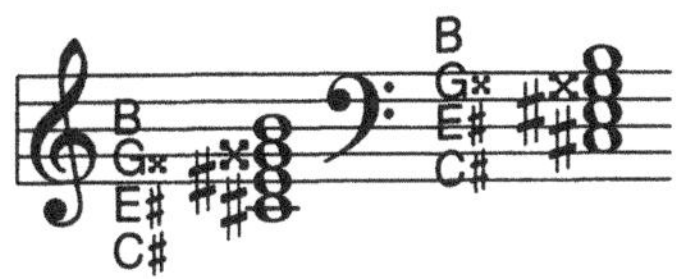

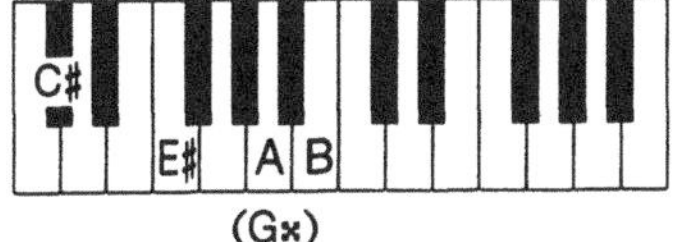

1st Inversion

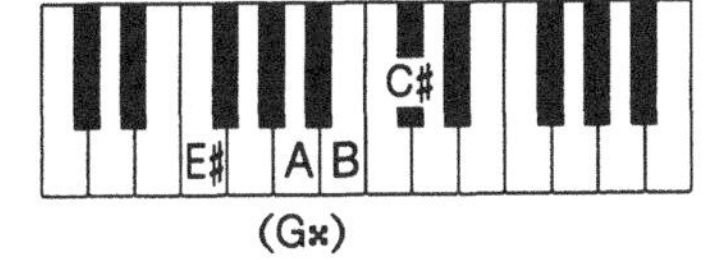

2nd Inversion

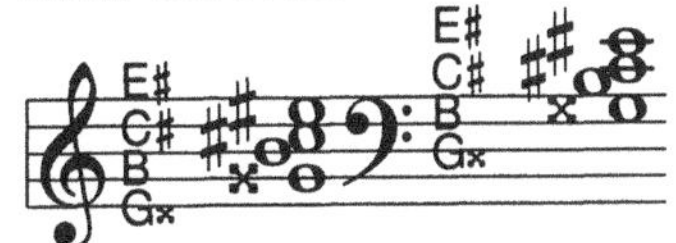

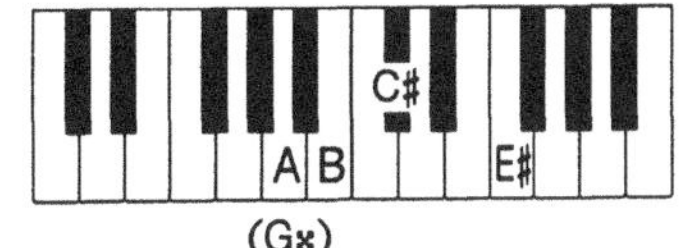

3rd Inversion

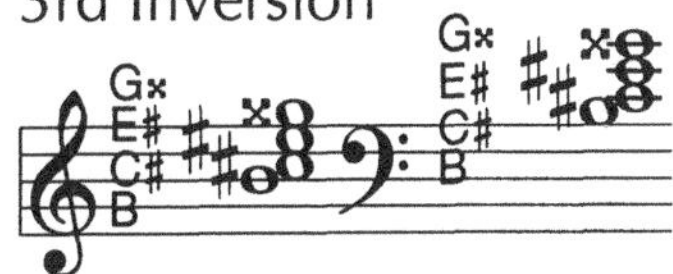

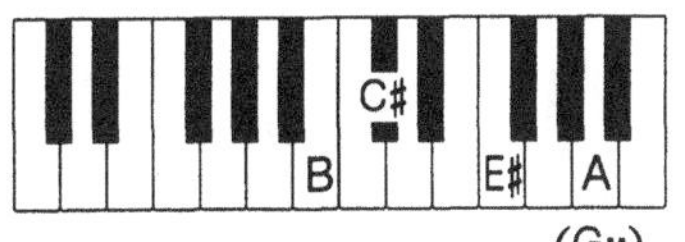

C♯7sus

Root Position

1st Inversion

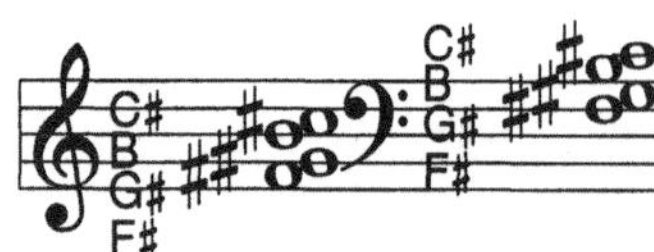

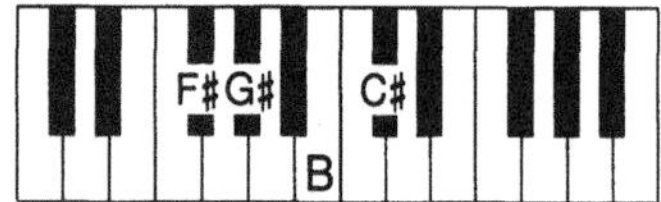

2nd Inversion

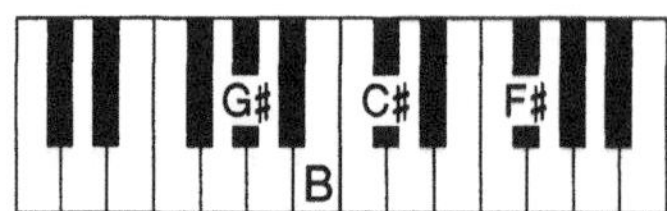

3rd Inversion

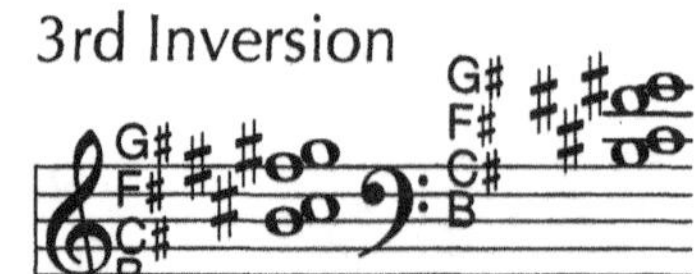

C♯m(add2), C♯m(add9)

Root Position

1st Inversion

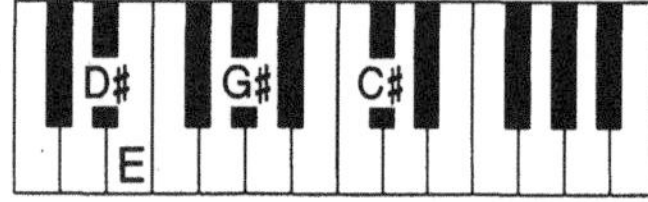

2nd Inversion

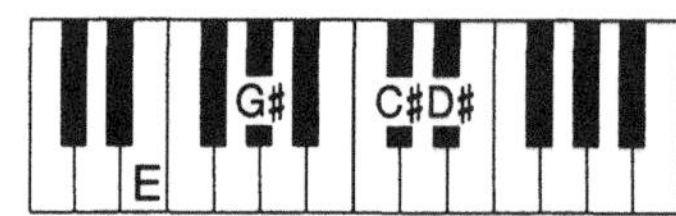

3rd Inversion

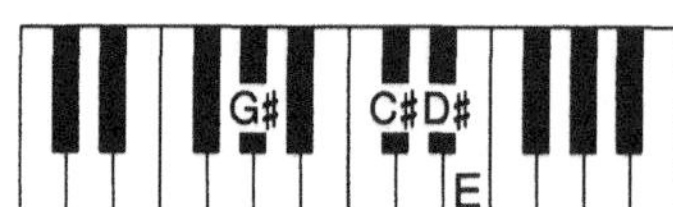

C♯m6

Root Position

1st Inversion

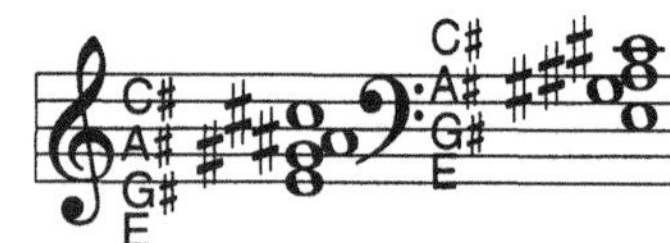

2nd Inversion

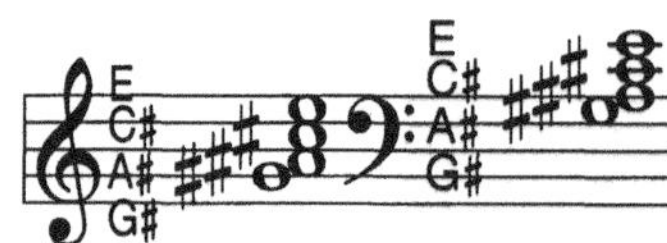

3rd Inversion

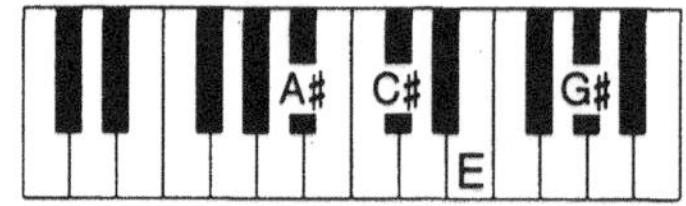

C♯m7

Root Position

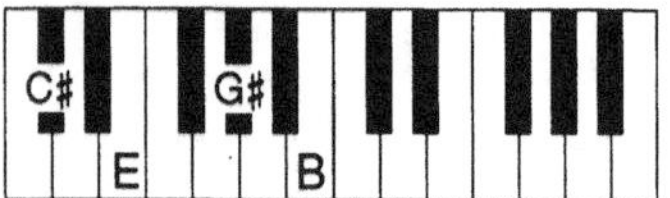

1st Inversion

2nd Inversion

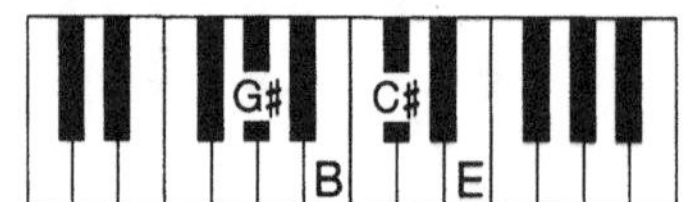

3rd Inversion

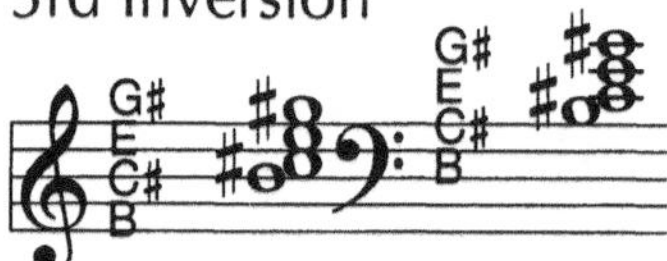

C♯m(maj7)

Root Position

1st Inversion

2nd Inversion

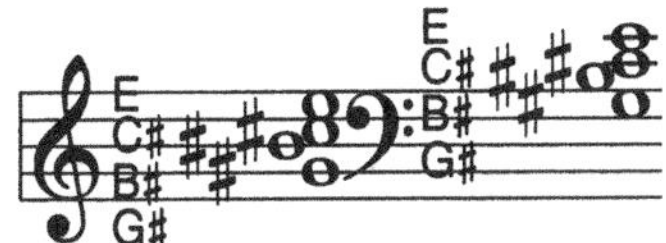

3rd Inversion

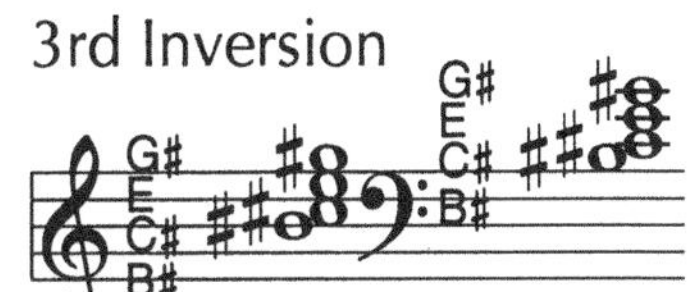

C♯m7♭5

Root Position

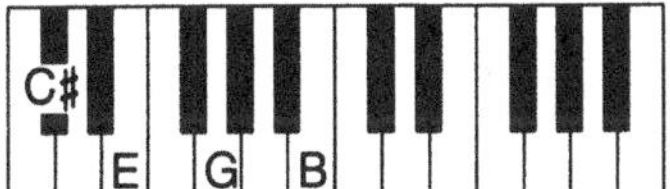

1st Inversion

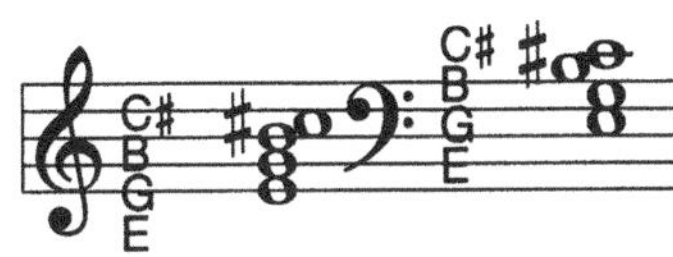

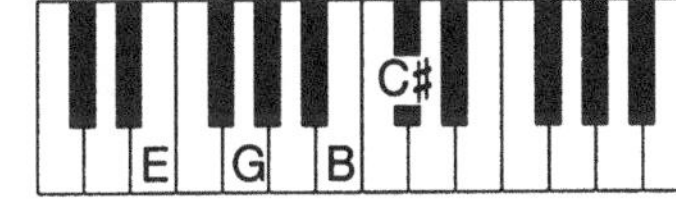

2nd Inversion

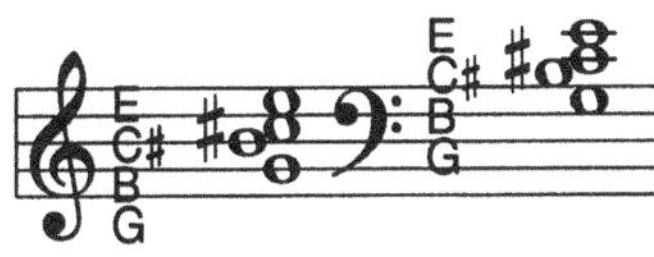

3rd Inversion

G E C♯ B G E C♯ B

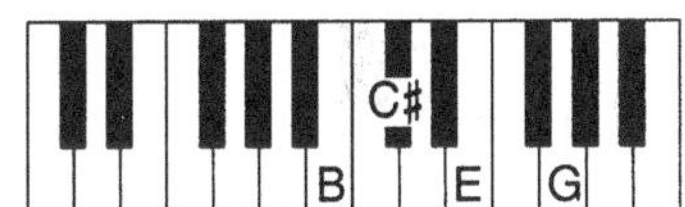

C♯dim7

Root Position

1st Inversion

2nd Inversion

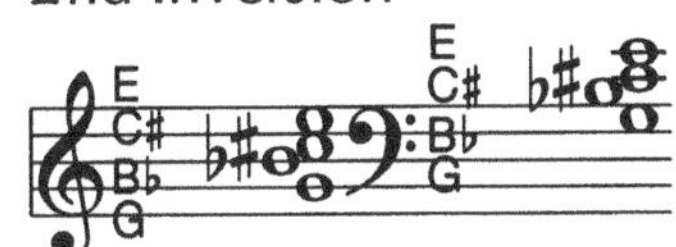

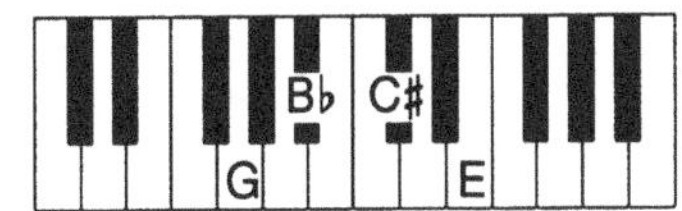

3rd Inversion

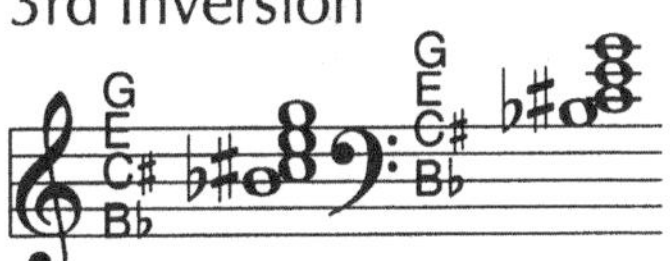

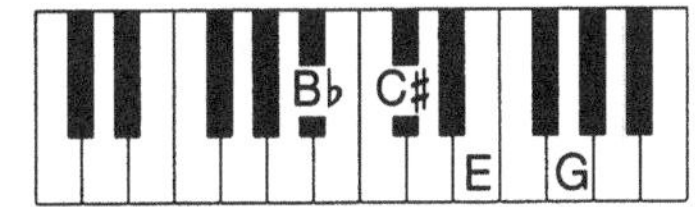

C♯dim(maj7)

Root Position

1st Inversion

2nd Inversion

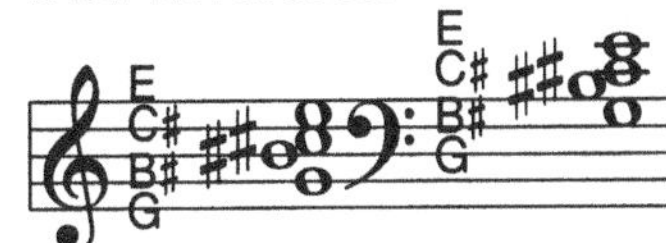

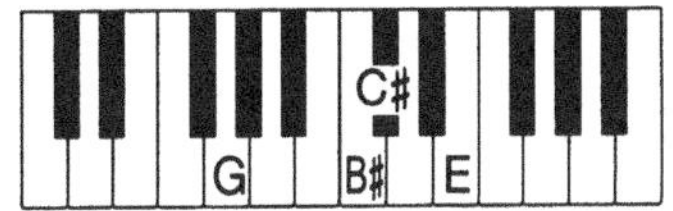

3rd Inversion

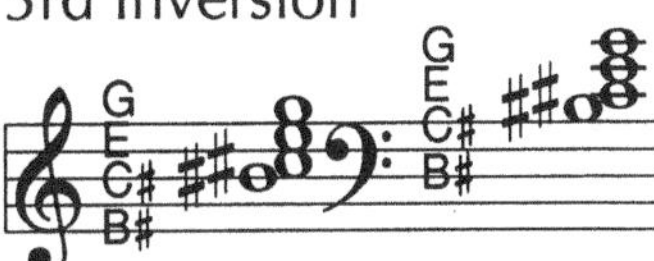

ADDITIONAL C♯/D♭ CHORDS

C♯5

C♯6/9

C♯maj6/9

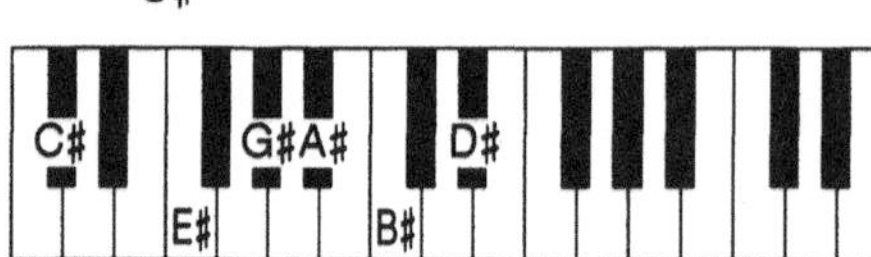

C♯maj7♯11

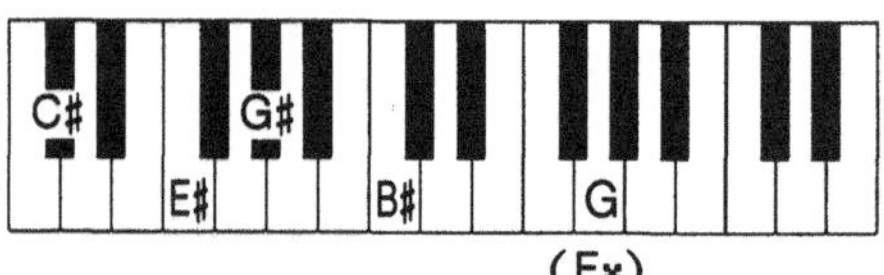

C♯maj9

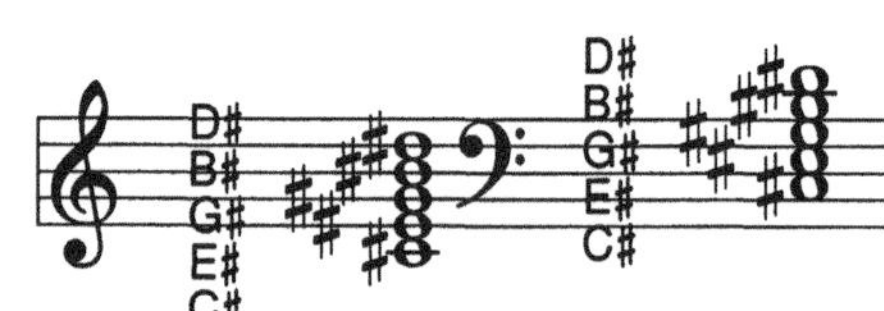

C♯maj9♭5

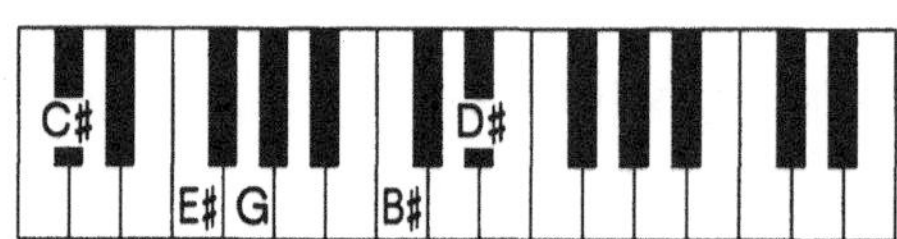

C♯maj9♯5

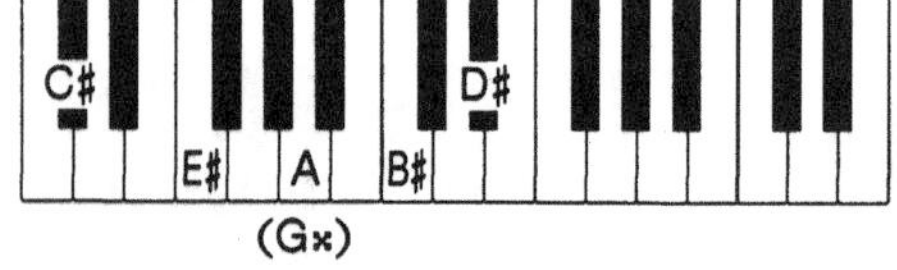

C♯maj9♯11

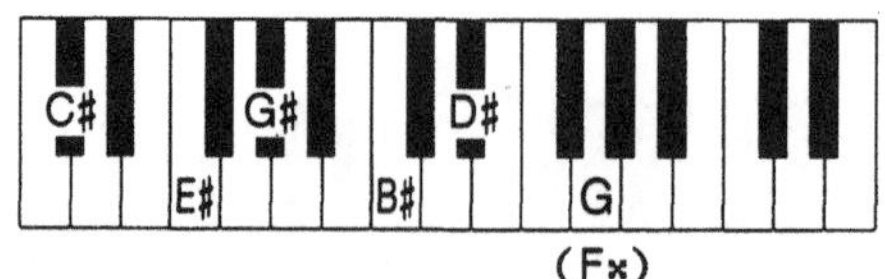

C♯maj13

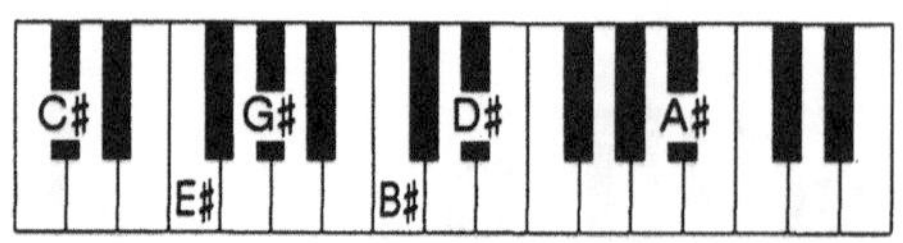

C♯maj13♭5

C♯maj13♯11

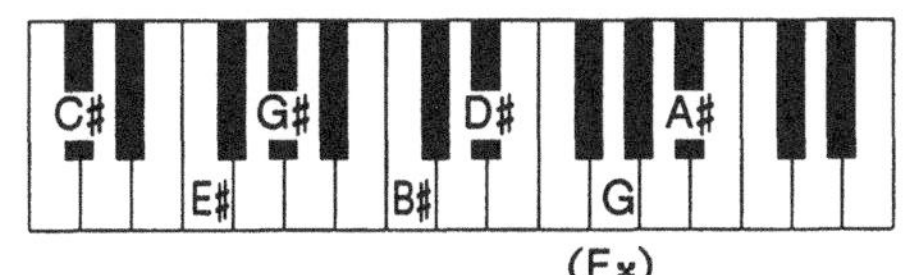

C♯7♭9

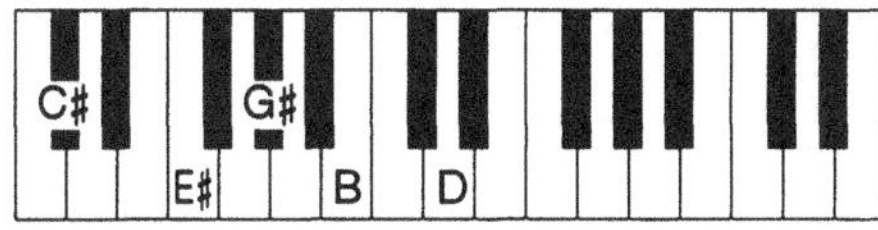

C♯7♯9

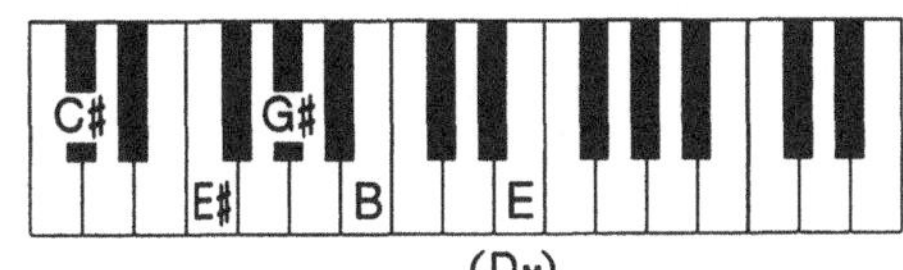

C♯7♯11

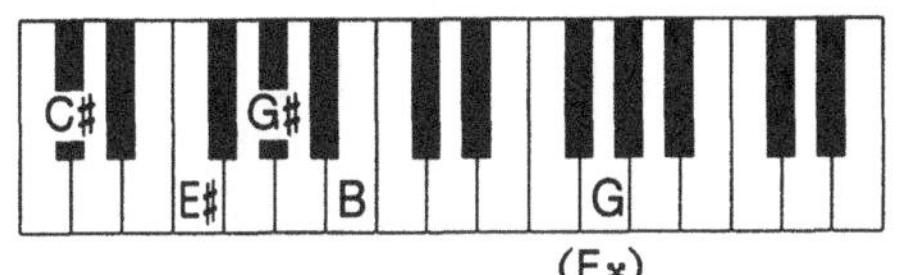

C♯7♭5(♭9)

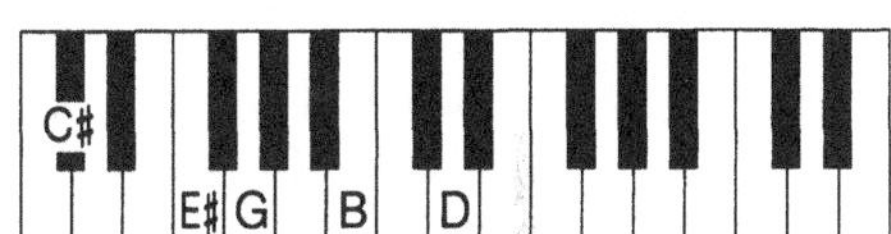

C♯7♭5(♯9)

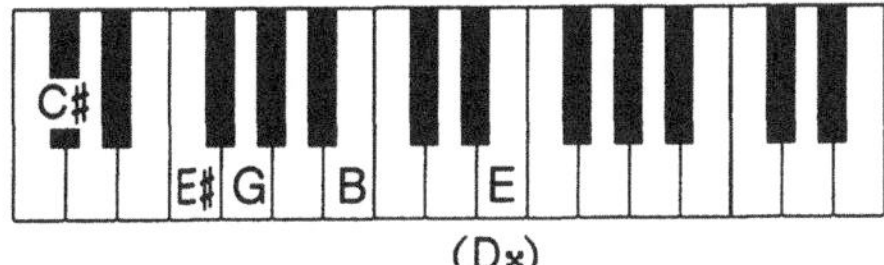

C♯7♯5(♭9)

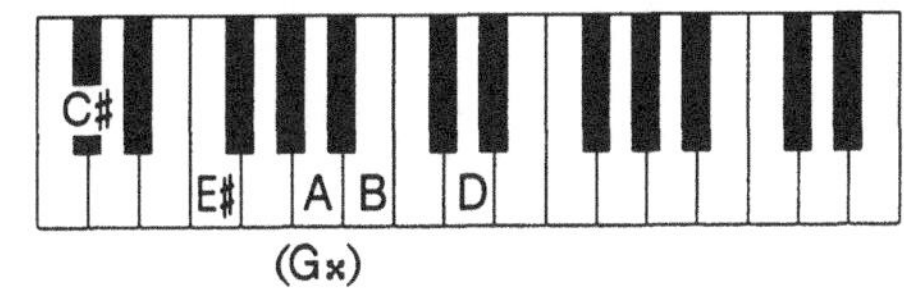

C♯7♯5(♯9)

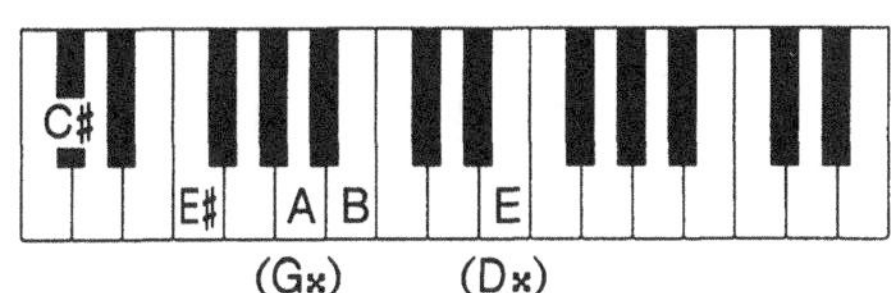

C♯7♭9(♯9)

C♯7(add13)

C♯7♭13

C♯7♭9(♯11)

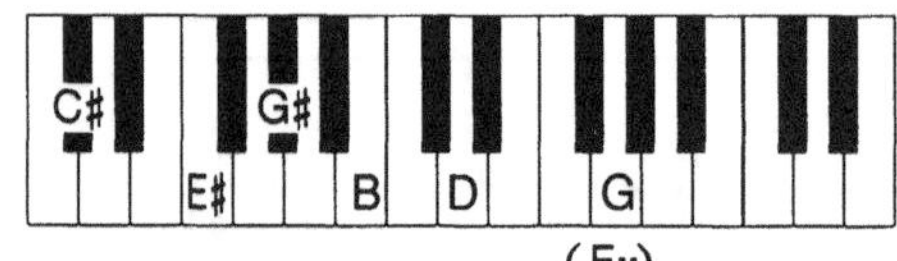

C♯7♯9(♯11)

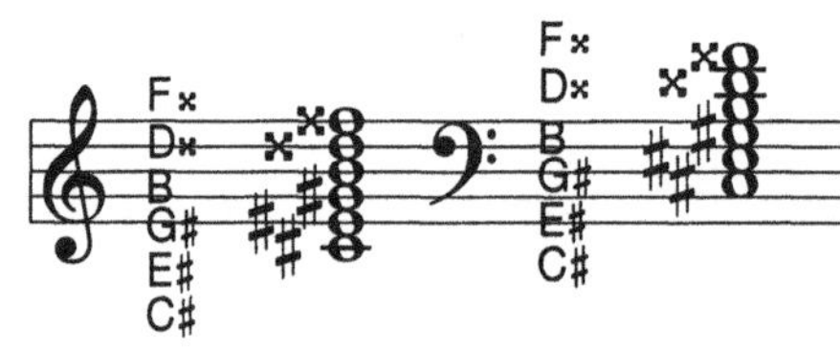

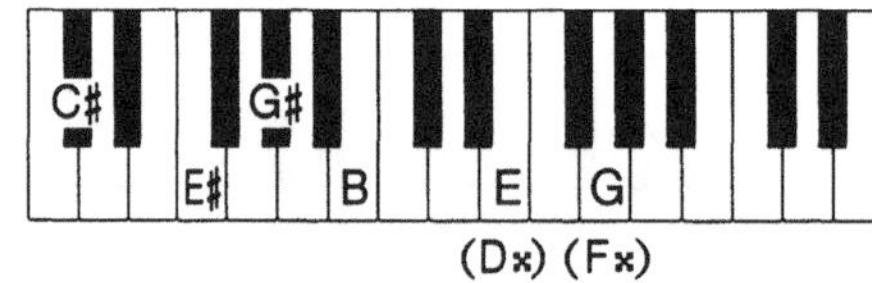

C♯7♭9(♭13)

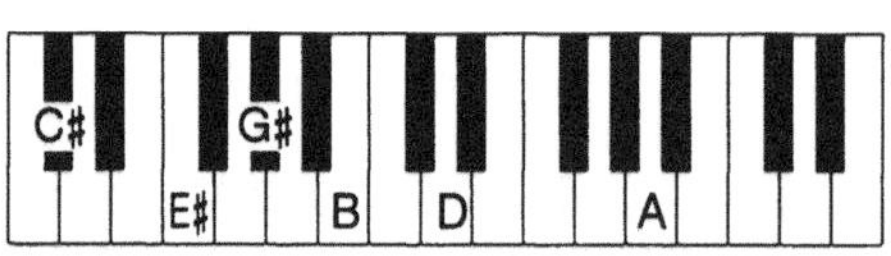

C♯7♯9(♭13)

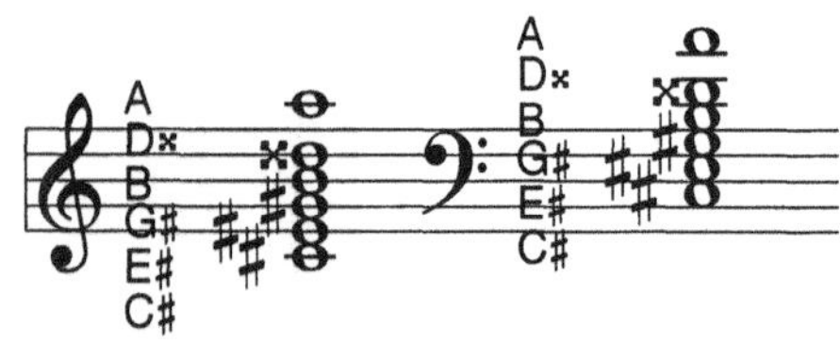

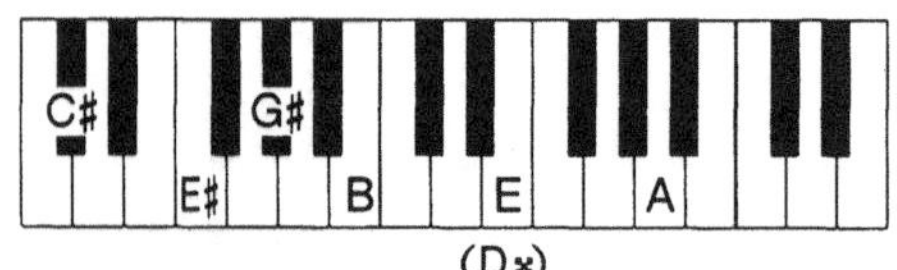

C♯7♯11(♭13)

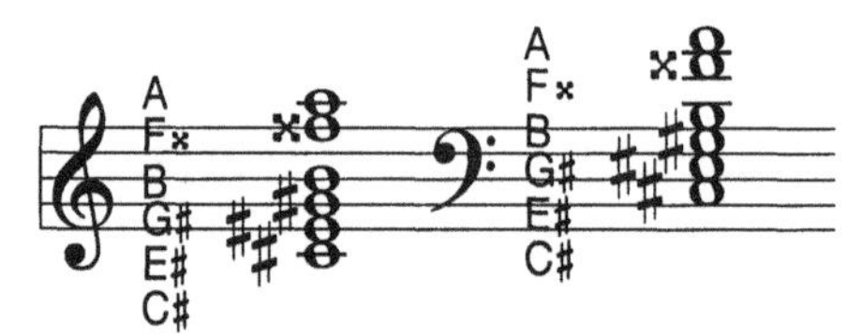

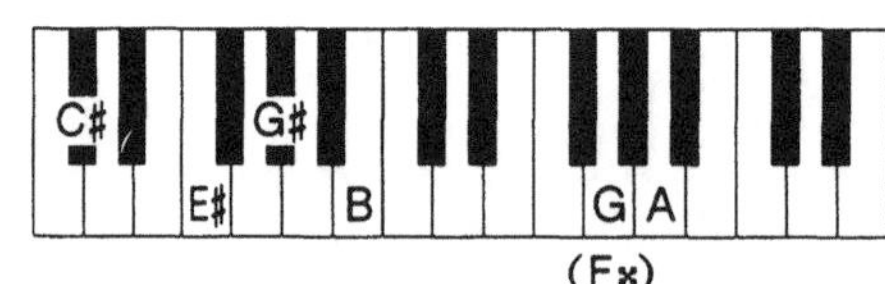

C♯7♭9(♯9,♯11)

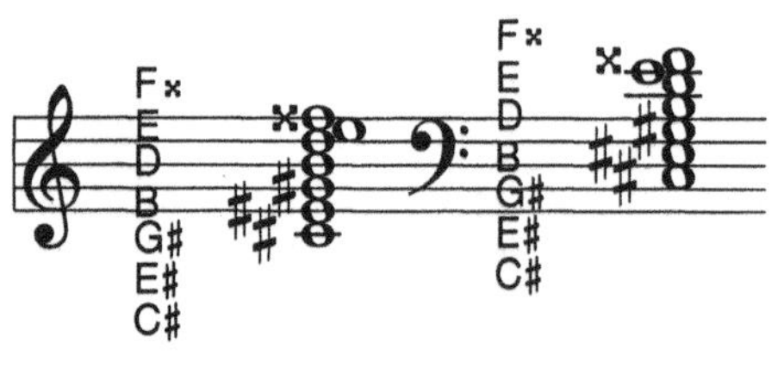

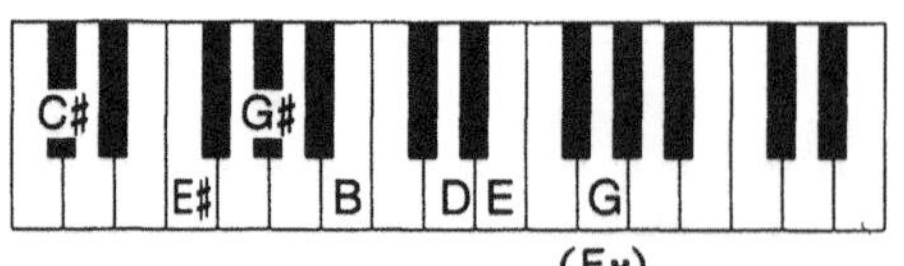

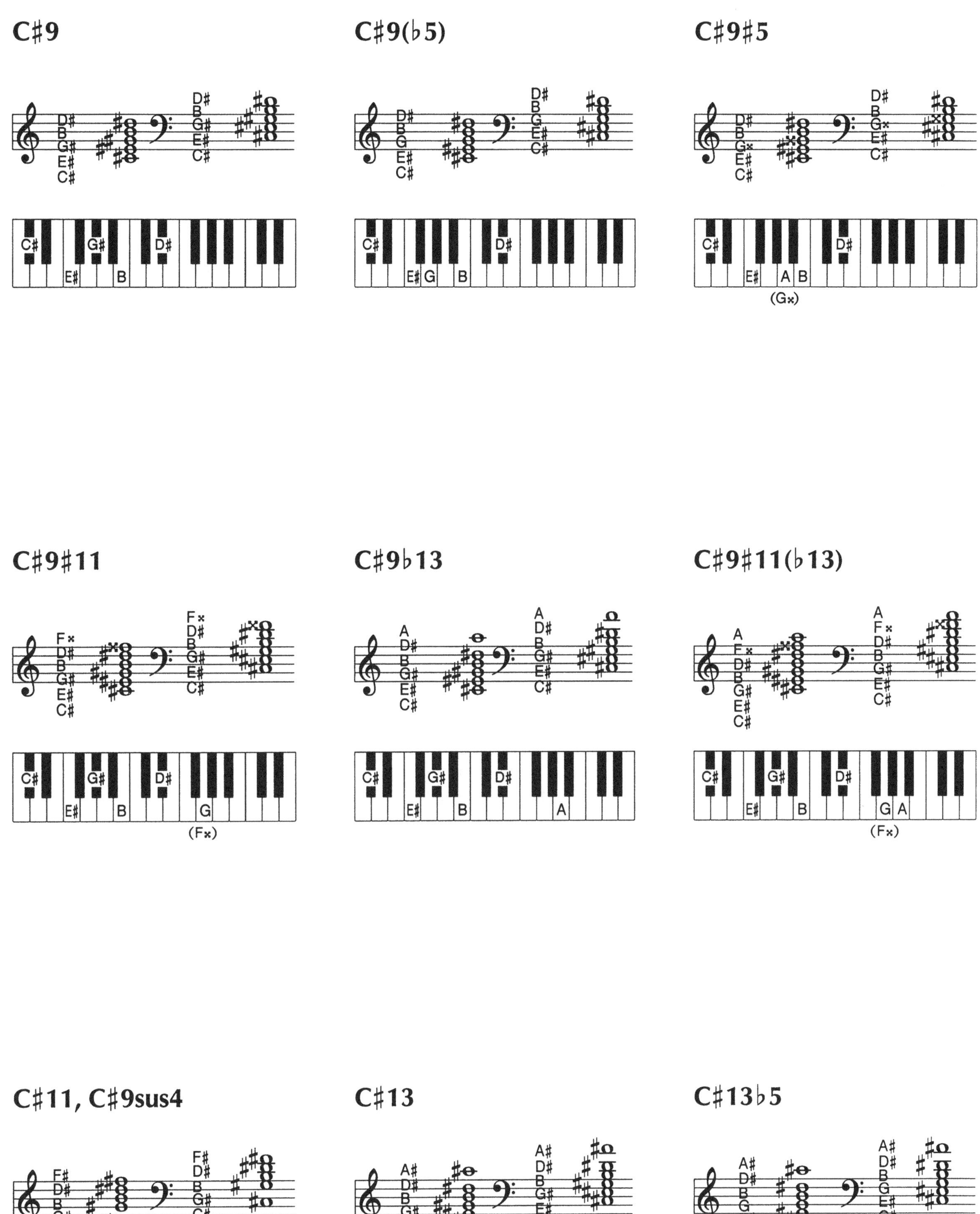

C♯9

C♯9(♭5)

C♯9♯5

C♯9♯11

C♯9♭13

C♯9♯11(♭13)

C♯11, C♯9sus4

C♯13

C♯13♭5

C♯13♭9

C♯13♯9

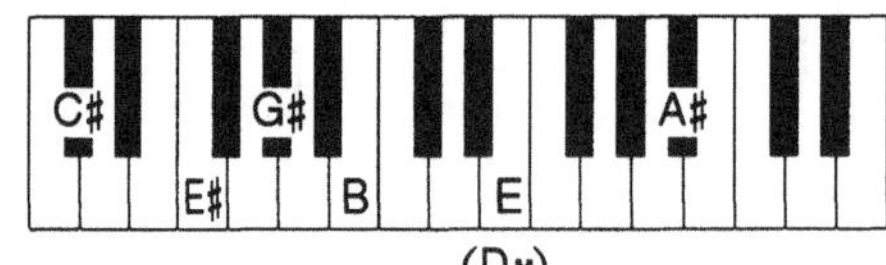

C♯13♯11

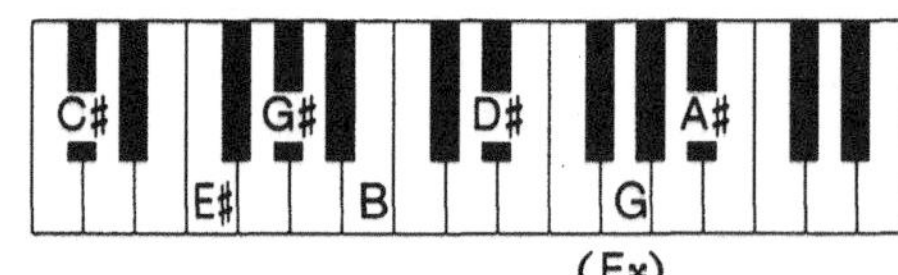

C♯13(sus4)

C♯m(♯5)

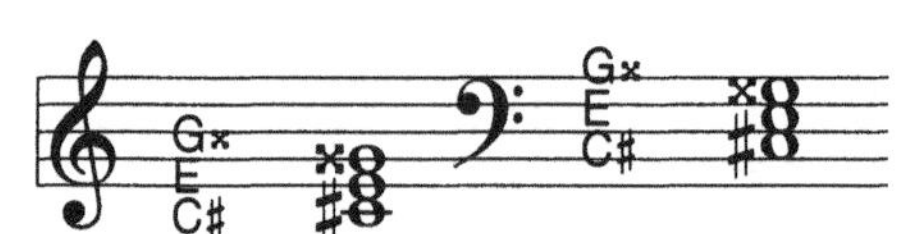

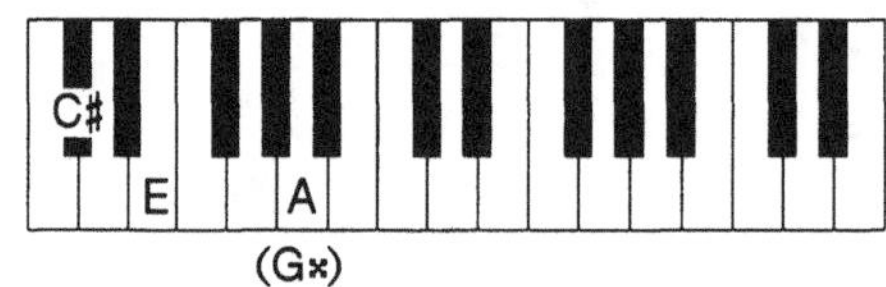

C♯m$^{6}_{9}$

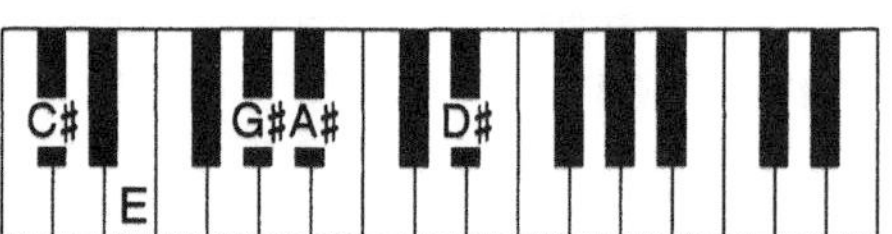

C♯m7(add4)

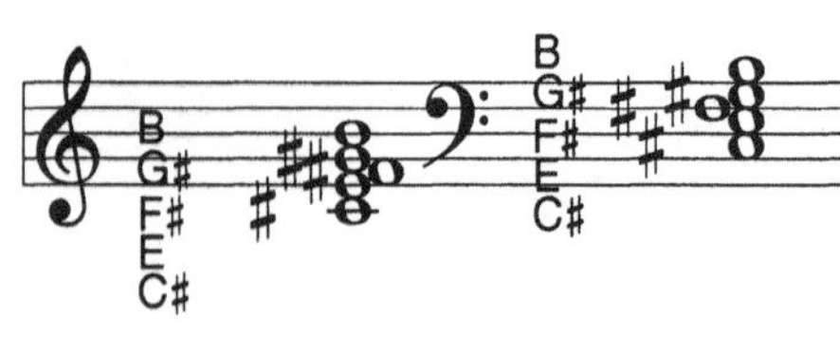

C♯m7(add11)

C♯m7♭5(♭9)

C♯m9

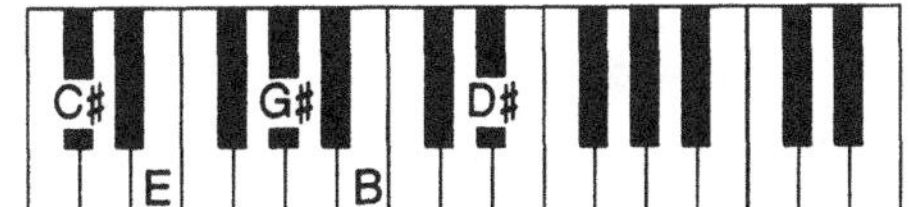

C♯m9(maj7)

C♯m9♭5

C♯m11

C♯m13

C♯dim7(add9)

C♯m11♭5

C♯m11(maj7)

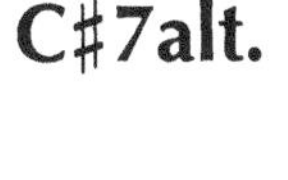

C♯7alt.

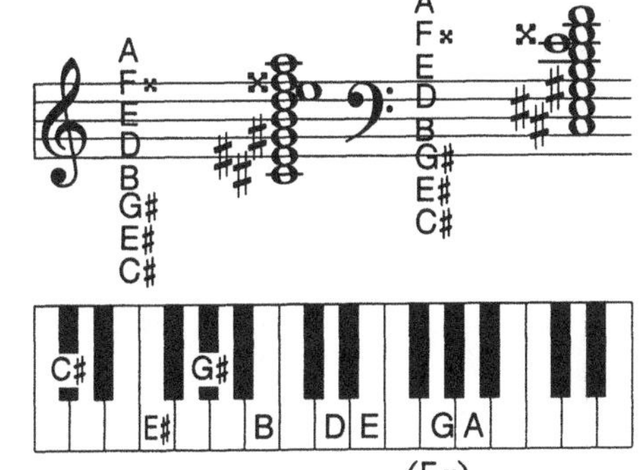

D CHORDS

D

Root Position

1st Inversion

2nd Inversion

Dm

Root Position

1st Inversion

2nd Inversion

D+

Root Position

1st Inversion

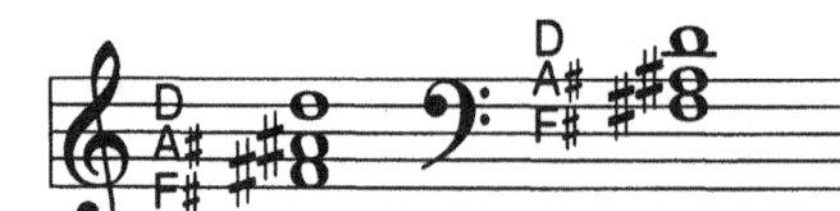

2nd Inversion

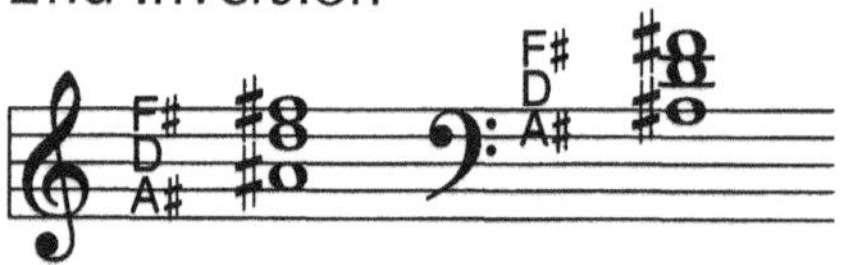

Ddim

Root Position

1st Inversion

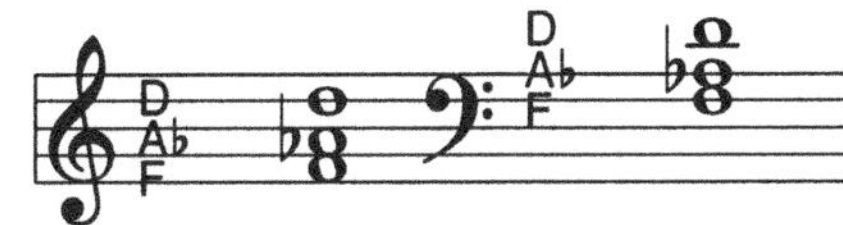

2nd Inversion

Dsus

Root Position

1st Inversion

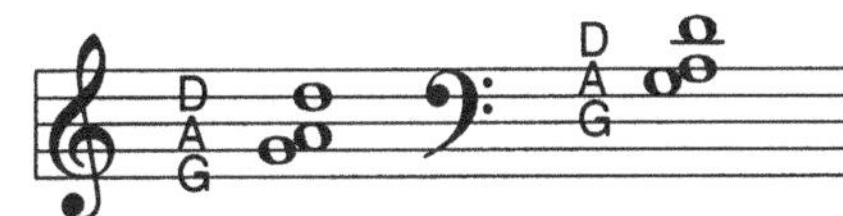

2nd Inversion

D(♭5)

Root Position

1st Inversion

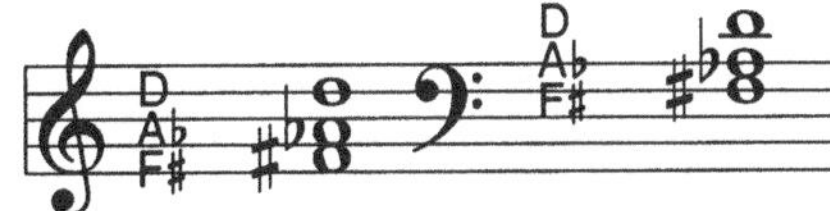

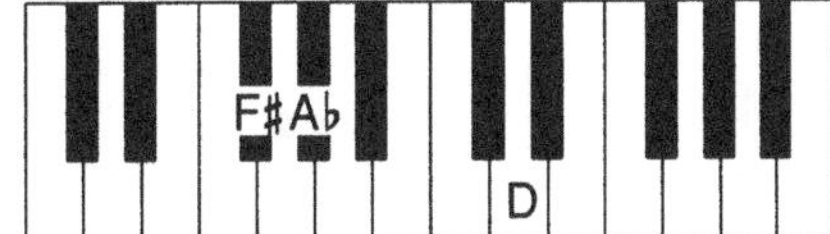

2nd Inversion

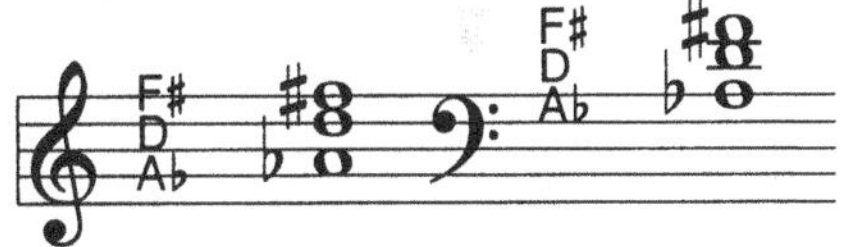

Dsus2

Root Position

1st Inversion

2nd Inversion

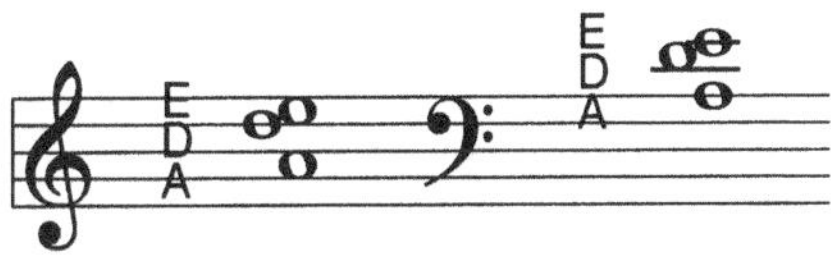

D6

Root Position

1st Inversion

2nd Inversion

3rd Inversion

D(add2), D(add9)

Root Position

1st Inversion

2nd Inversion

3rd Inversion

Dmaj7

Root Position

1st Inversion

2nd Inversion

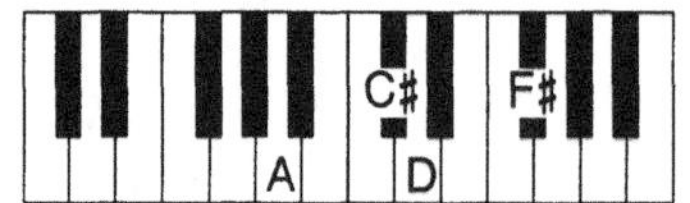

3rd Inversion

Dmaj7♭5

Root Position

1st Inversion

2nd Inversion

3rd Inversion

Dmaj7♯5

Root Position

1st Inversion

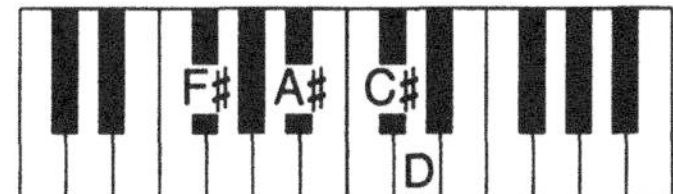

2nd Inversion

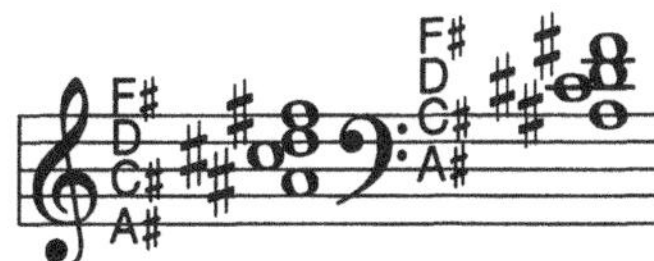

3rd Inversion

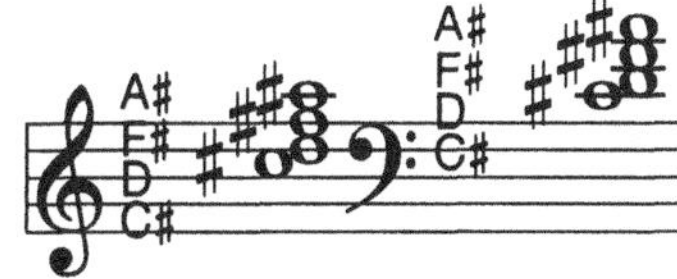

D7

Root Position

1st Inversion

2nd Inversion

3rd Inversion

D7♭5

Root Position

1st Inversion

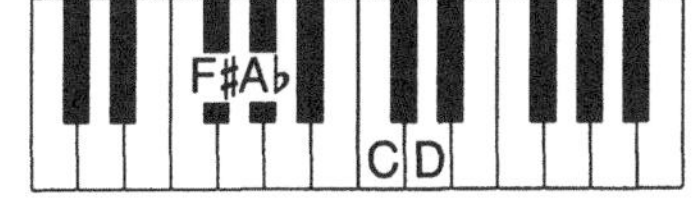

2nd Inversion

3rd Inversion

D7♯5

Root Position

1st Inversion

2nd Inversion

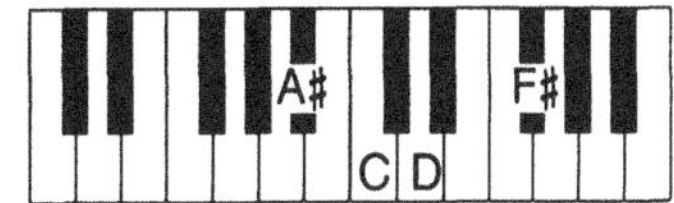

3rd Inversion

D7sus

Root Position

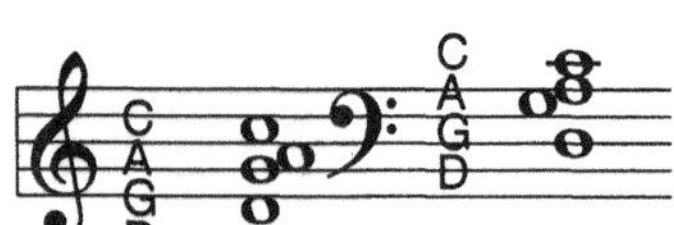

1st Inversion

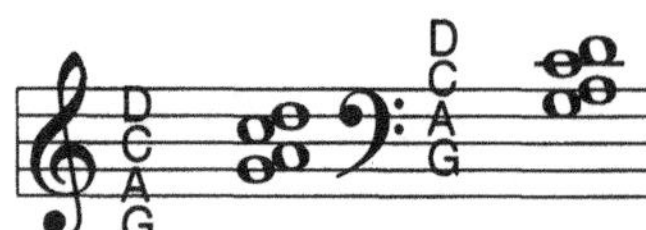

2nd Inversion

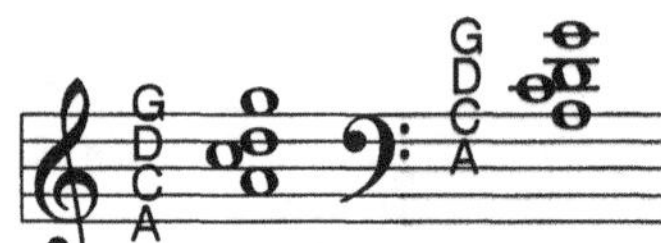

3rd Inversion

Dm(add2), Dm(add9)

Root Position

1st Inversion

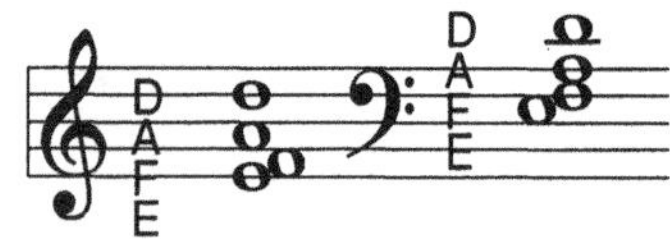

2nd Inversion

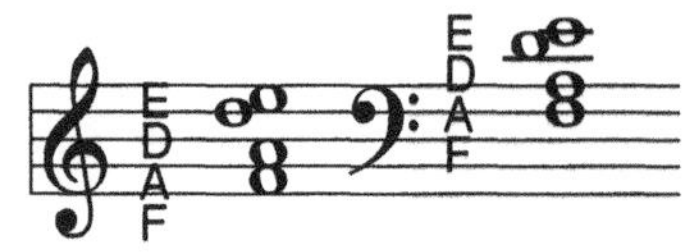

3rd Inversion

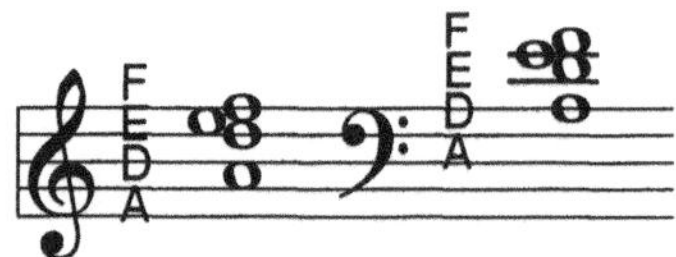

Dm6

Root Position

1st Inversion

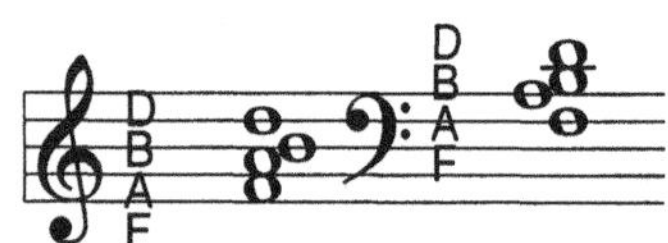

2nd Inversion

3rd Inversion

Dm7

Root Position

1st Inversion

2nd Inversion

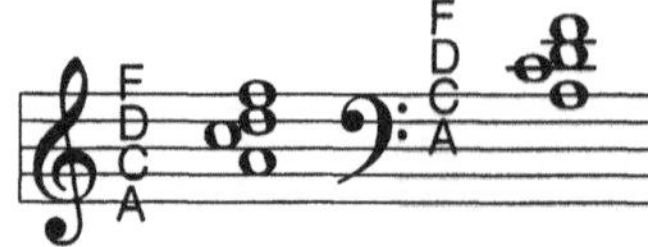

3rd Inversion

Dm(maj7)

Root Position

1st Inversion

2nd Inversion

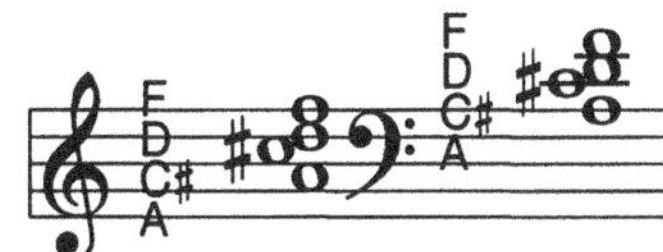

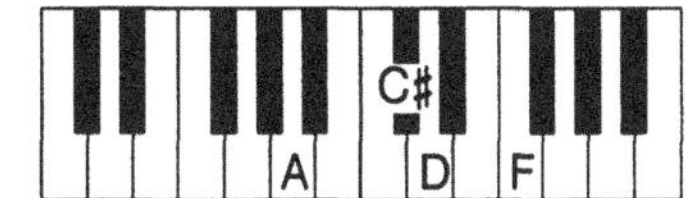

3rd Inversion

Dm7♭5

Root Position

1st Inversion

2nd Inversion

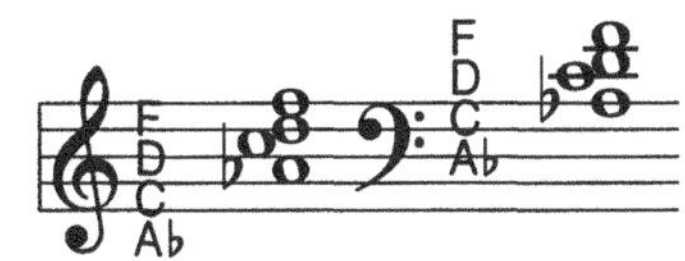

3rd Inversion

Ddim7

Root Position

1st Inversion

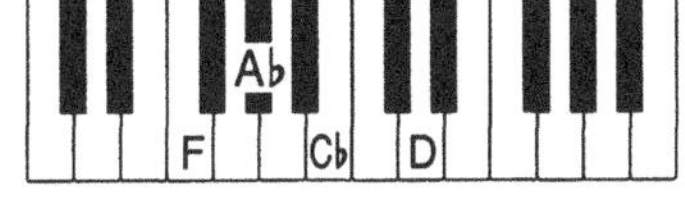

2nd Inversion

3rd Inversion

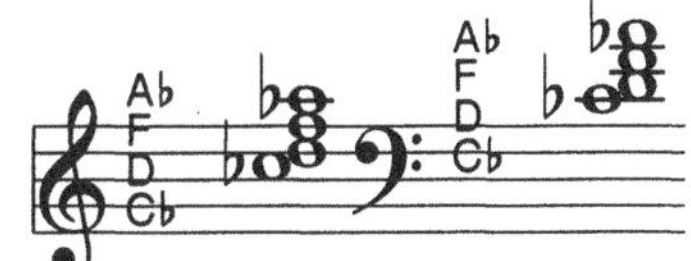

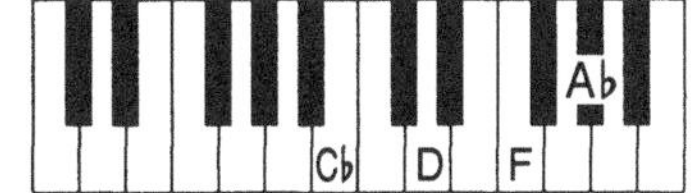

Ddim(maj7)

Root Position

1st Inversion

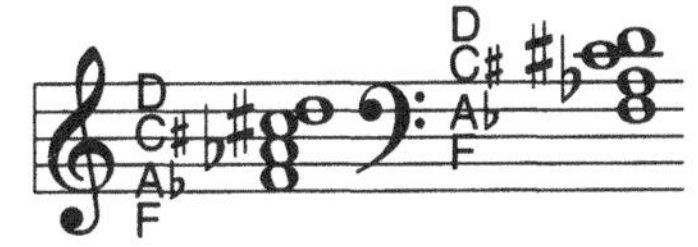

2nd Inversion

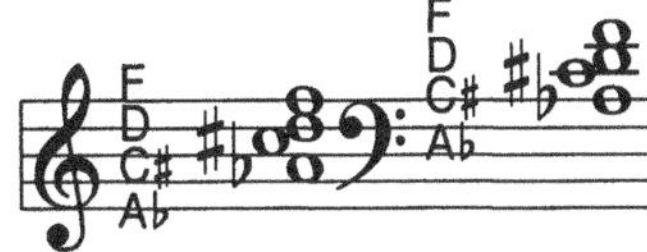

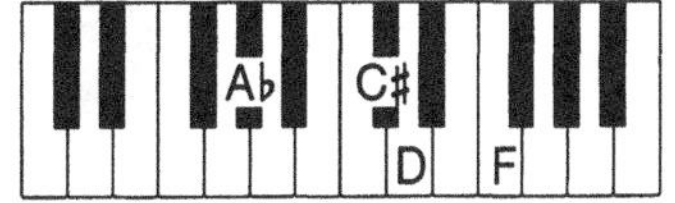

3rd Inversion

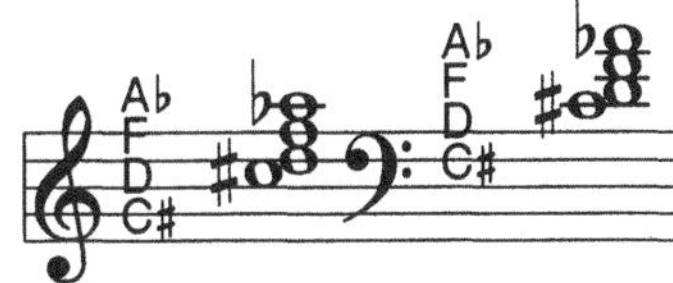

ADDITIONAL D CHORDS

D5

D$^{6}_{9}$

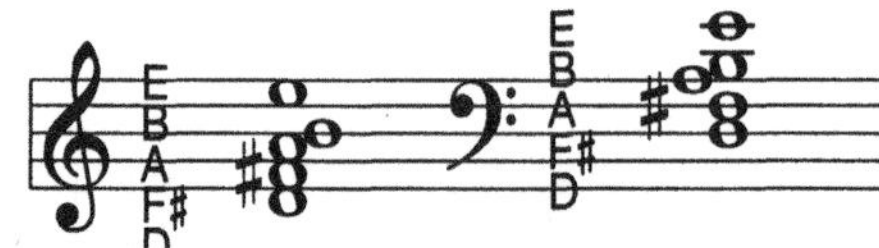

Dmaj$^{6}_{9}$

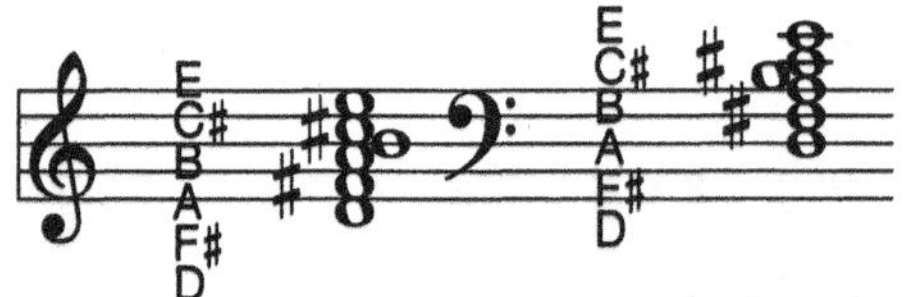

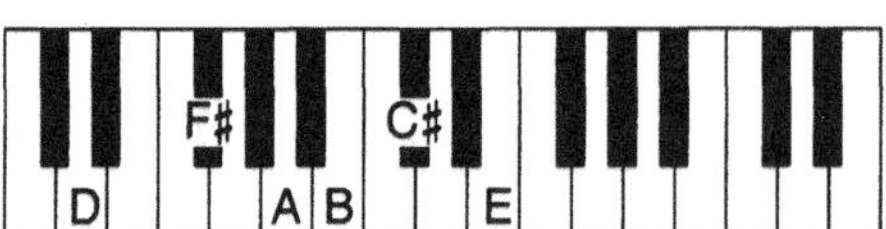

Dmaj7♯11

Dmaj9

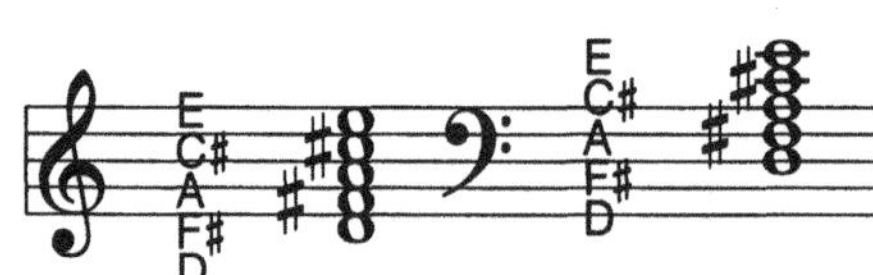

Dmaj9♭5

Dmaj9♯5

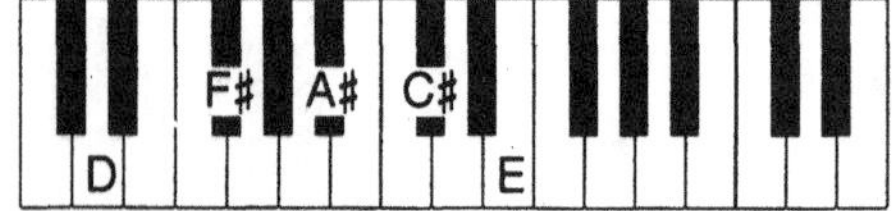

Dmaj9♯11

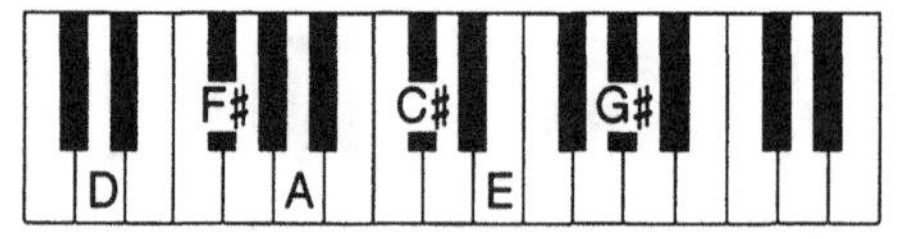

Dmaj13

Dmaj13♭5

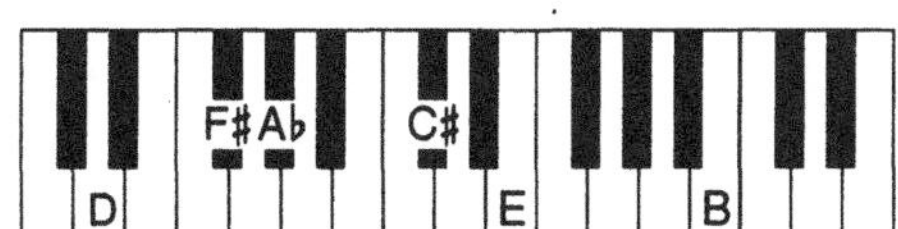

Dmaj13♯11

D7♭9

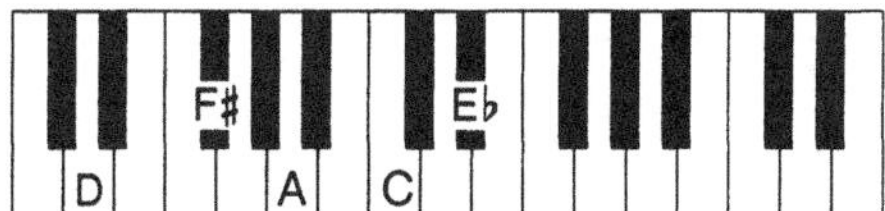

D7♯9

D7♯11

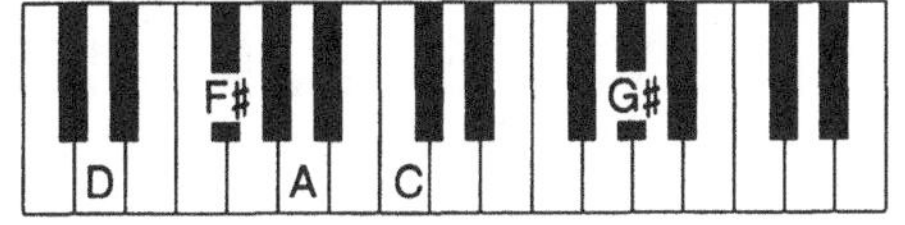

D7♭5(♭9)

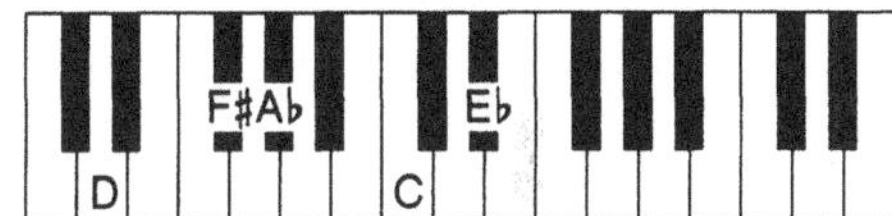

D7♭5(♯9)

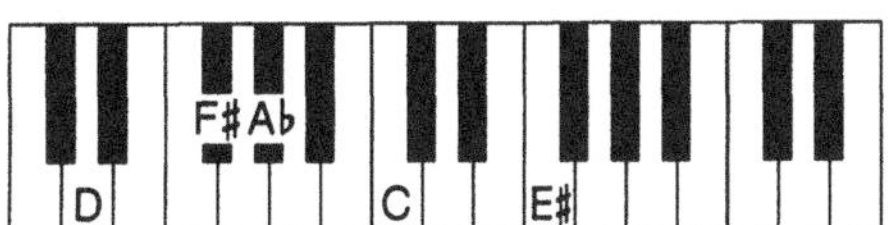

D7♯5(♭9)

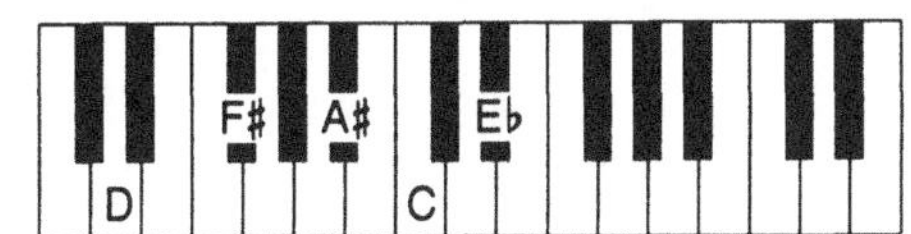

D7♯5(♯9)

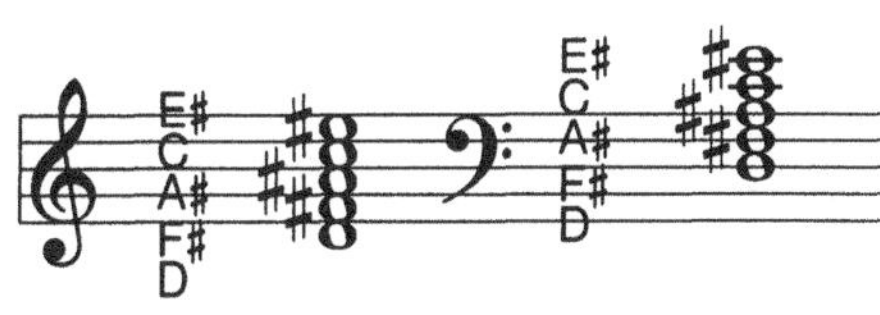

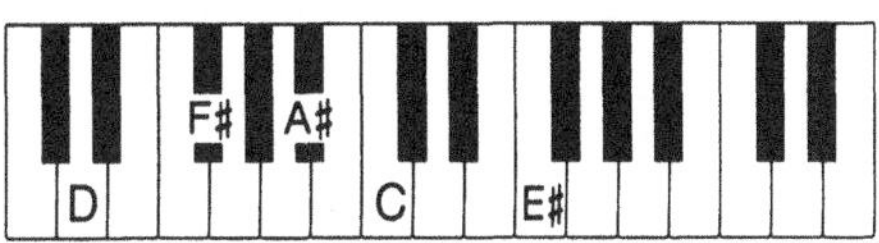

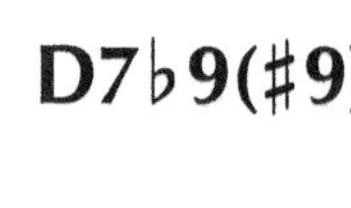

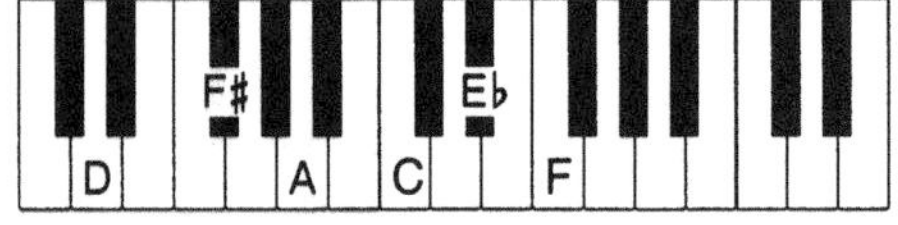

D7(add13)

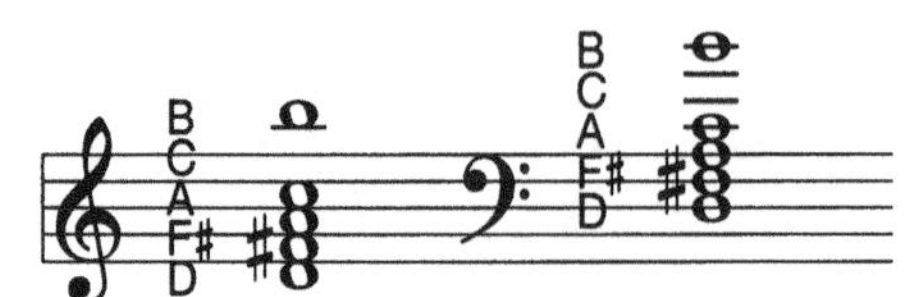

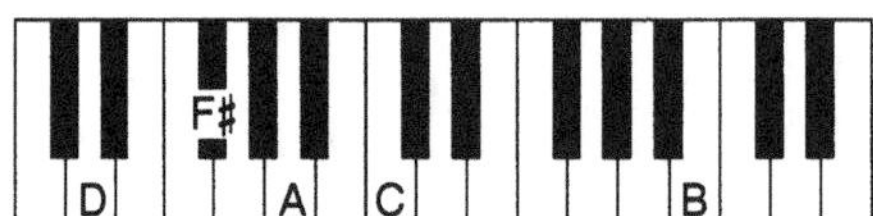

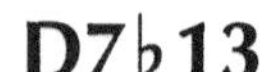

D7♭9(♯11)

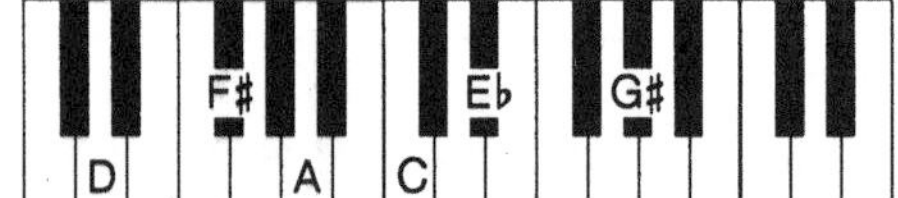

D7♯9(♯11)

D7♭9(♭13)

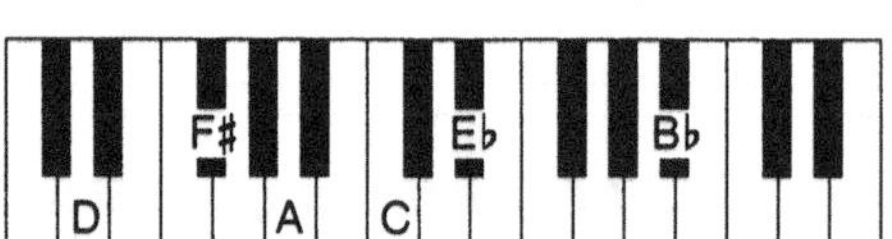

D7♯9(♭13)

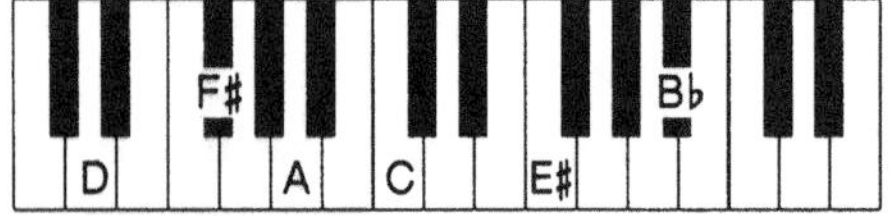

D7♯11(♭13)

D7♭9(♯9,♯11)

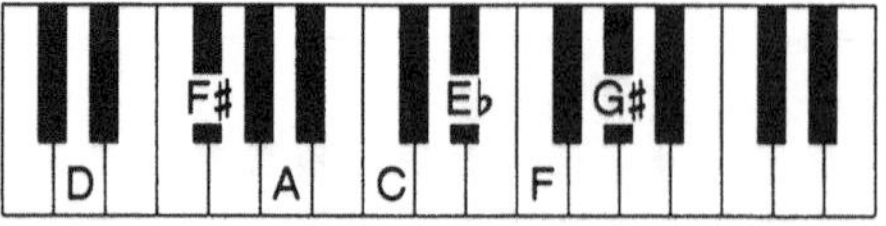

D9

D9(♭5)

D9♯5

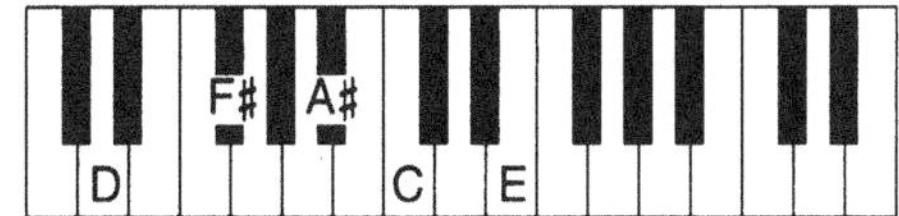

D9♯11

D9♭13

D9♯11(♭13)

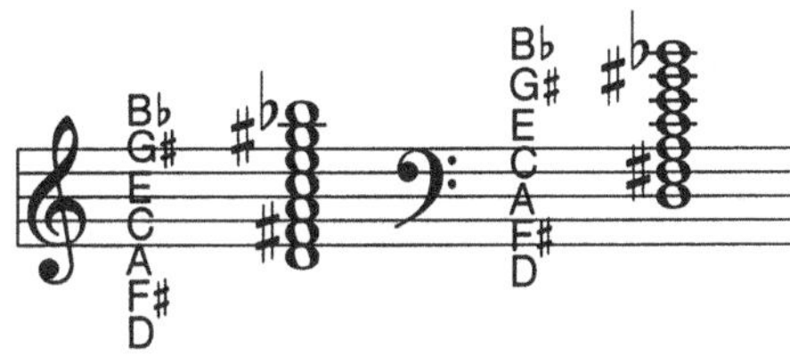

D11, D9sus4

D13

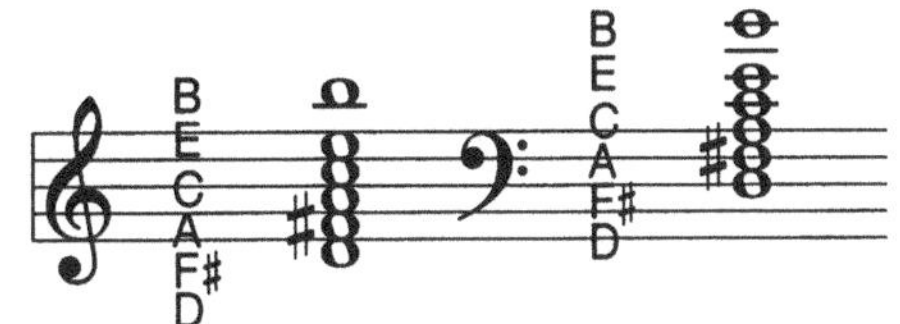

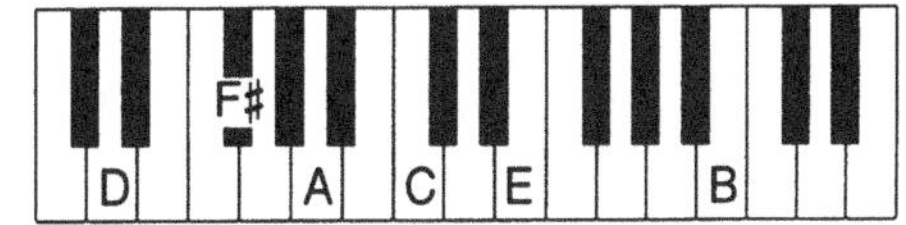

D13♭5

D13♭9

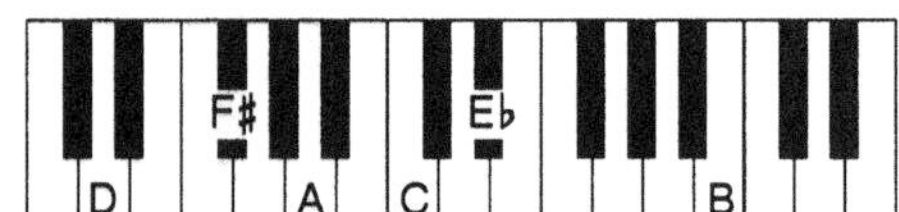

D13♯9

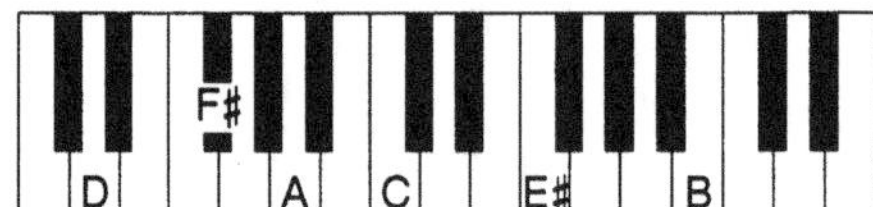

D13♯11

D13(sus4)

Dm(♯5)

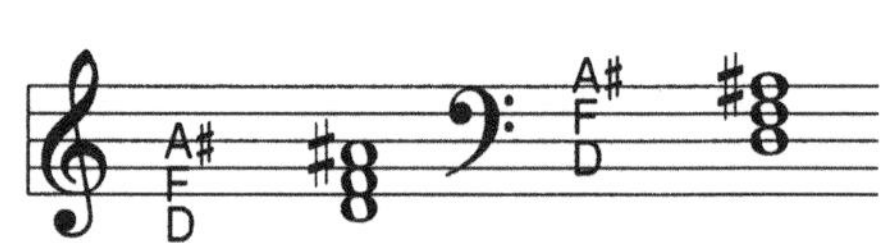

Dm$^6_9$

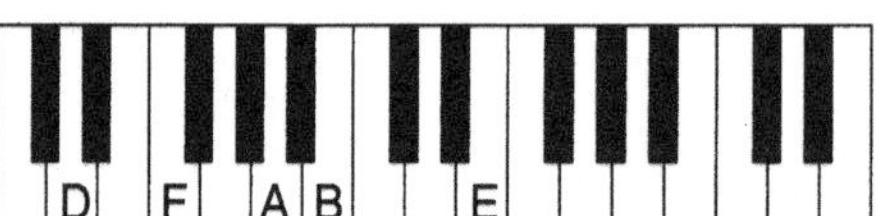

Dm7(add4)

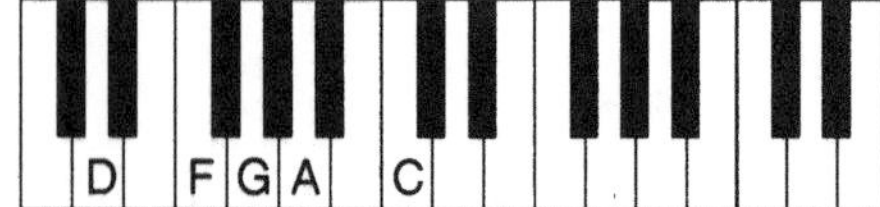

Dm7(add11)

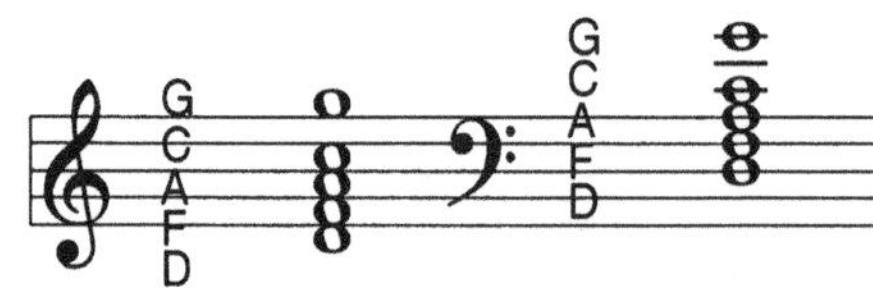

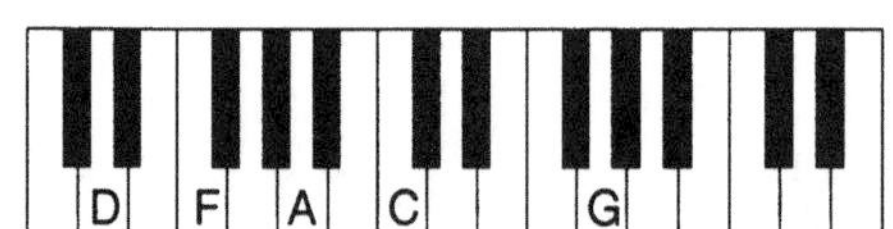

Dm7♭5(♭9)

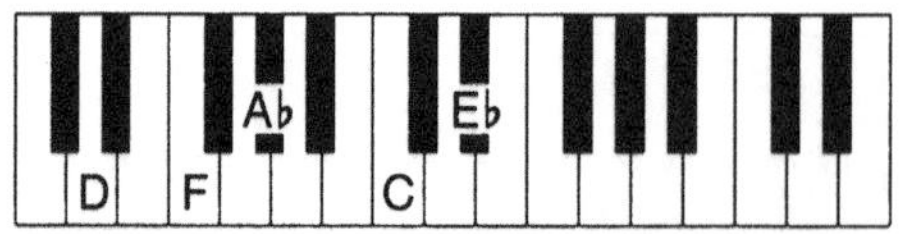

Dm9

Dm9(maj7)

Dm9♭5

Dm11

Dm13

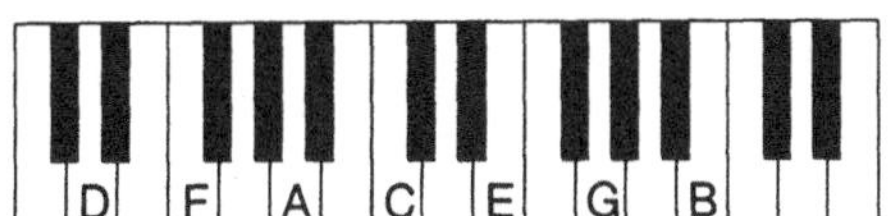

Ddim7(add9)

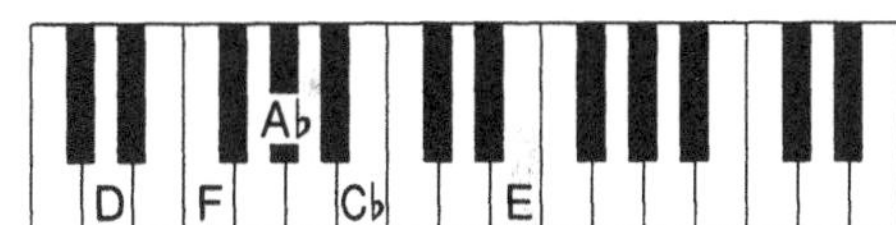

Dm11♭5

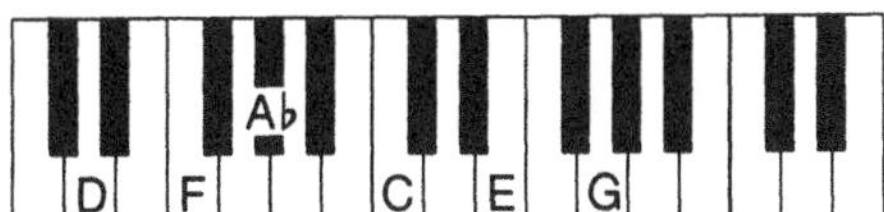

Dm11(maj7)

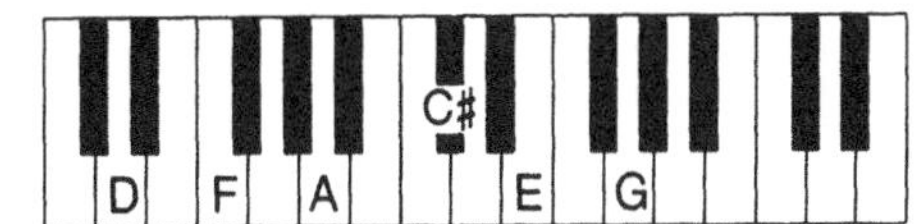

D7alt.

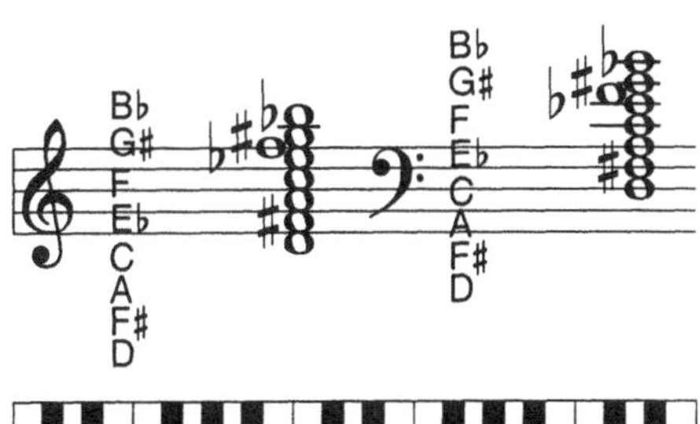

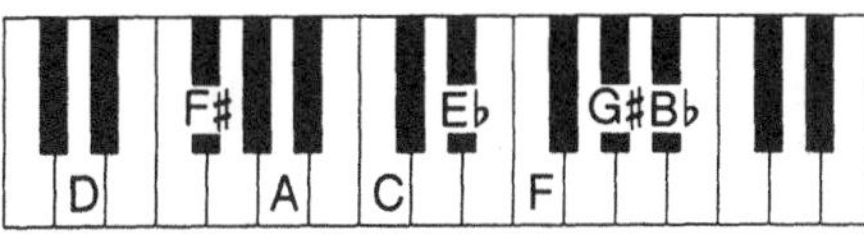

E♭ CHORDS

E♭

Root Position

1st Inversion

2nd Inversion

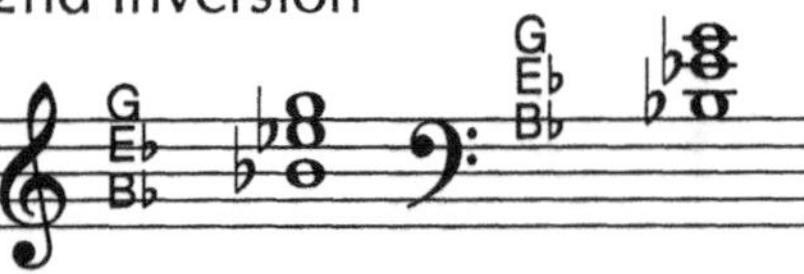

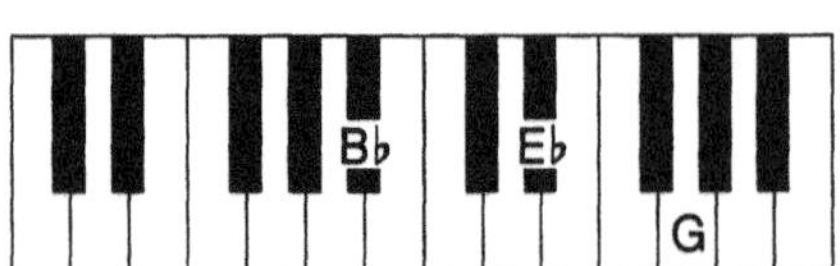

E♭m

Root Position

1st Inversion

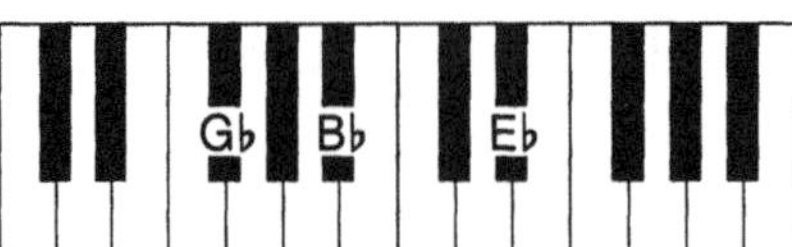

2nd Inversion

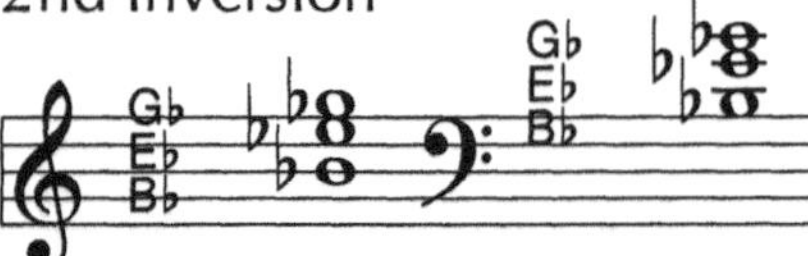

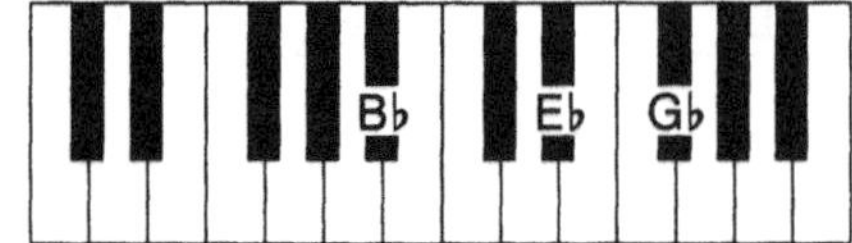

E♭+

Root Position

1st Inversion

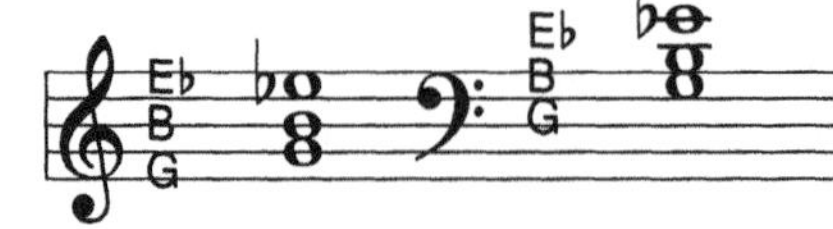

2nd Inversion

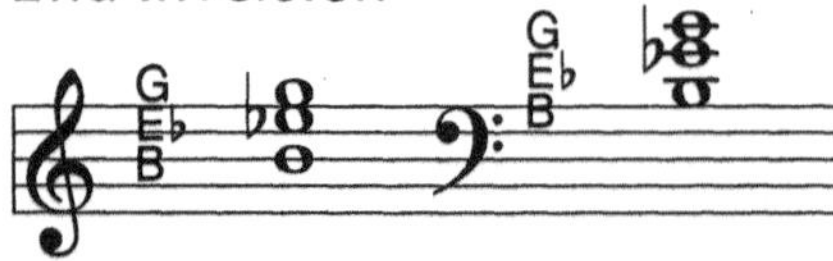

E♭dim

Root Position

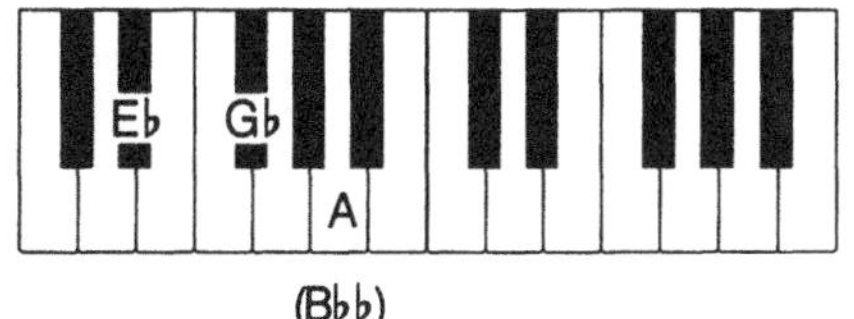

1st Inversion

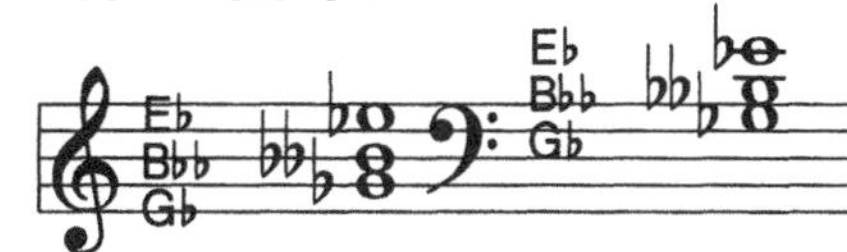

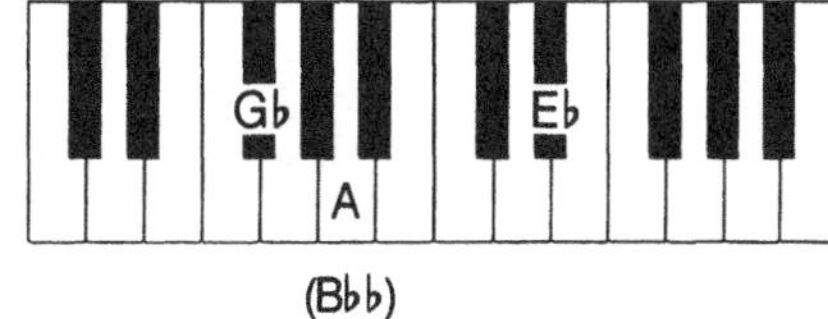

2nd Inversion

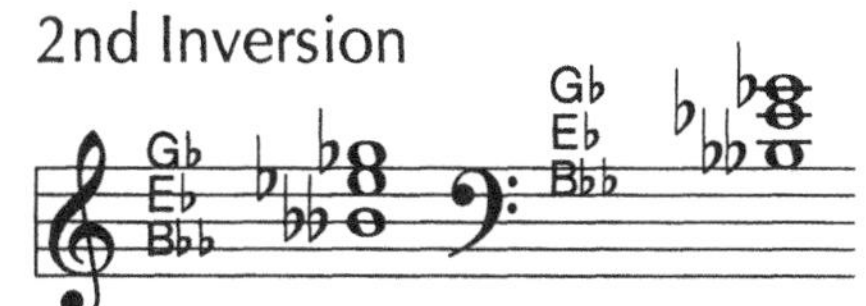

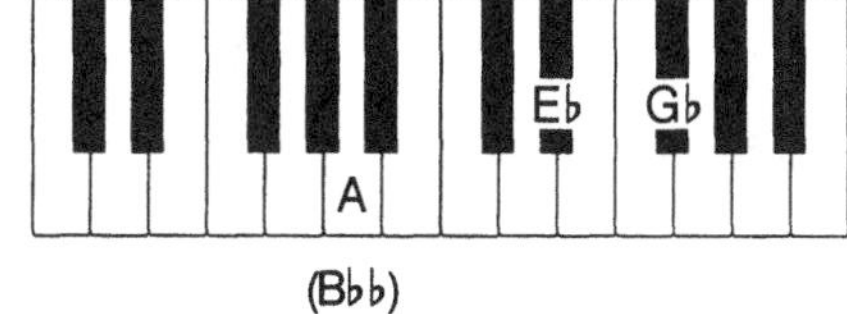

E♭sus

Root Position

1st Inversion

2nd Inversion

E♭(♭5)

Root Position

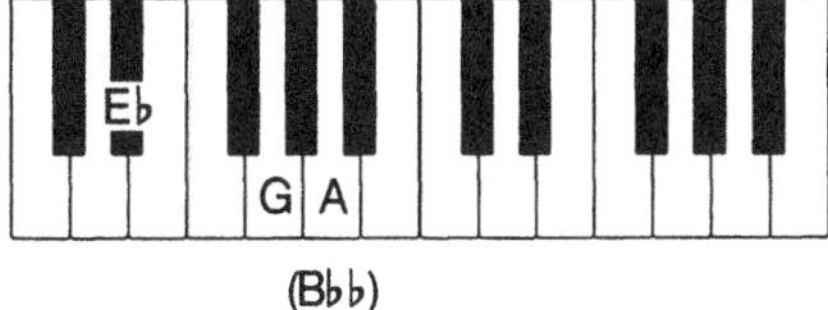

1st Inversion

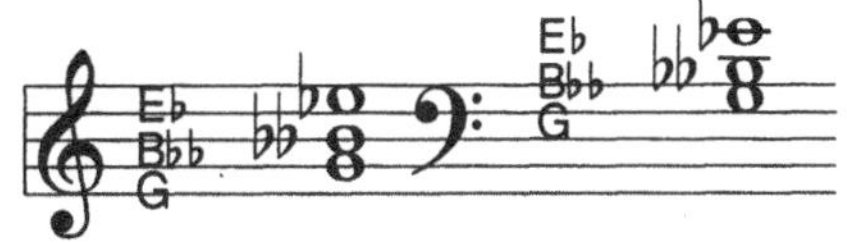

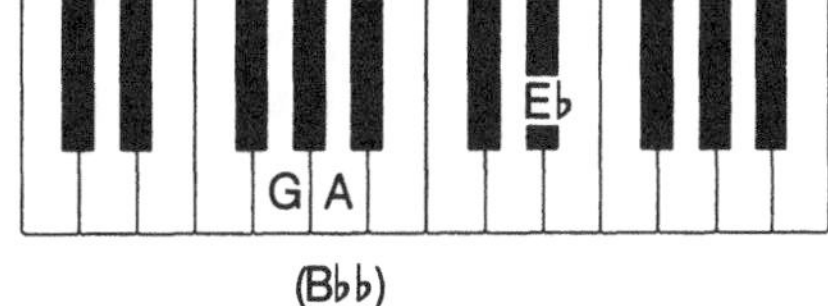

2nd Inversion

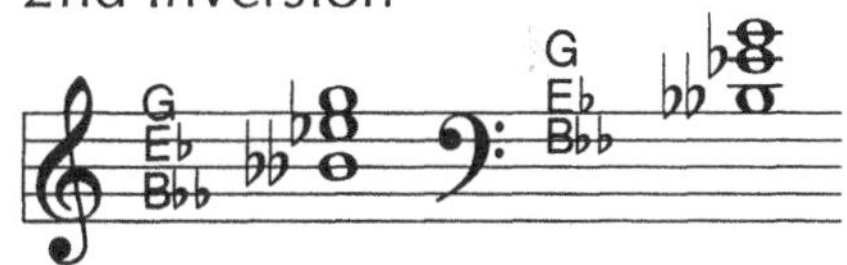

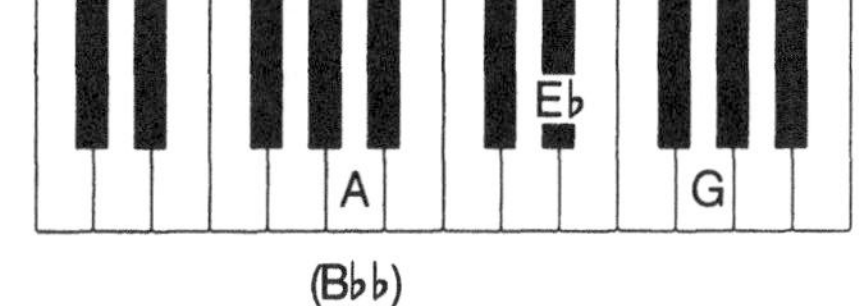

E♭sus2

Root Position

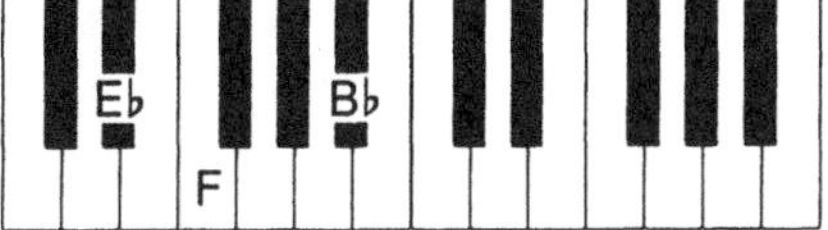

1st Inversion

2nd Inversion

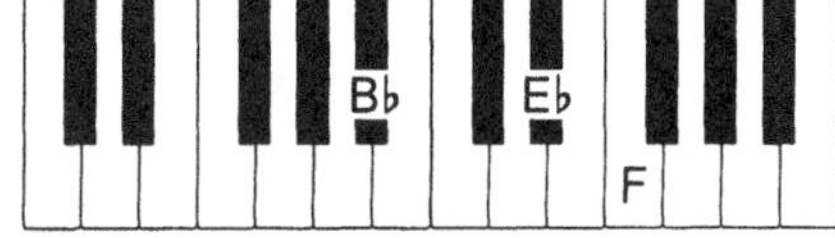

E♭6

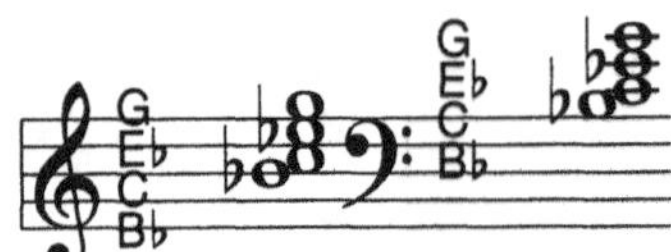

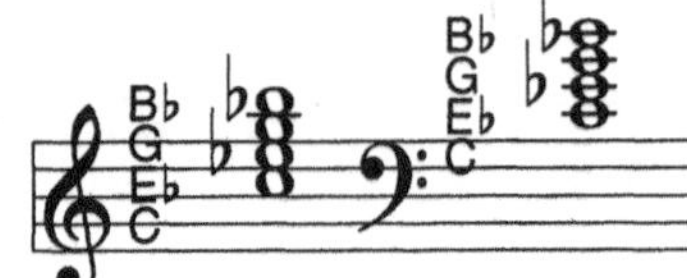

E♭(add2), E♭(add9)

Root Position

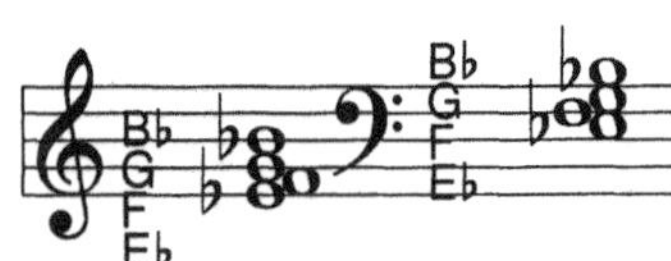

1st Inversion

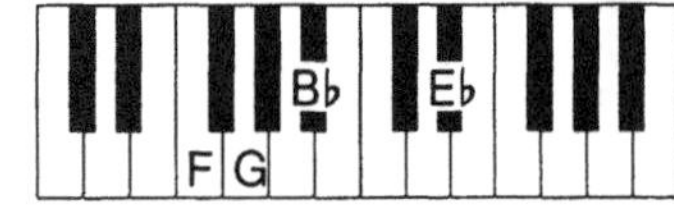

2nd Inversion

3rd Inversion

E♭maj7

Root Position

1st Inversion

2nd Inversion

3rd Inversion

E♭maj7♭5

Root Position

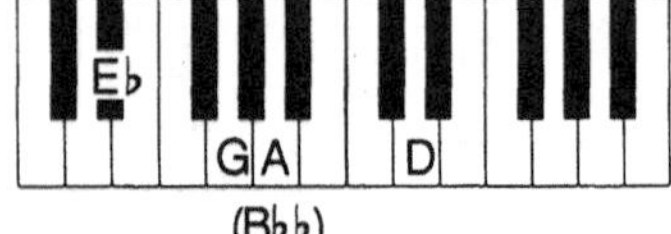

1st Inversion

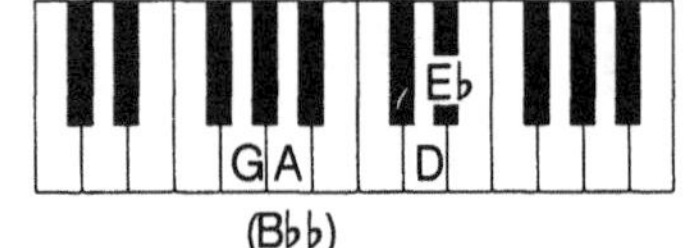

2nd Inversion

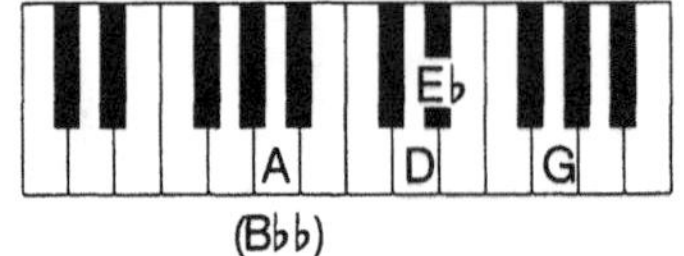

3rd Inversion

E♭maj7♯5

E♭7

Root Position

1st Inversion

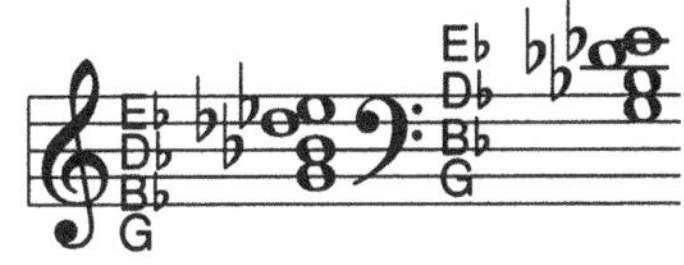

2nd Inversion

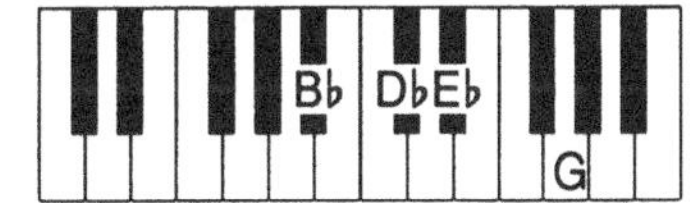

3rd Inversion

E♭7♭5

Root Position

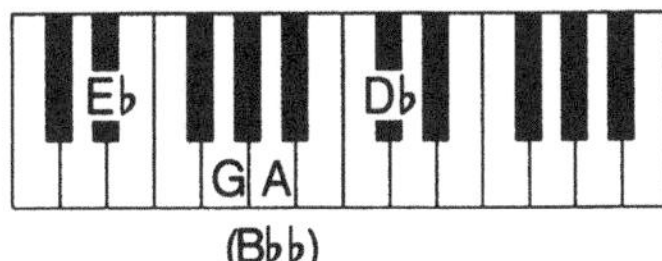

1st Inversion

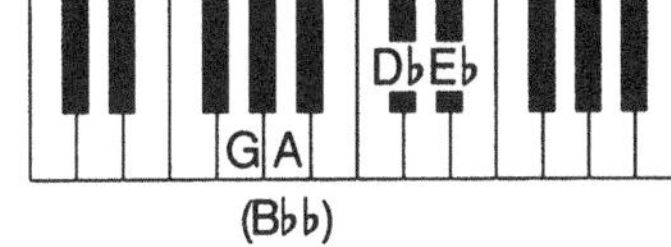

2nd Inversion

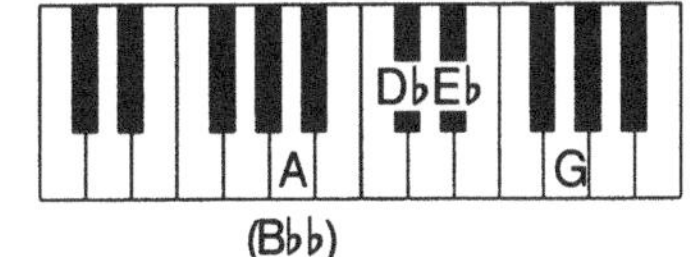

3rd Inversion

E♭7♯5

Root Position

1st Inversion

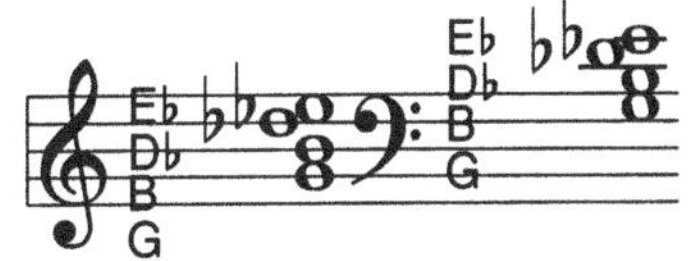

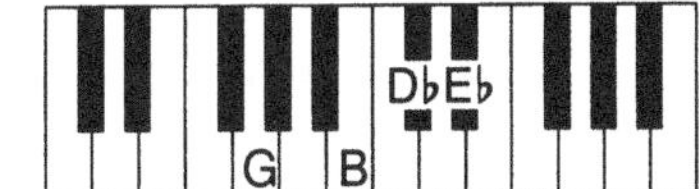

2nd Inversion

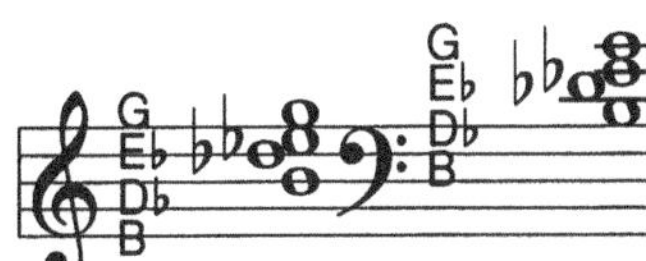

3rd Inversion

E♭7sus

Root Position

1st Inversion

2nd Inversion

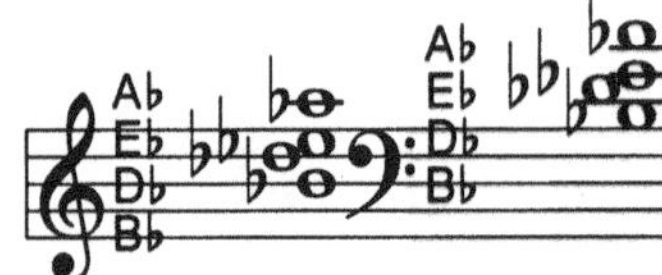

3rd Inversion

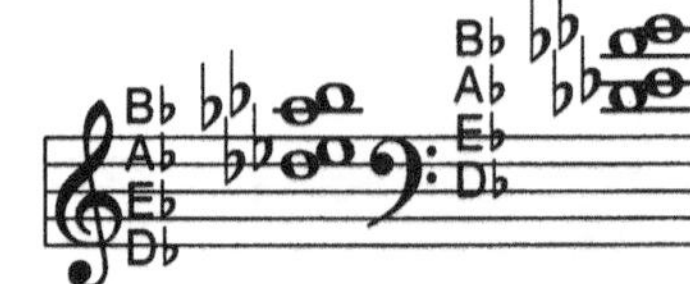

E♭m(add2), E♭m(add9)

Root Position

1st Inversion

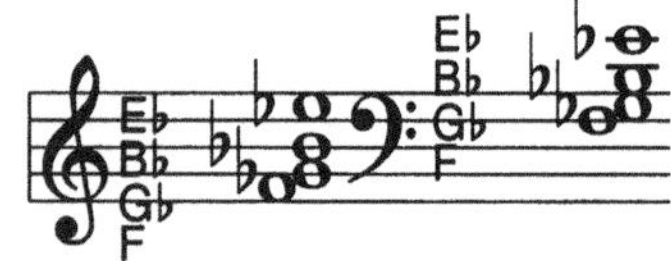

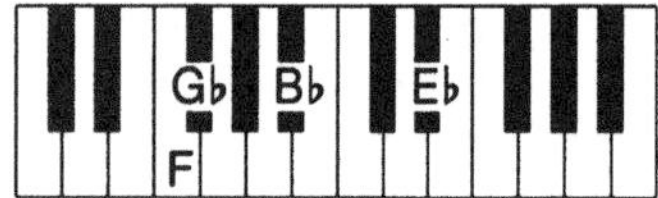

2nd Inversion

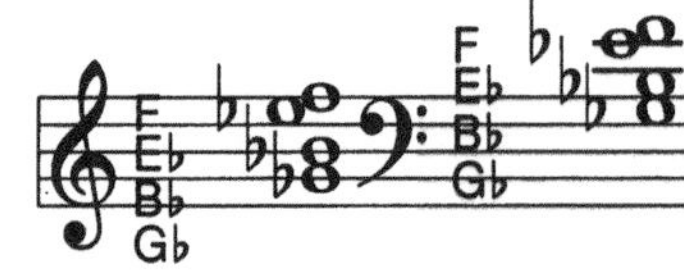

3rd Inversion

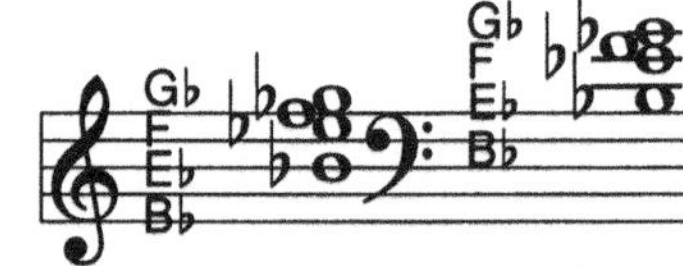

E♭m6

Root Position

1st Inversion

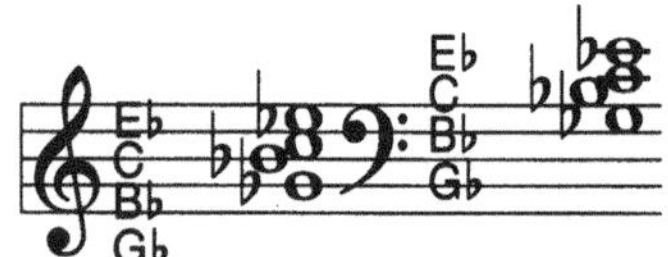

2nd Inversion

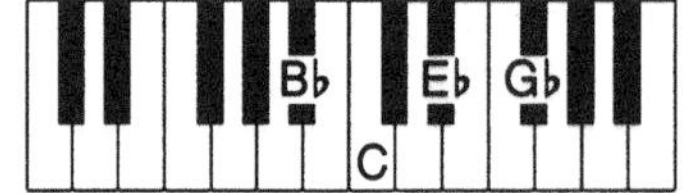

3rd Inversion

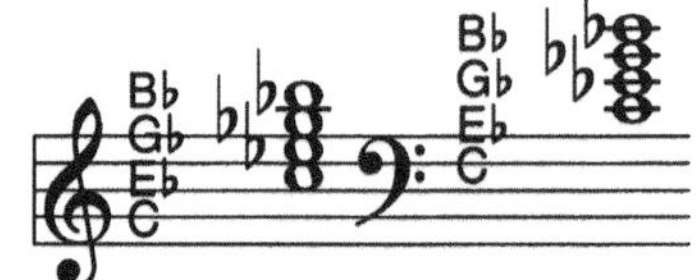

E♭m7

Root Position

1st Inversion

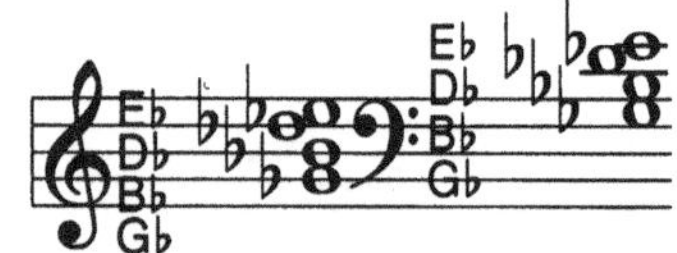

2nd Inversion

3rd Inversion

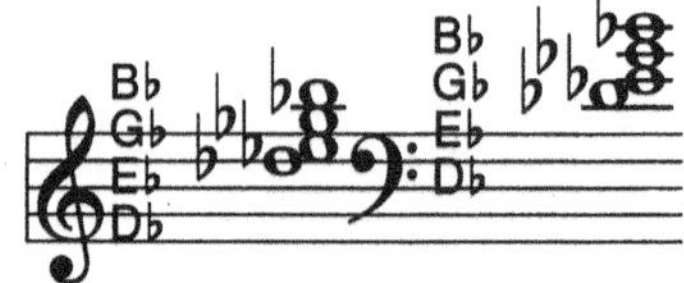

E♭m(maj7)

Root Position

1st Inversion

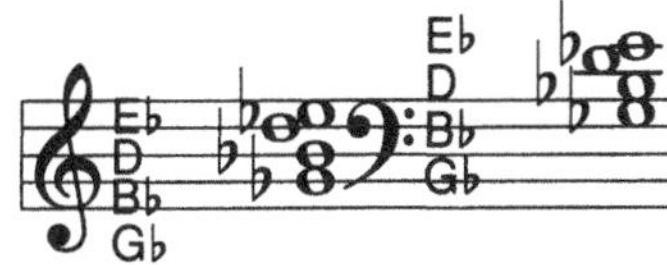

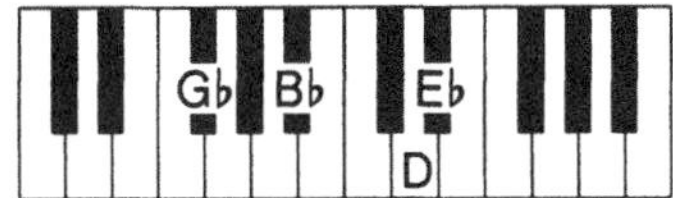

2nd Inversion

3rd Inversion

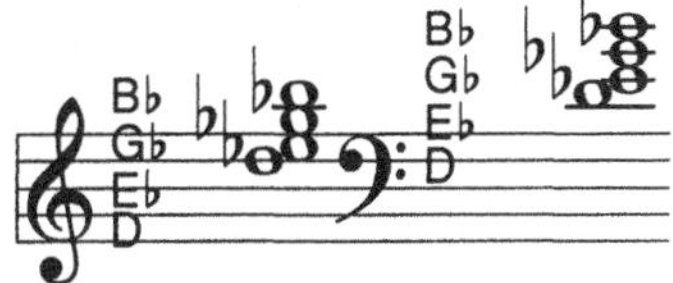

E♭m7♭5

Root Position

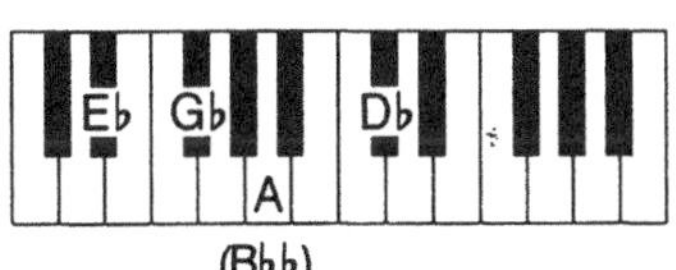

1st Inversion

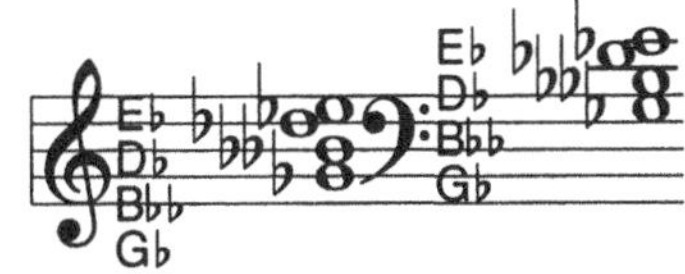

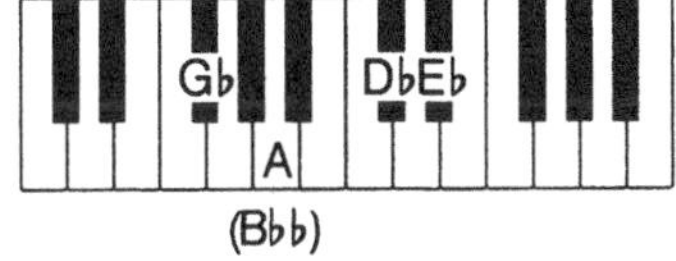

2nd Inversion

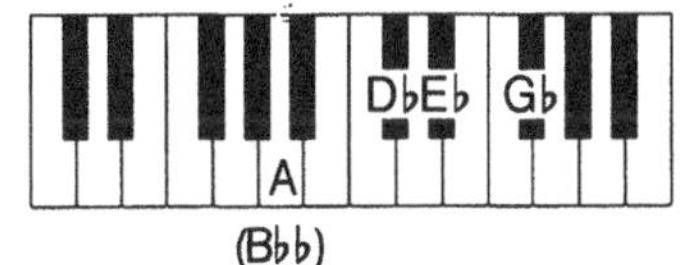

3rd Inversion

E♭dim7

Root Position

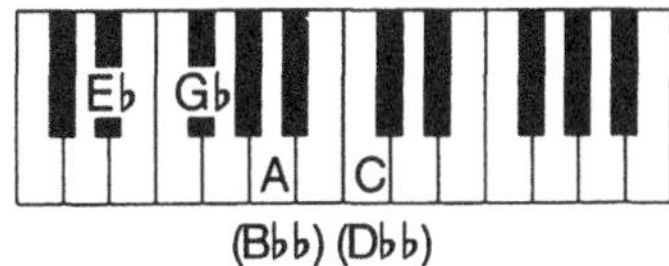

1st Inversion

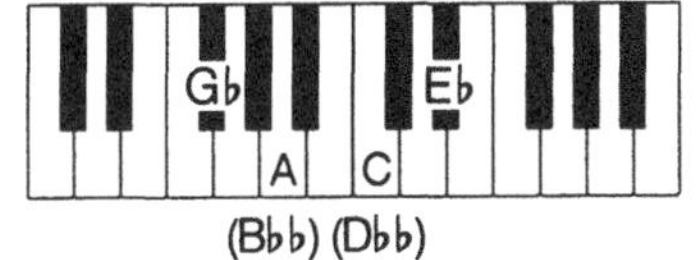

2nd Inversion

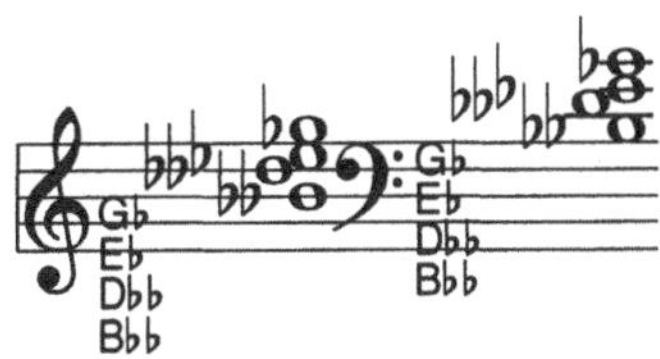

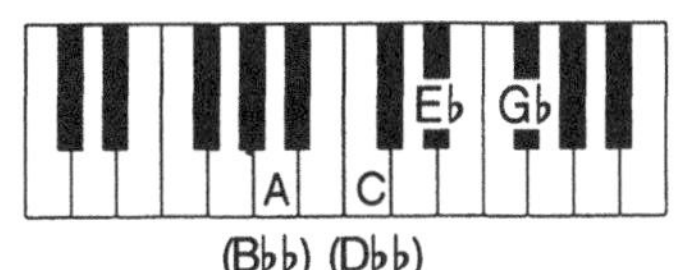

3rd Inversion

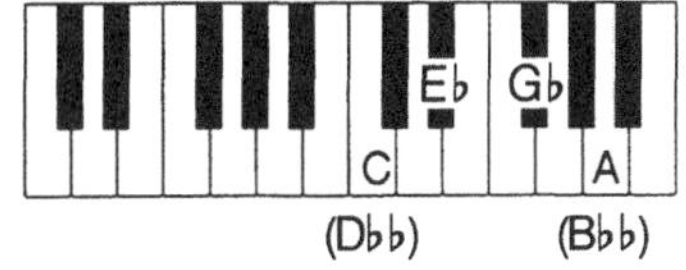

E♭dim(maj7)

Root Position

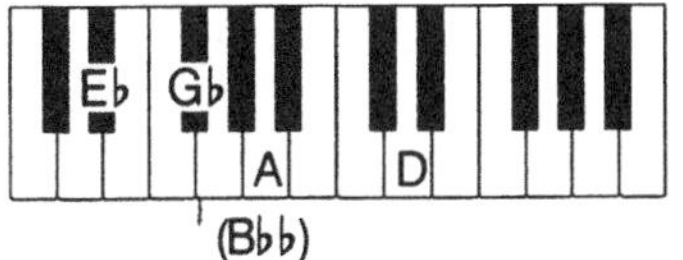

1st Inversion

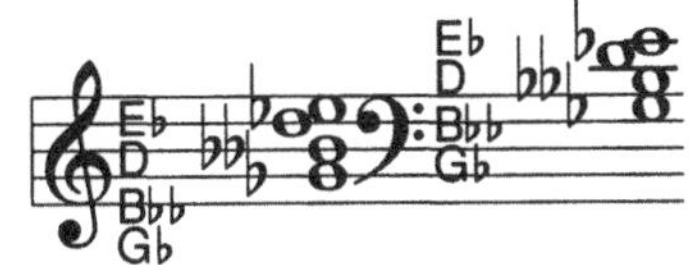

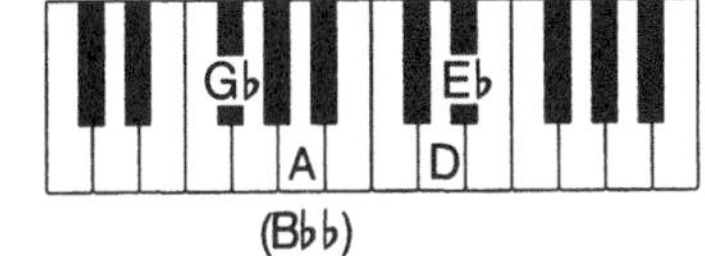

2nd Inversion

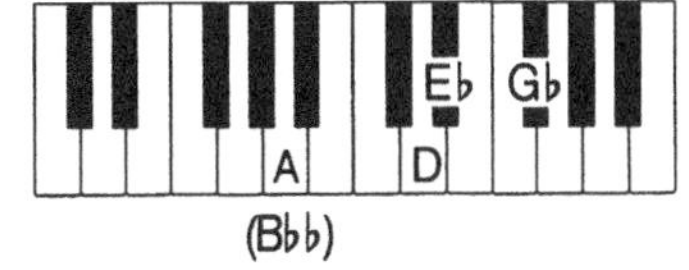

3rd Inversion

ADDITIONAL E♭ CHORDS

E♭5

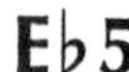

E♭ 6/9

E♭maj 6/9

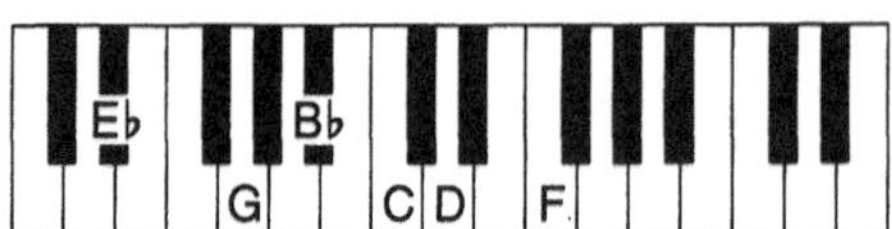

E♭maj7♯11

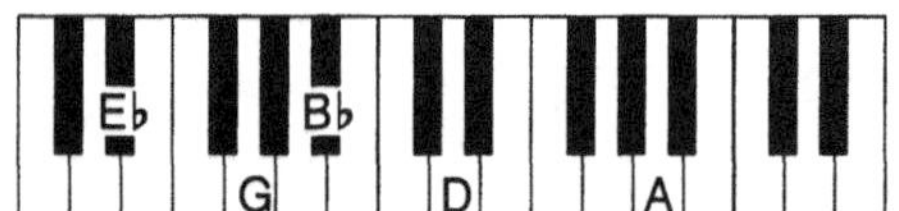

E♭maj9

E♭maj9♭5

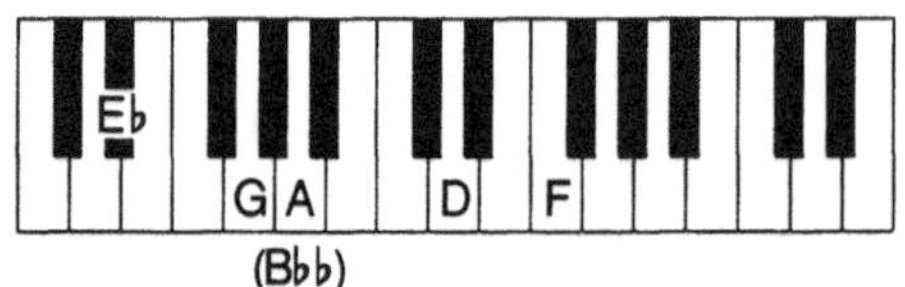

E♭maj9♯5

E♭maj9♯11

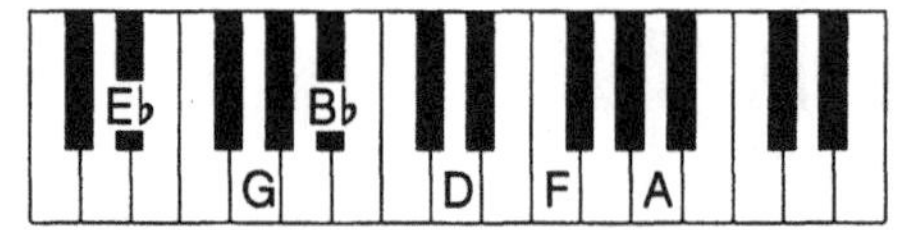

E♭maj13

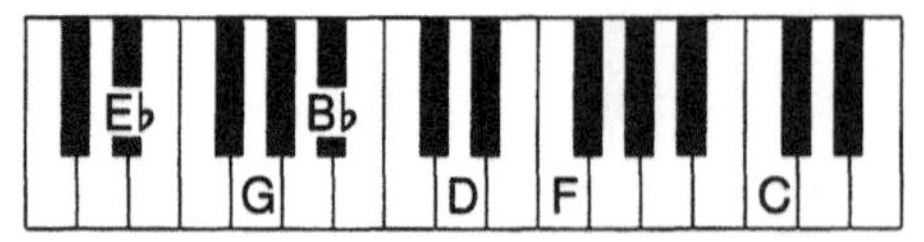

E♭maj13♭5

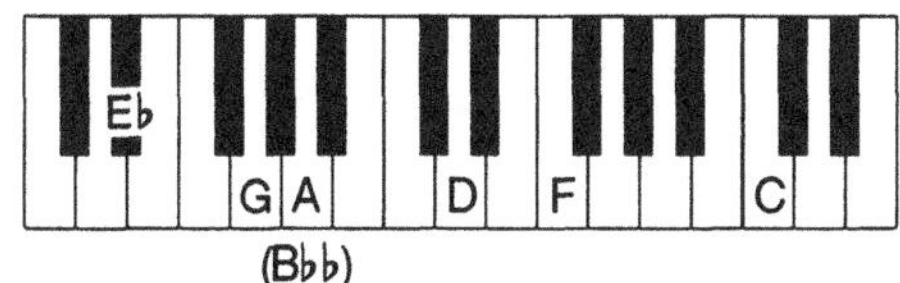

E♭maj13♯11

E♭7♭9

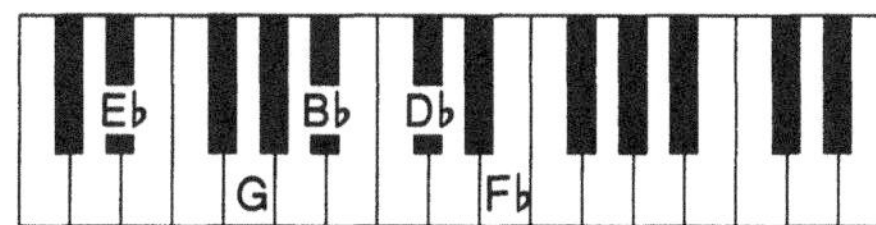

E♭7♯9

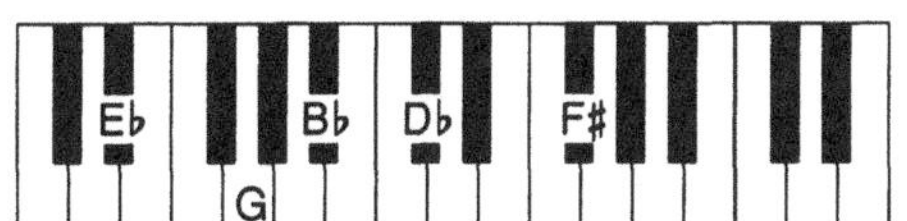

E♭7♯11

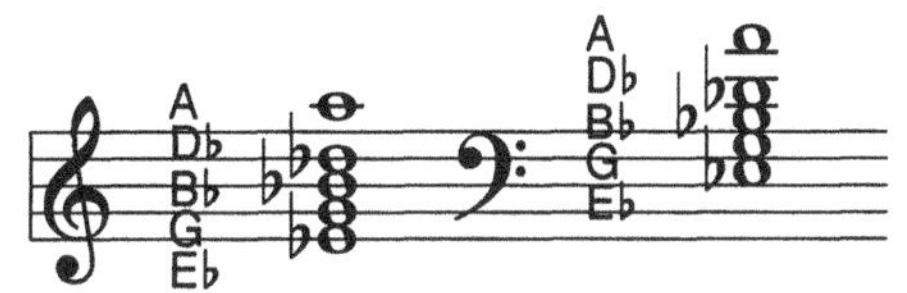

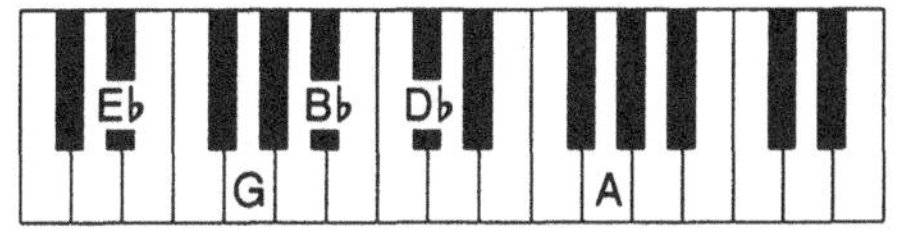

E♭7♭5(♭9)

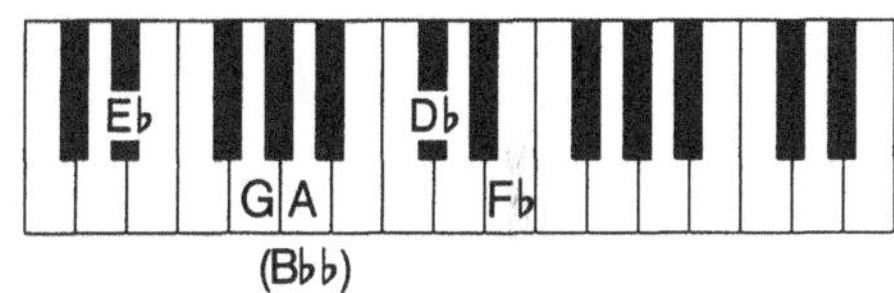

E♭7♭5(♯9)

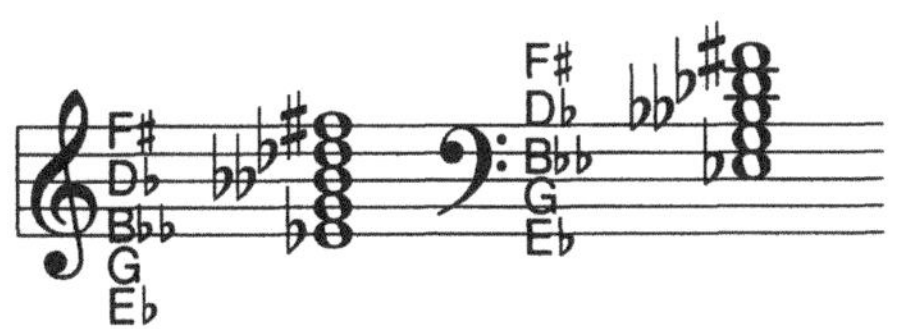

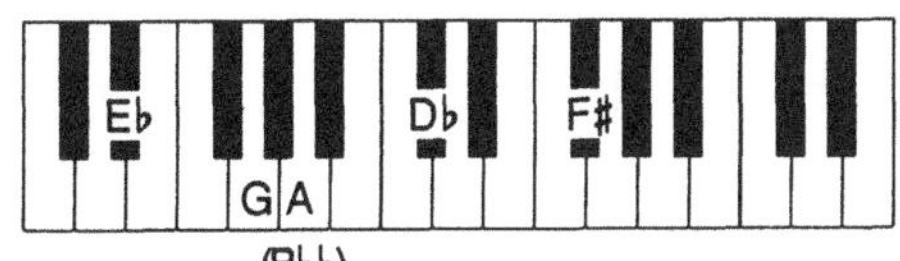

E♭7♯5(♭9)

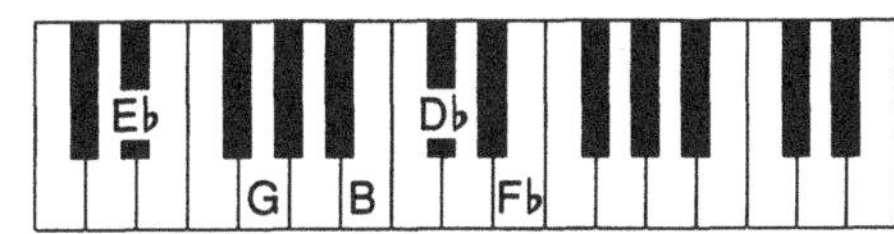

E♭7♯5(♯9)

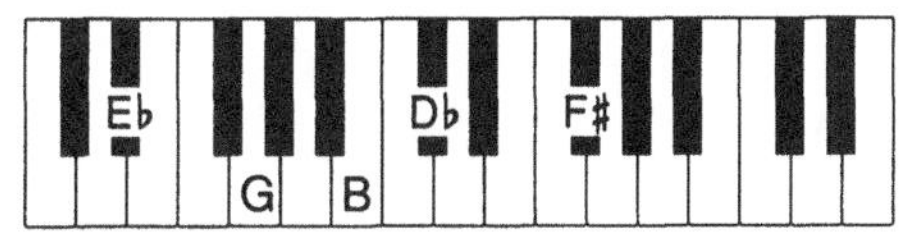

E♭7♭9(♯9)

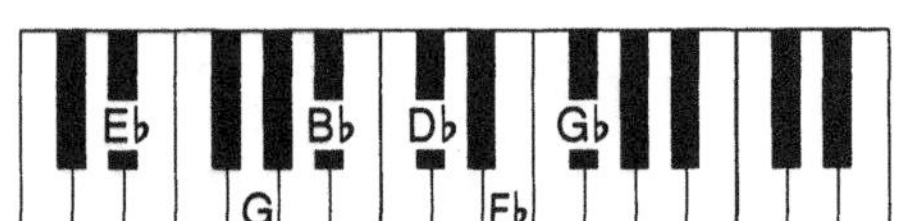

E♭7(add13)

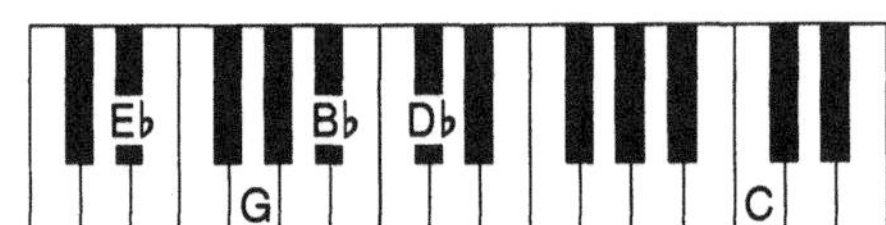

E♭7♭13

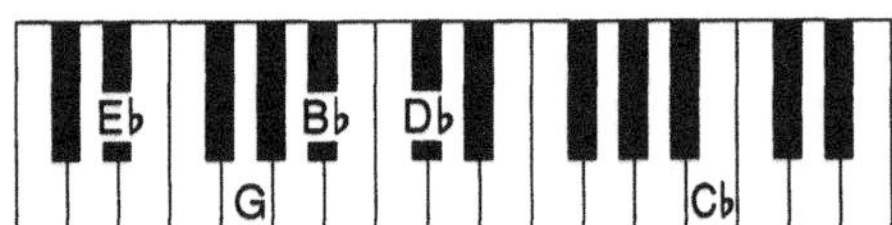

E♭7♭9(♯11)

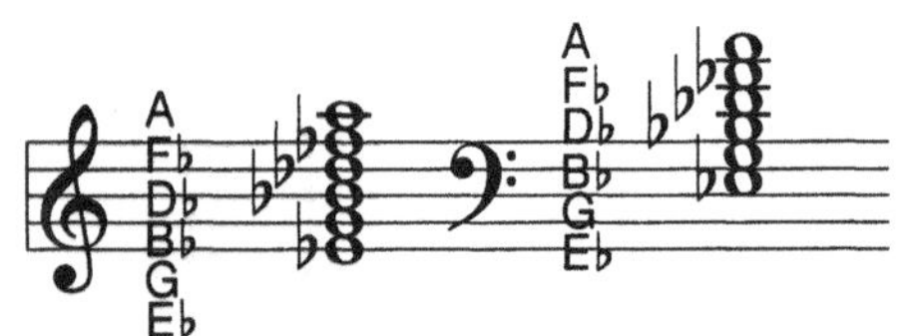

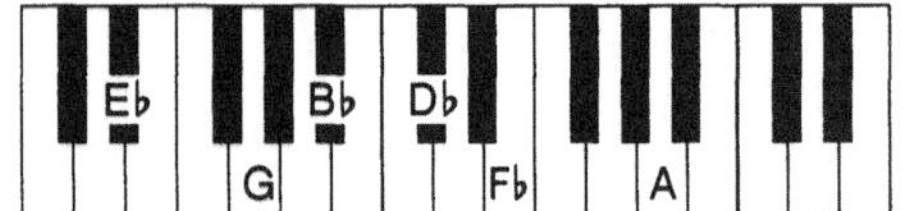

E♭7♯9(♯11)

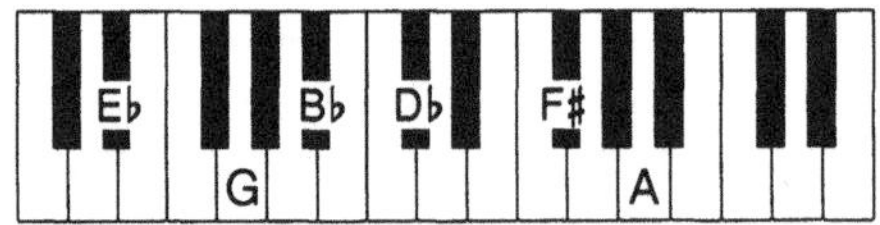

E♭7♭9(♭13)

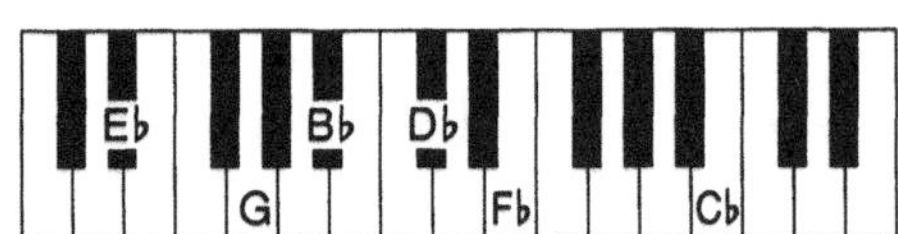

E♭7♯9(♭13)

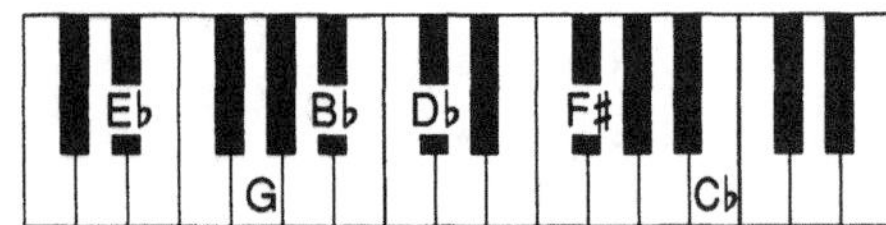

E♭7♯11(♭13)

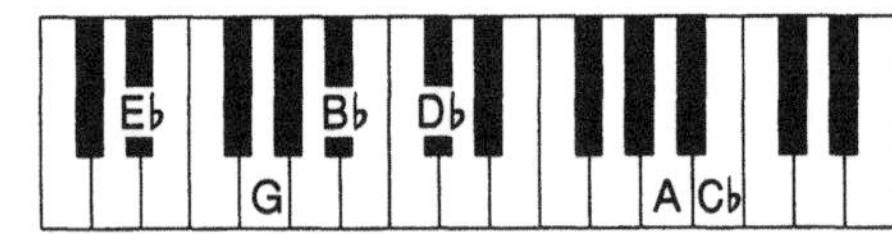

E♭7♭9(♯9,♯11)

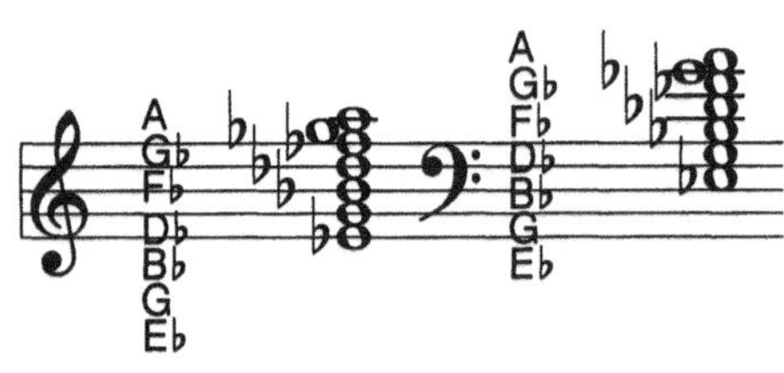

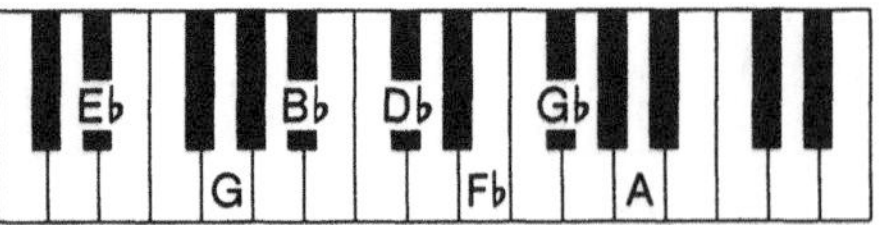

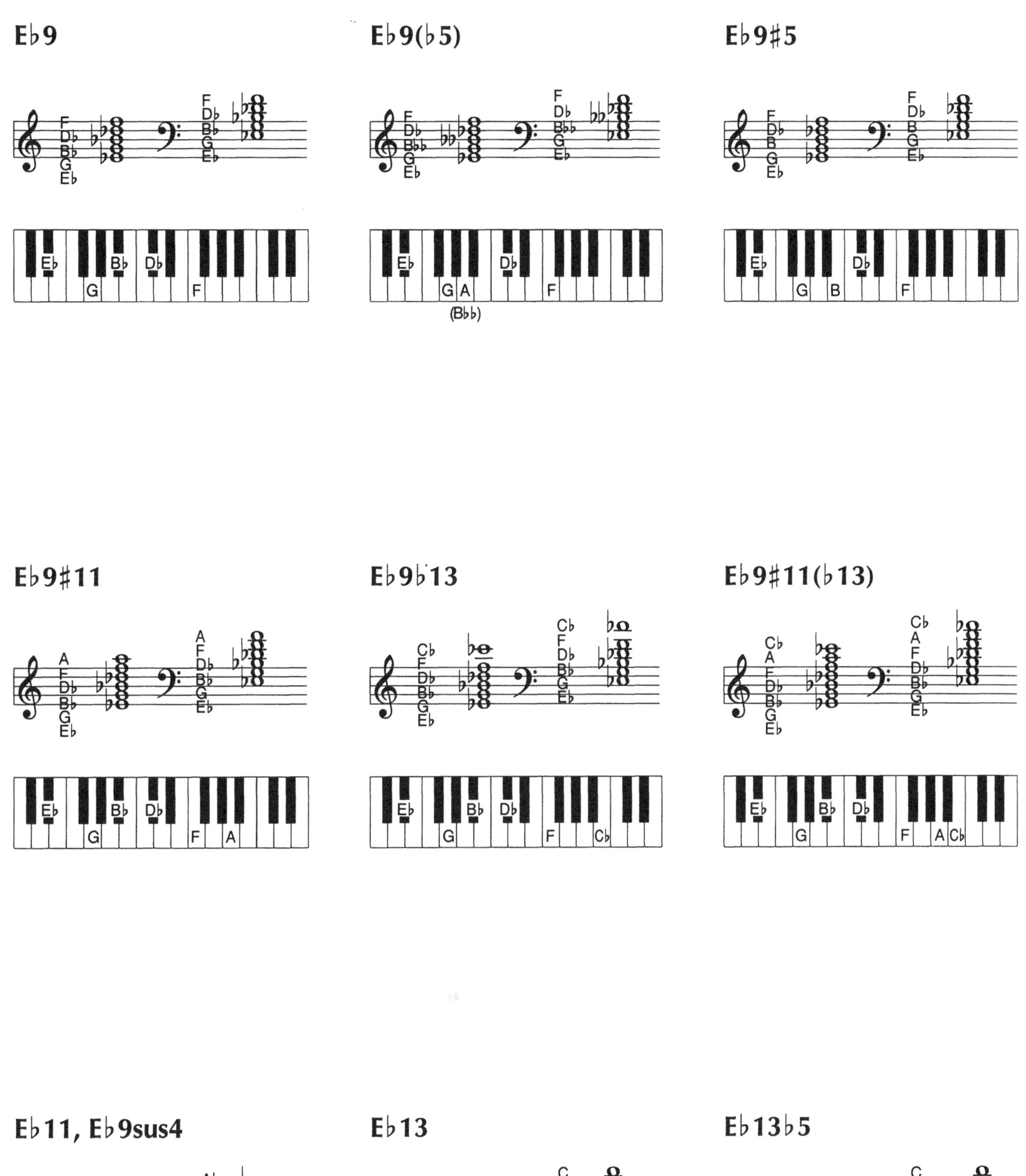

E♭11, E♭9sus4

A♭
F
D♭
B♭
E♭

E♭ B♭ D♭ A♭
F

E♭13

C
F
D♭
B♭
G
E♭

E♭ B♭ D♭
G F C

E♭13♭5

C
F
D♭
B♭♭
G
E♭

E♭ D♭
G A F C
(B♭♭)

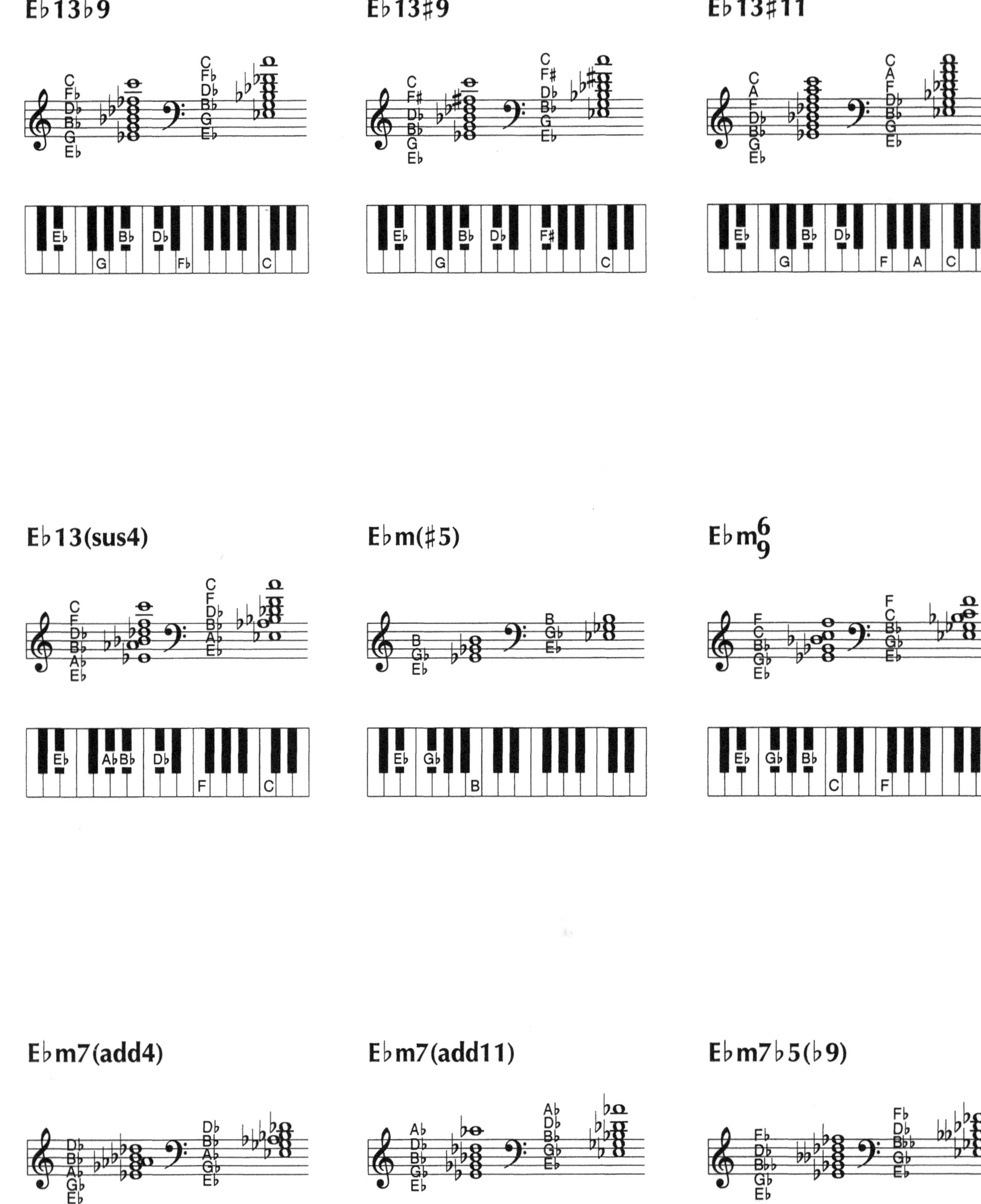
E♭13♭9
C
F♭
D♭
B♭
G
E♭
E♭
B♭
D♭
G
F♭
C
E♭13♯9
C
F♯
D♭
B♭
G
E♭
E♭
B♭
D♭
F♯
G
C
E♭13♯11
C
A
F
D♭
B♭
G
E♭
E♭
B♭
D♭
G
F
A
C
E♭13(sus4)
C
F
D♭
B♭
A♭
E♭
E♭
A♭
B♭
D♭
F
C
E♭m(♯5)
B
G♭
E♭
E♭
G♭
B
E♭m6/9
F
C
B♭
G♭
E♭
E♭
G♭
B♭
C
F
E♭m7(add4)
D♭
B♭
A♭
G♭
E♭
E♭
G♭
A♭
B♭
D♭
E♭m7(add11)
A♭
D♭
B♭
G♭
E♭
E♭
G♭
B♭
D♭
A♭
E♭m7♭5(♭9)
F♭
D♭
B♭♭
G♭
E♭
E♭
G♭
D♭
A
F♭
(B♭♭)

E♭m9

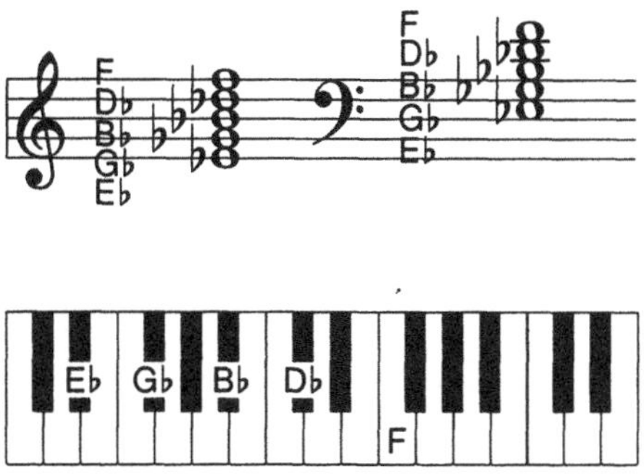

F
D♭
B♭
G♭
E♭
F
D♭
B♭
G♭
E♭
E♭ G♭ B♭ D♭
F

E♭m9(maj7)

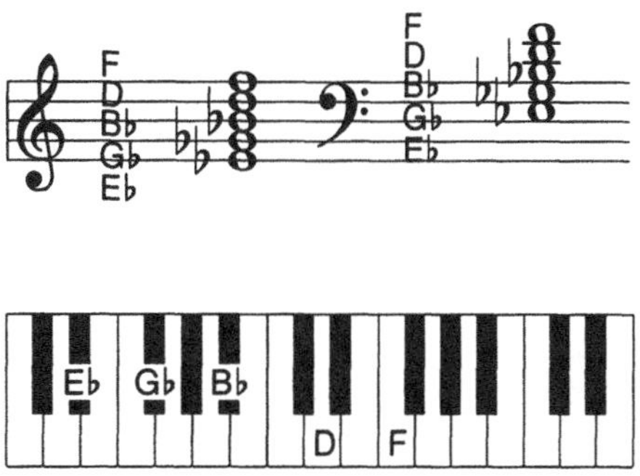

F
D
B♭
G♭
E♭
F
D
B♭
G♭
E♭
E♭ G♭ B♭
D F

E♭m9♭5

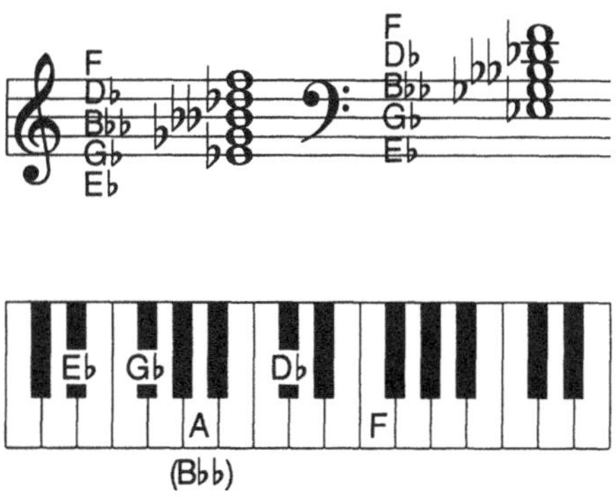

F
D♭
B♭♭
G♭
E♭
F
D♭
B♭♭
G♭
E♭
E♭ G♭ D♭
A F
(B♭♭)

E♭m11

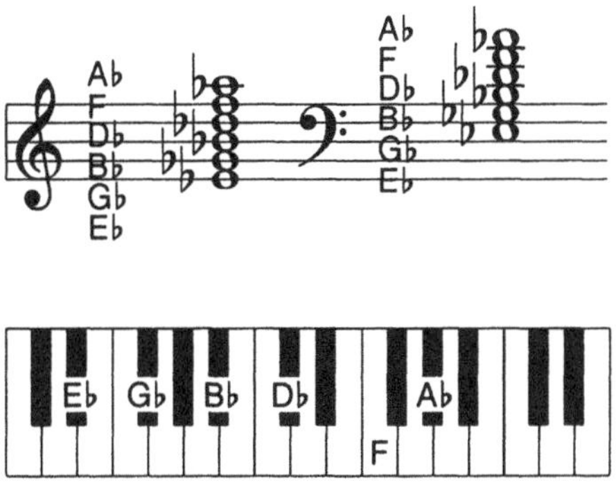

A♭
F
D♭
B♭
G♭
E♭
A♭
F
D♭
B♭
G♭
E♭
E♭ G♭ B♭ D♭ A♭
F

E♭m13

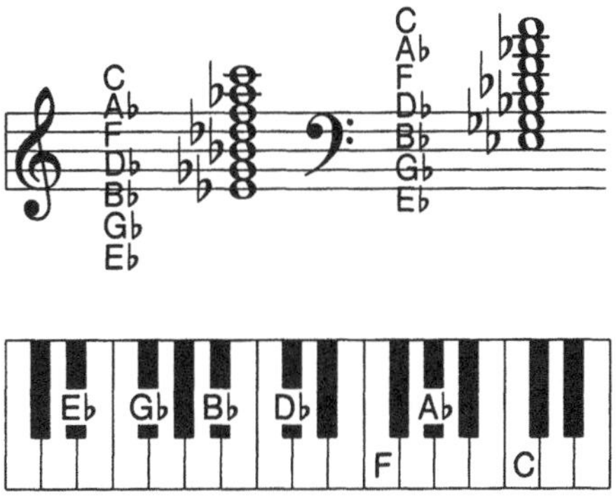

C
A♭
F
D♭
B♭
G♭
E♭
C
A♭
F
D♭
B♭
G♭
E♭
E♭ G♭ B♭ D♭ A♭
F C

E♭dim7(add9)

F
D♭♭
B♭♭
G♭
E♭
F
D♭♭
B♭♭
G♭
E♭
E♭ G♭
A C F
(B♭♭) (D♭♭)

E♭m11♭5

A♭
F
D♭
B♭♭
G♭
E♭
A♭
F
D♭
B♭♭
G♭
E♭
E♭ G♭ D♭ A♭
A F
(B♭♭)

E♭m11(maj7)

A♭
F
D
B♭
G♭
E♭
A♭
F
D
B♭
G♭
E♭
E♭ G♭ B♭ A♭
D F

E♭7alt.

C♭
A
G♭
F♭
D♭
B♭
G
E♭
C♭
A
G♭
F♭
D♭
B♭
G
E♭
E♭ B♭ D♭ G♭
G F♭ A C♭

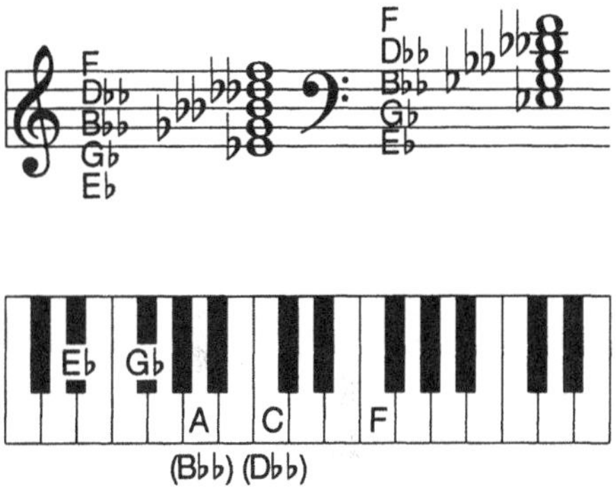

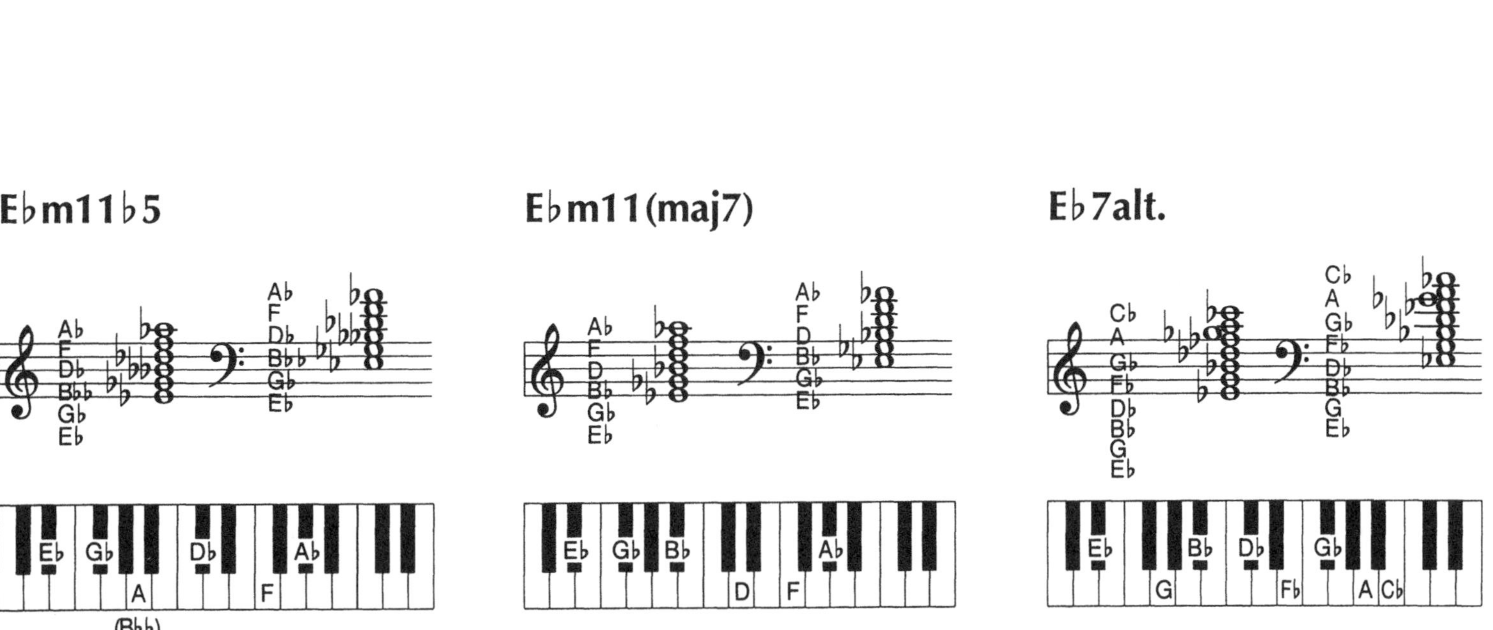

E CHORDS

E

Root Position

1st Inversion

2nd Inversion

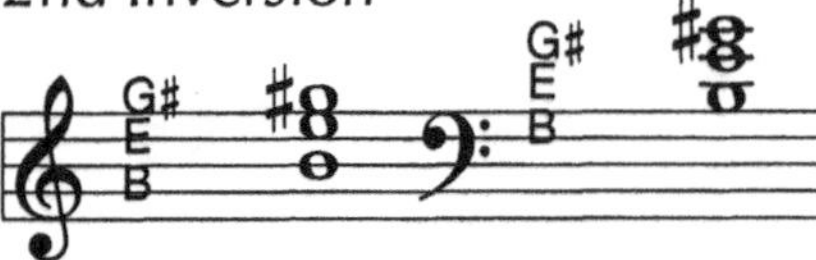

Em

Root Position

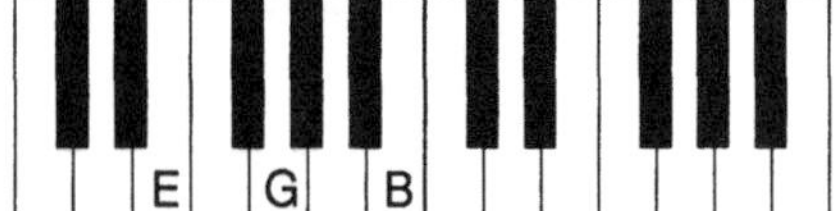

1st Inversion

2nd Inversion

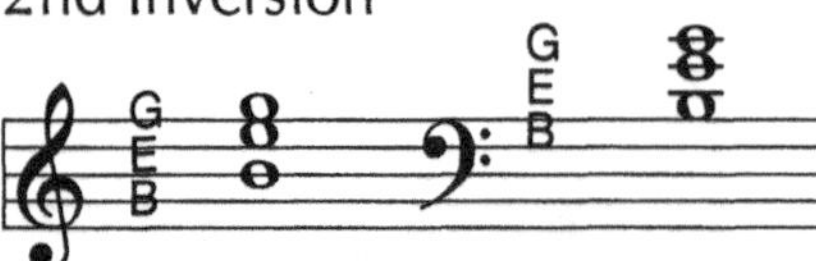

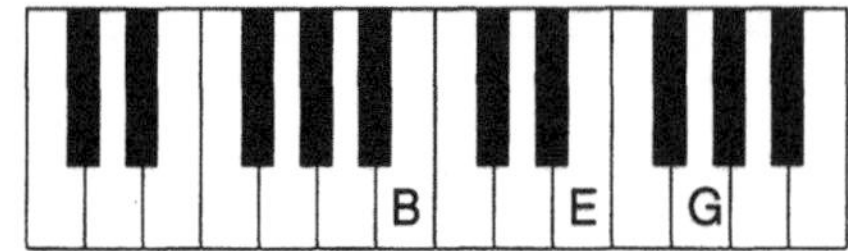

E+

Root Position

1st Inversion

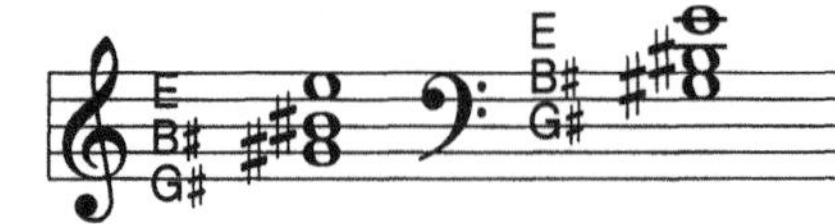

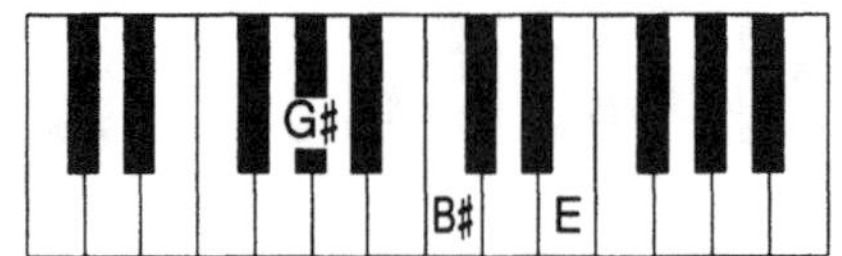

2nd Inversion

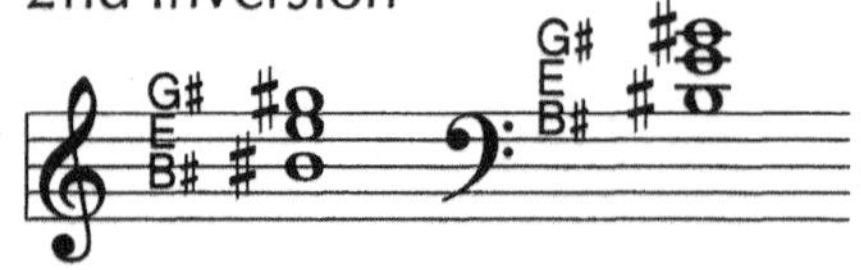

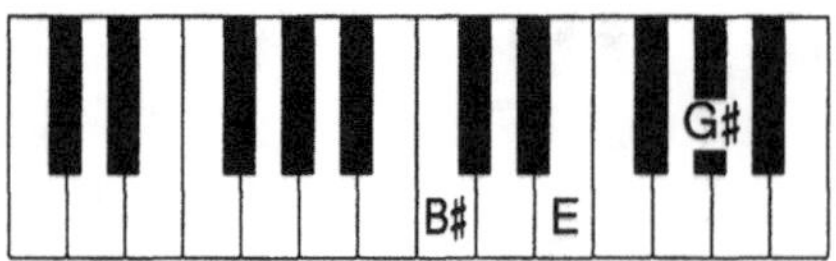

Edim

Root Position

1st Inversion

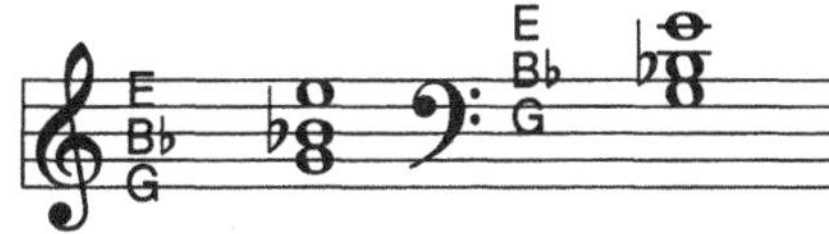

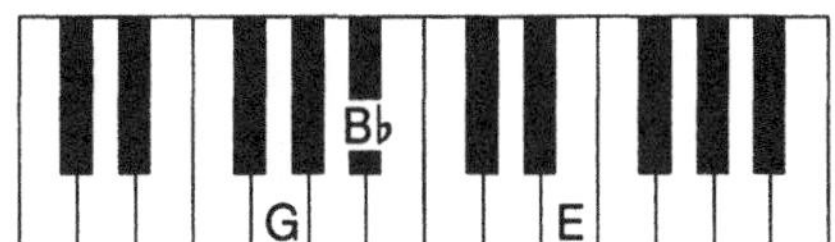

2nd Inversion

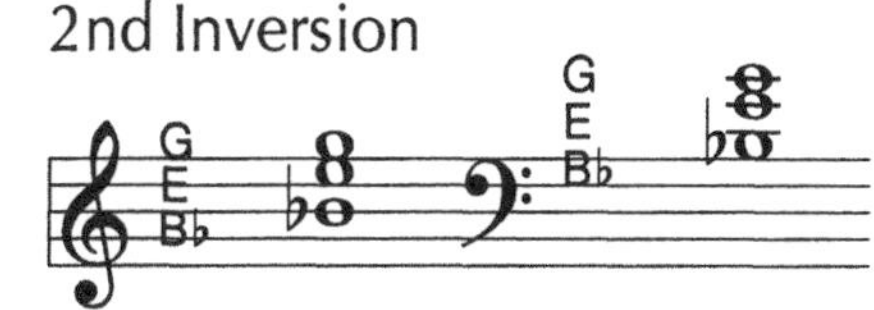

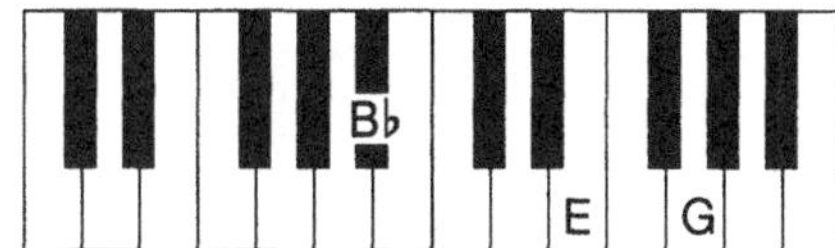

Esus

Root Position

1st Inversion

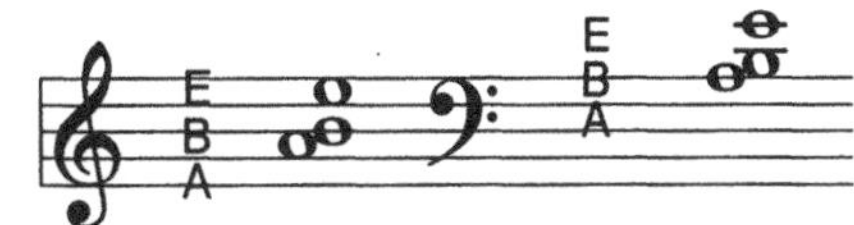

2nd Inversion

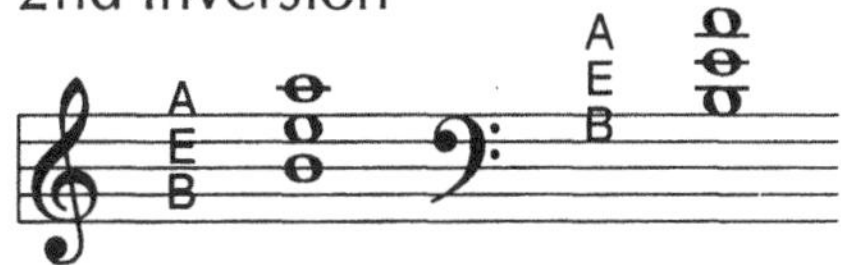

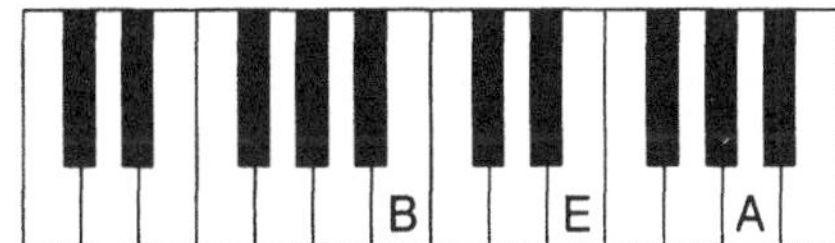

E(♭5)

Root Position

1st Inversion

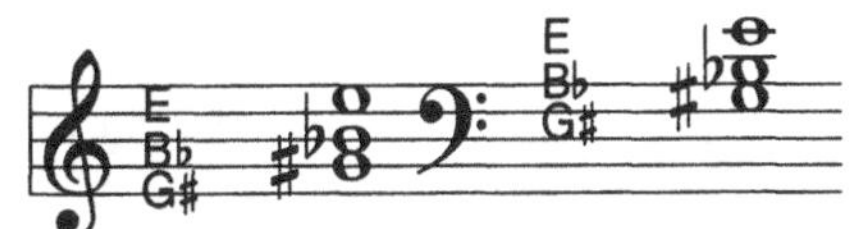

2nd Inversion

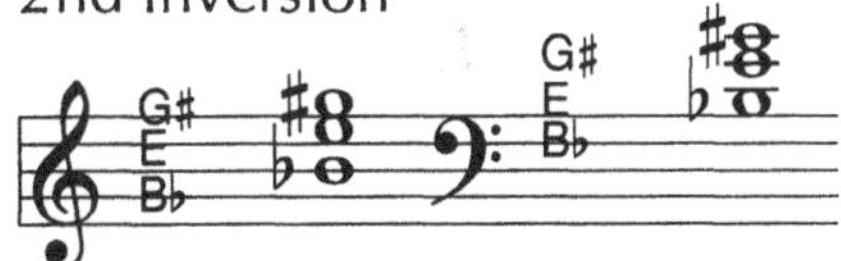

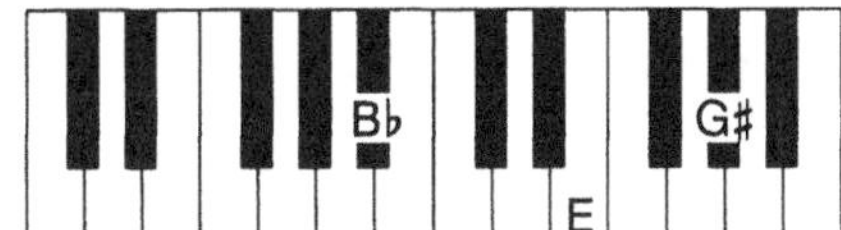

Esus2

Root Position

1st Inversion

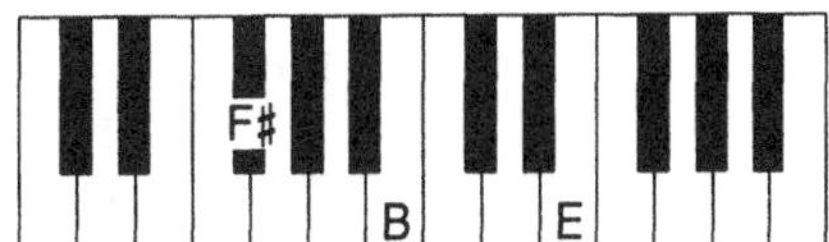

2nd Inversion

E6

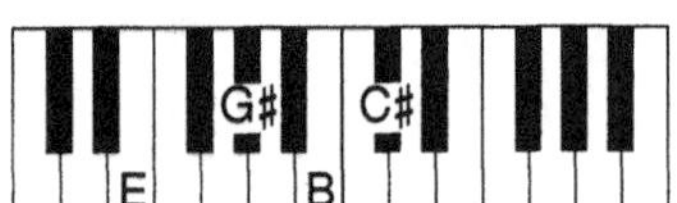

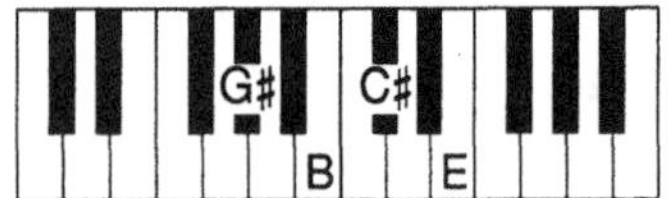

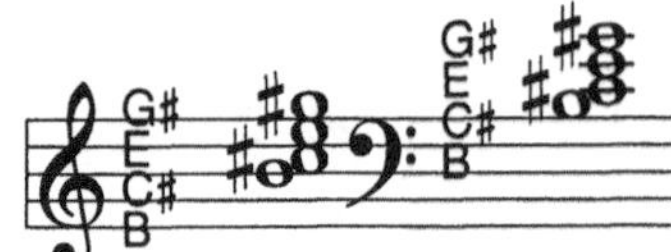

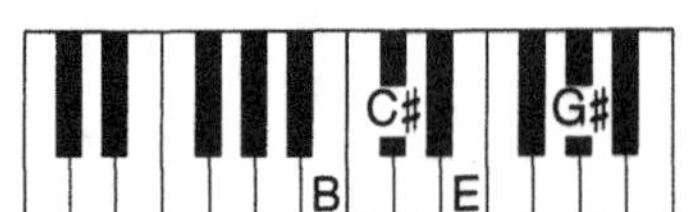

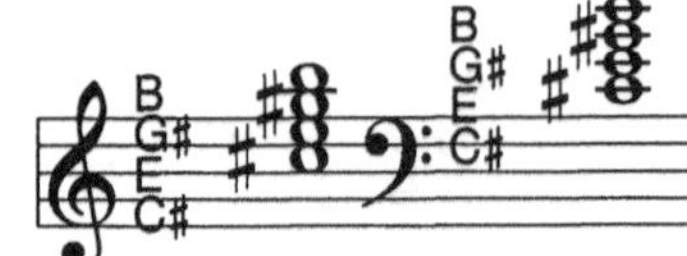

E(add2), E(add9)

Root Position

1st Inversion

2nd Inversion

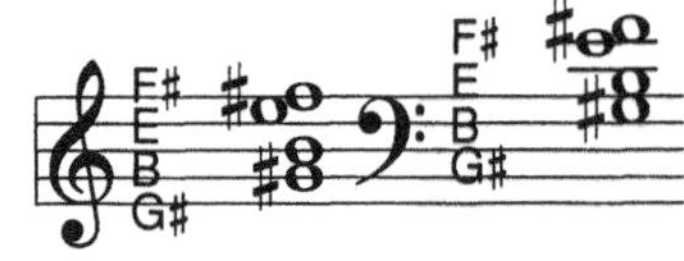

3rd Inversion

Emaj7

Root Position

1st Inversion

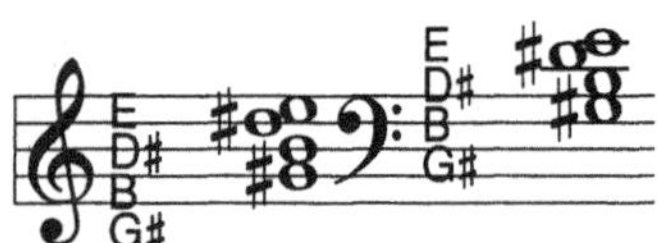

2nd Inversion

3rd Inversion

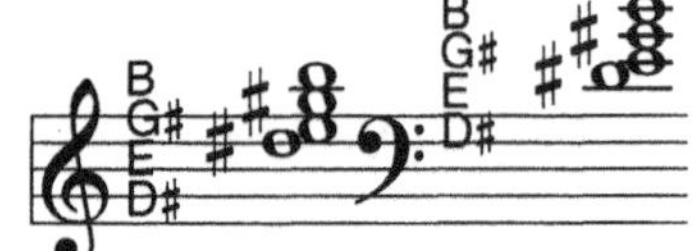

Emaj7♭5

Root Position

1st Inversion

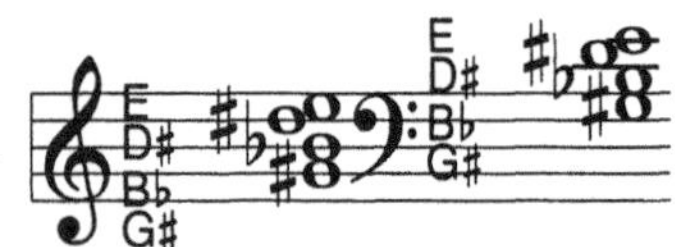

2nd Inversion

3rd Inversion

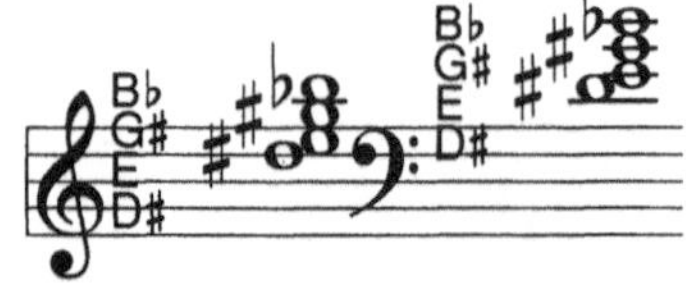

Emaj7♯5

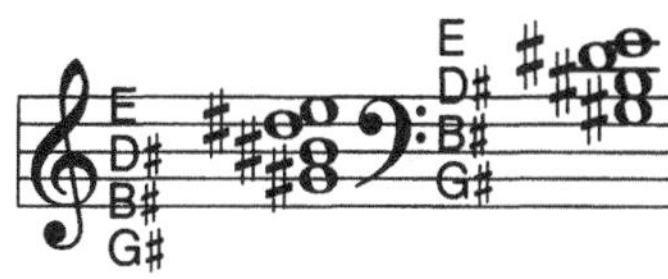

2nd Inversion

3rd Inversion

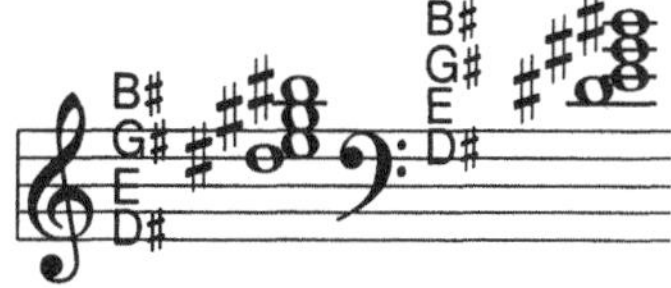

E7

Root Position

1st Inversion

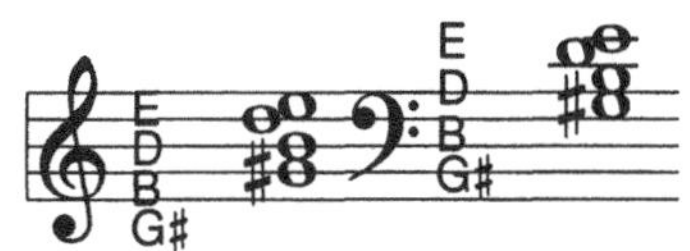

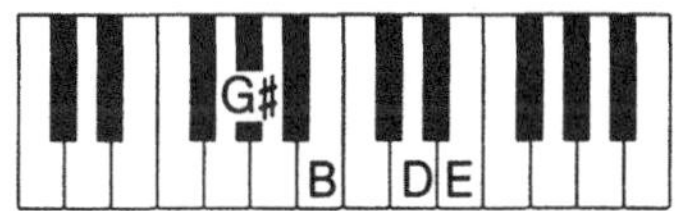

2nd Inversion

3rd Inversion

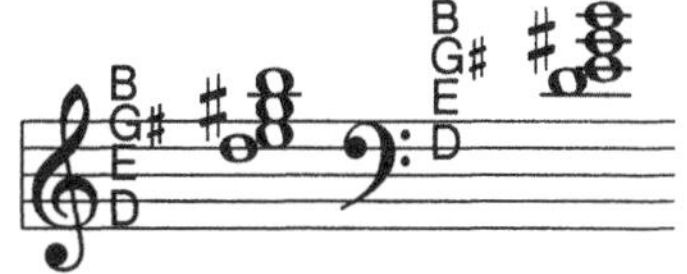

E7♭5

Root Position

1st Inversion

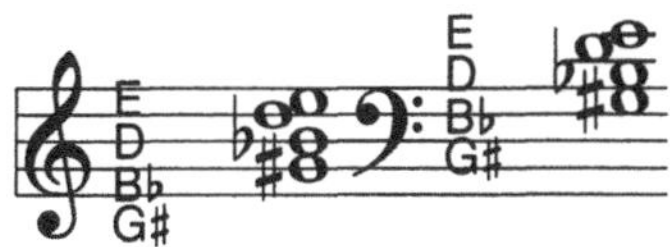

2nd Inversion

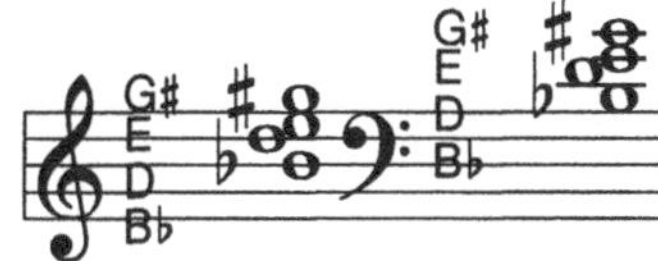

3rd Inversion

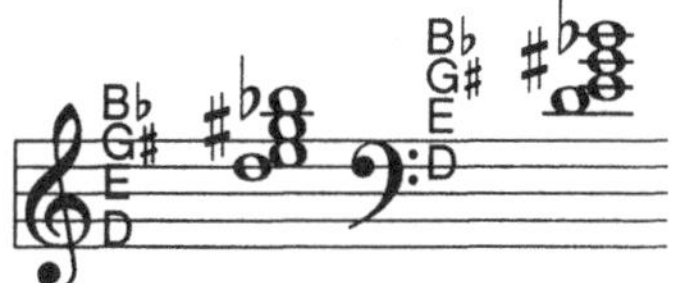

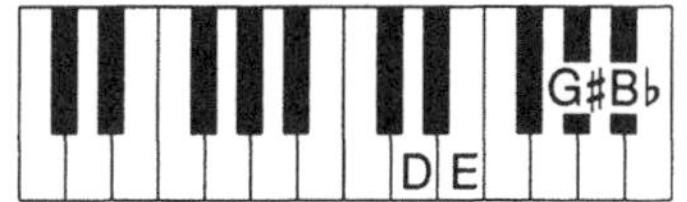

E7♯5

Root Position

1st Inversion

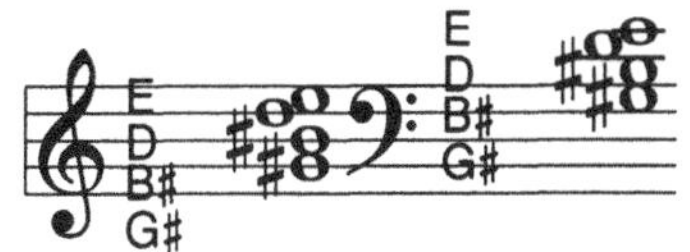

2nd Inversion

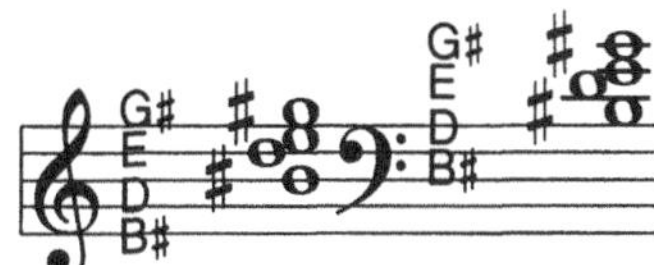

3rd Inversion

E7sus

Root Position

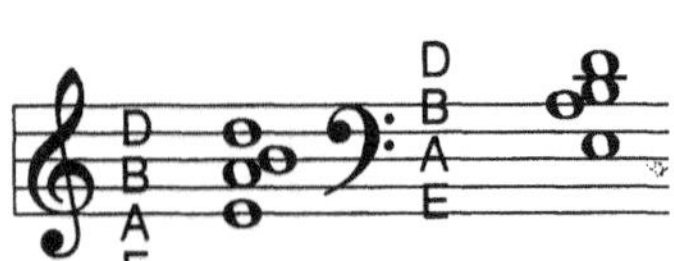

1st Inversion

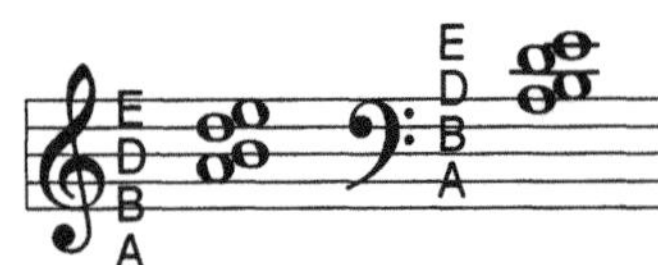

2nd Inversion

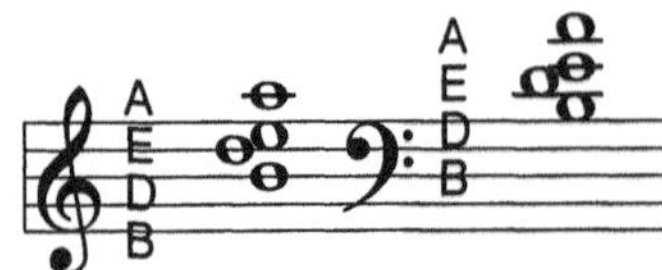

3rd Inversion

Em(add2), Em(add9)

Root Position

1st Inversion

2nd Inversion

3rd Inversion

Em6

Root Position

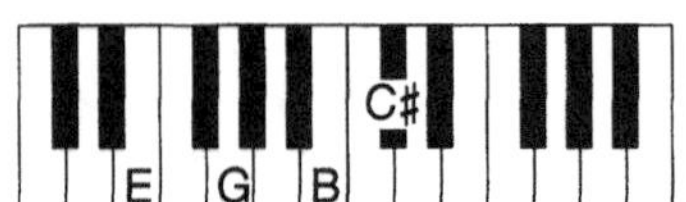

1st Inversion

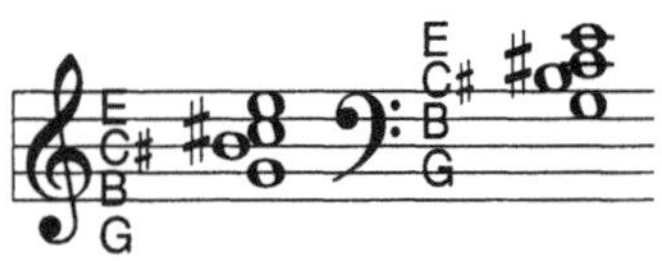

2nd Inversion

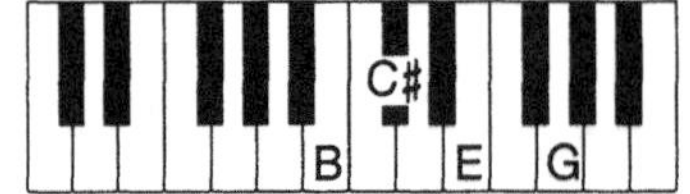

3rd Inversion

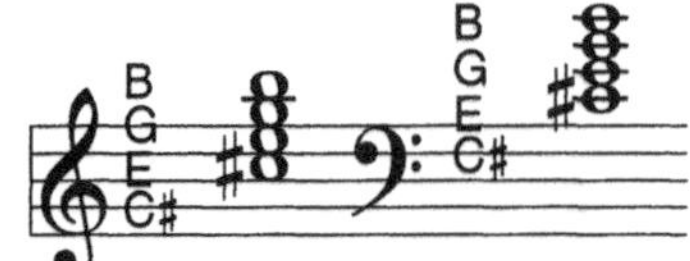

Em7

Root Position

1st Inversion

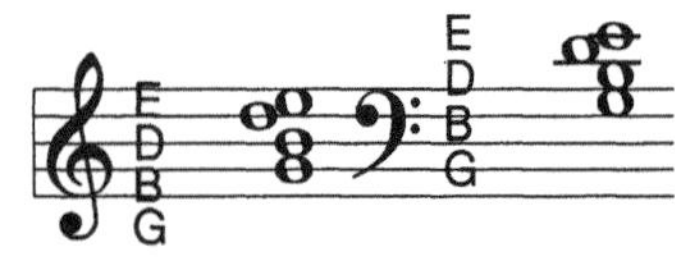

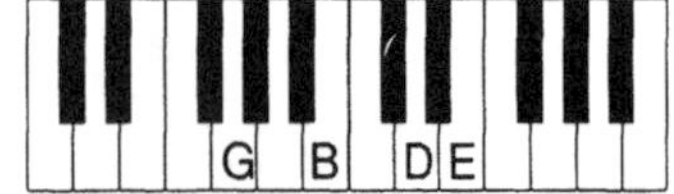

2nd Inversion

3rd Inversion

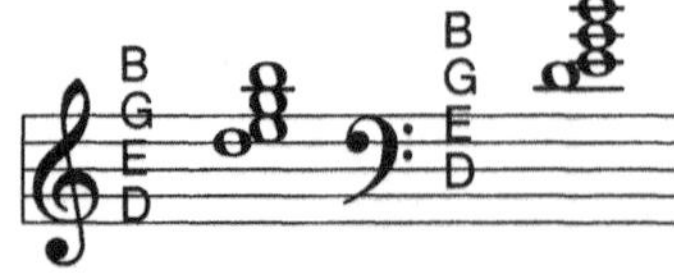

Em(maj7)

Root Position

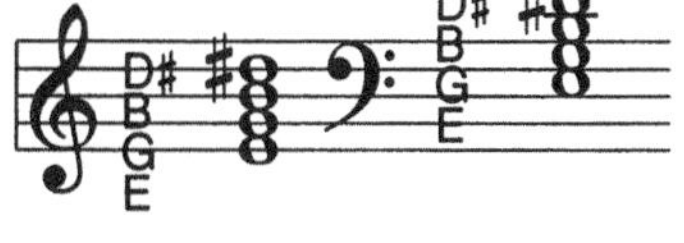

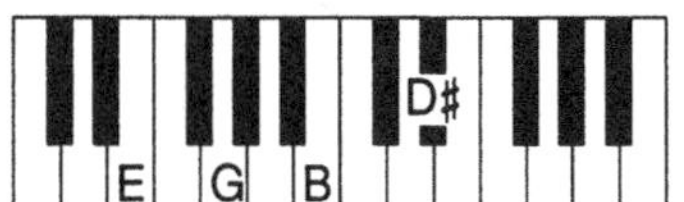

1st Inversion

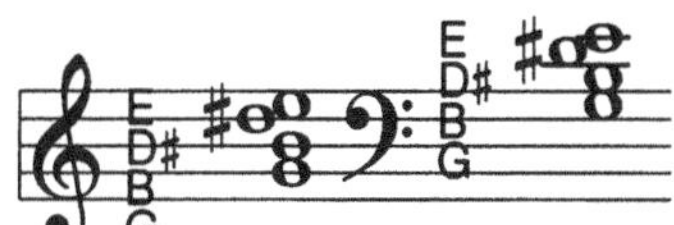

2nd Inversion

3rd Inversion

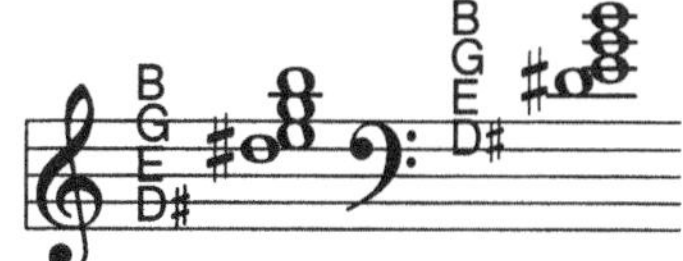

Em7♭5

Root Position

1st Inversion

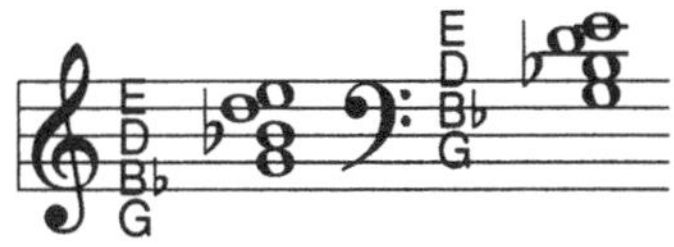

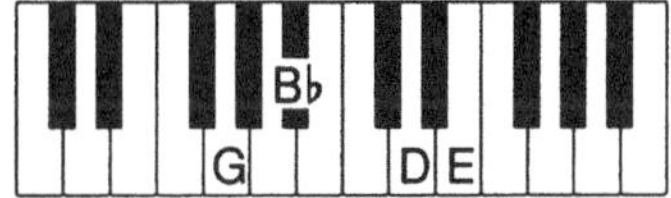

2nd Inversion

3rd Inversion

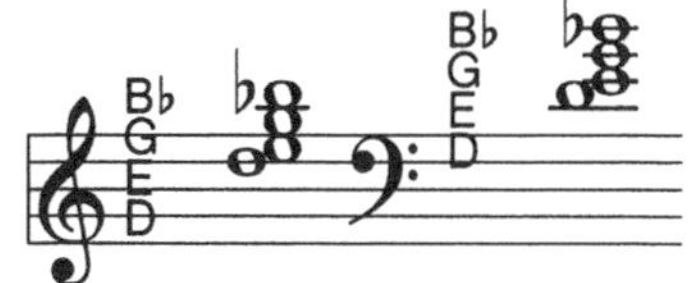

Edim7

Root Position

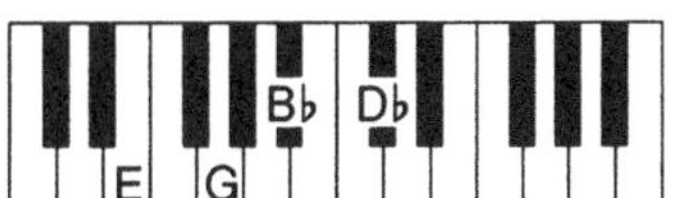

1st Inversion

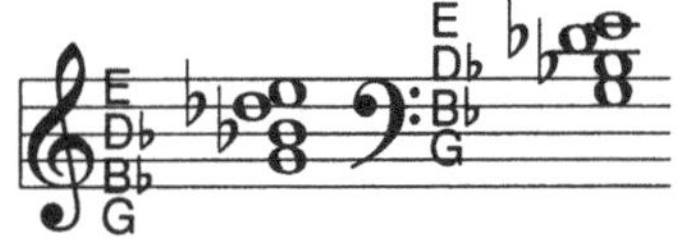

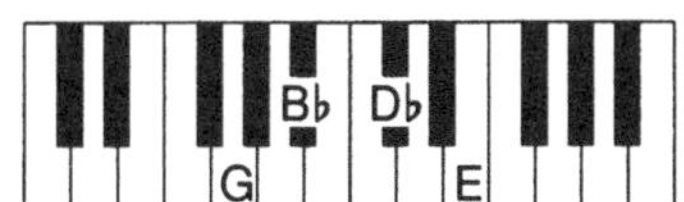

2nd Inversion

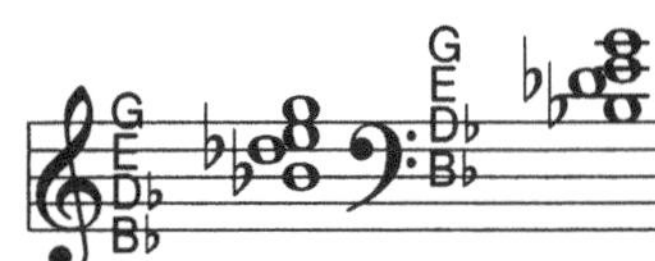

3rd Inversion

Edim(maj7)

Root Position

1st Inversion

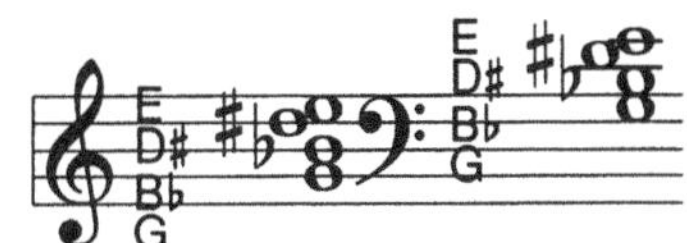

2nd Inversion

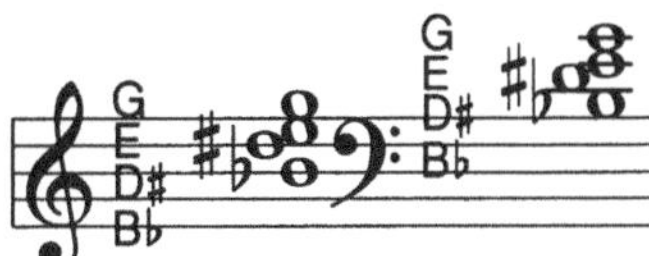

3rd Inversion

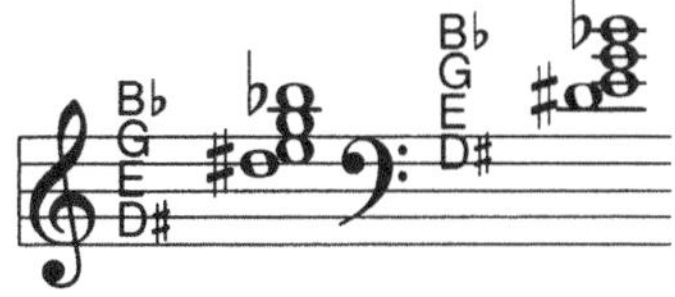

ADDITIONAL E CHORDS

E5

E$^{6}_{9}$

Emaj $^{6}_{9}$

Emaj7#11

Emaj9

Emaj9♭5

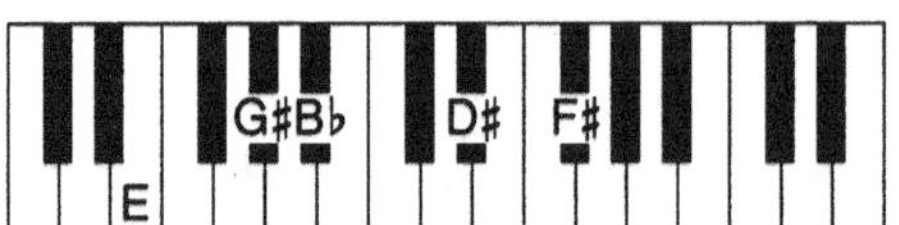

Emaj9#5

Emaj9#11

Emaj13

Emaj13♭5

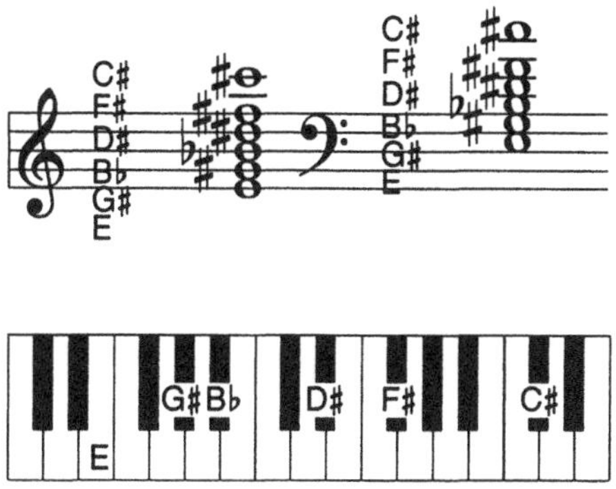

Emaj13♯11

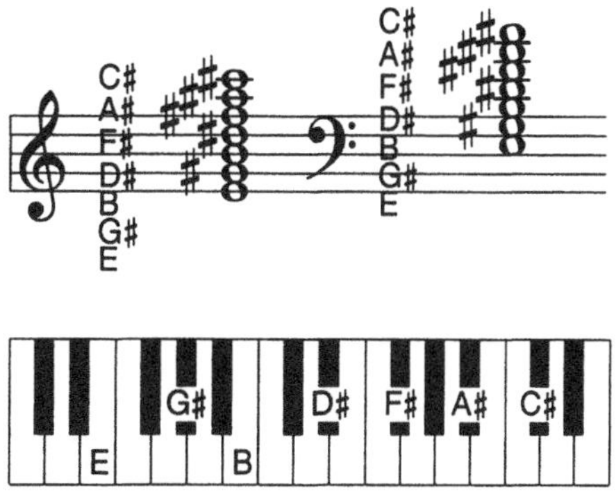

E7♭9

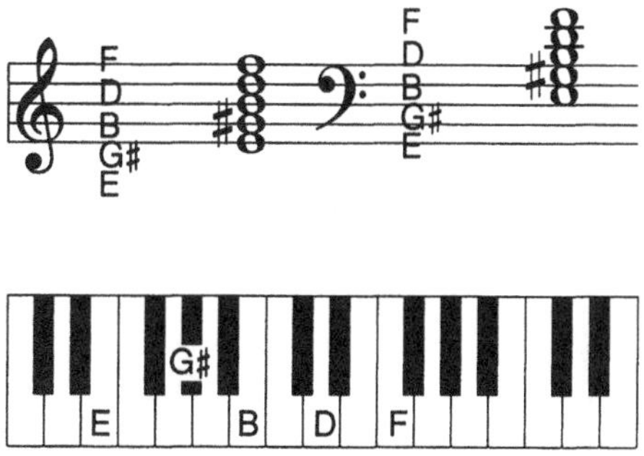

E7♯9

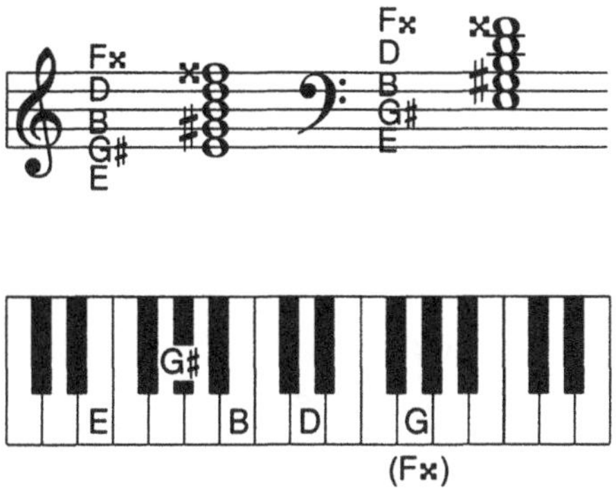

E7♯11

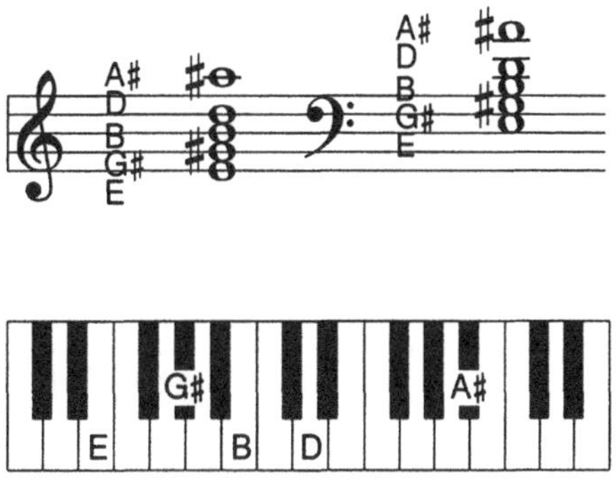

E7♭5(♭9)

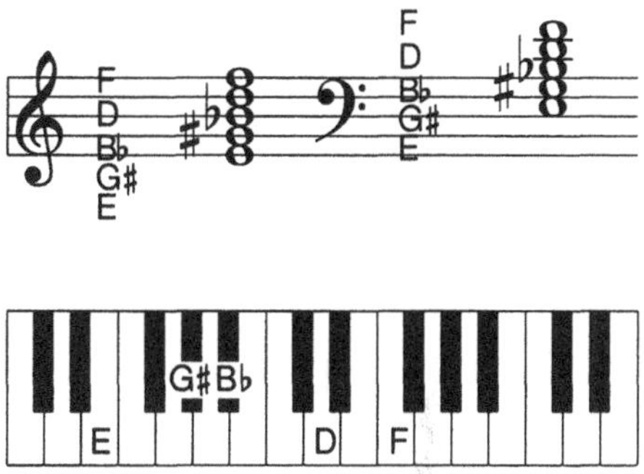

E7♭5(♯9)

E7♯5(♭9)

E7♯5(♯9)

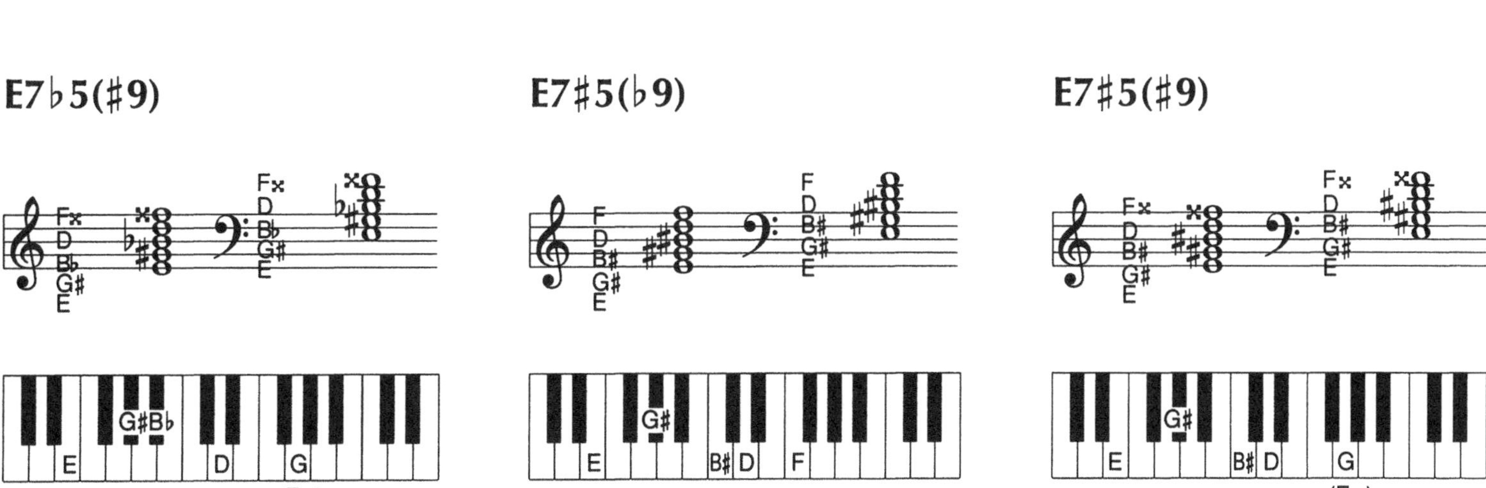

E7♭9(♯9)

E7(add13)

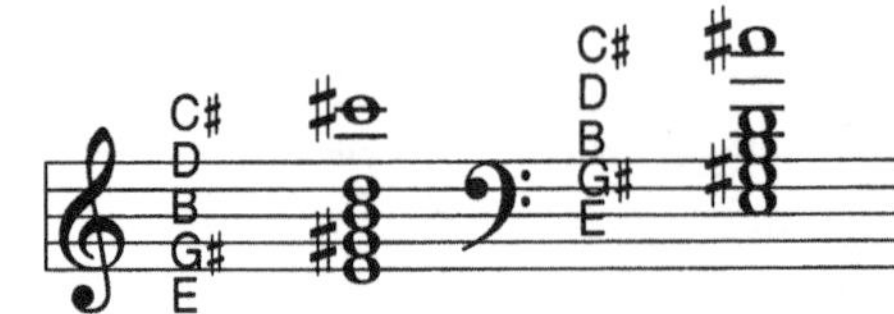

E7♭13

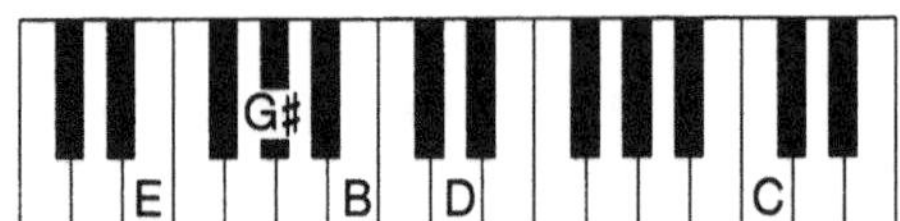

E7♭9(♯11)

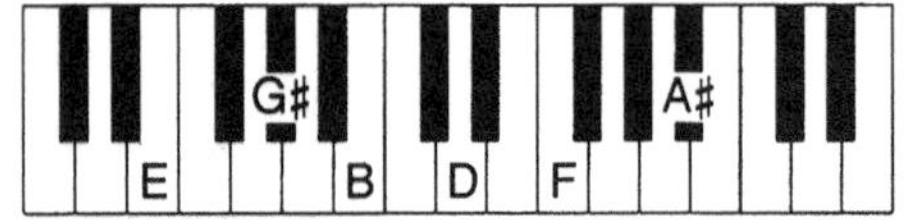

E7♯9(♯11)

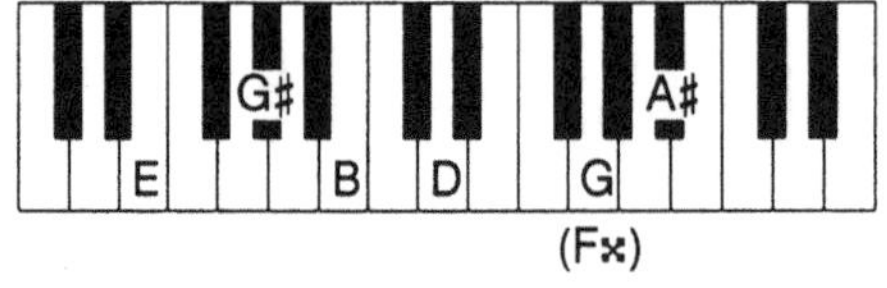

E7♭9(♭13)

E7♯9(♭13)

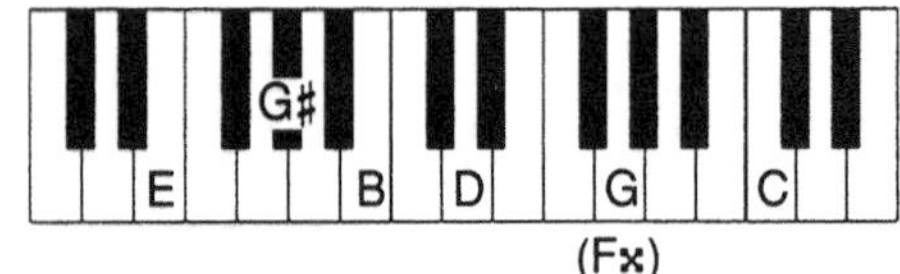

E7♯11(♭13)

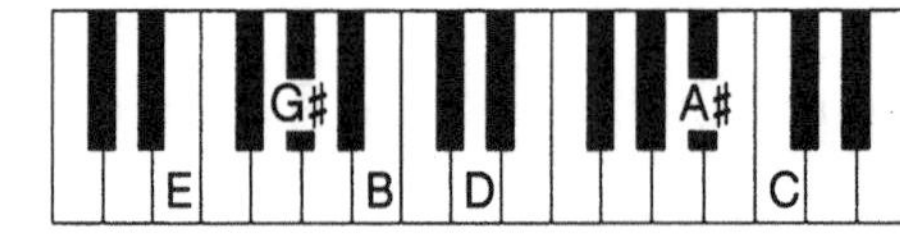

E7♭9(♯9,♯11)

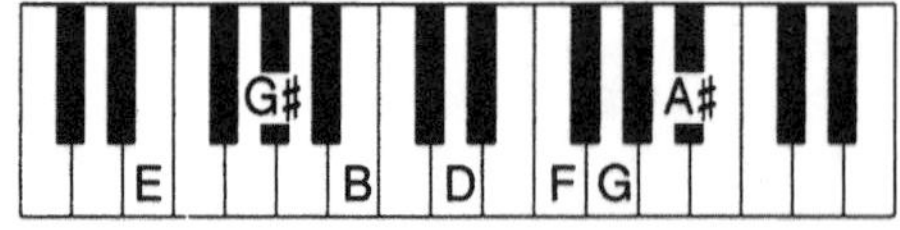

E9

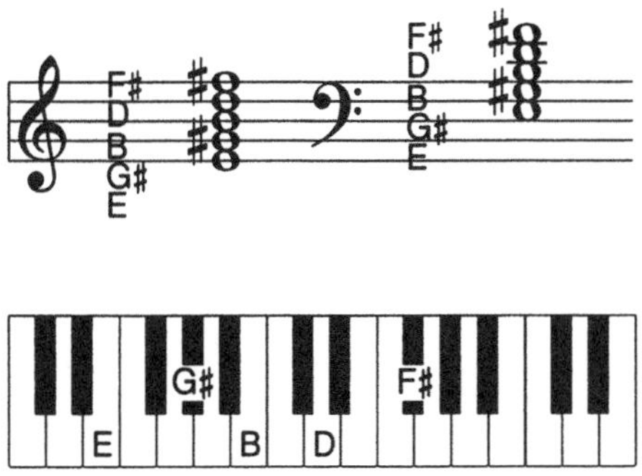

F♯ D B G♯ E
F♯ D B G♯ E
G♯ F♯
E B D

E9(♭5)

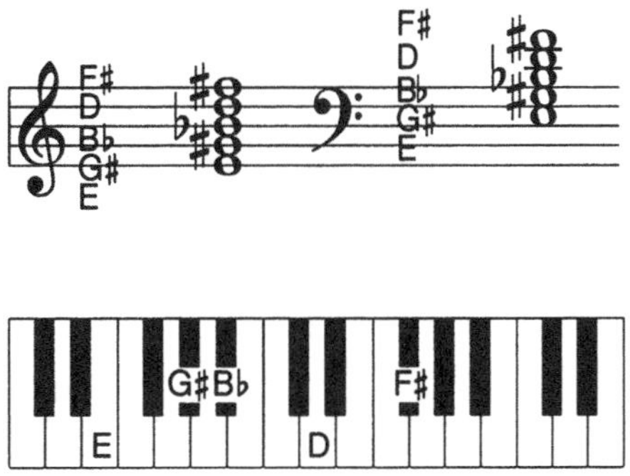

F♯ D B♭ G♯ E
F♯ D B♭ G♯ E
G♯ B♭ F♯
E D

E9♯5

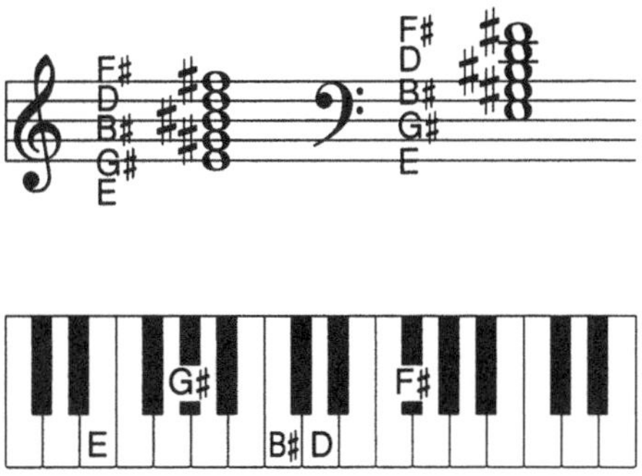

F♯ D B♯ G♯ E
F♯ D B♯ G♯ E
G♯ F♯
E B♯ D

E9♯11

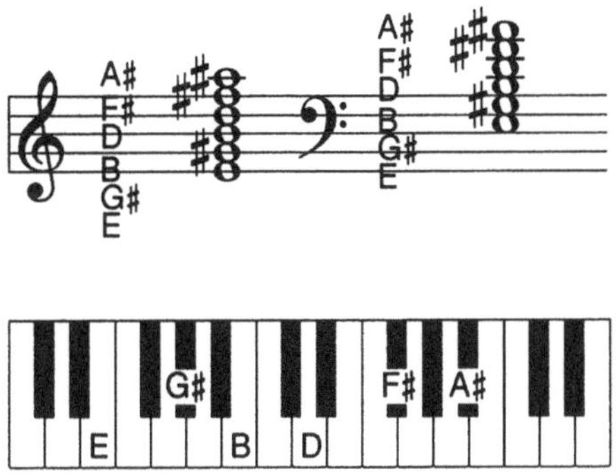

A♯ F♯ D B G♯ E
A♯ F♯ D B G♯ E
G♯ F♯ A♯
E B D

E9♭13

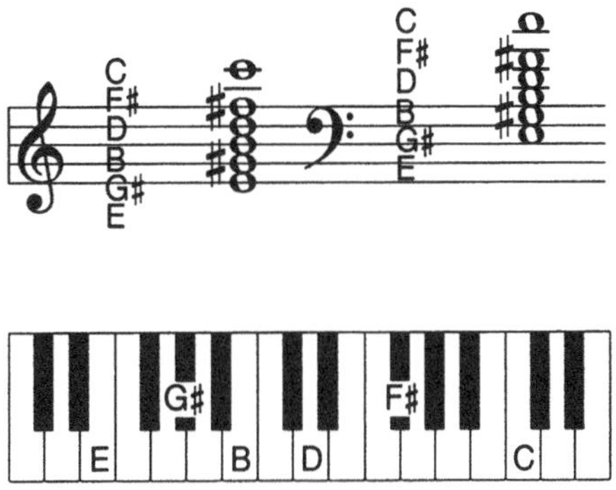

C F♯ D B G♯ E
C F♯ D B G♯ E
G♯ F♯
E B D C

E9♯11(♭13)

C A♯ F♯ D B G♯ E
C A♯ F♯ D B G♯ E
G♯ F♯ A♯
E B D C

E11, E9sus4

A F♯ D B E
A F♯ D B E
F♯
E B D A

E13

C♯ F♯ D B G♯ E
C♯ F♯ D B G♯ E
G♯ F♯ C♯
E B D

E13♭5

C♯ F♯ D B♭ G♯ E
C♯ F♯ D B♭ G♯ E
G♯ B♭ F♯ C♯
E D

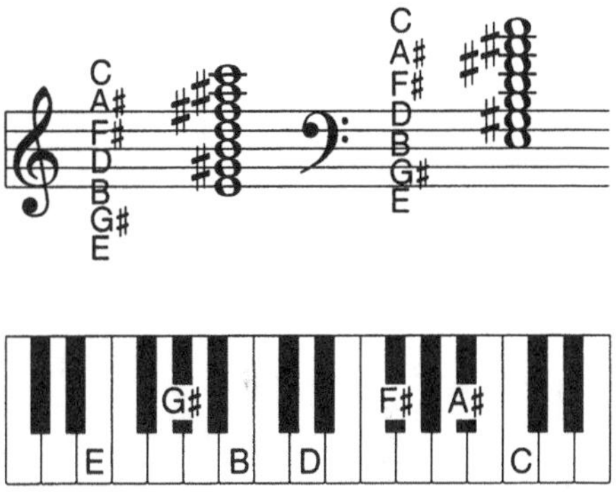

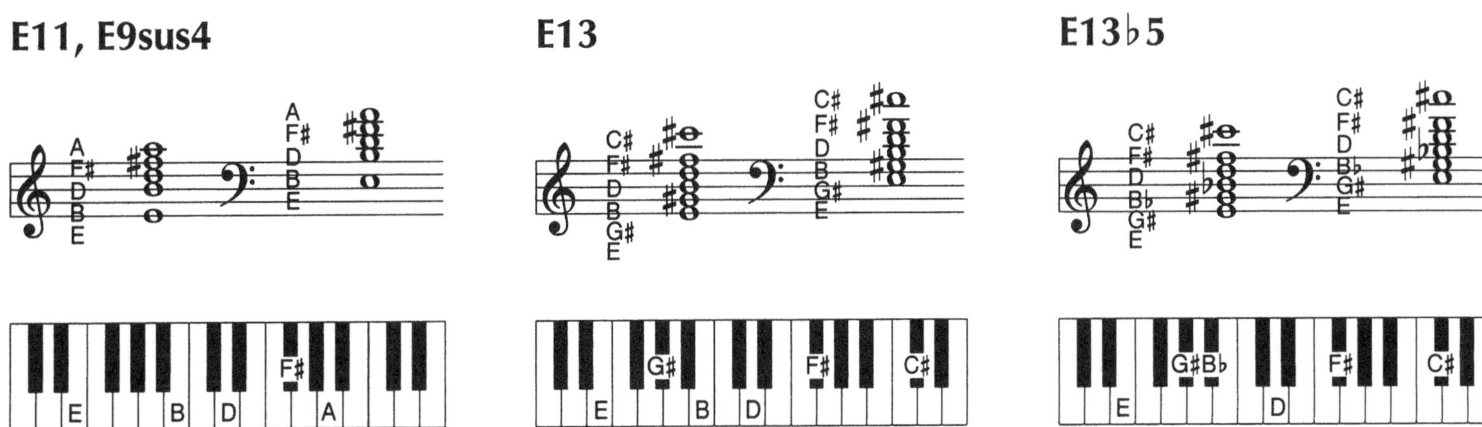

E13♭9

E13♯9

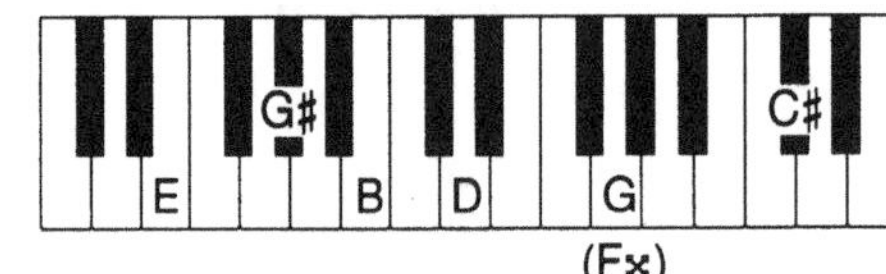

E13♯11

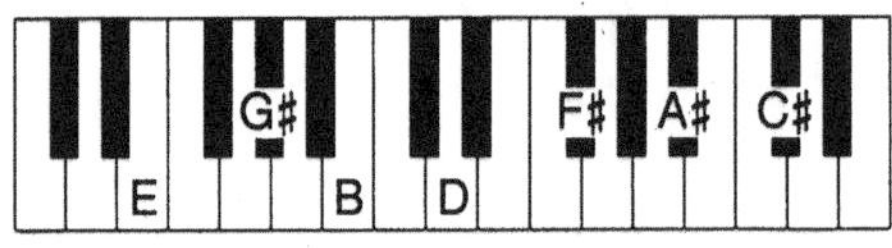

E13(sus4)

Em(♯5)

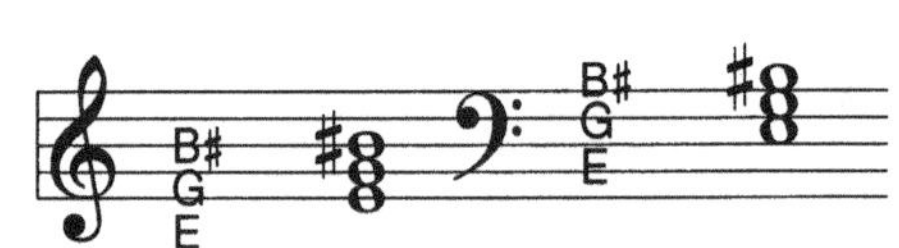

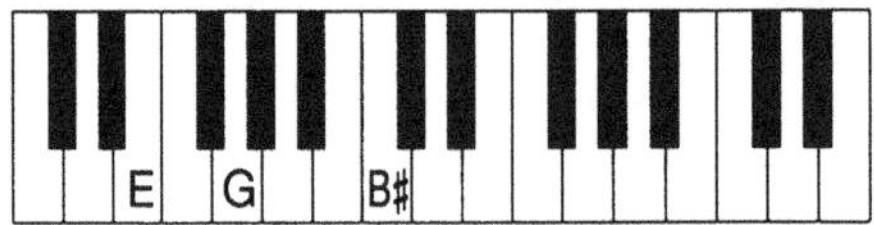

Em$^{6}_{9}$

Em7(add4)

Em7(add11)

Em7♭5(♭9)

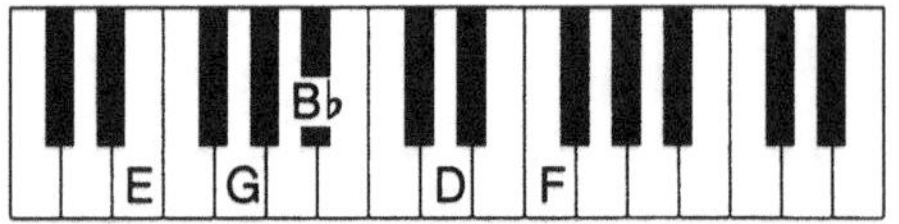

Em9

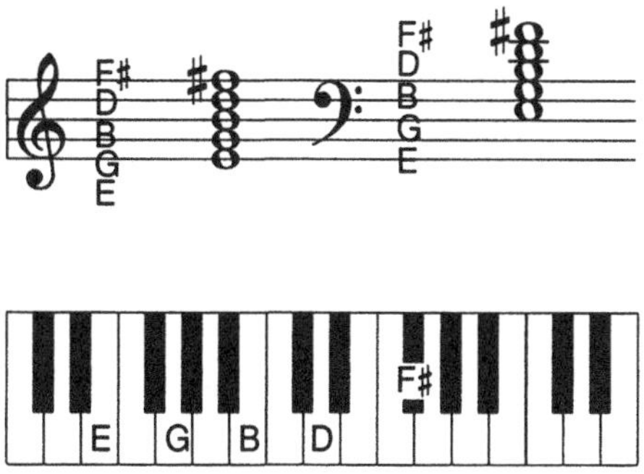

F♯ D B G E

F♯ D B G E

E G B D F♯

Em9(maj7)

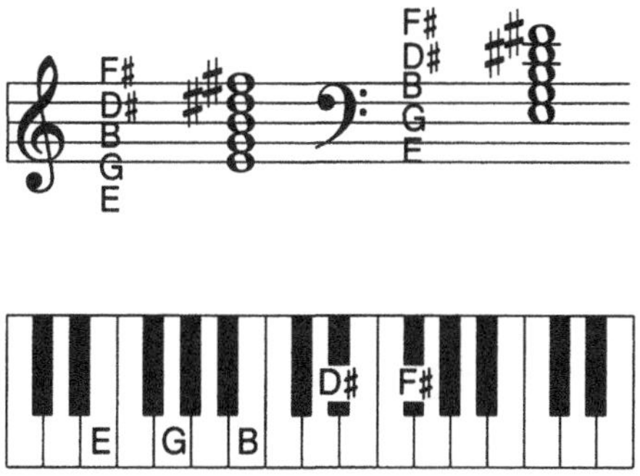

F♯ D♯ B G E

F♯ D♯ B G E

E G B D♯ F♯

Em9♭5

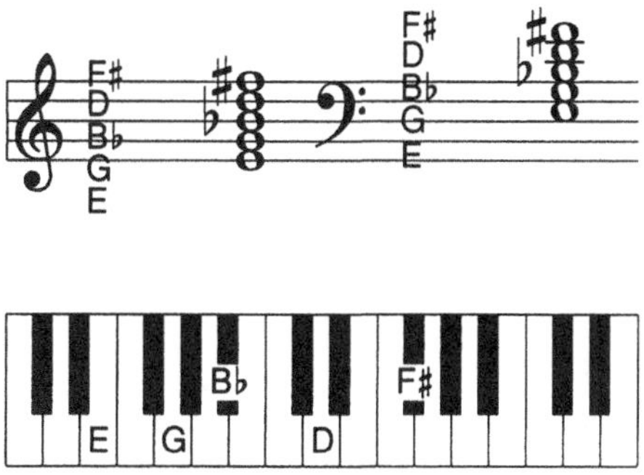

F♯ D B♭ G E

F♯ D B♭ G E

E G B♭ D F♯

Em11

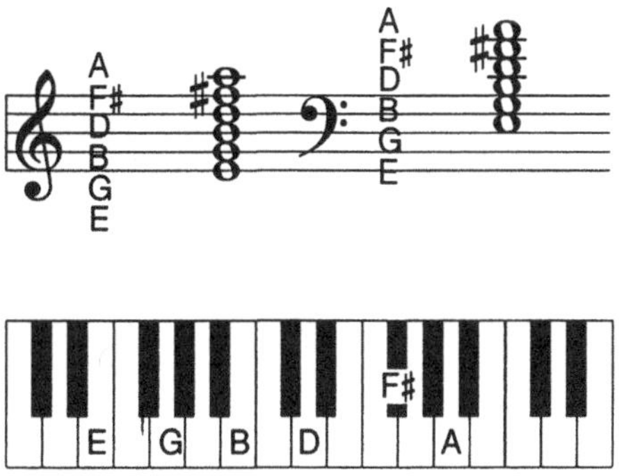

A F♯ D B G E

A F♯ D B G E

E G B D F♯ A

Em13

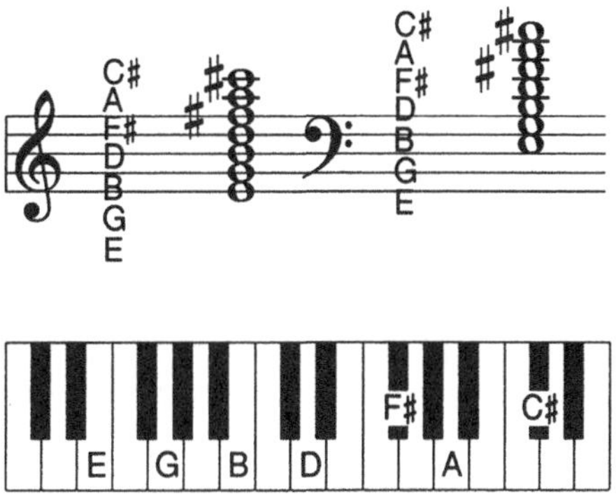

C♯ A F♯ D B G E

C♯ A F♯ D B G E

E G B D F♯ A C♯

Edim7(add9)

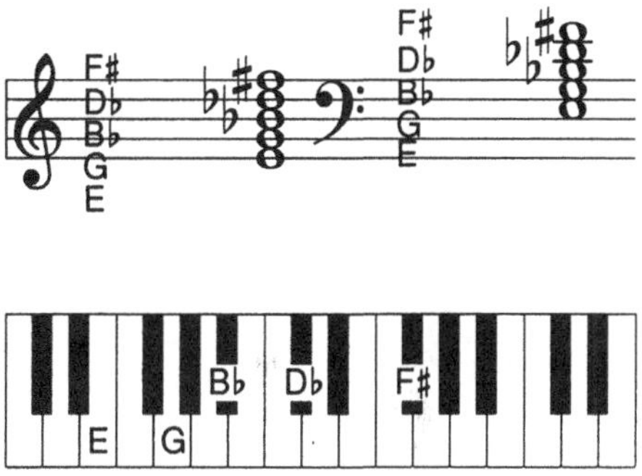

F♯ D♭ B♭ G E

F♯ D♭ B♭ G E

E G B♭ D♭ F♯

Em11♭5

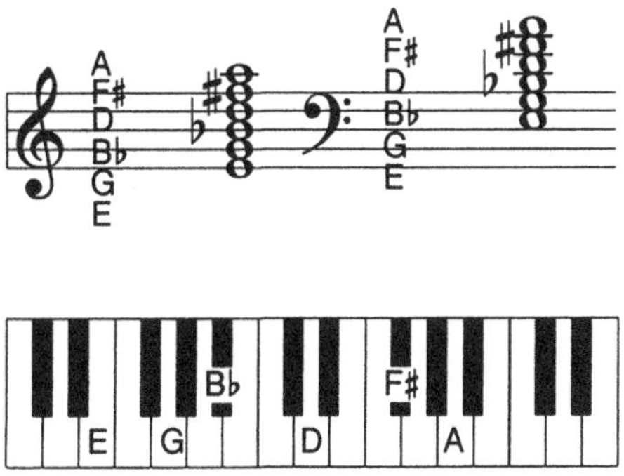

A F♯ D B♭ G E

A F♯ D B♭ G E

E G B♭ D F♯ A

Em11(maj7)

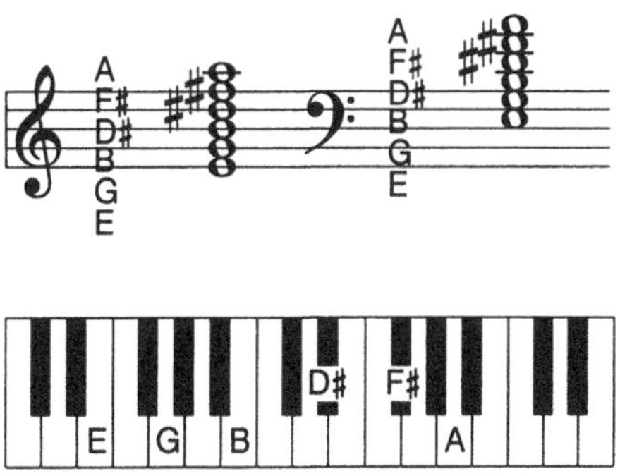

A F♯ D♯ B G E

A F♯ D♯ B G E

E G B D♯ F♯ A

E7alt.

C A♯ G F D B G♯ E

C A♯ G F D B G♯ E

E G♯ B D F G A♯ C

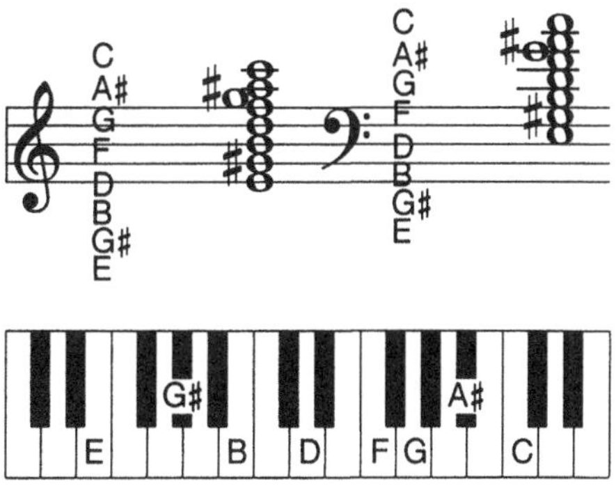

F CHORDS

F

Root Position

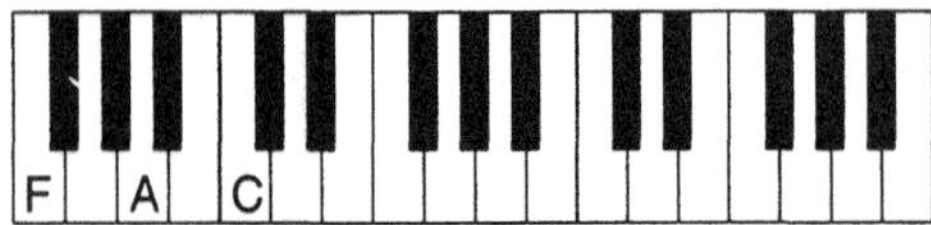

1st Inversion

2nd Inversion

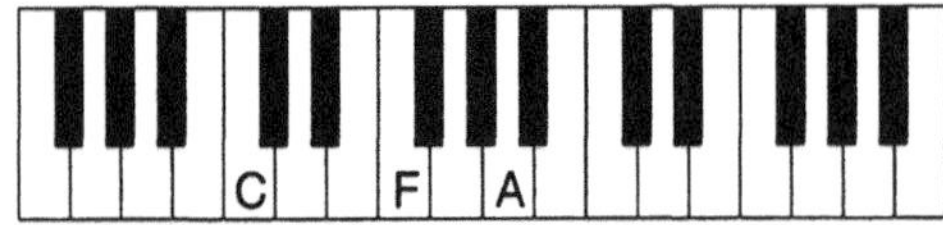

Fm

Root Position

1st Inversion

2nd Inversion

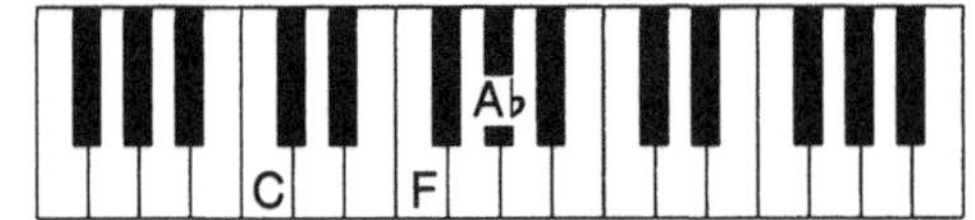

F+

Root Position

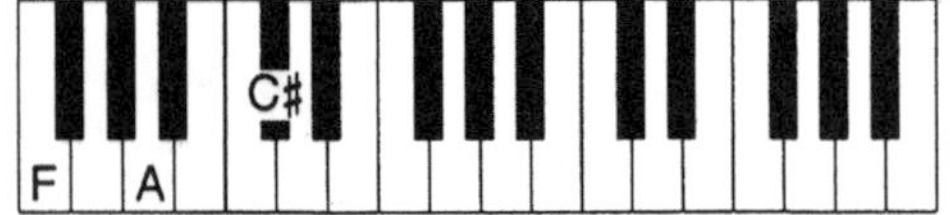

1st Inversion

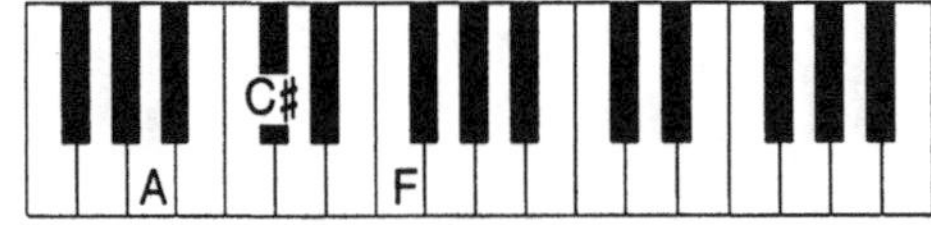

2nd Inversion

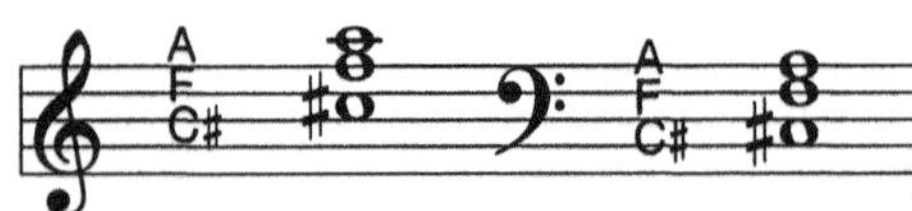

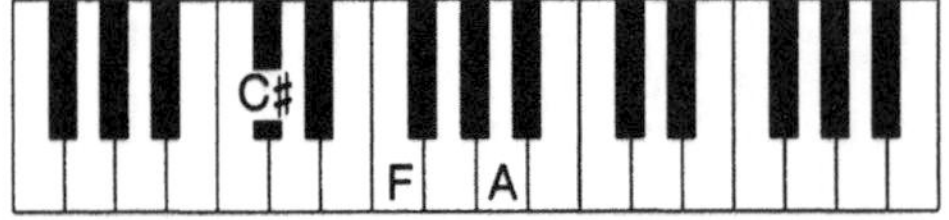

Fdim

Root Position

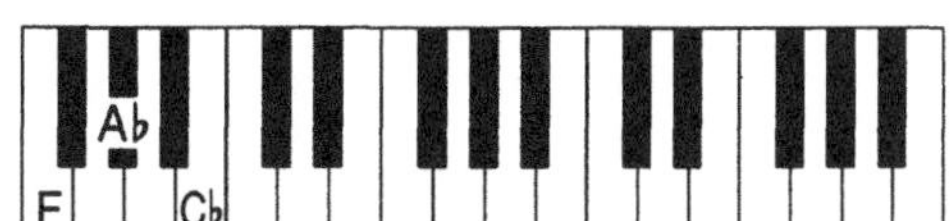

1st Inversion

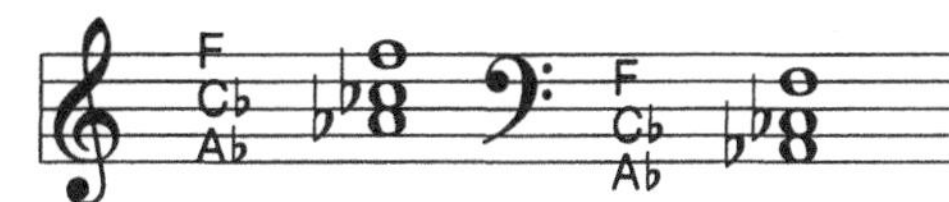

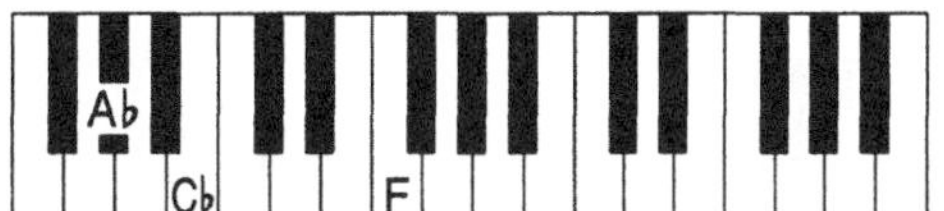

2nd Inversion

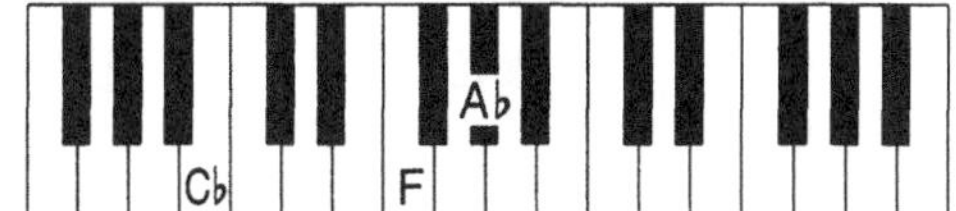

Fsus

Root Position

1st Inversion

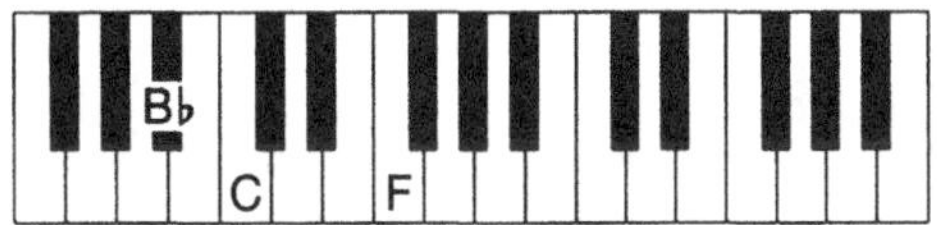

2nd Inversion

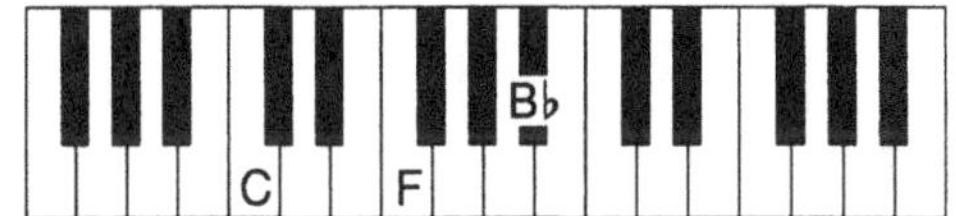

F(♭5)

Root Position

1st Inversion

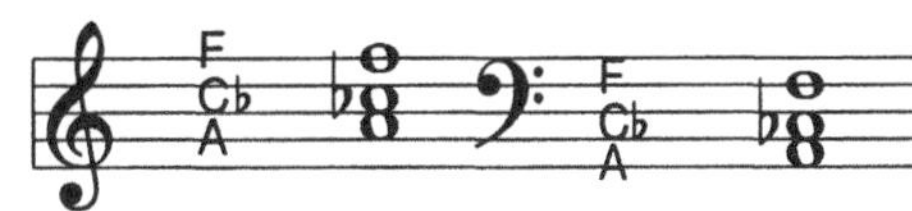

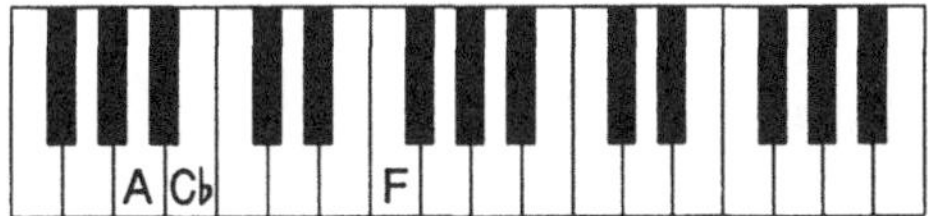

2nd Inversion

Fsus2

Root Position

1st Inversion

2nd Inversion

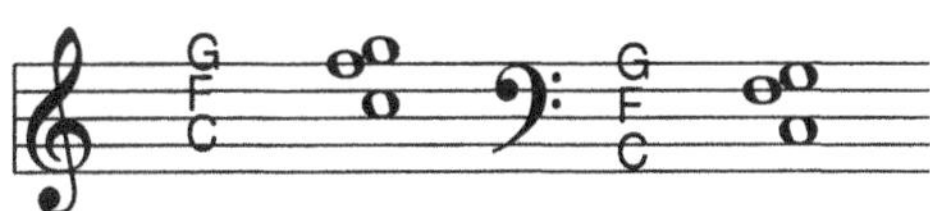

F6

1st Inversion

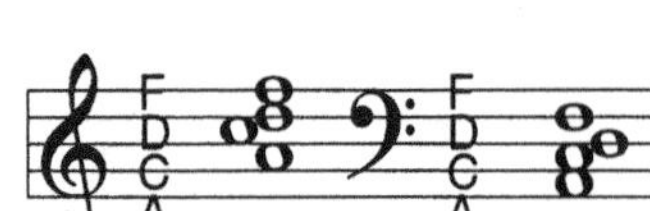

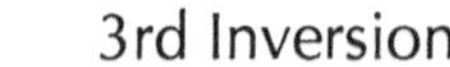

F(add2), F(add9)

Root Position

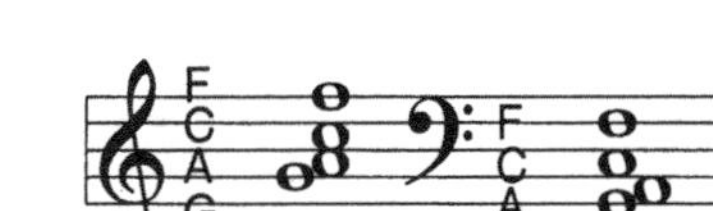

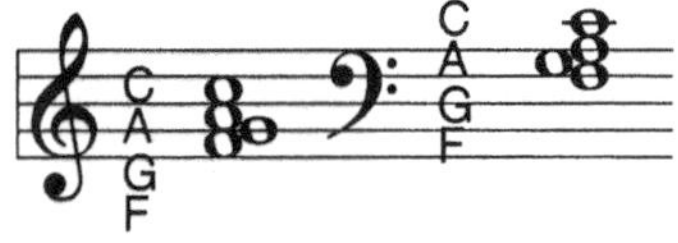

1st Inversion

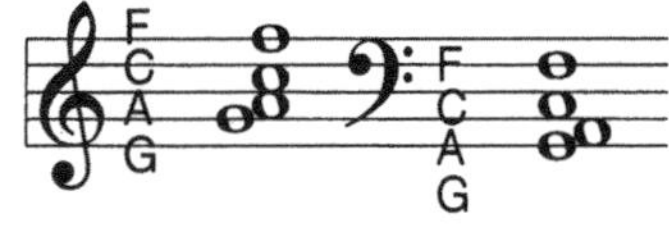

2nd Inversion

3rd Inversion

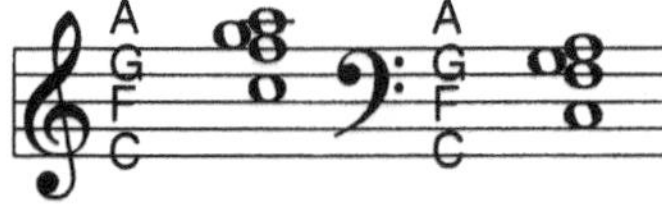

A C F G

C F G A

Fmaj7

Root Position

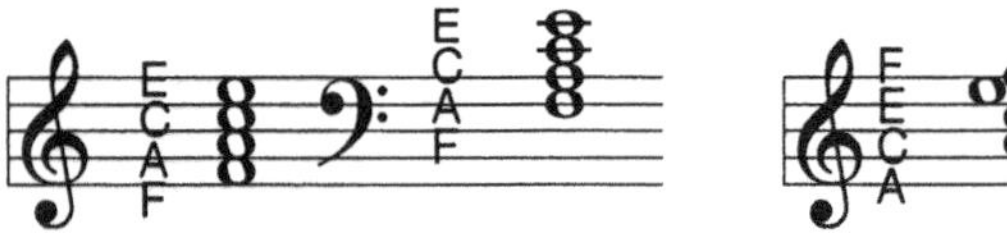

1st Inversion

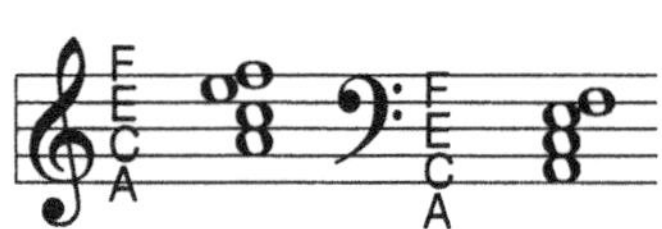

2nd Inversion

3rd Inversion

C E F A

E F A C

Fmaj7♭5

Root Position

1st Inversion

F
E
C♭
A
F
E
C♭
A

2nd Inversion

3rd Inversion

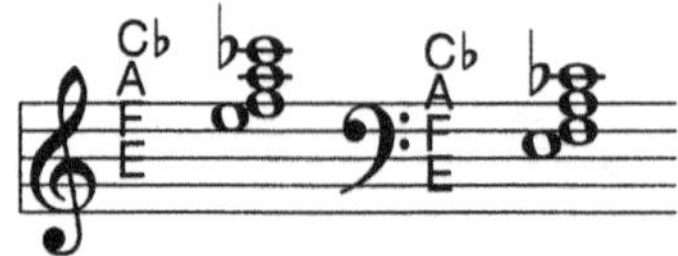

F A C♭ E

A C♭ E F

Fmaj7♯5

Root Position | 1st Inversion | 2nd Inversion | 3rd Inversion

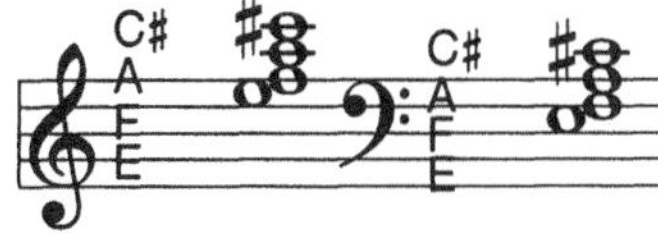

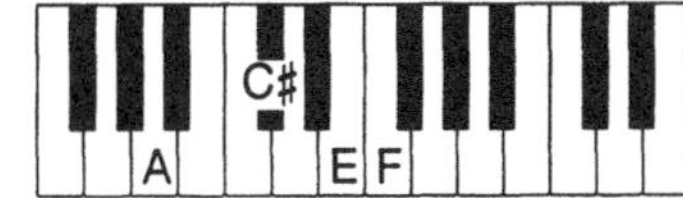

C♯ E F A

C♯ E F A

F7

Root Position | 1st Inversion | 2nd Inversion | 3rd Inversion

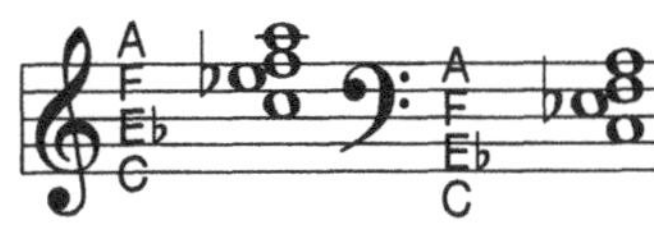

E♭ C F A

E♭ F A C

F7♭5

Root Position | 1st Inversion | 2nd Inversion | 3rd Inversion

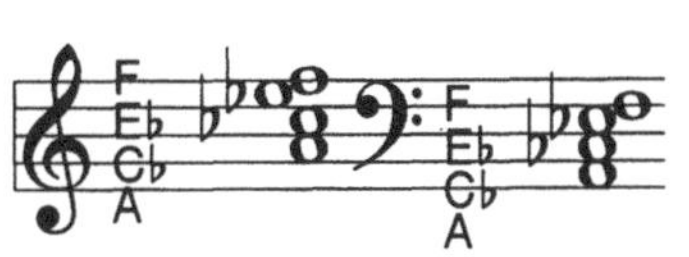

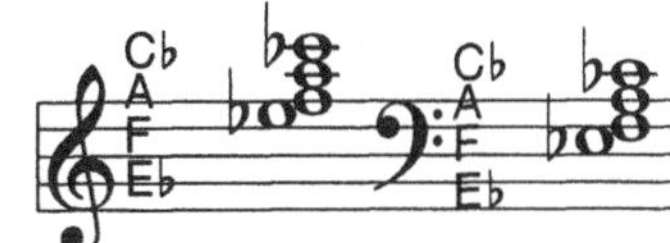

E♭ C♭ F A

E♭ F A C♭

F7♯5

Root Position | 1st Inversion | 2nd Inversion | 3rd Inversion

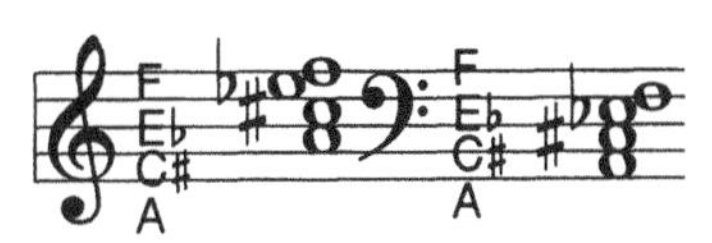

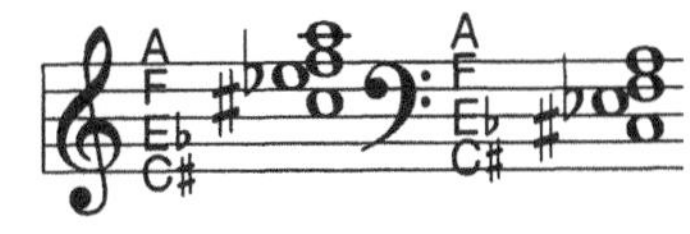

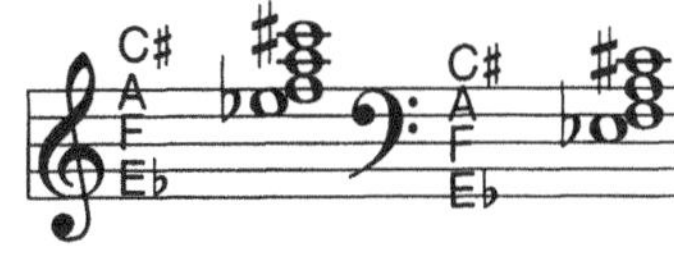

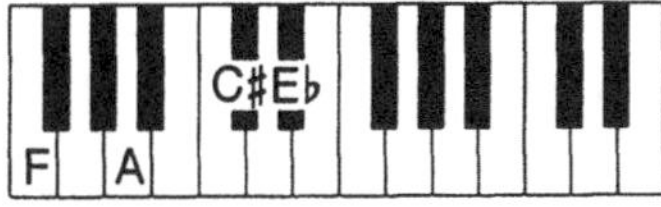

F7sus

Root Position

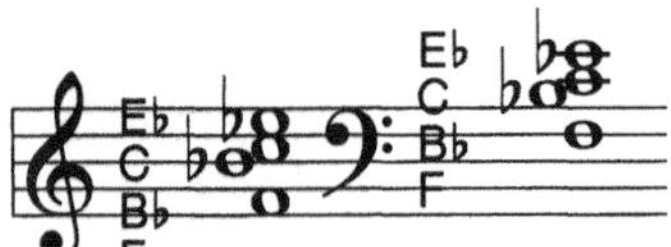

1st Inversion

2nd Inversion

3rd Inversion

Fm(add2), Fm(add9)

Root Position

1st Inversion

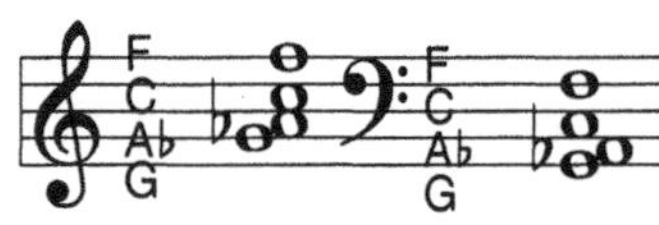

2nd Inversion

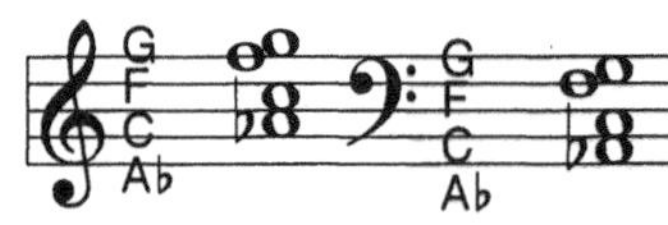

3rd Inversion

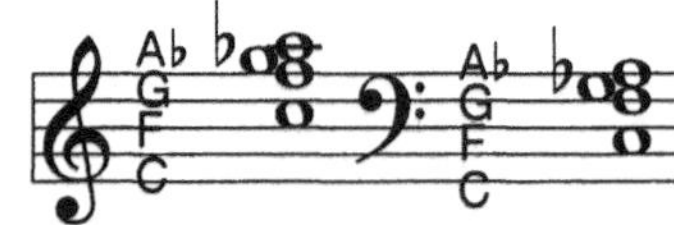

Fm6

Root Position

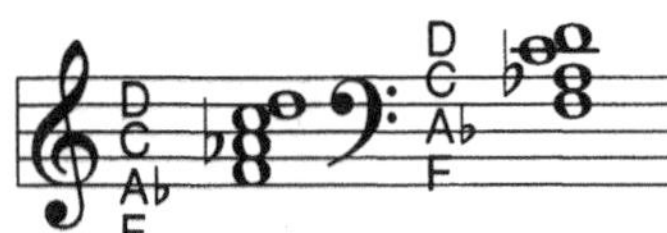

1st Inversion

2nd Inversion

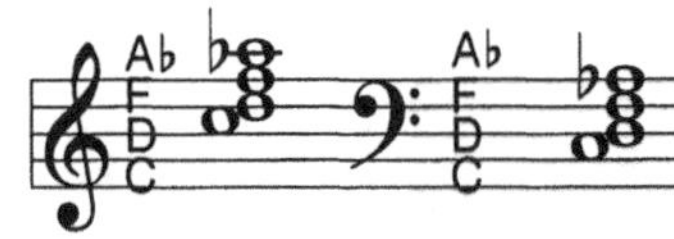

3rd Inversion

Fm7

Root Position

1st Inversion

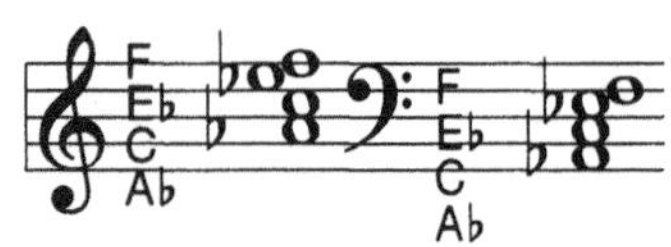

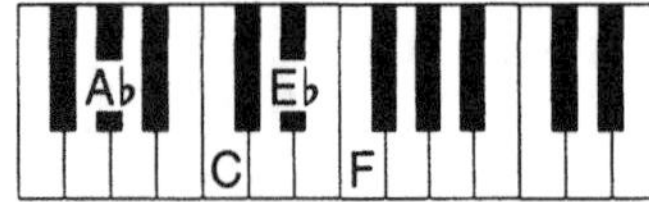

2nd Inversion

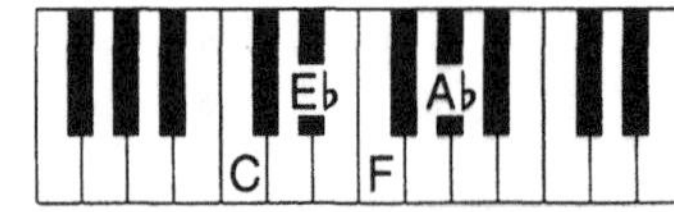

3rd Inversion

Fm(maj7)

2nd Inversion

Fm7♭5

Root Position

1st Inversion

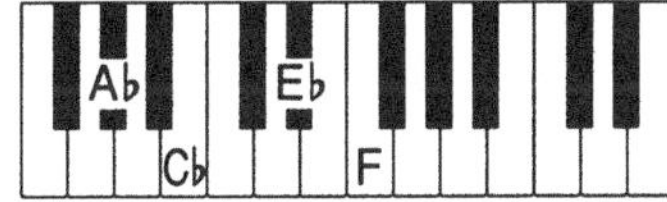

2nd Inversion

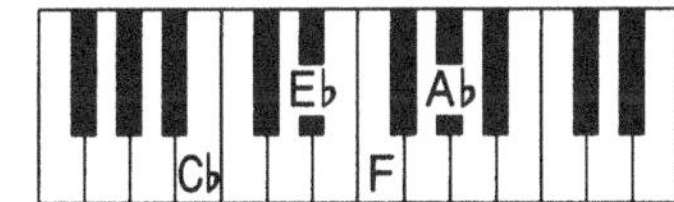

3rd Inversion

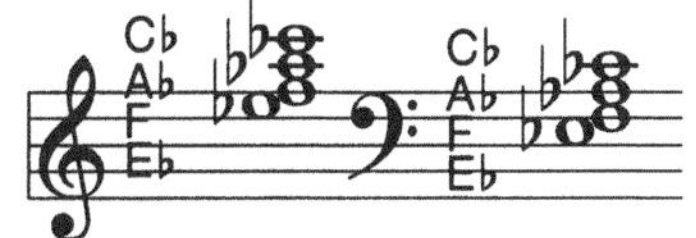

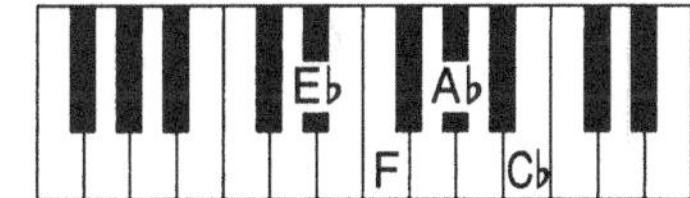

Fdim7

Root Position

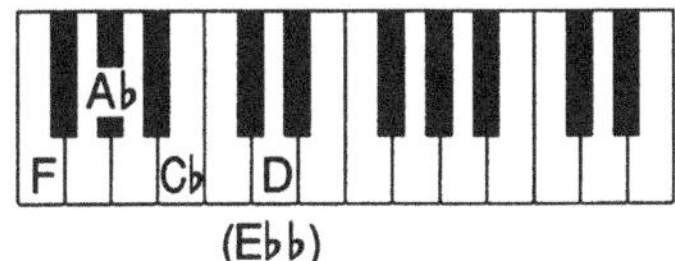

1st Inversion

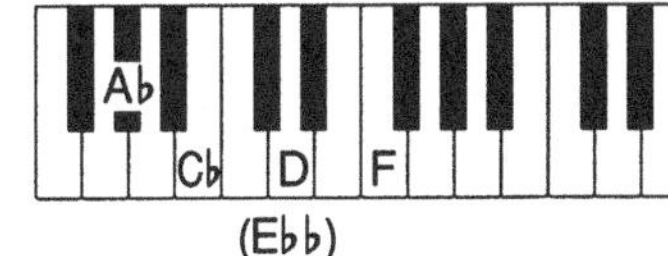

2nd Inversion

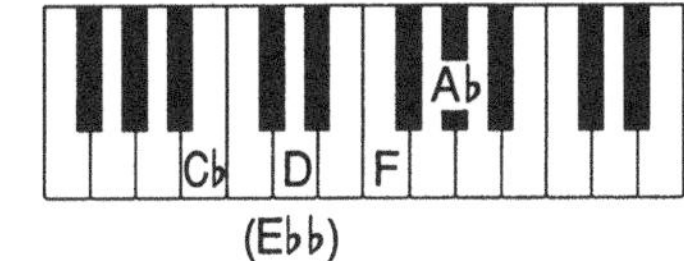

3rd Inversion

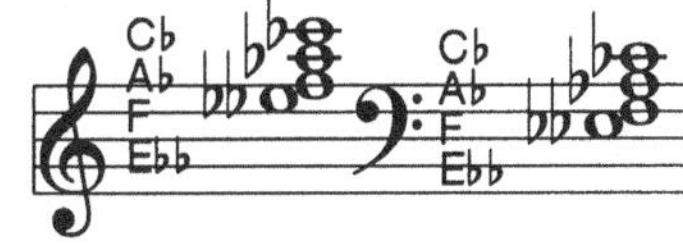

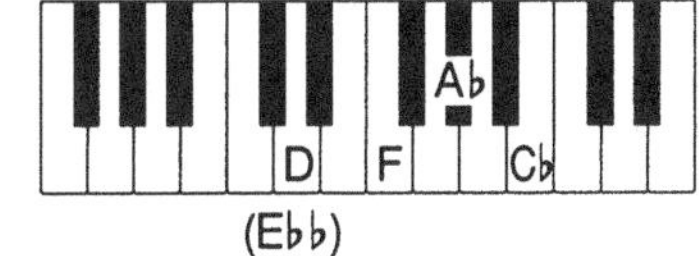

Fdim(maj7)

Root Position

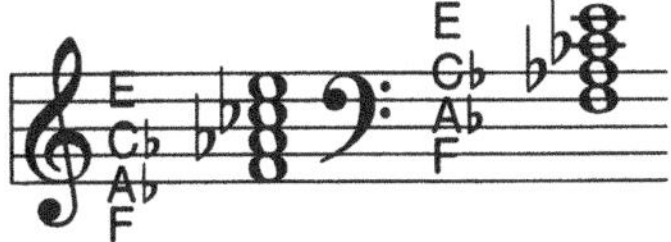

1st Inversion

2nd Inversion

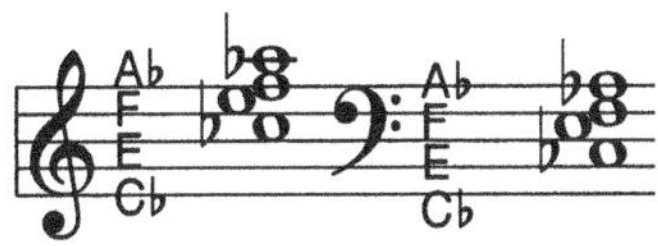

3rd Inversion

ADDITIONAL F CHORDS

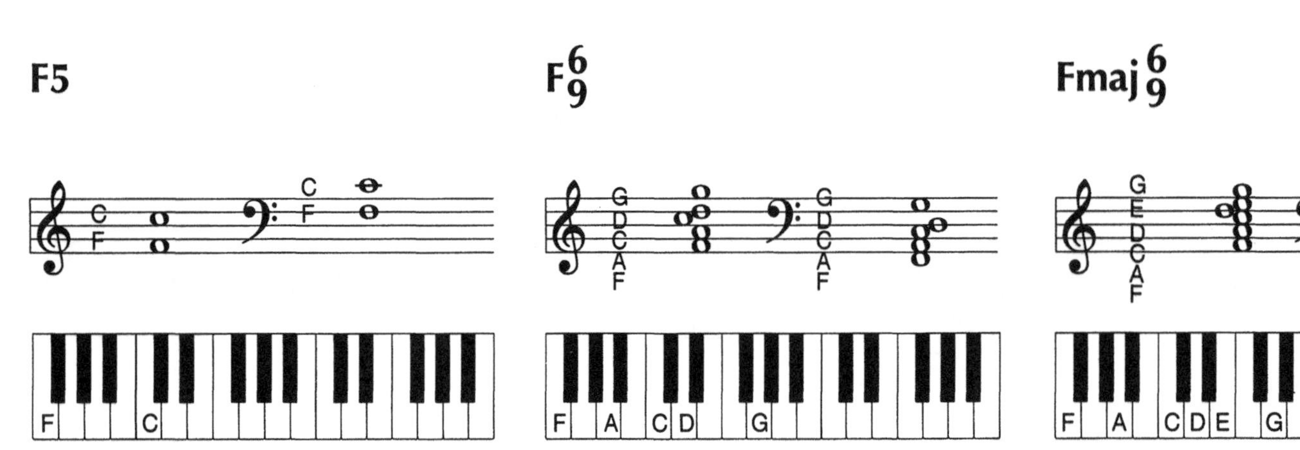

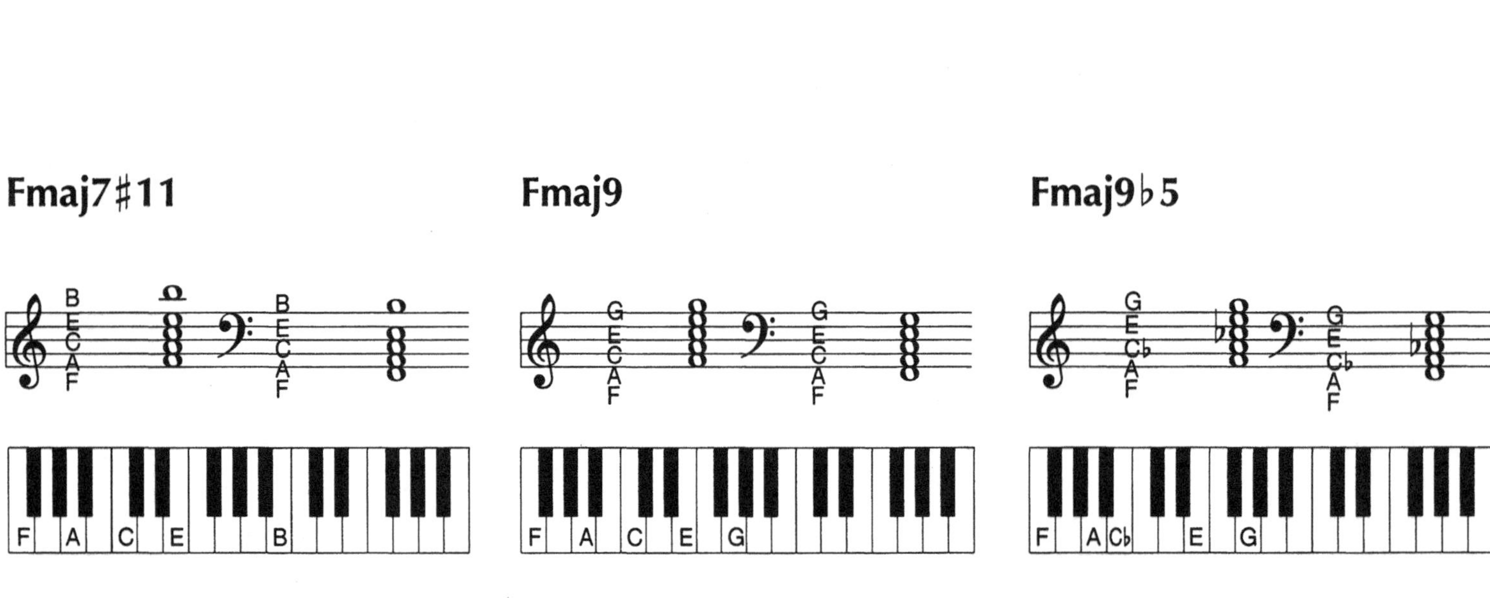

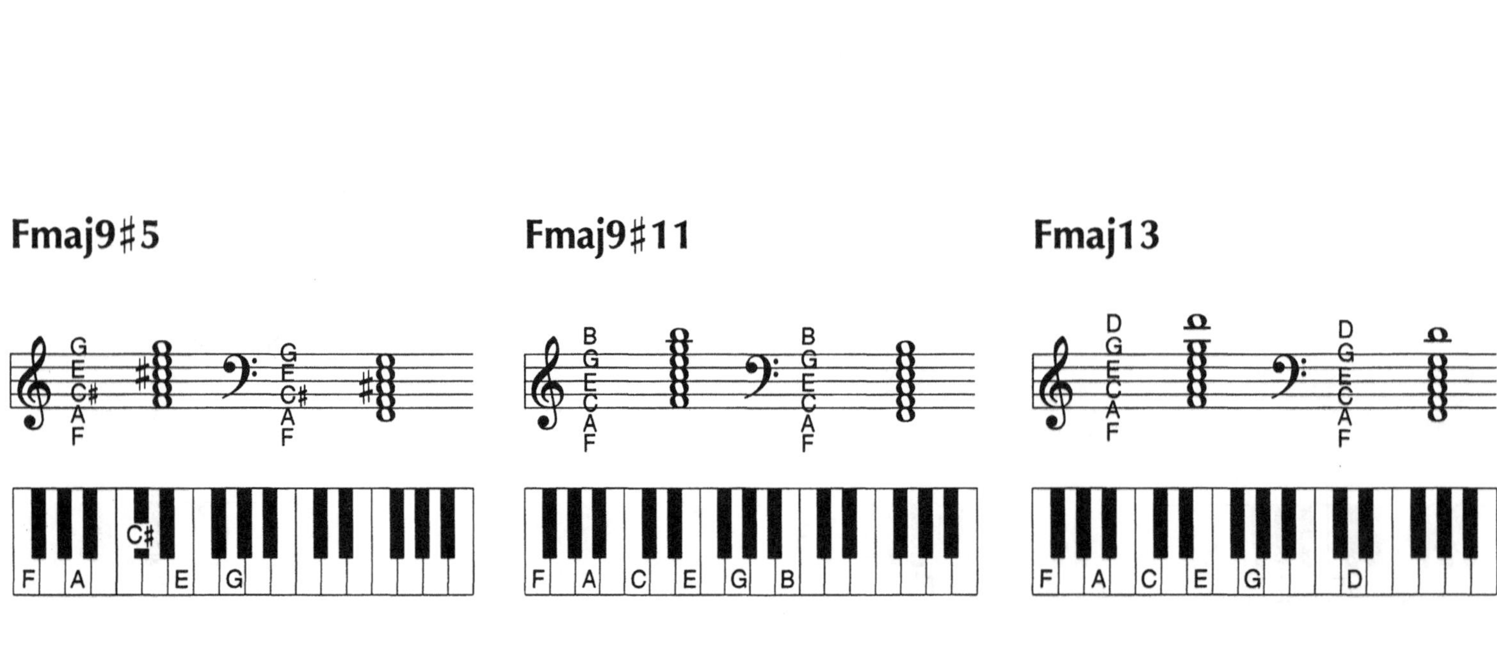

Fmaj13♭5

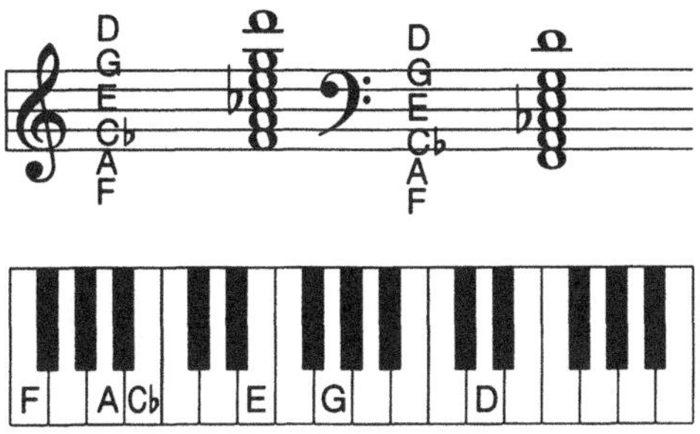

Fmaj13♯11

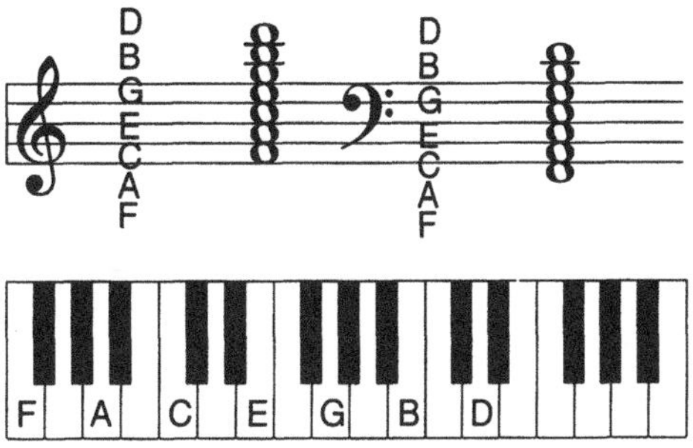

F7♭9

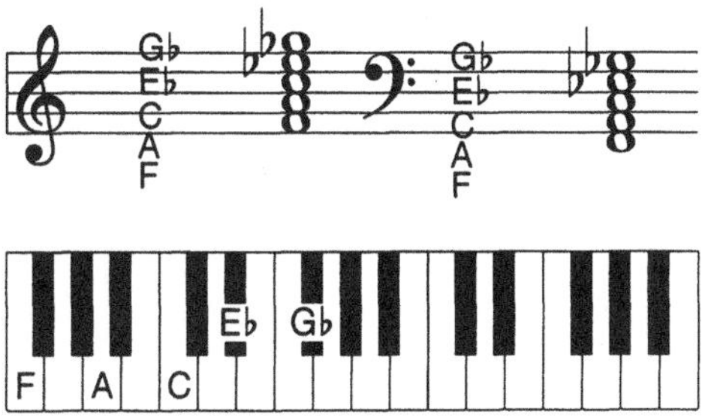

F7♯9

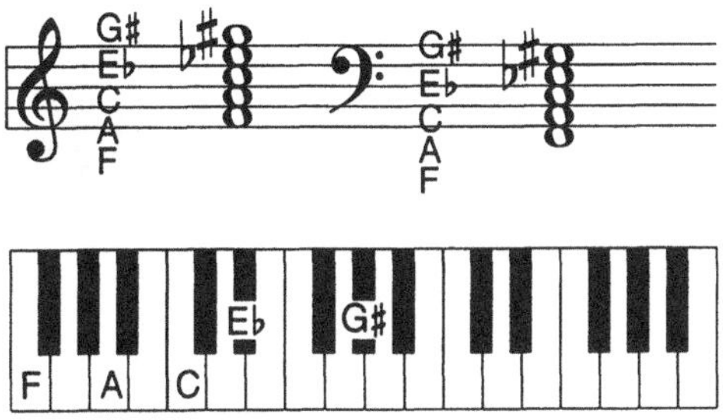

F7♯11

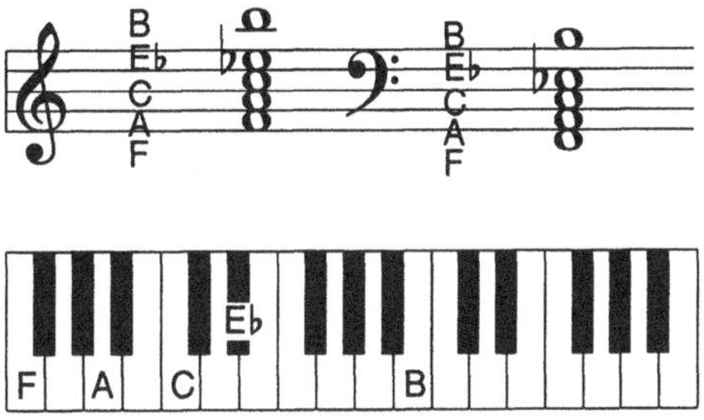

F7♭5(♭9)

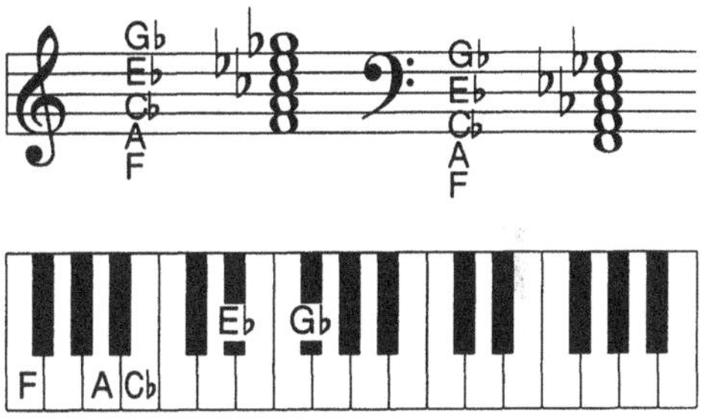

F7♭5(♯9)

F7♯5(♭9)

F7♯5(♯9)

F7♭9(♯9)

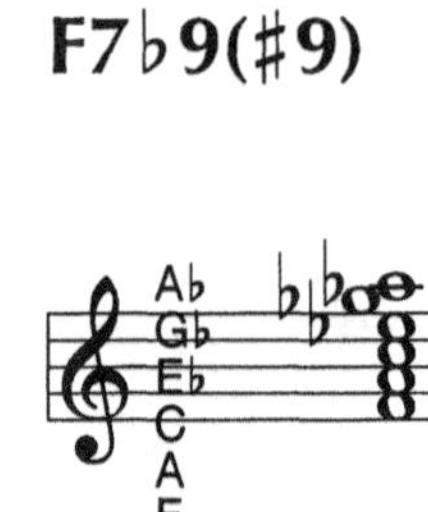

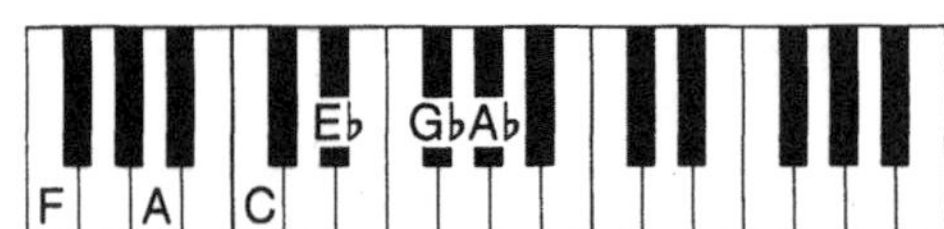

F7(add13)

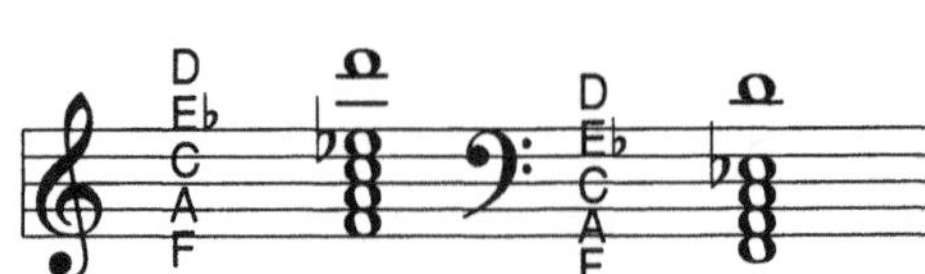

F7♭13

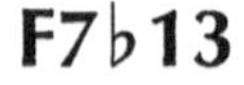

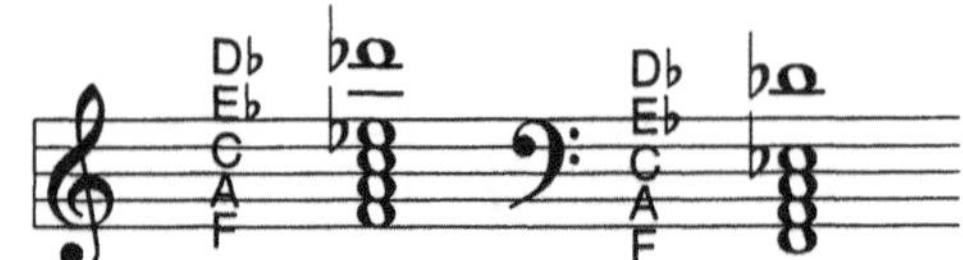

F7♭9(♯11)

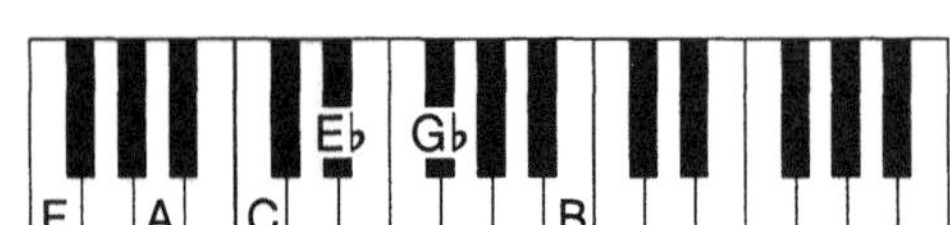

F7♯9(♯11)

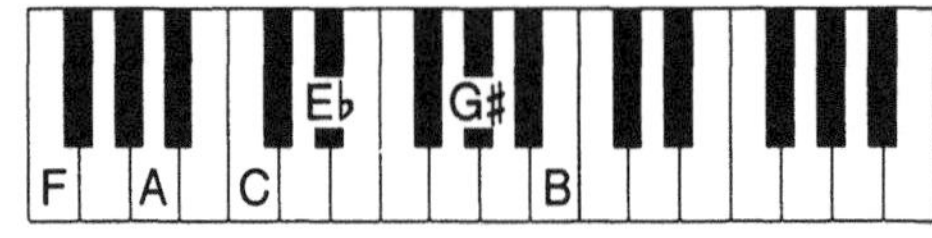

F7♭9(♭13)

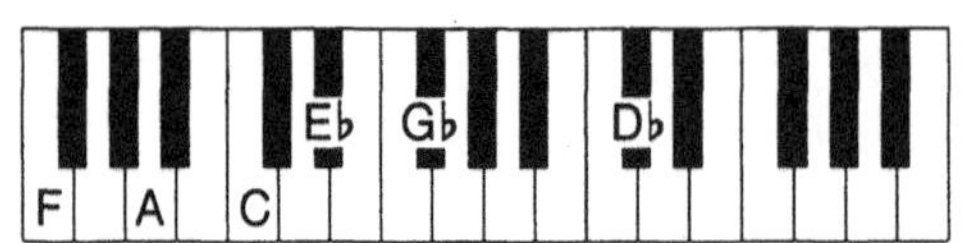

F7♯9(♭13)

F7♯11(♭13)

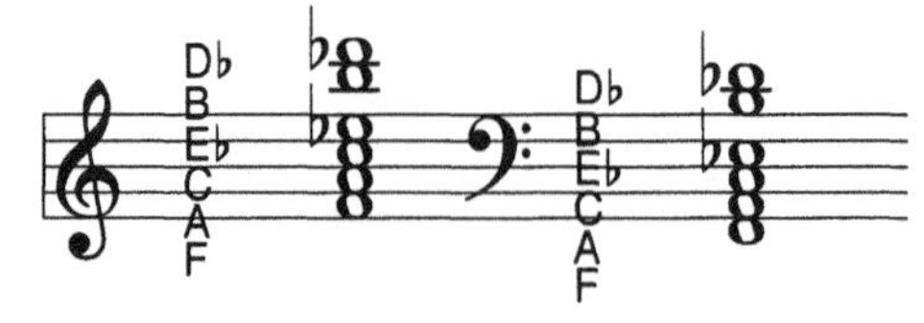

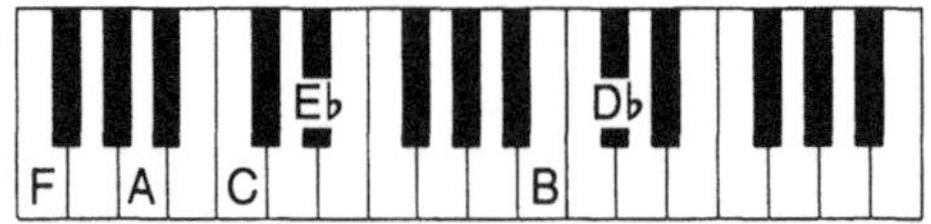

F7♭9(♯9,♯11)

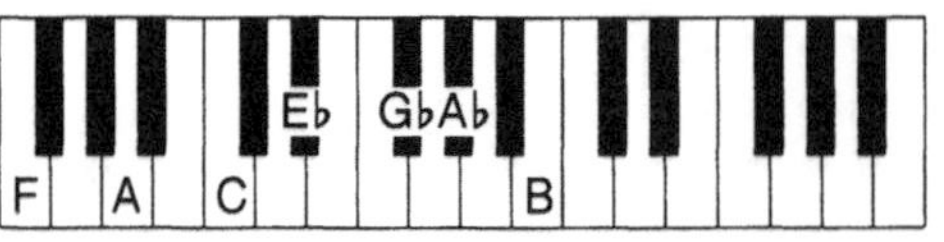

F9

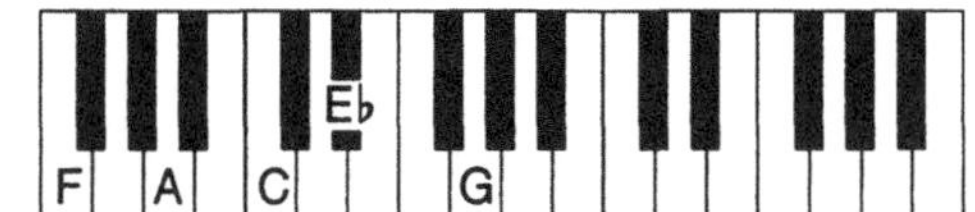

F9(♭5)

F9♯5

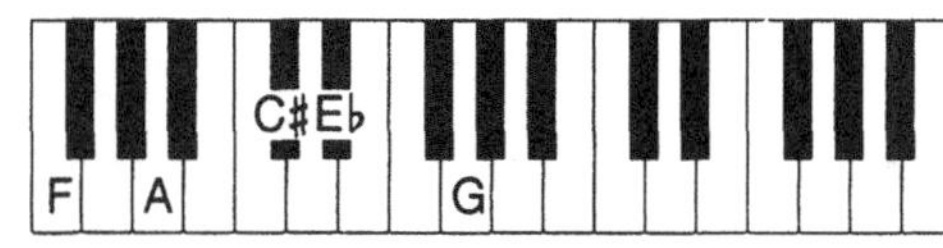

F9♯11

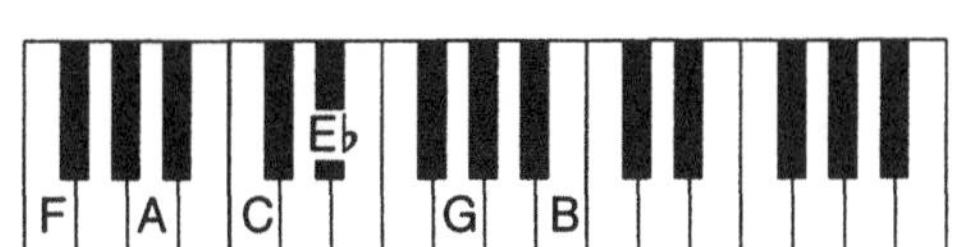

F9♭13

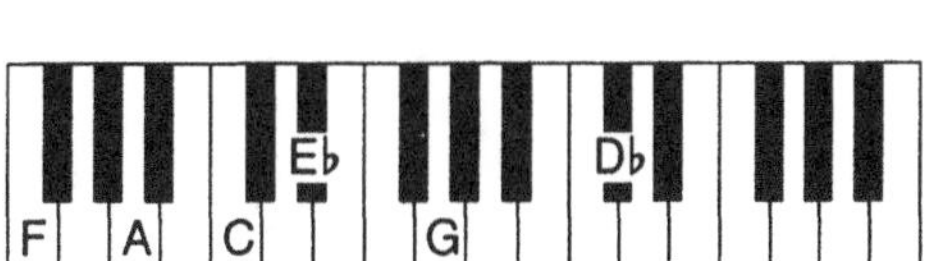

F9♯11(♭13)

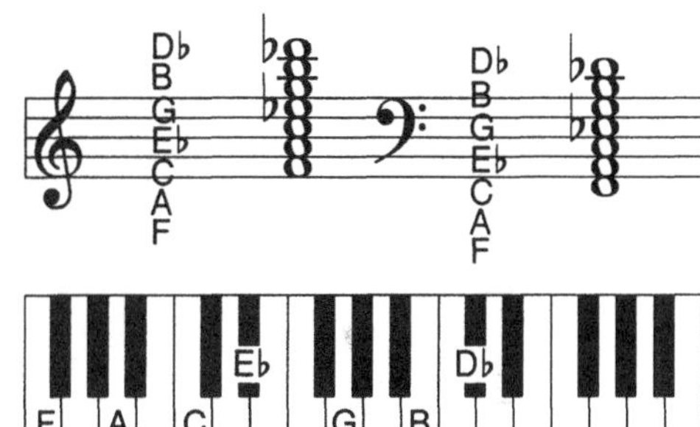

F11, F9sus4

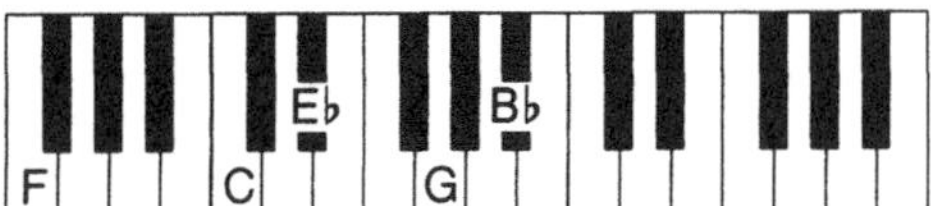

F13

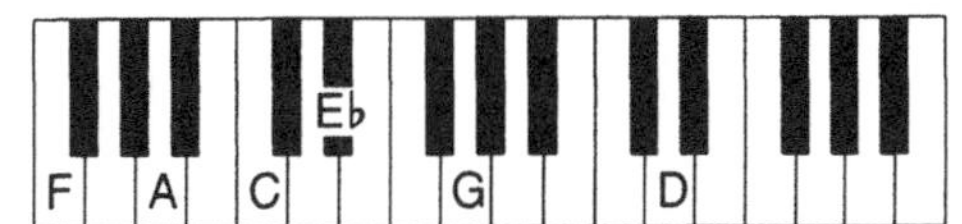

F13♭5

F13♭9

F13♯9

F13♯11

F13(sus4)

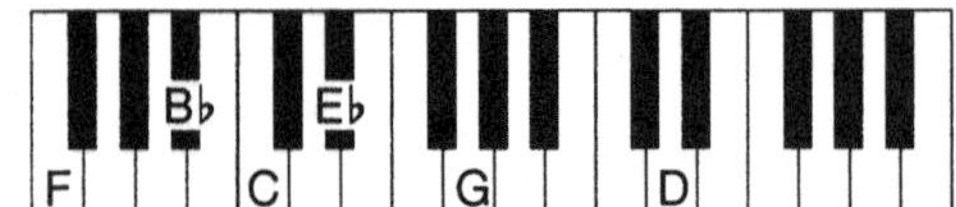

Fm(♯5)

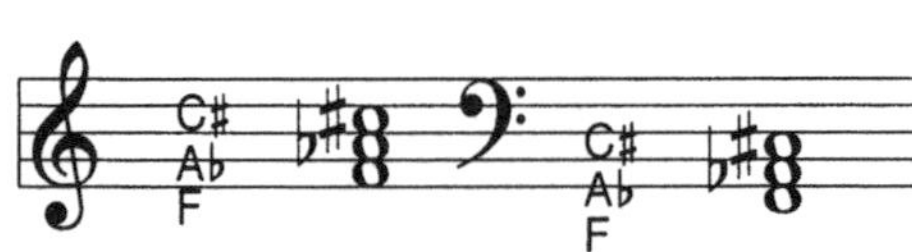

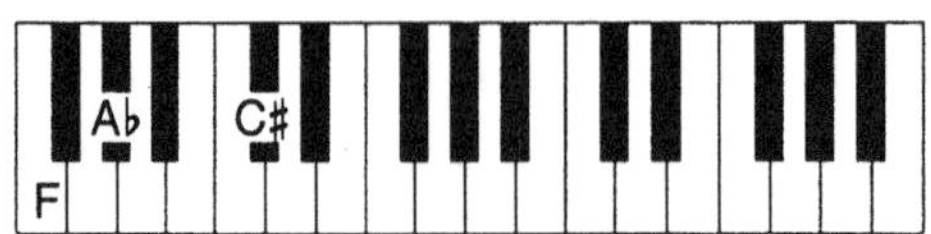

Fm$^{6}_{9}$

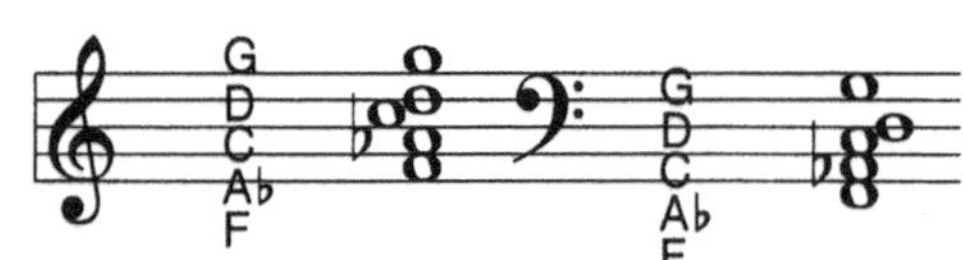

Fm7(add4)

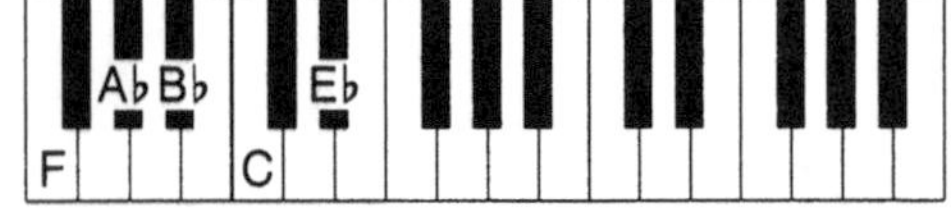

Fm7(add11)

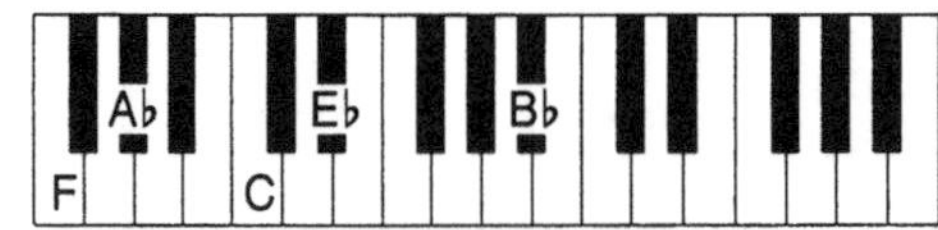

Fm7♭5(♭9)

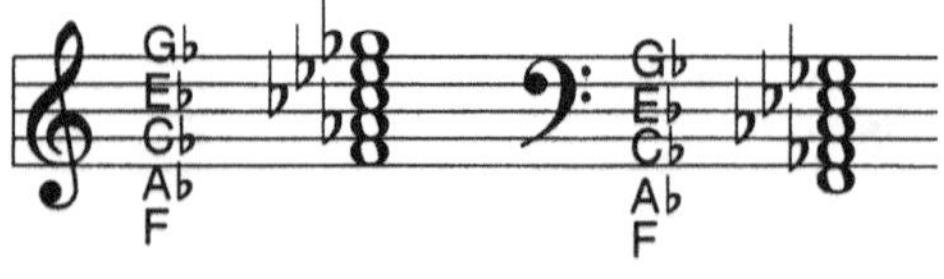

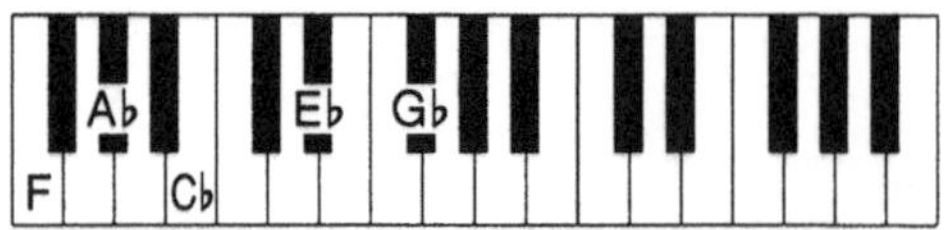

Fm9

Fm9(maj7)

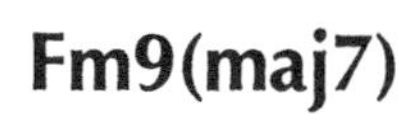

Fm9♭5

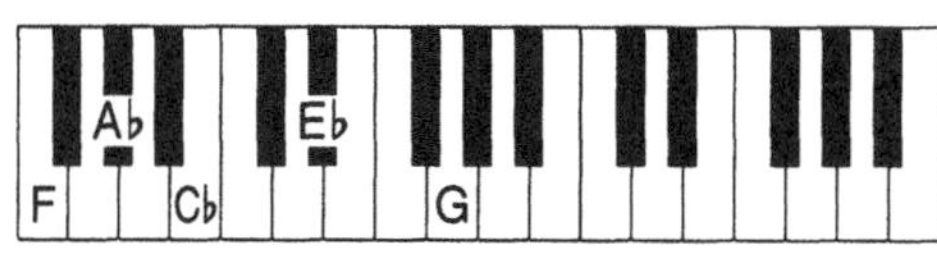

Fm11

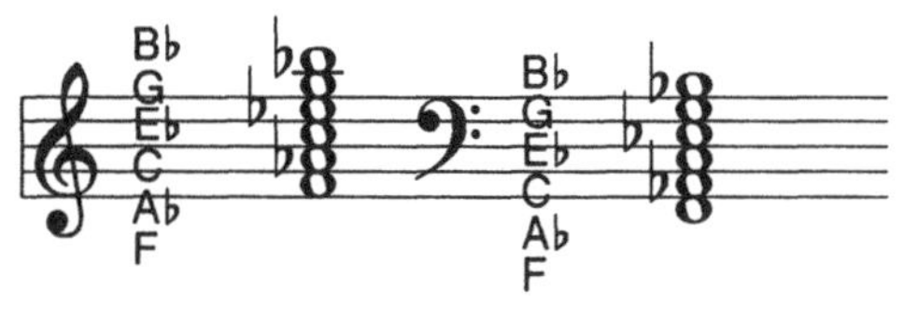

Fm13

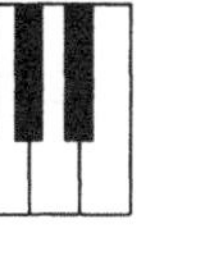

Fdim7(add9)

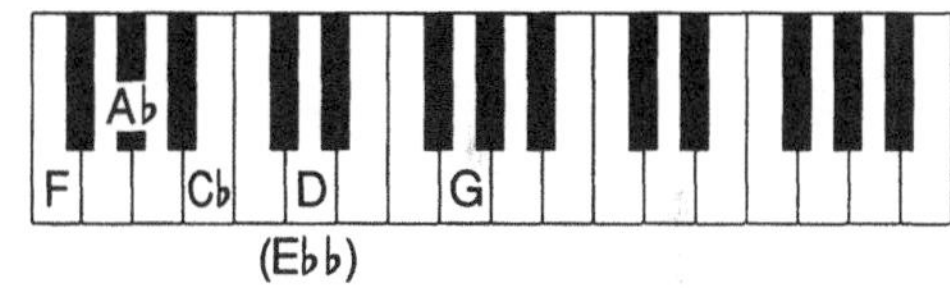

Fm11♭5

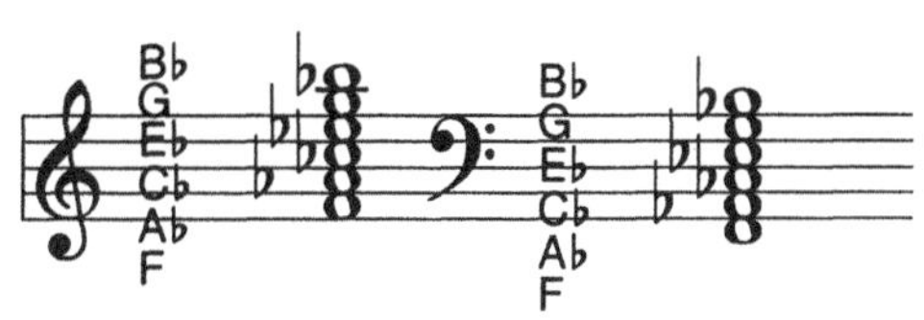

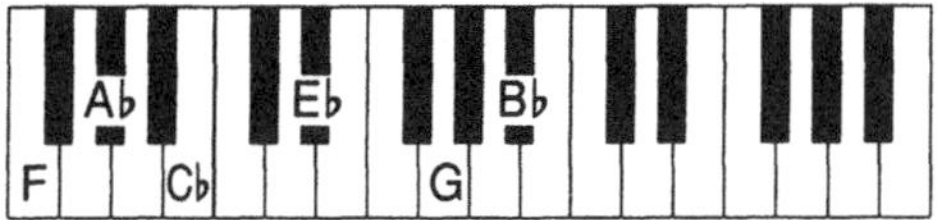

Fm11(maj7)

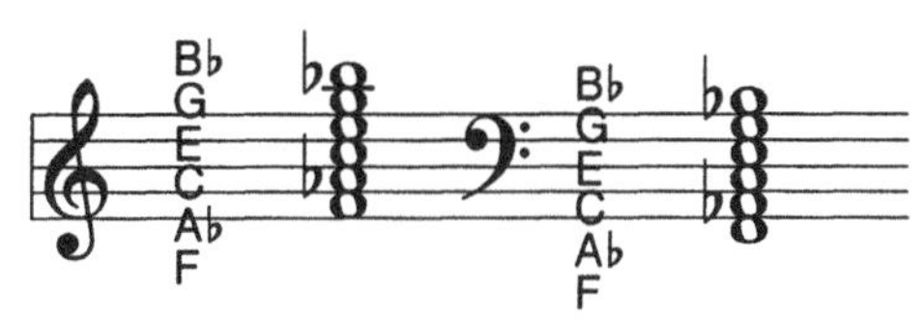

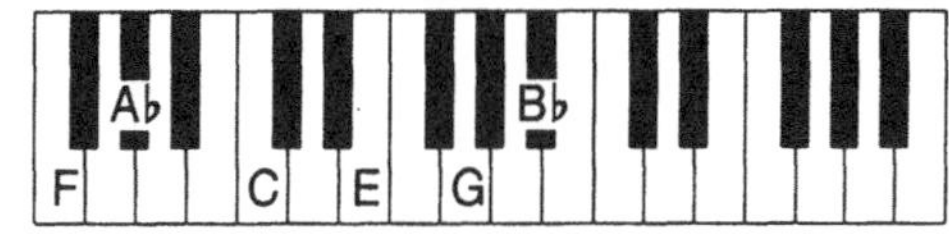

F7alt.

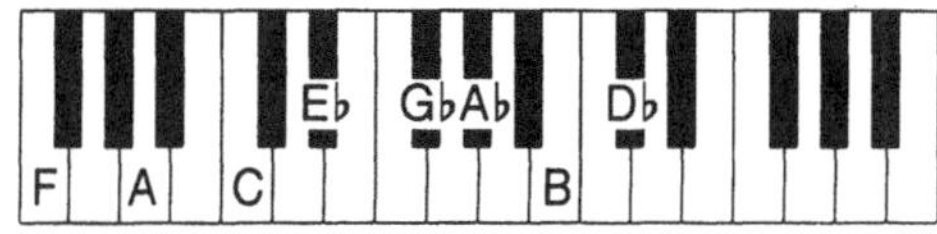

F♯/G♭ CHORDS

F♯

Root Position

1st Inversion

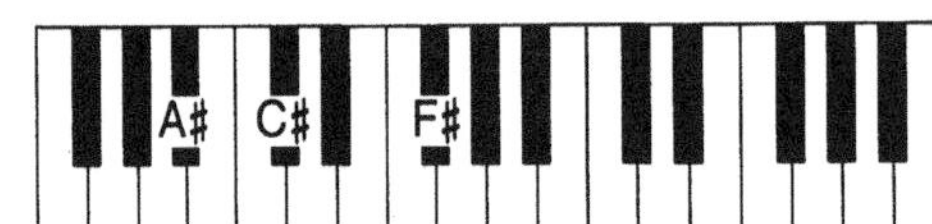

2nd Inversion

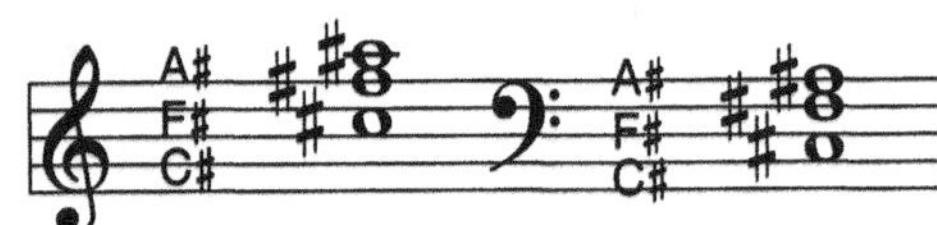

F♯m

Root Position

1st Inversion

2nd Inversion

C♯ F♯ A

F♯+

Root Position

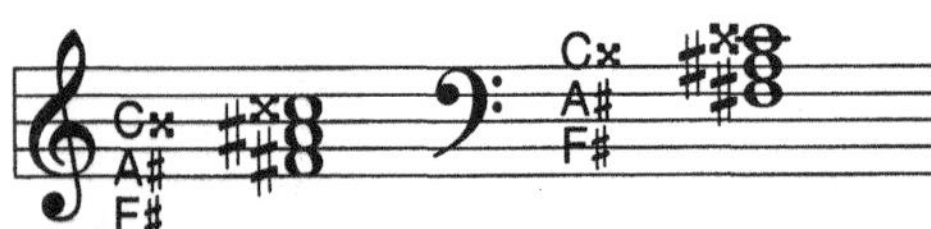

F♯ A♯ D (C𝄪)

1st Inversion

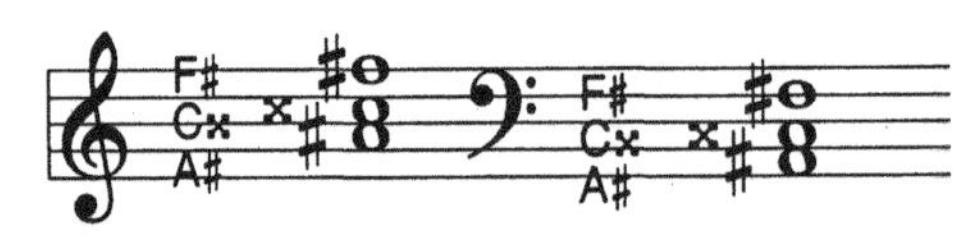

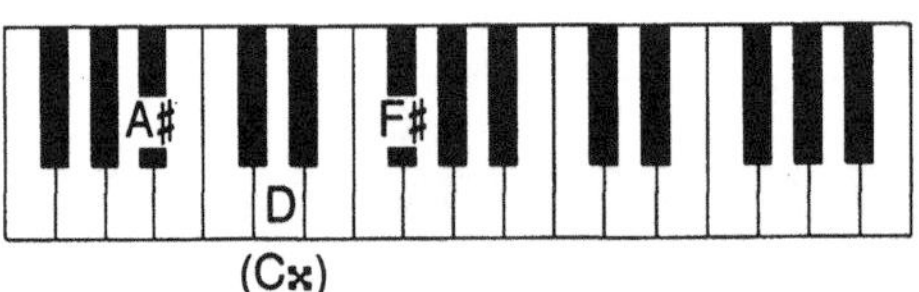

2nd Inversion

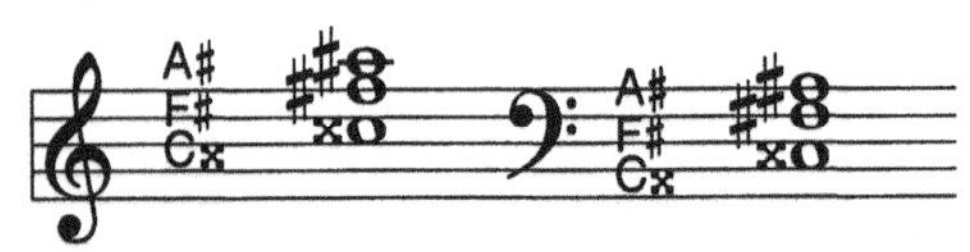

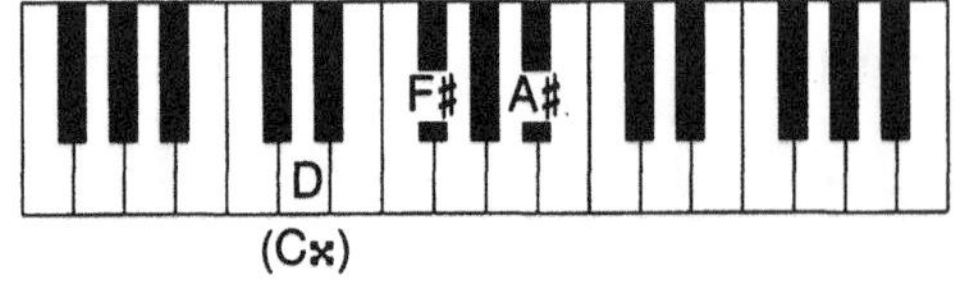

F♯dim

Root Position

1st Inversion

2nd Inversion

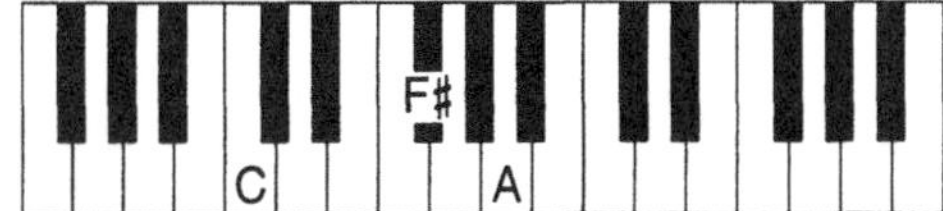

F♯sus

Root Position

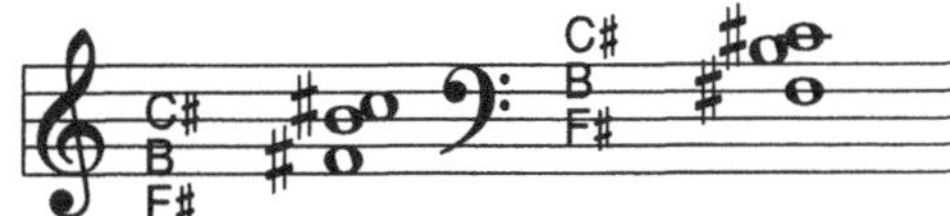

1st Inversion

2nd Inversion

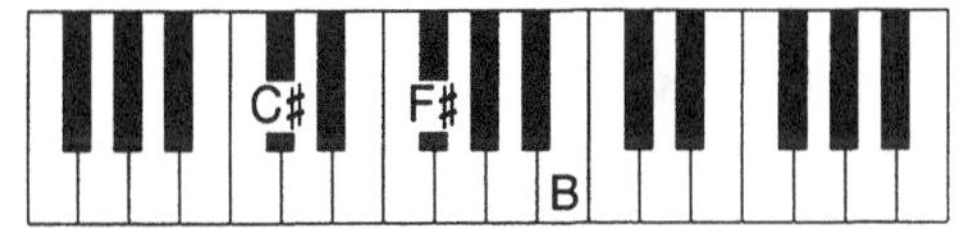

F♯(♭5)

Root Position

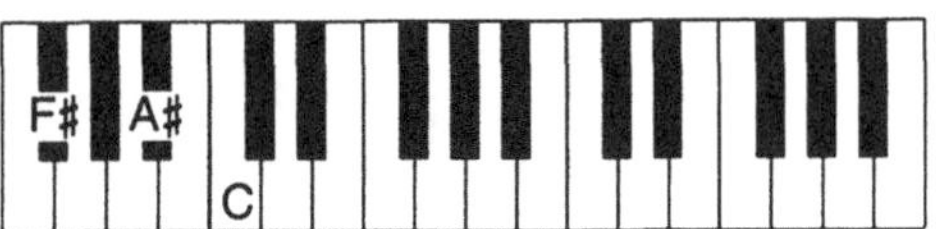

1st Inversion

2nd Inversion

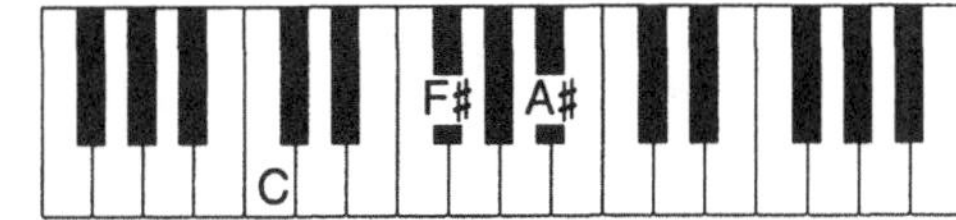

F♯sus2

Root Position

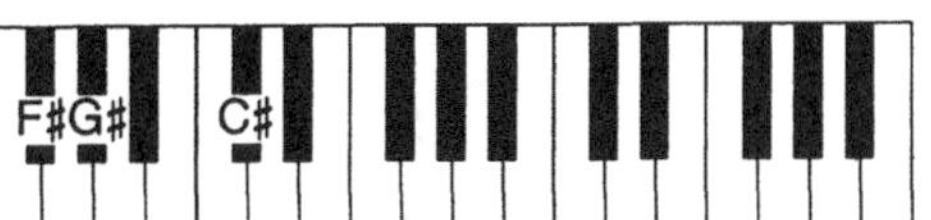

1st Inversion

2nd Inversion

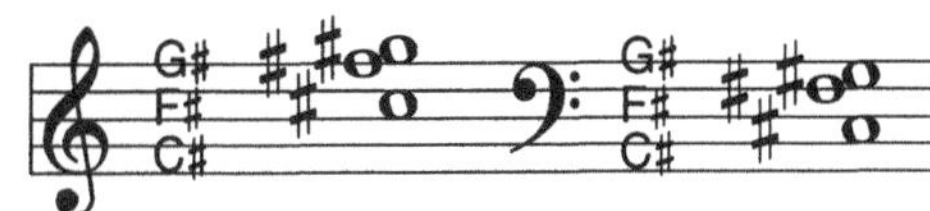

F♯6

Root Position

1st Inversion

2nd Inversion

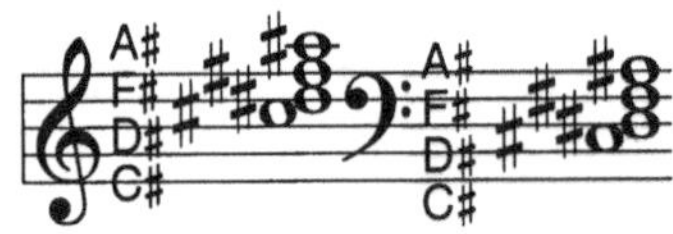

3rd Inversion

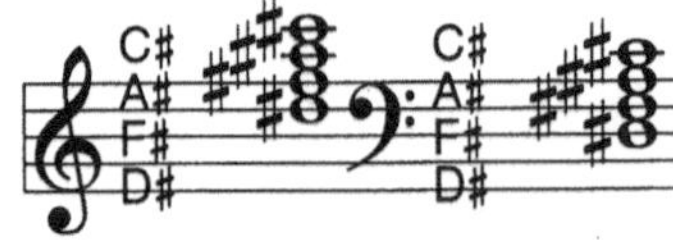

F♯(add2), F♯(add9)

Root Position

1st Inversion

2nd Inversion

3rd Inversion

F♯maj7

Root Position

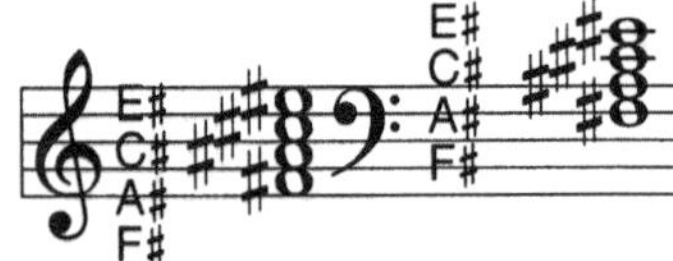

1st Inversion

2nd Inversion

3rd Inversion

F♯maj7♭5

Root Position

1st Inversion

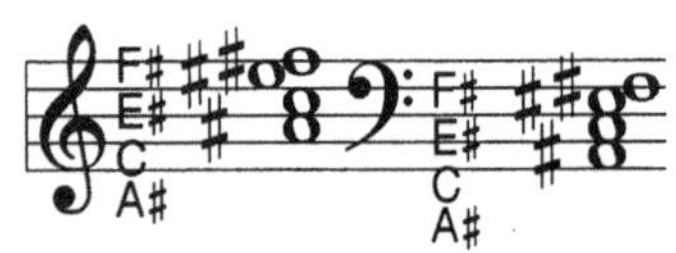

2nd Inversion

3rd Inversion

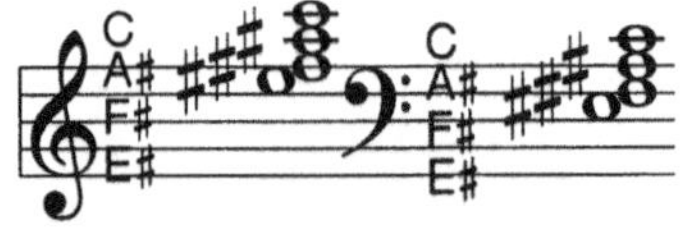

F♯maj7♯5

Root Position

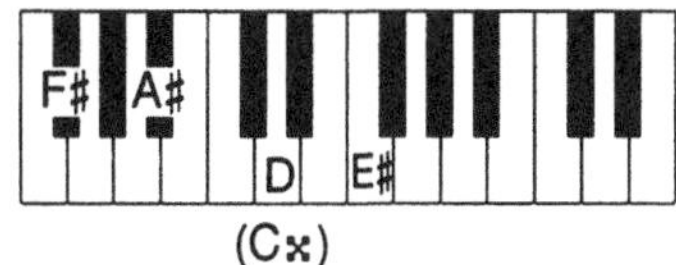

1st Inversion

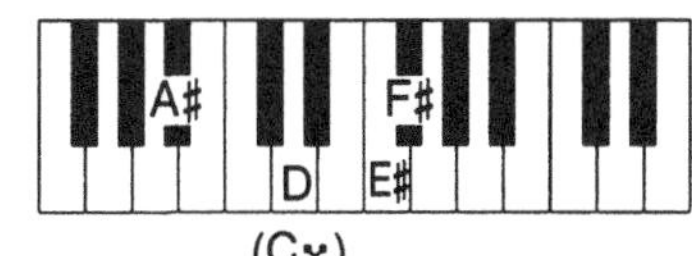

2nd Inversion

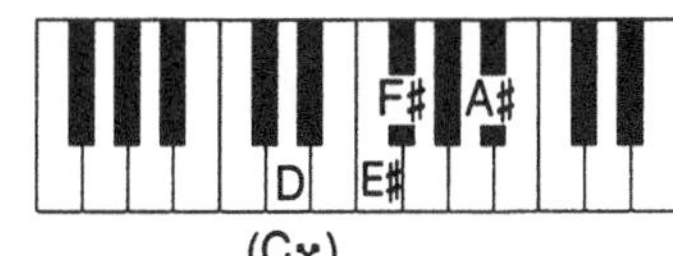

3rd Inversion

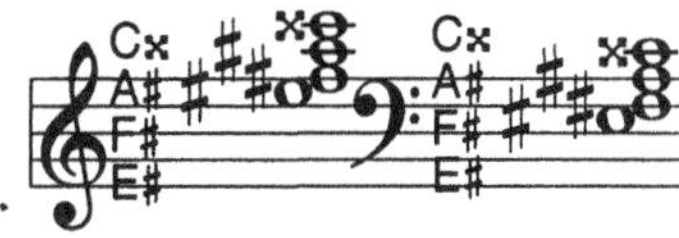

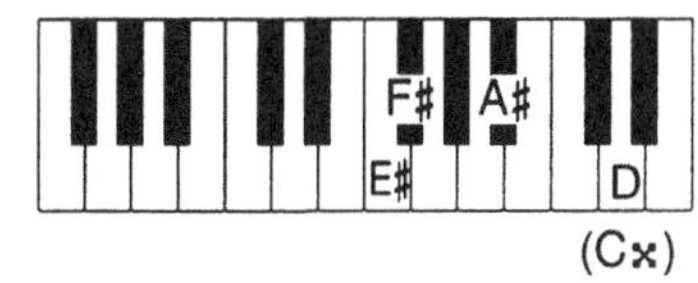

F♯7

Root Position

1st Inversion

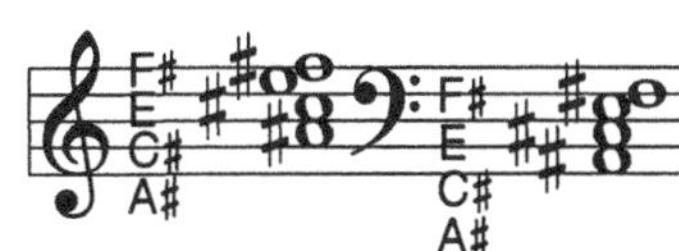

2nd Inversion

3rd Inversion

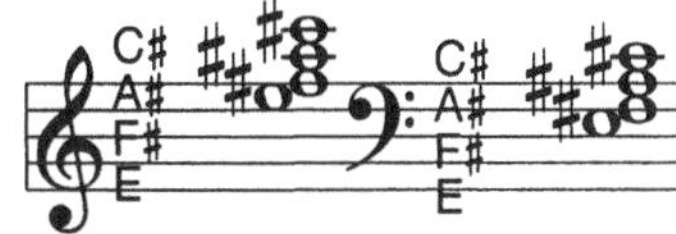

F♯7♭5

Root Position

1st Inversion

2nd Inversion

F♯ A♯
C E

3rd Inversion

F♯ A♯
E C

F♯7♯5

Root Position

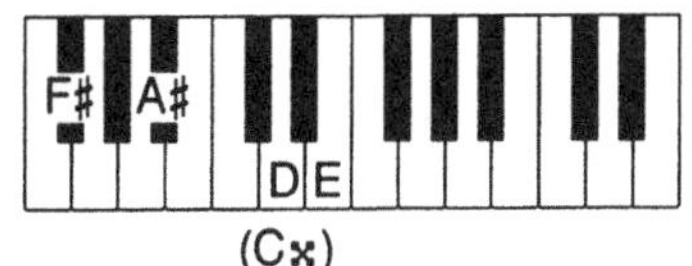

1st Inversion

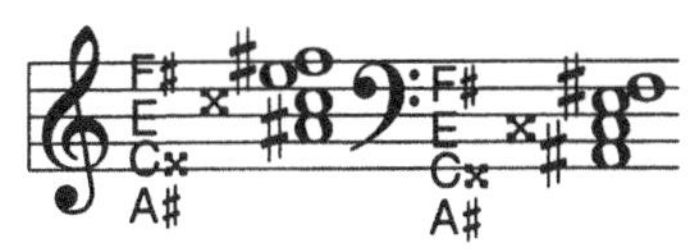

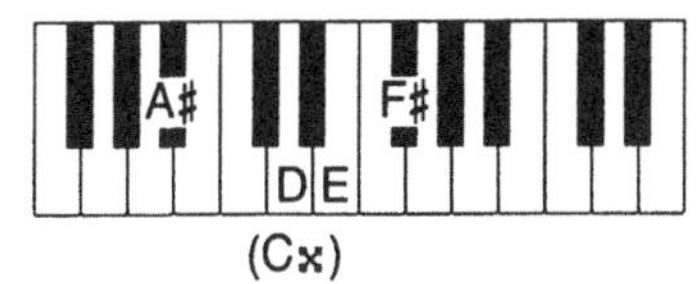

2nd Inversion

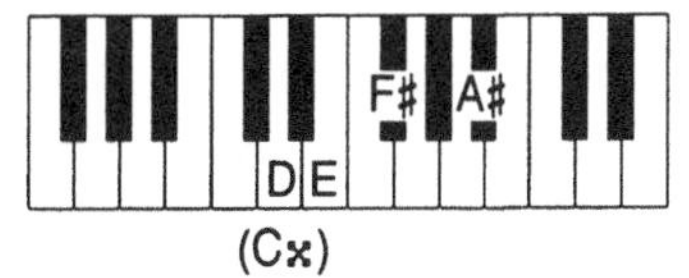

3rd Inversion

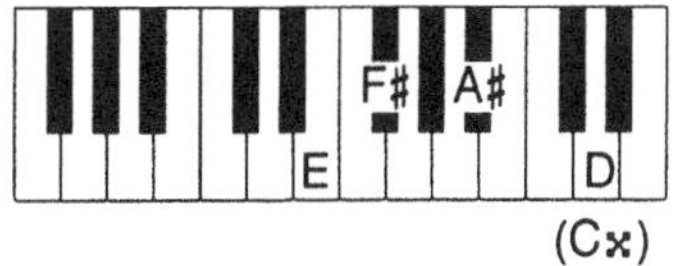

F♯7sus

Root Position

1st Inversion

2nd Inversion

3rd Inversion

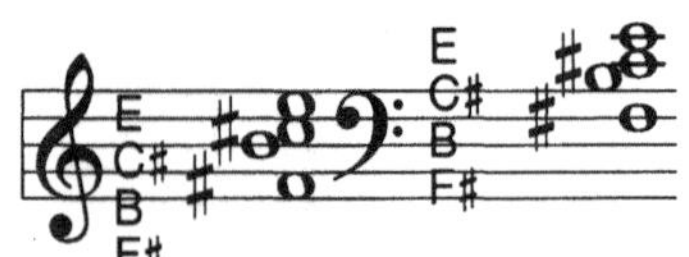

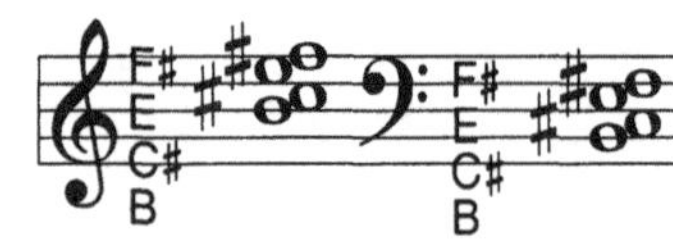

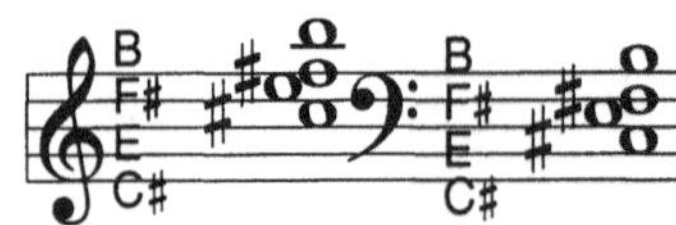

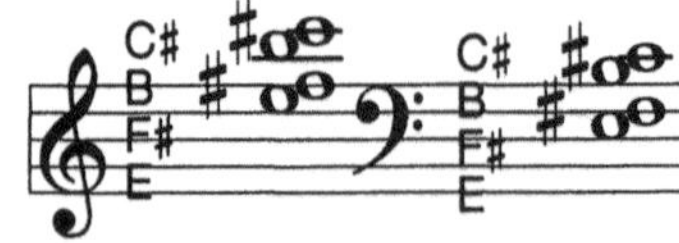

F♯m(add2), F♯m(add9)

Root Position

1st Inversion

2nd Inversion

3rd Inversion

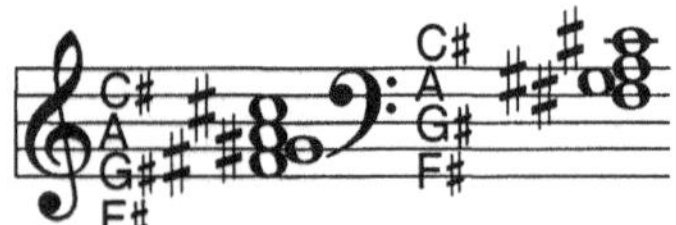

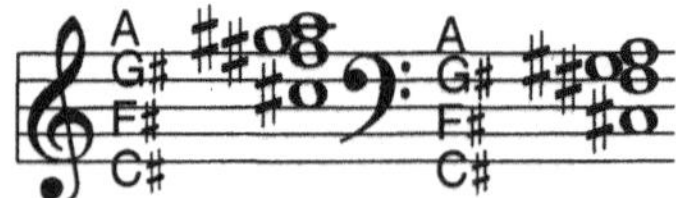

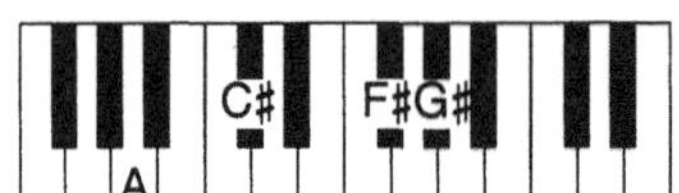

F♯m6

Root Position

1st Inversion

2nd Inversion

3rd Inversion

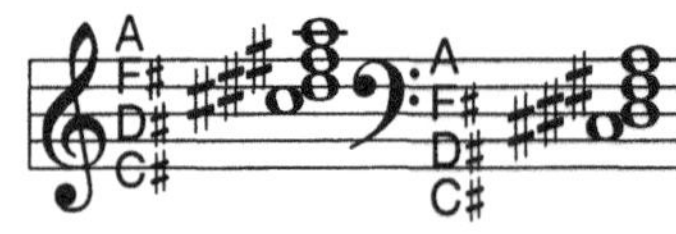

F♯m7

Root Position

1st Inversion

2nd Inversion

3rd Inversion

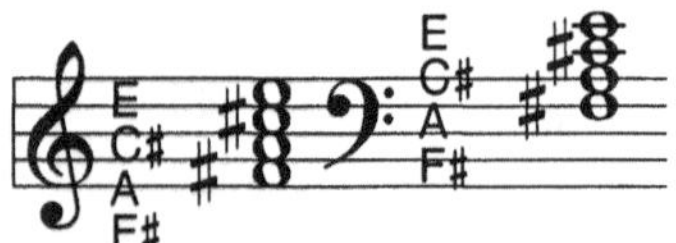

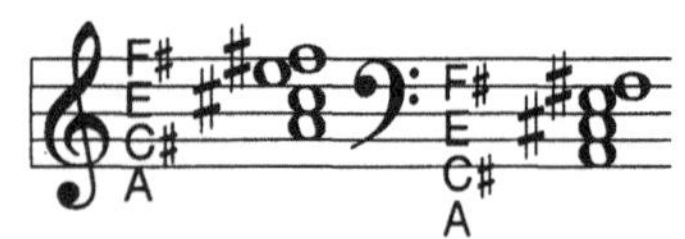

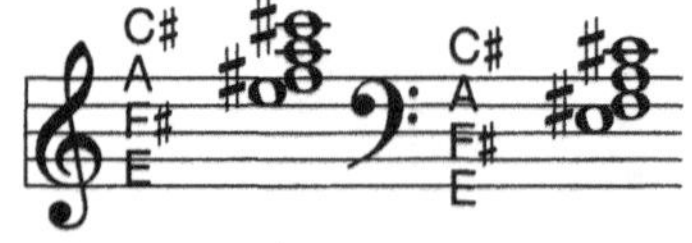

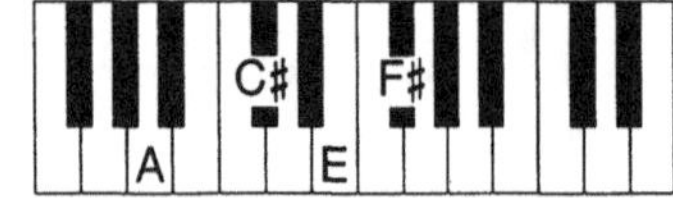

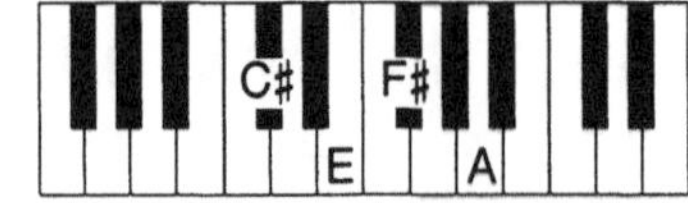

F♯m(maj7)

Root Position

1st Inversion

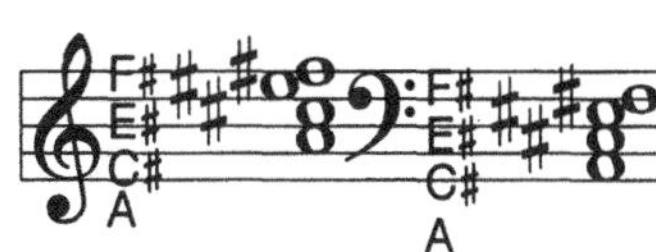

2nd Inversion

3rd Inversion

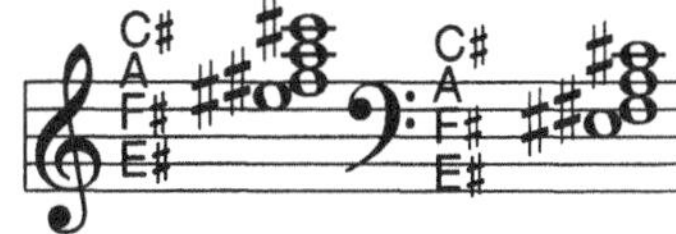

F♯m7♭5

Root Position

1st Inversion

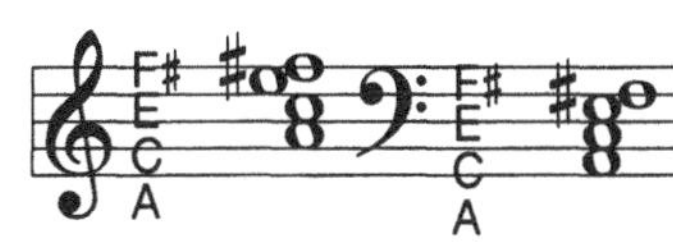

2nd Inversion

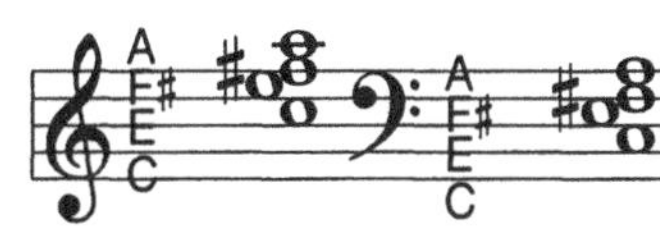

3rd Inversion

F♯dim7

Root Position

1st Inversion

2nd Inversion

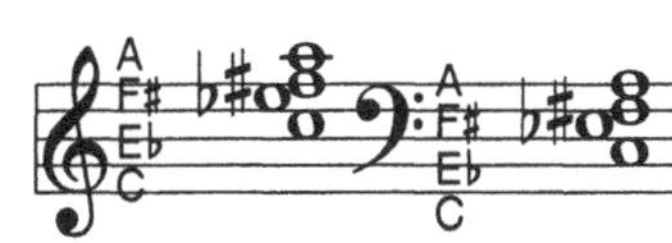

3rd Inversion

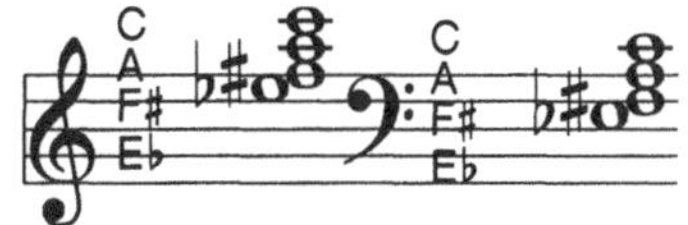

F♯dim(maj7)

Root Position

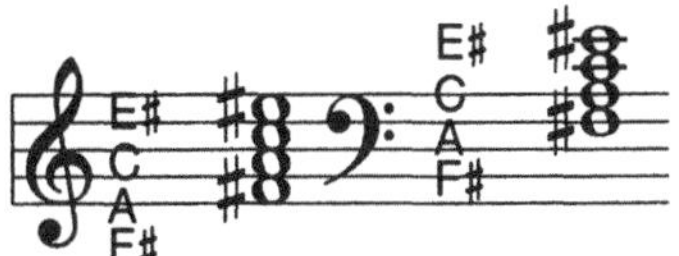

1st Inversion

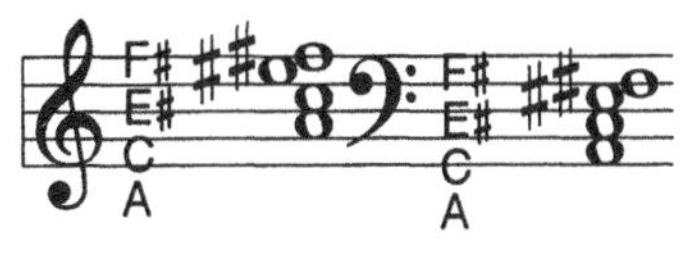

2nd Inversion

3rd Inversion

ADDITIONAL F♯/G♭ CHORDS

F♯5

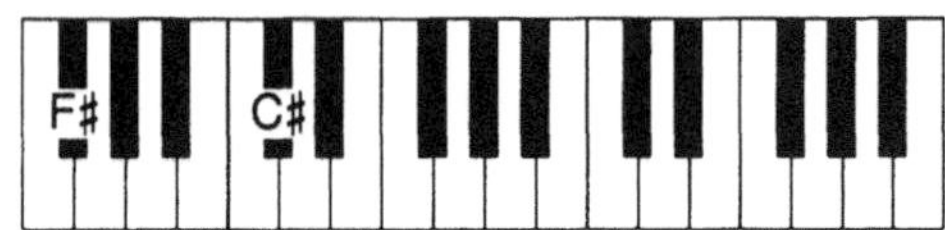

F♯6/9

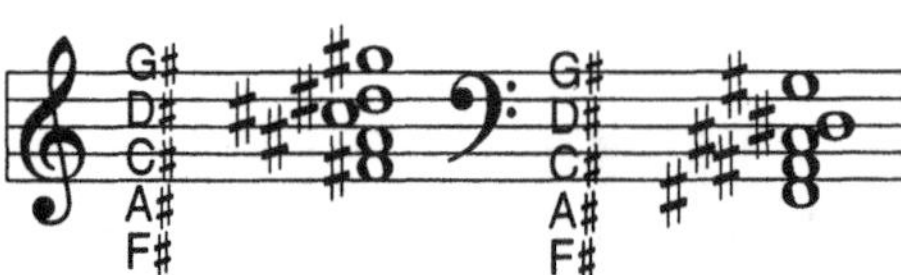

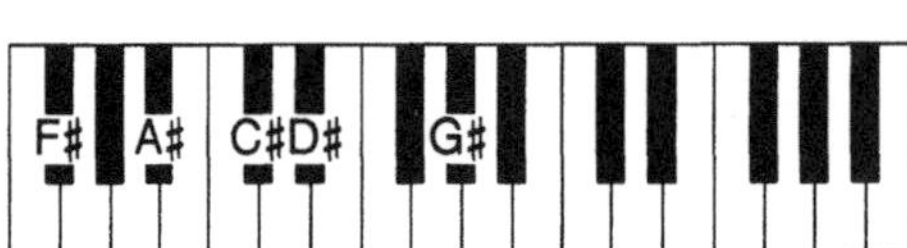

F♯maj6/9

F♯maj7♯11

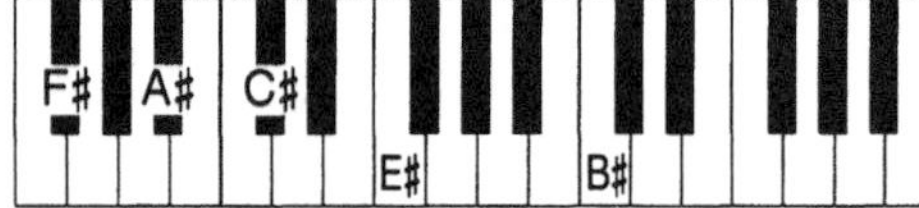

F♯maj9

F♯maj9♭5

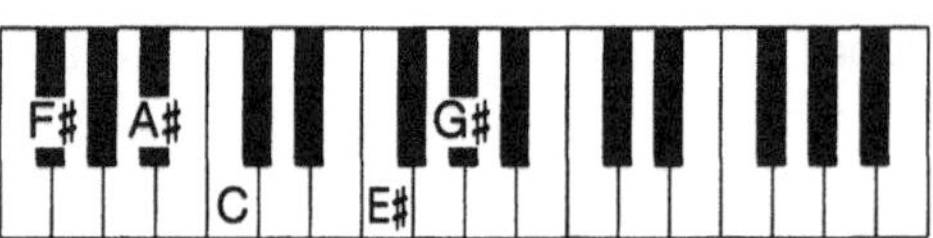

F♯maj9♯5

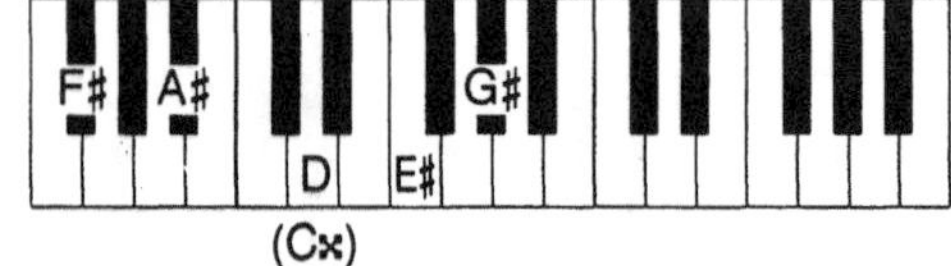

F♯maj9♯11

F♯maj13

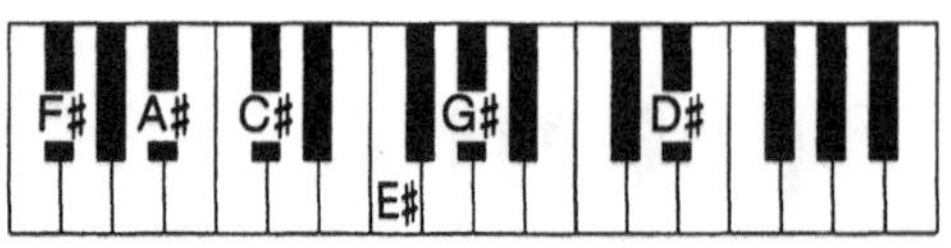

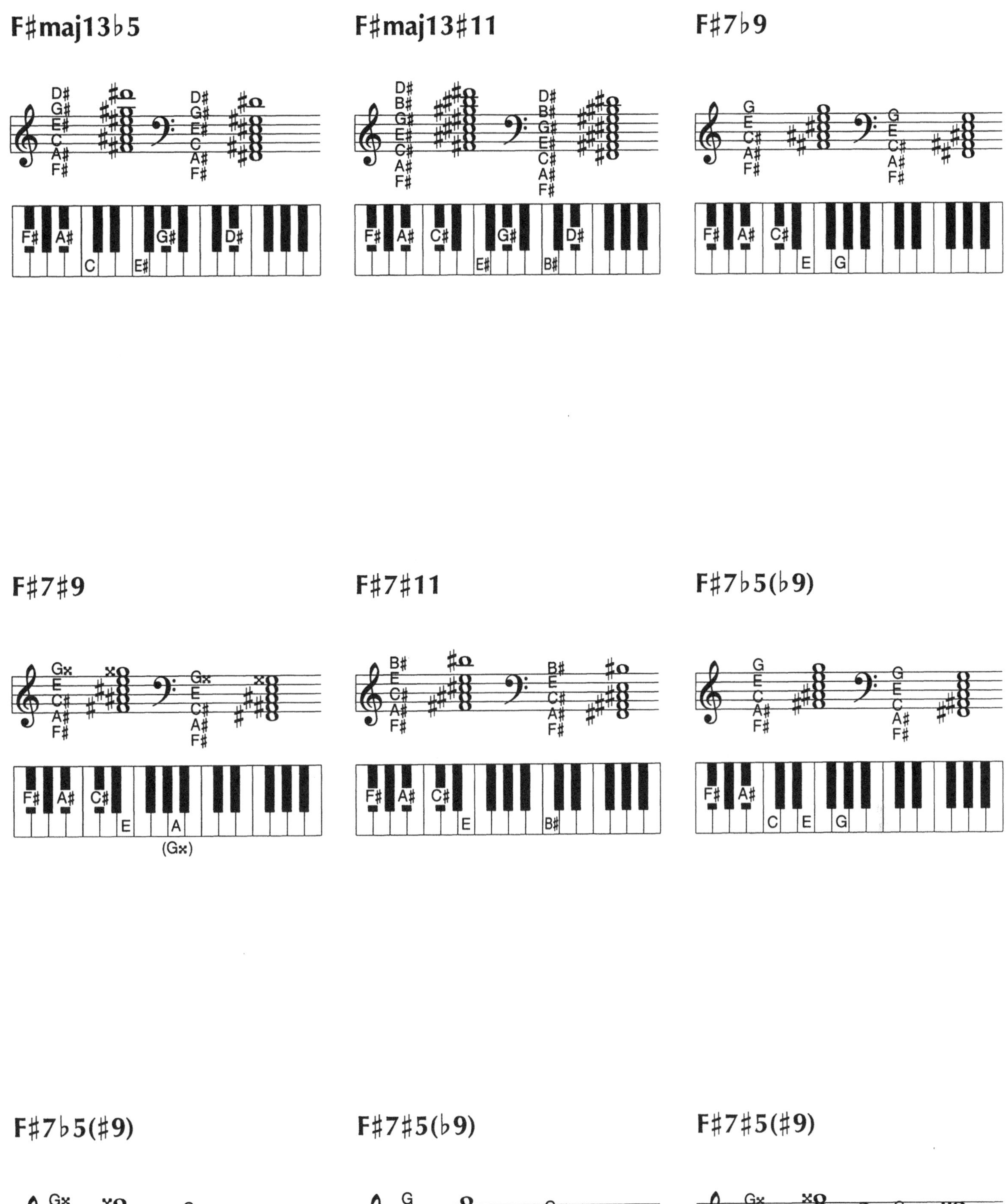
F♯maj13♭5
D♯ G♯ E♯ C A♯ F♯
F♯ A♯ C E♯ G♯ D♯
F♯maj13♯11
D♯ B♯ G♯ E♯ C♯ A♯ F♯
F♯ A♯ C♯ E♯ G♯ B♯ D♯
F♯7♭9
G E C♯ A♯ F♯
F♯ A♯ C♯ E G
F♯7♯9
Gx E C♯ A♯ F♯
F♯ A♯ C♯ E A
(Gx)
F♯7♯11
B♯ E C♯ A♯ F♯
F♯ A♯ C♯ E B♯
F♯7♭5(♭9)
G E C A♯ F♯
F♯ A♯ C E G
F♯7♭5(♯9)
Gx E C A♯ F♯
F♯ A♯ C E A
(Gx)
F♯7♯5(♭9)
G E Cx A♯ F♯
F♯ A♯ D E G
(Cx)
F♯7♯5(♯9)
Gx E Cx A♯ F♯
F♯ A♯ D E A
(Cx) (Gx)

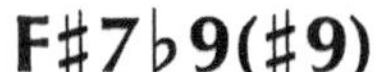

F♯7♭9(♯9)

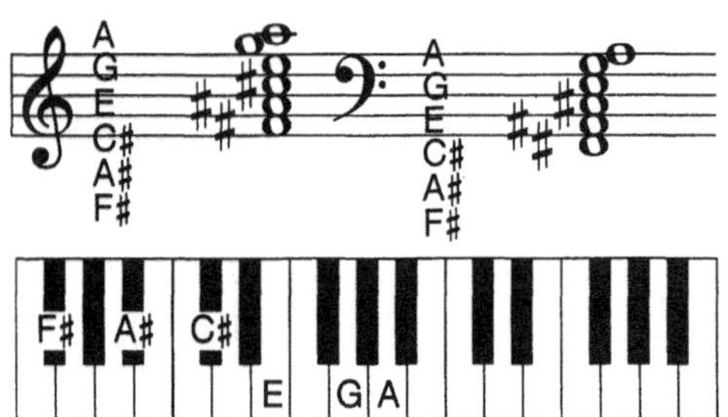

F♯7(add13)

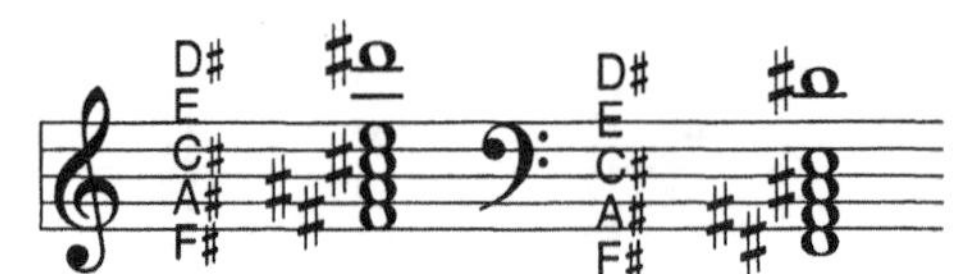

F♯7♭13

F♯7♭9(♯11)

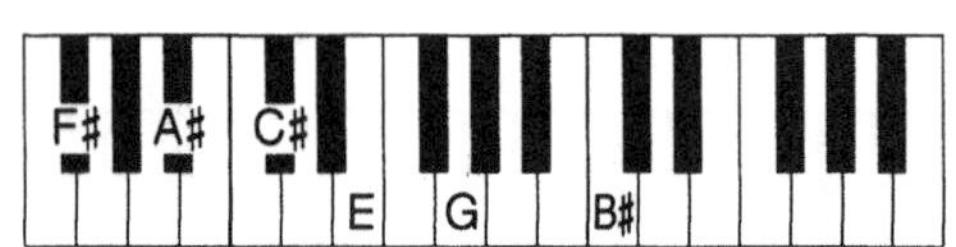

F♯7♯9(♯11)

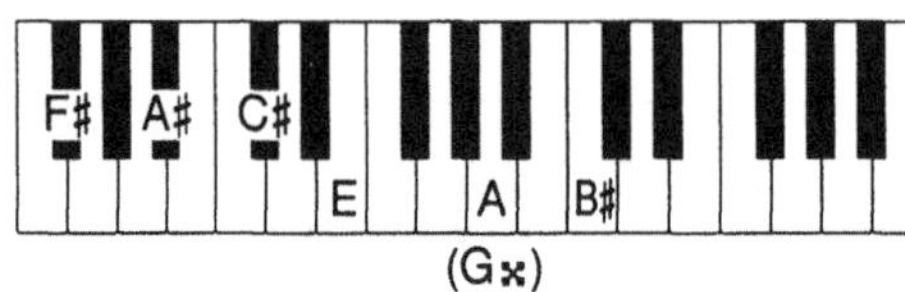

F♯7♭9(♭13)

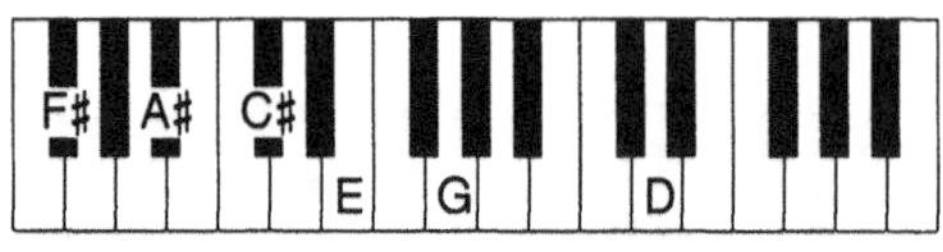

F♯7♯9(♭13)

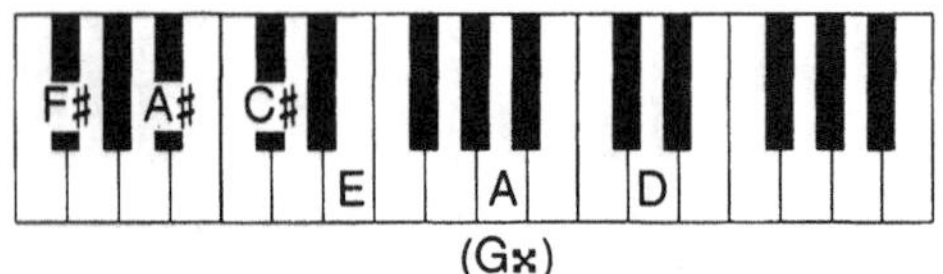

F♯7♯11(♭13)

F♯7♭9(♯9,♯11)

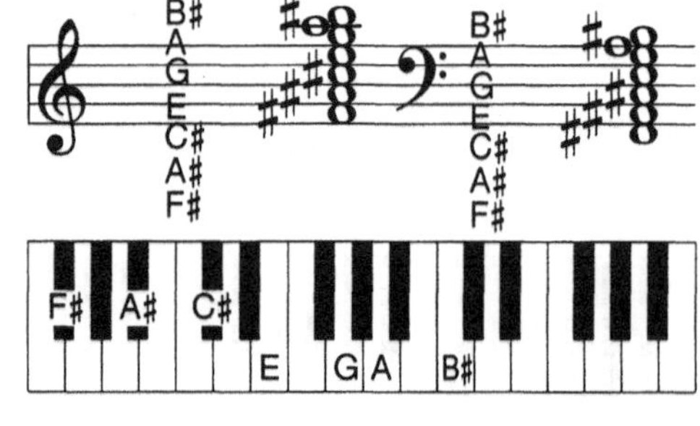

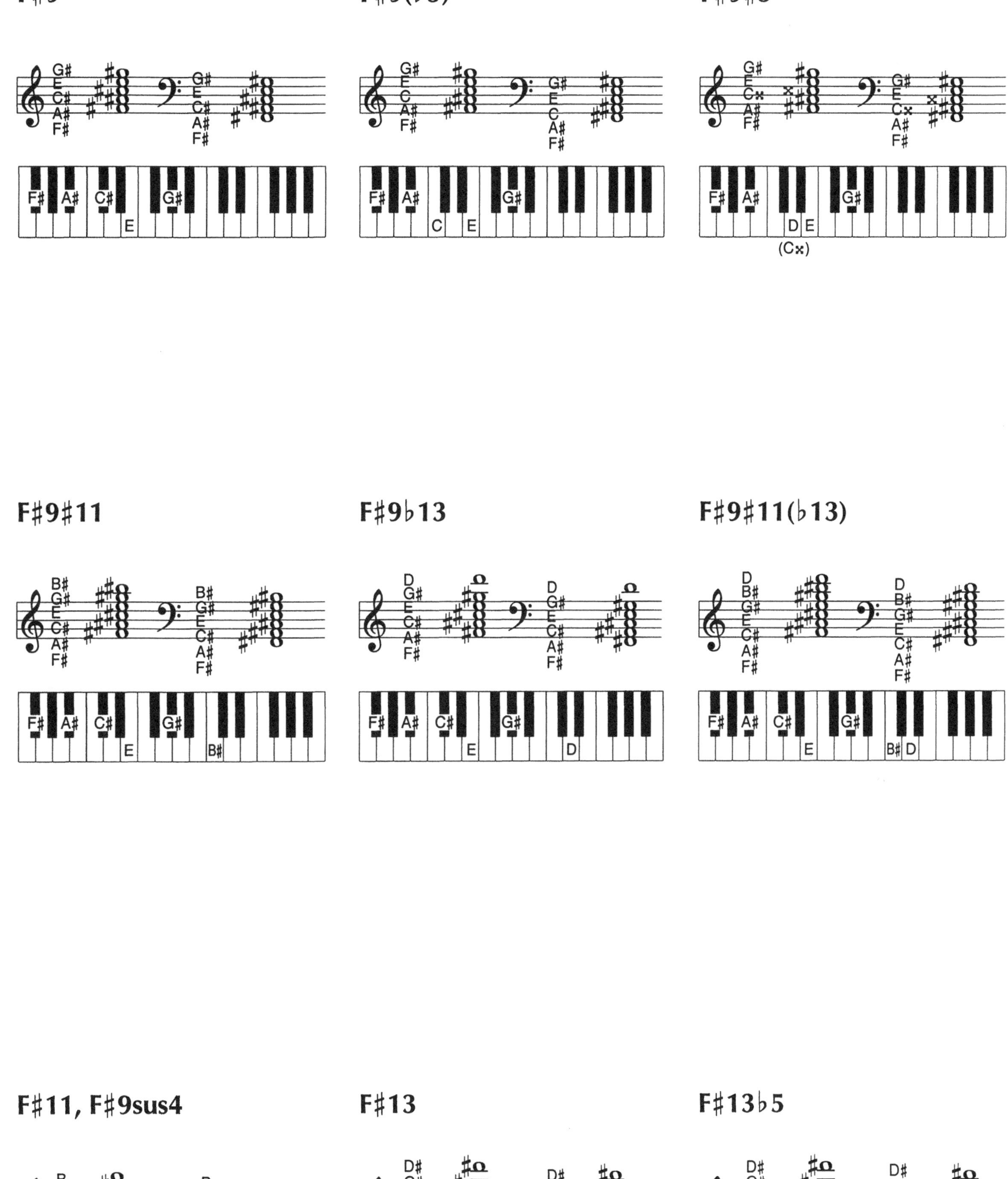
F♯9
F♯ A♯ C♯ G♯ E
F♯9(♭5)
F♯ A♯ G♯ C E
F♯9♯5
F♯ A♯ G♯ D E
(C𝄪)
F♯9♯11
F♯ A♯ C♯ G♯ E B♯
F♯9♭13
F♯ A♯ C♯ G♯ E D
F♯9♯11(♭13)
F♯ A♯ C♯ G♯ E B♯ D
F♯11, F♯9sus4
F♯ C♯ G♯ E B
F♯13
F♯ A♯ C♯ G♯ D♯ E
F♯13♭5
F♯ A♯ G♯ D♯ C E

F♯13♭9

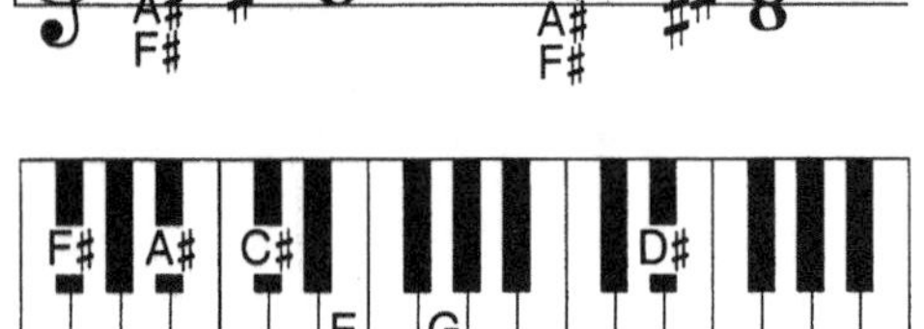

F♯13♯9

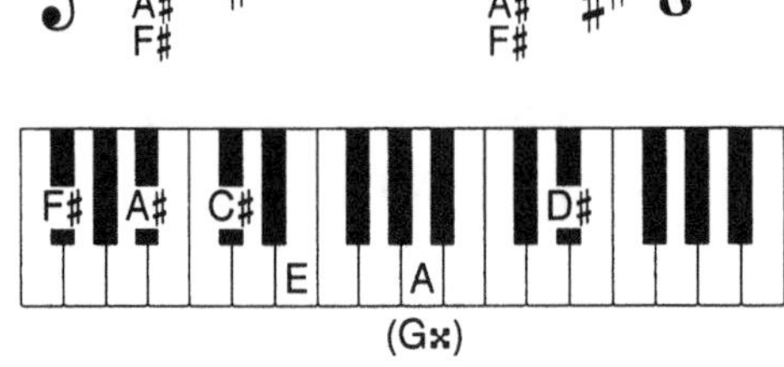

F♯13♯11

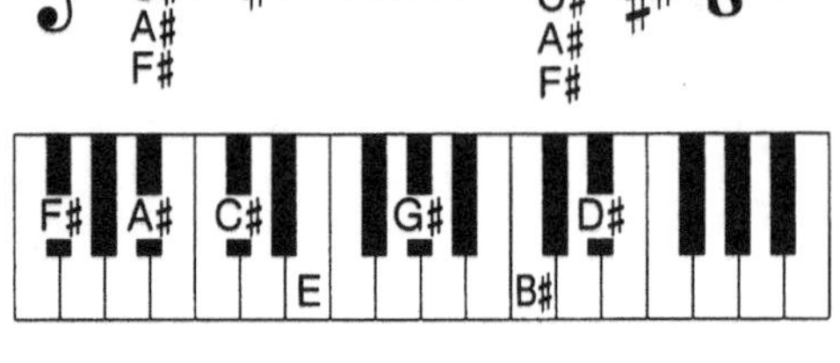

F♯13(sus4)

F♯m(♯5)

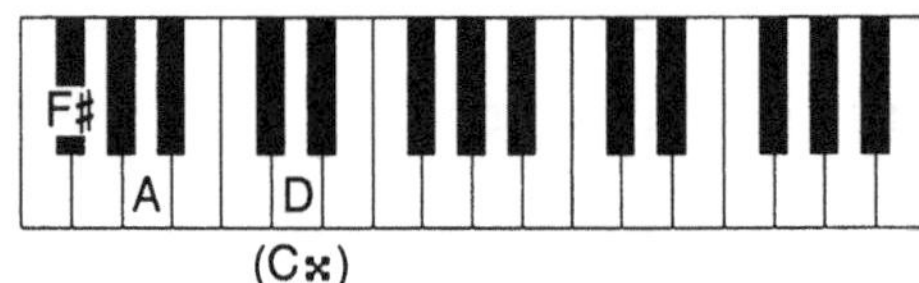

F♯m$^{6}_{9}$

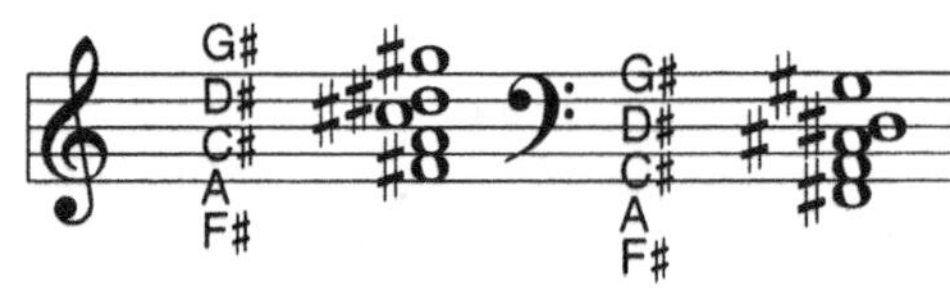

F♯m7(add4)

F♯m7(add11)

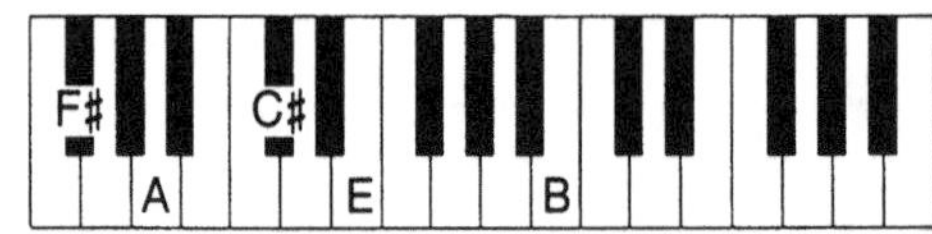

F♯m7♭5(♭9)

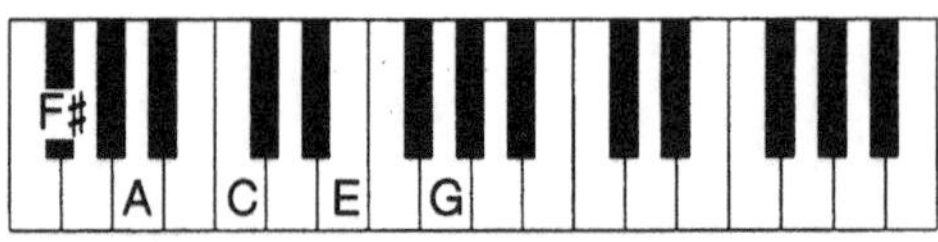

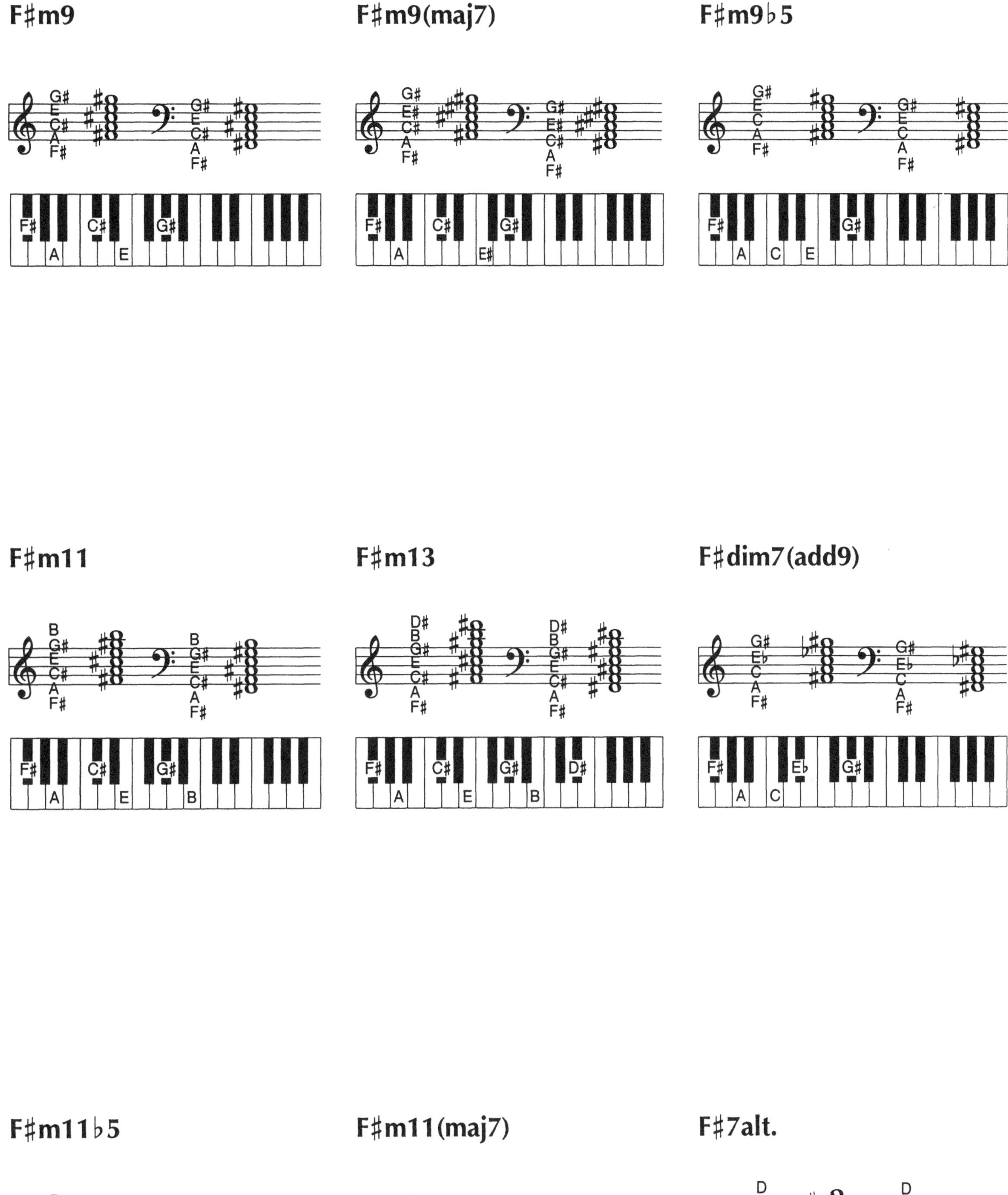
F♯m9
F♯m9(maj7)
F♯m9♭5
F♯m11
F♯m13
F♯dim7(add9)
F♯m11♭5
F♯m11(maj7)
F♯7alt.

G CHORDS

G

Root Position

1st Inversion

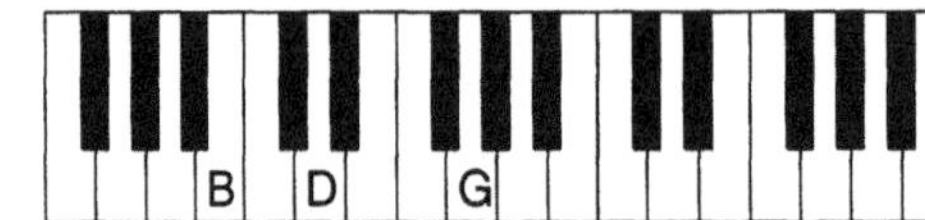

2nd Inversion

Gm

Root Position

1st Inversion

2nd Inversion

G+

Root Position

1st Inversion

2nd Inversion

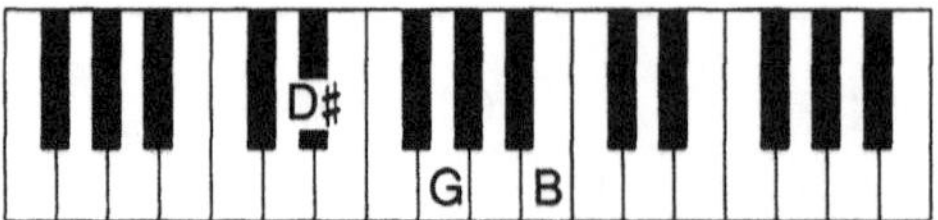

Gdim

Root Position

1st Inversion

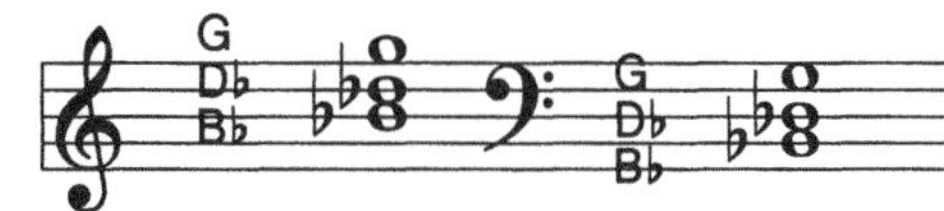

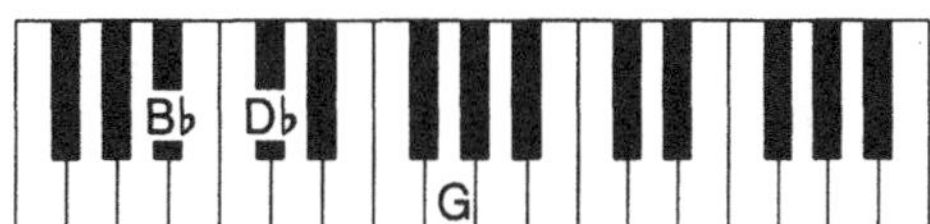

2nd Inversion

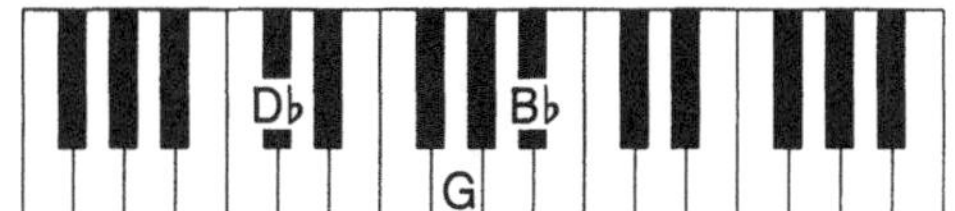

Gsus

Root Position

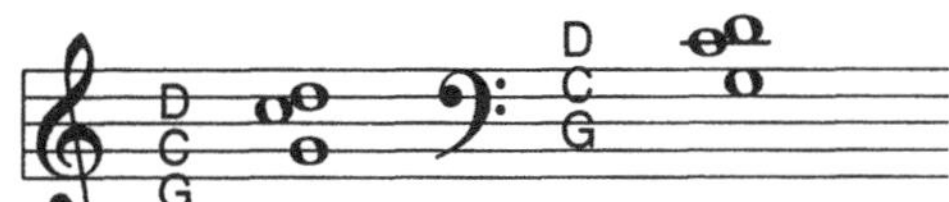

1st Inversion

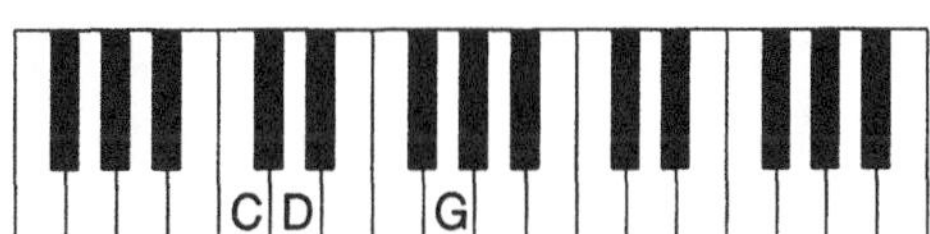

2nd Inversion

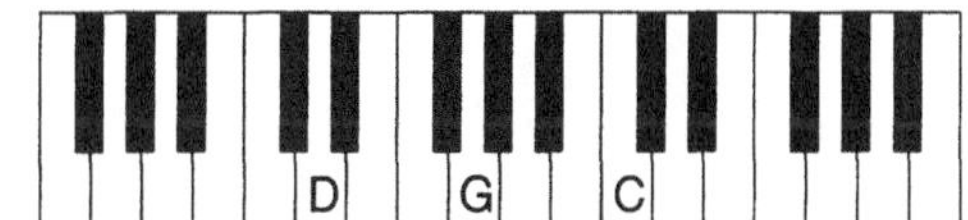

G(♭5)

Root Position

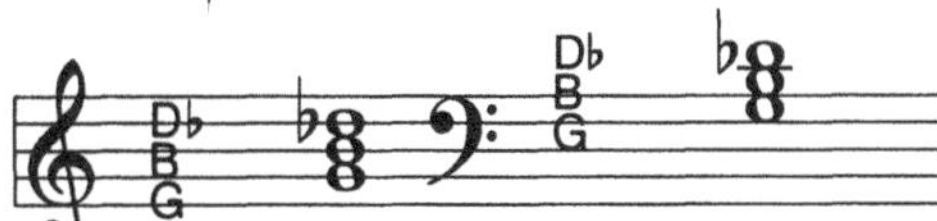

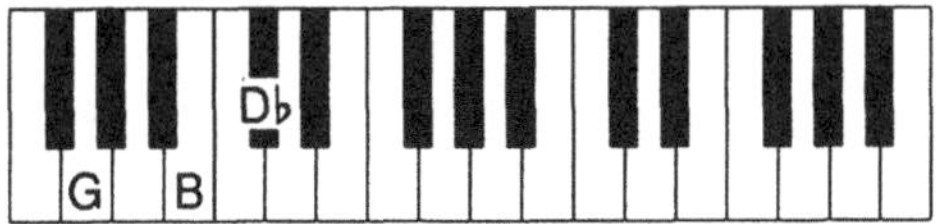

1st Inversion

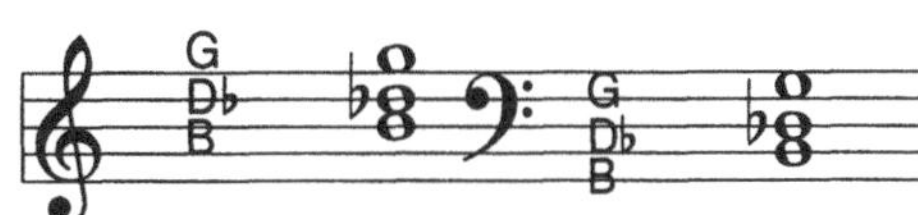

2nd Inversion

Gsus2

Root Position

1st Inversion

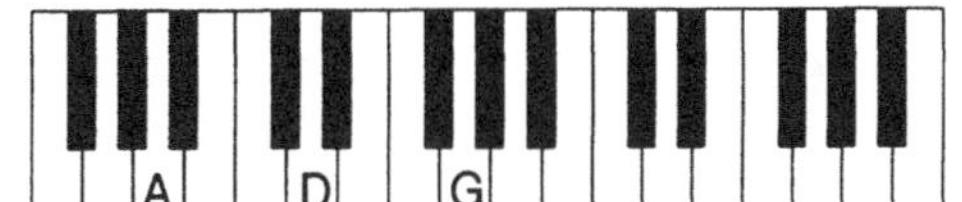

2nd Inversion

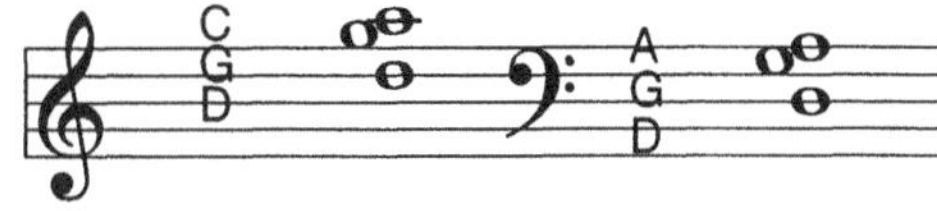

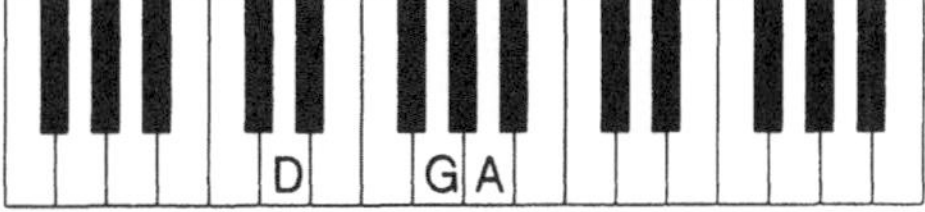

G6

Root Position

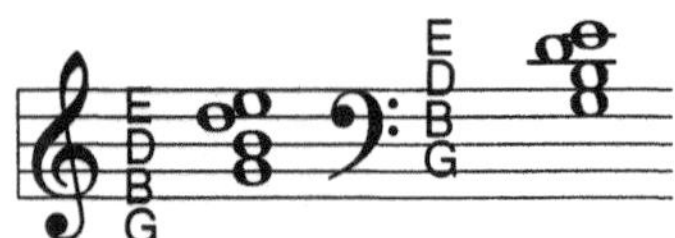

1st Inversion

2nd Inversion

3rd Inversion

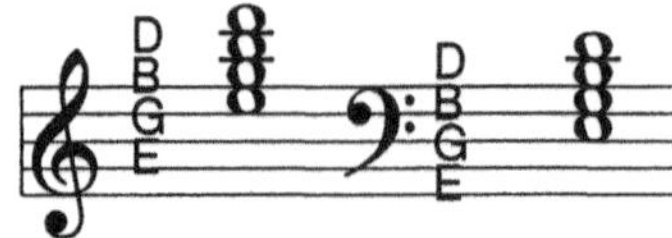

G(add2), G(add9)

Root Position

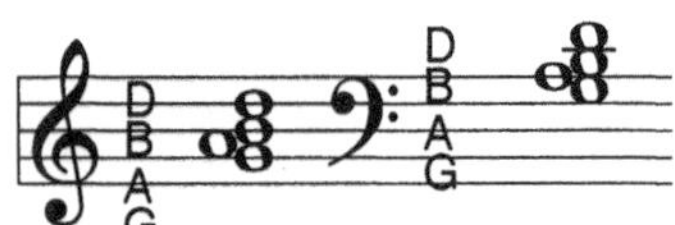

1st Inversion

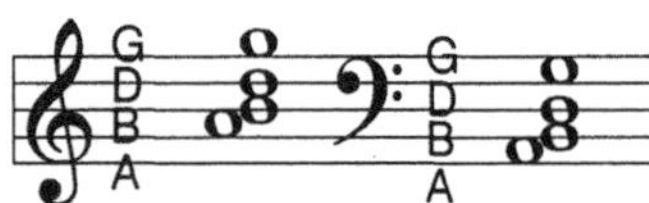

2nd Inversion

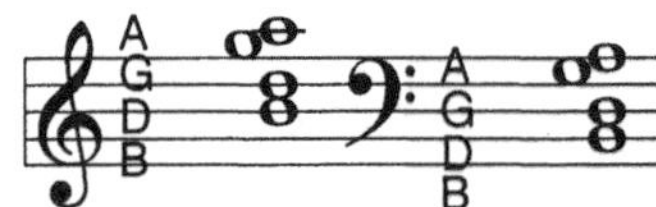

3rd Inversion

Gmaj7

Root Position

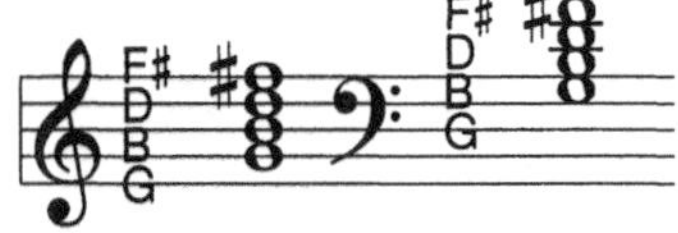

1st Inversion

2nd Inversion

3rd Inversion

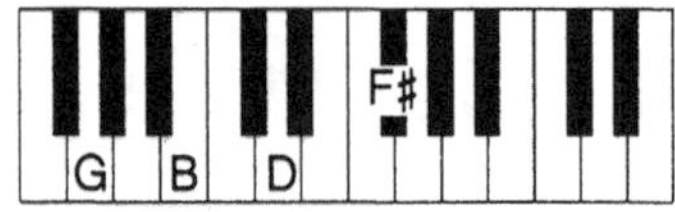

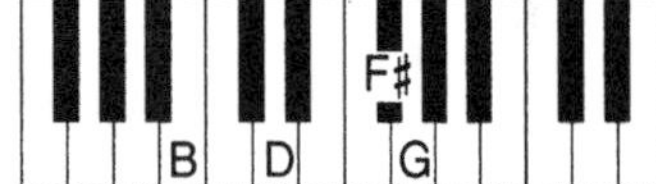

Gmaj7♭5

Root Position

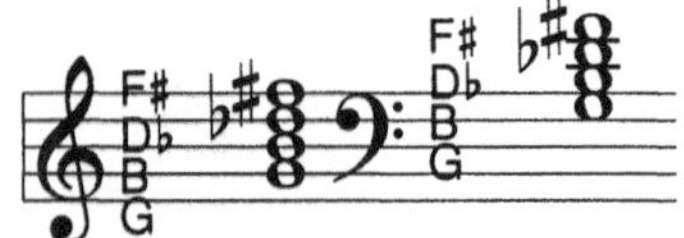

1st Inversion

2nd Inversion

3rd Inversion

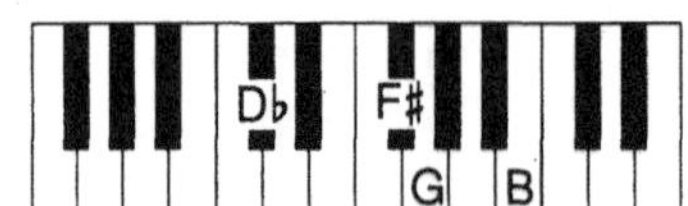

Gmaj7♯5

Root Position

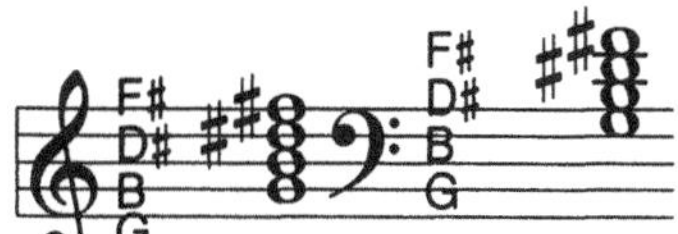

1st Inversion

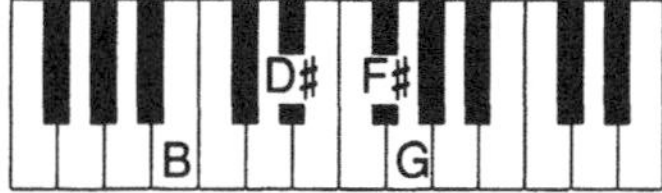

2nd Inversion

3rd Inversion

G7

Root Position

1st Inversion

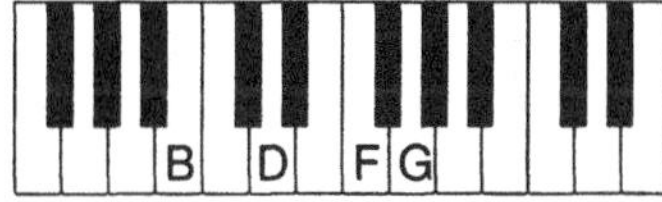

2nd Inversion

3rd Inversion

G7♭5

Root Position

1st Inversion

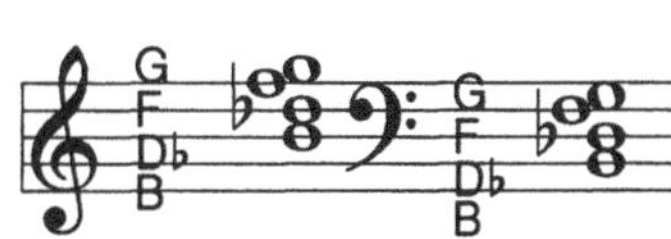

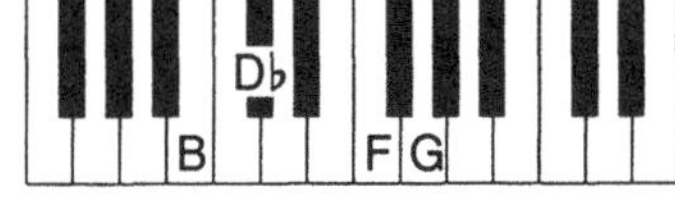

2nd Inversion

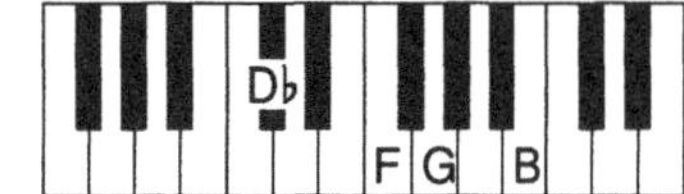

3rd Inversion

G7♯5

Root Position

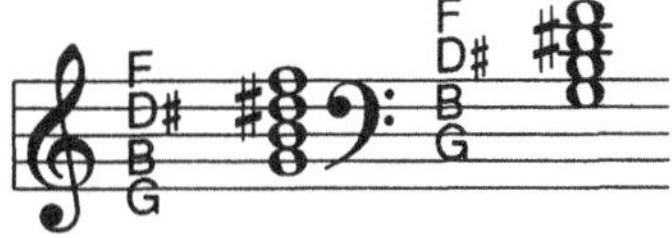

1st Inversion

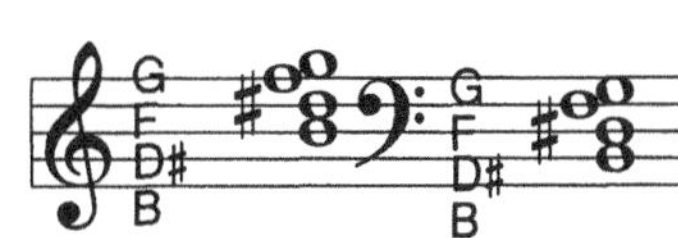

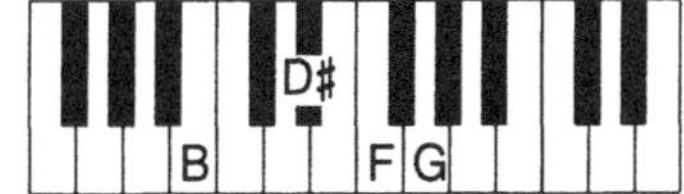

2nd Inversion

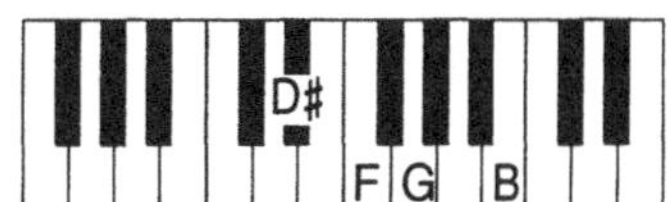

3rd Inversion

G7sus

Root Position

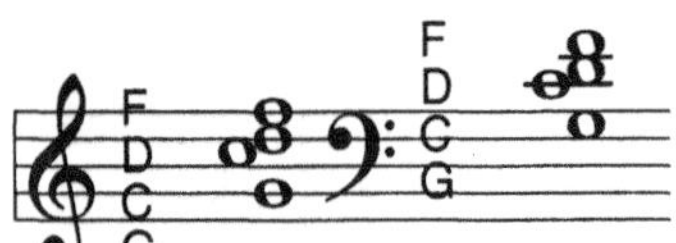

1st Inversion

2nd Inversion

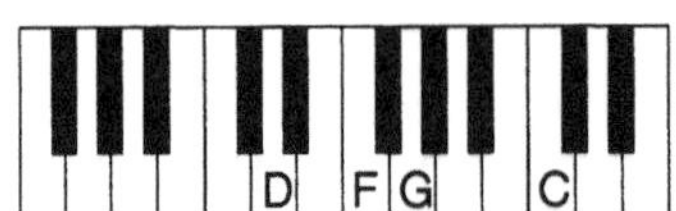

3rd Inversion

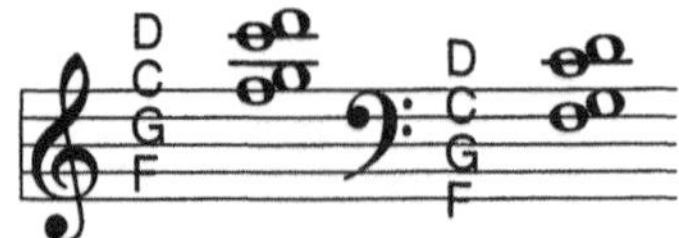

Gm(add2), Gm(add9)

Root Position

1st Inversion

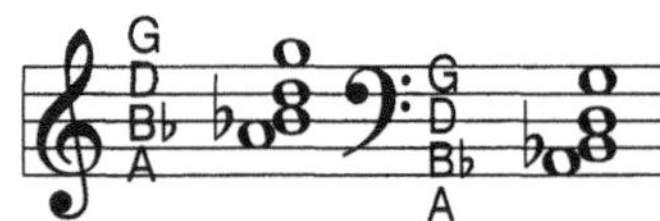

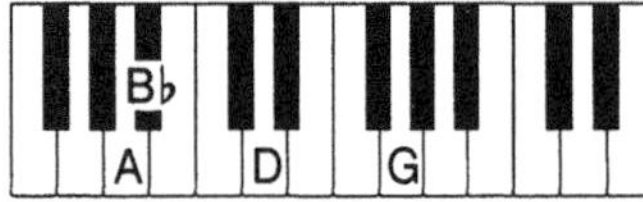

2nd Inversion

3rd Inversion

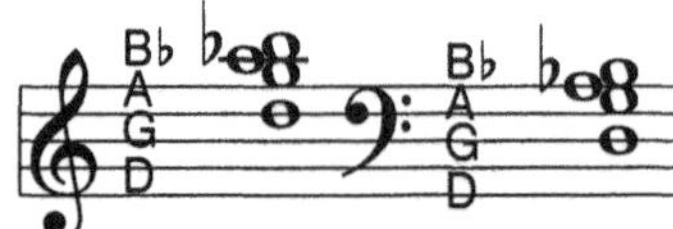

Gm6

Root Position

1st Inversion

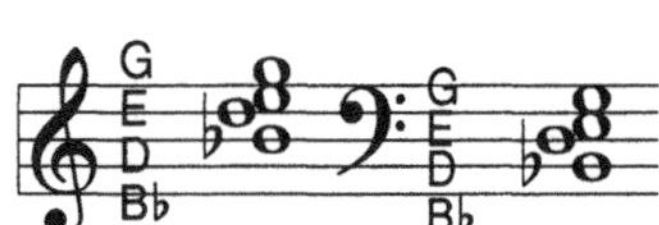

2nd Inversion

3rd Inversion

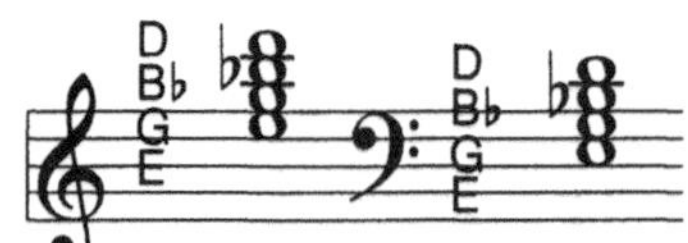

Gm7

Root Position

1st Inversion

2nd Inversion

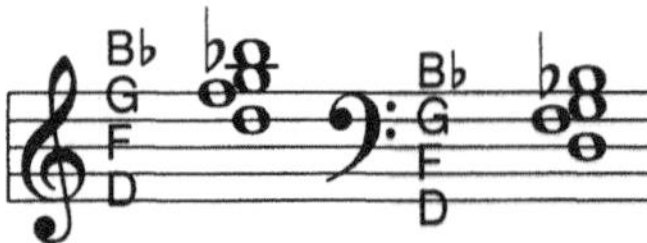

3rd Inversion

Gm(maj7)

2nd Inversion

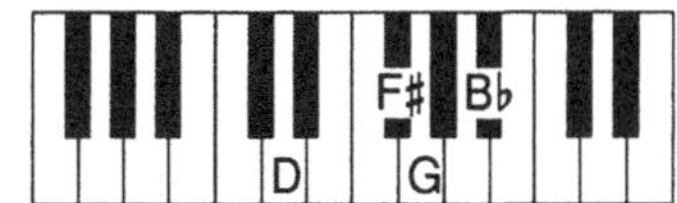

3rd Inversion

Gm7♭5

Root Position

1st Inversion

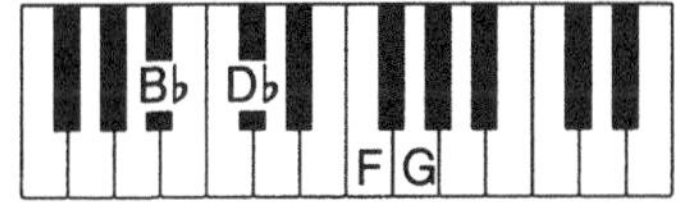

2nd Inversion

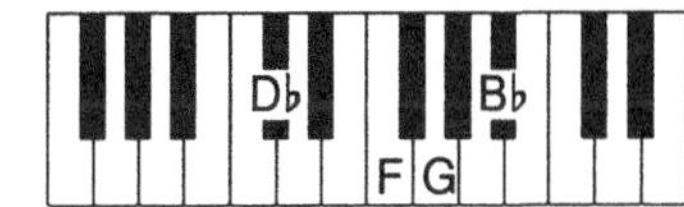

3rd Inversion

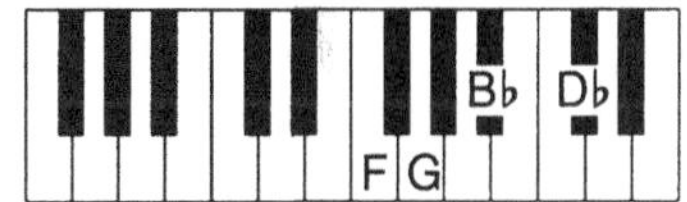

Gdim7

Root Position

1st Inversion

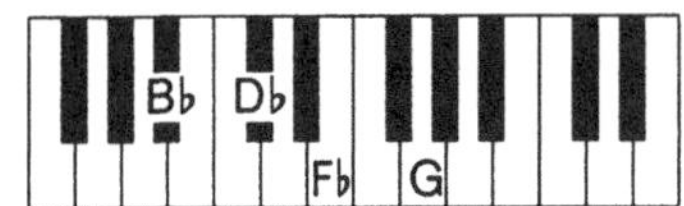

2nd Inversion

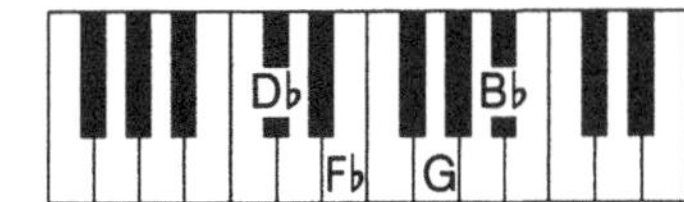

3rd Inversion

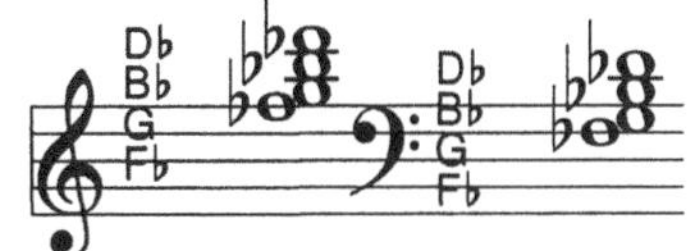

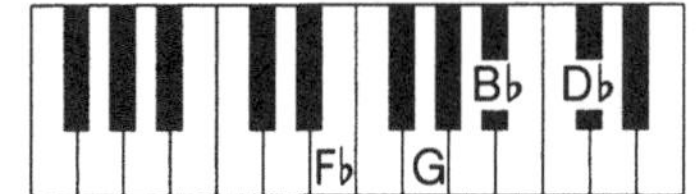

Gdim(maj7)

Root Position

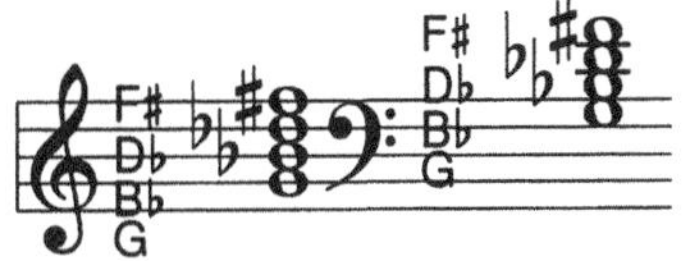

1st Inversion

2nd Inversion

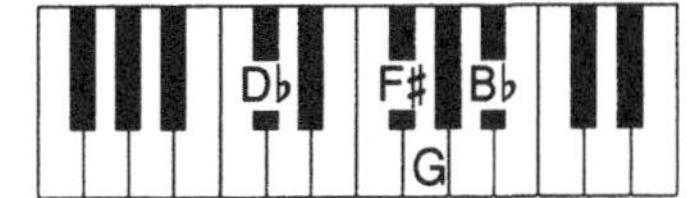

3rd Inversion

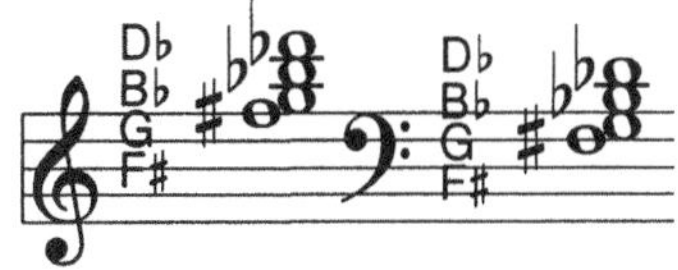

ADDITIONAL G CHORDS

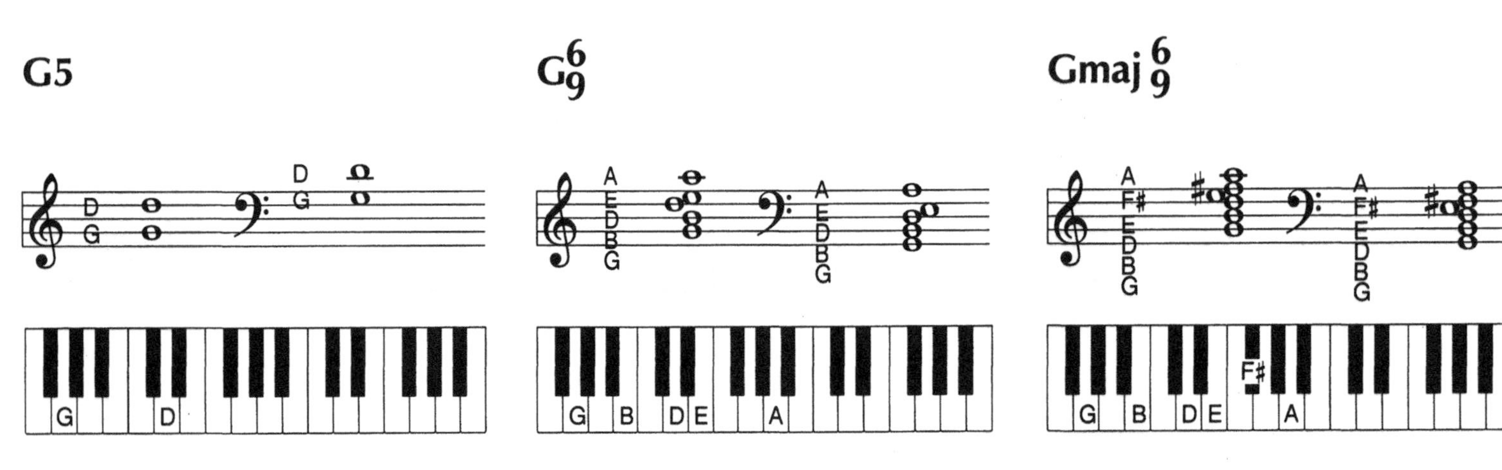

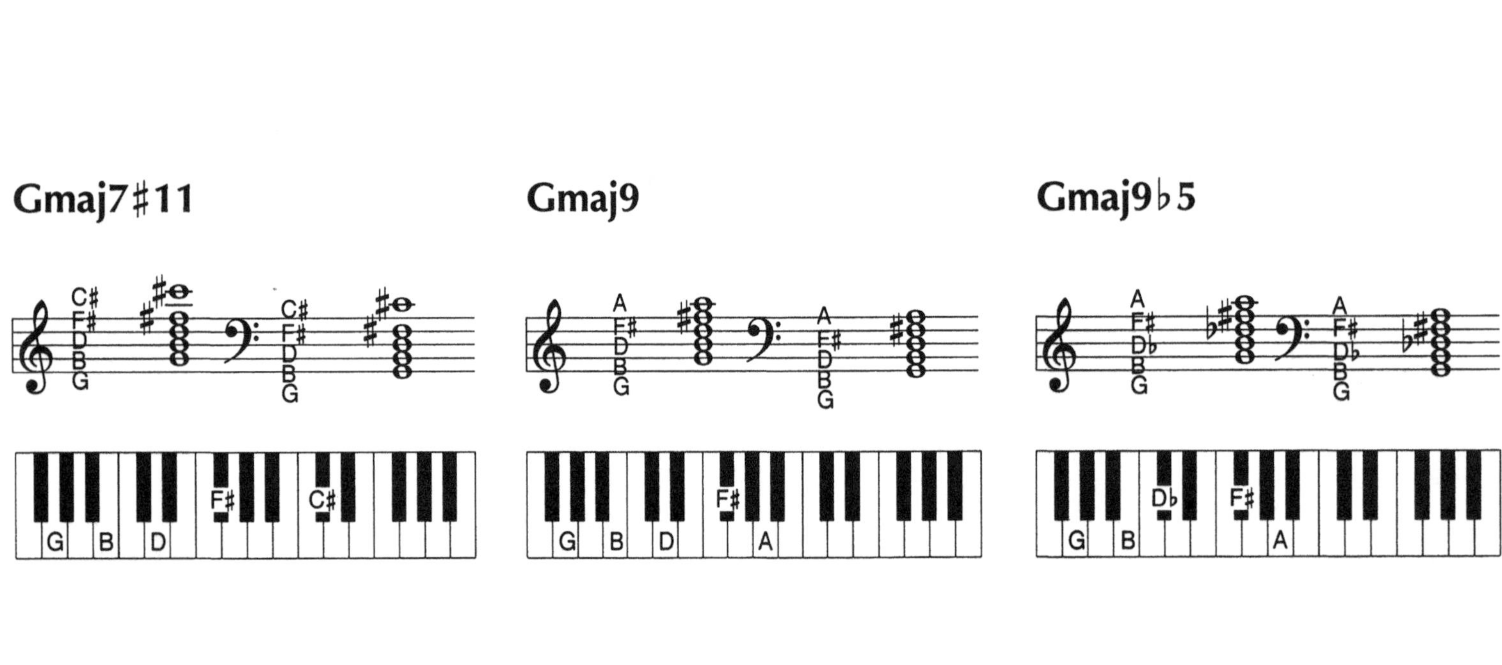

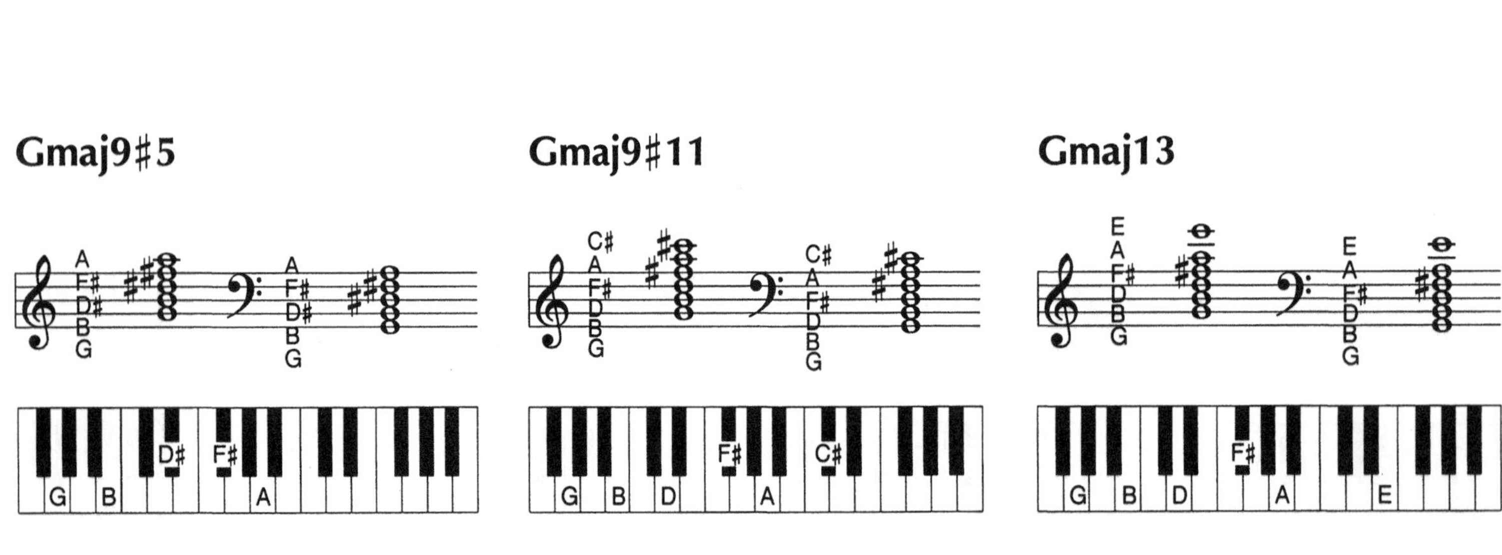

Gmaj13♭5

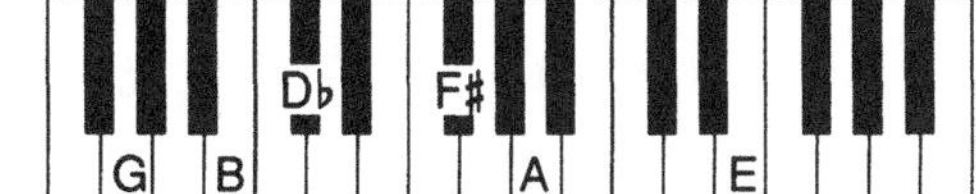

Gmaj13♯11

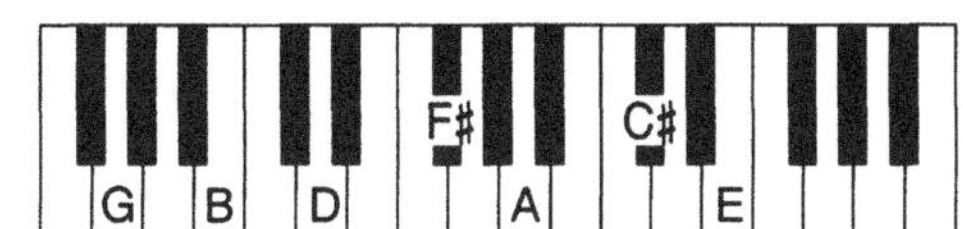

G7♭9

G7♯9

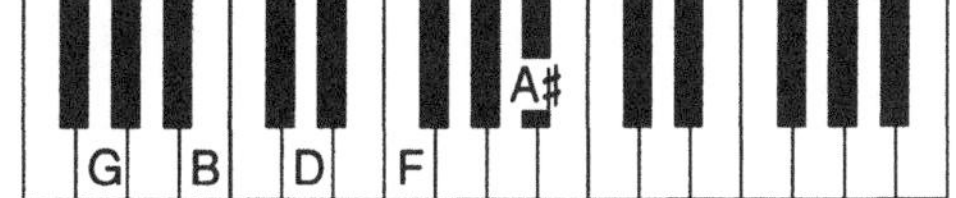

G7♯11

G7♭5(♭9)

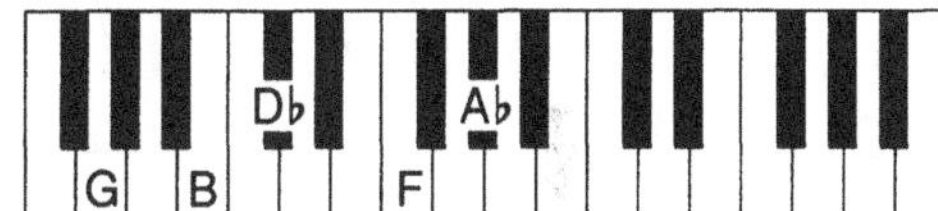

G7♭5(♯9)

G7♯5(♭9)

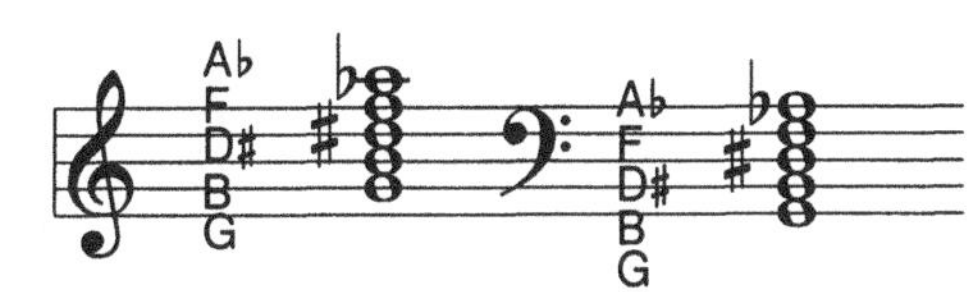

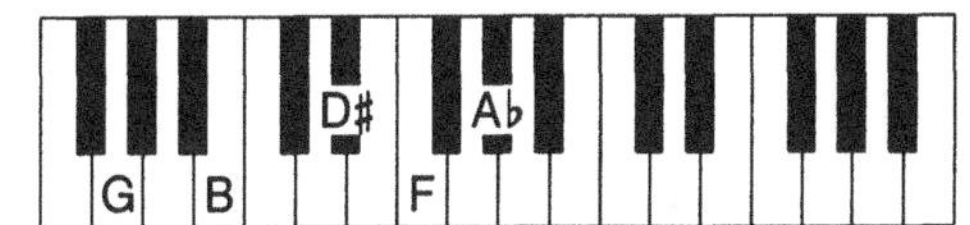

G7♯5(♯9)

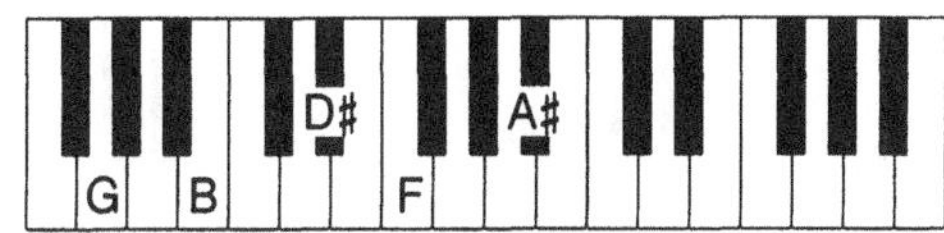

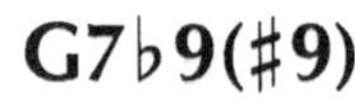

G7♭9(♯9)

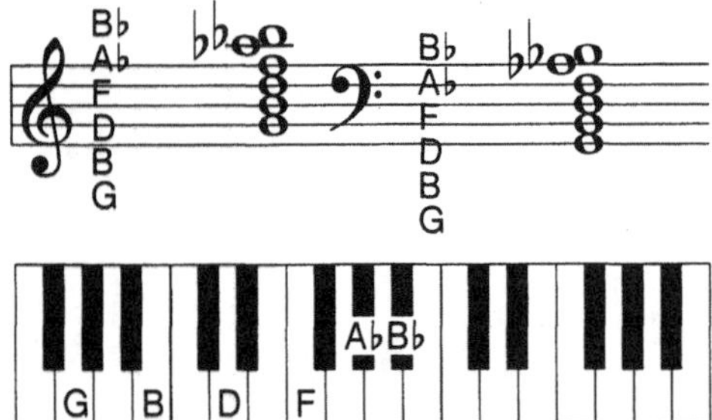

G7(add13)

G7♭13

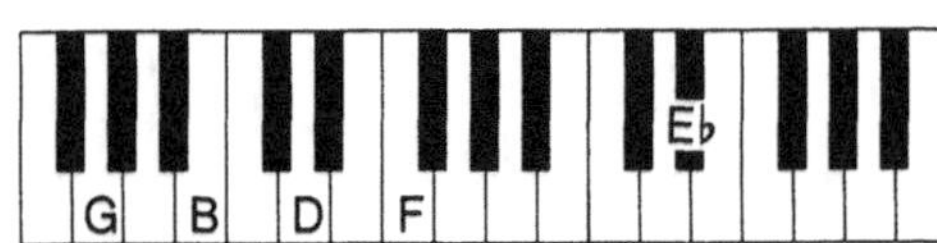

G7♭9(♯11)

G7♯9(♯11)

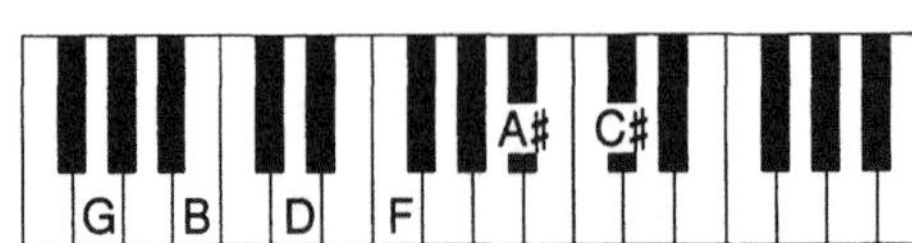

G7♭9(♭13)

G7♯9(♭13)

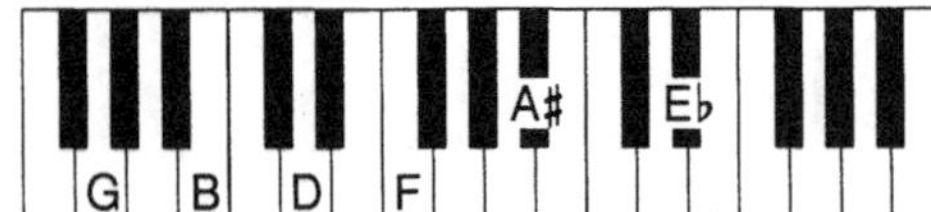

G7♯11(♭13)

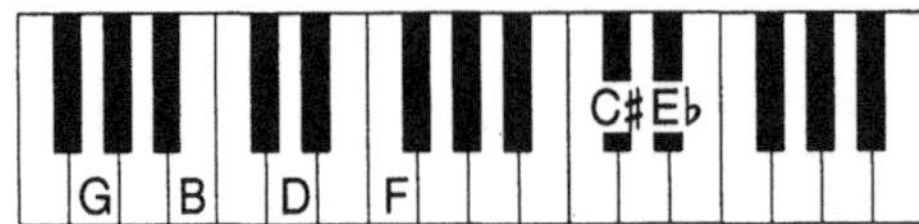

G7♭9(♯9,♯11)

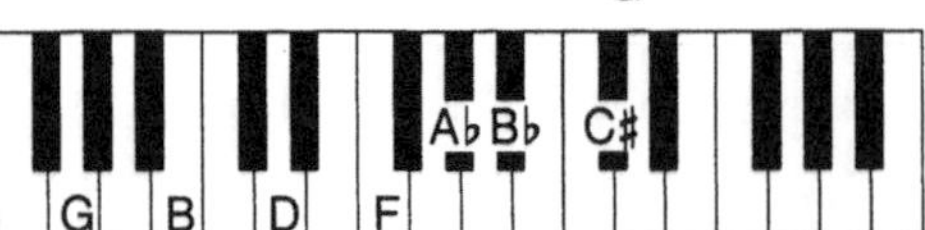

G9

G9(♭5)

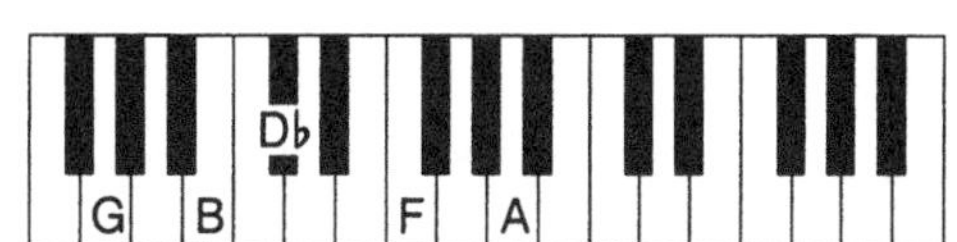

G9♯5

G9♯11

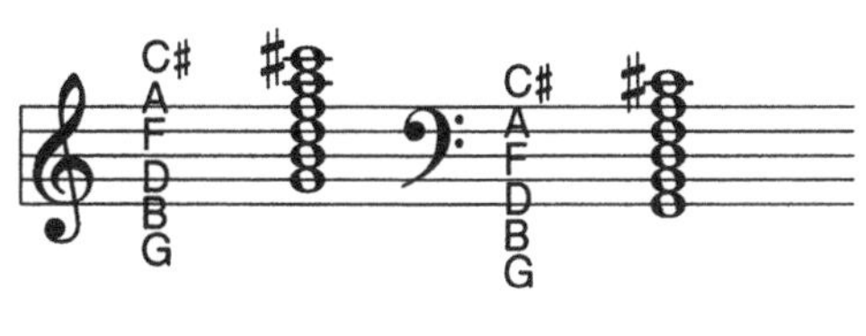

G9♭13

G9♯11(♭13)

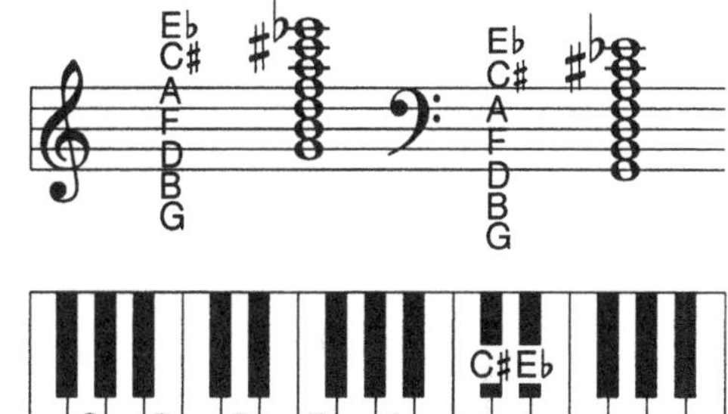

G11, G9sus4

G13

G13♭5

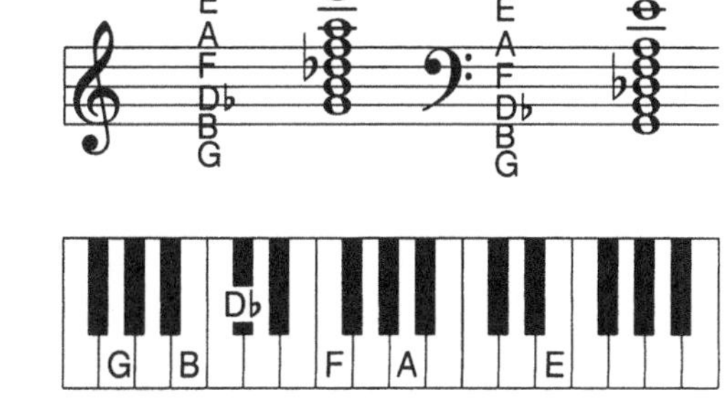

G13♭9

G13♯9

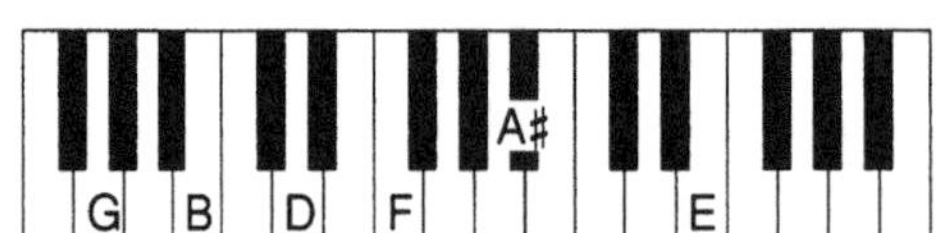

G13♯11

C♯
G B D F A E

G13(sus4)

Gm(♯5)

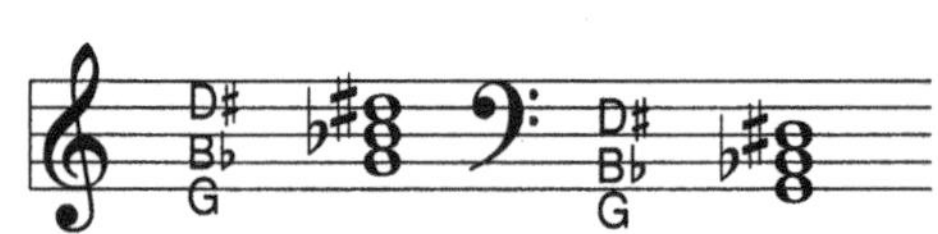

Gm$^{6}_{9}$

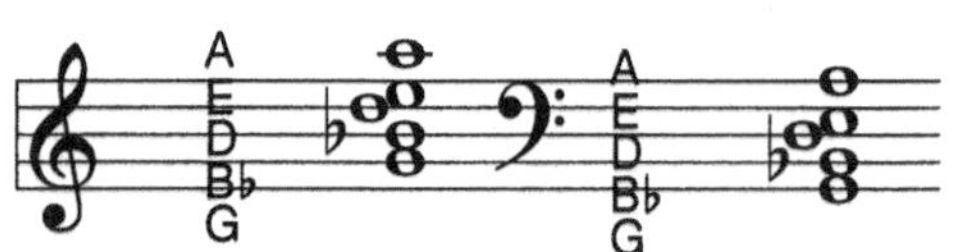

B♭
G D E A

Gm7(add4)

Gm7(add11)

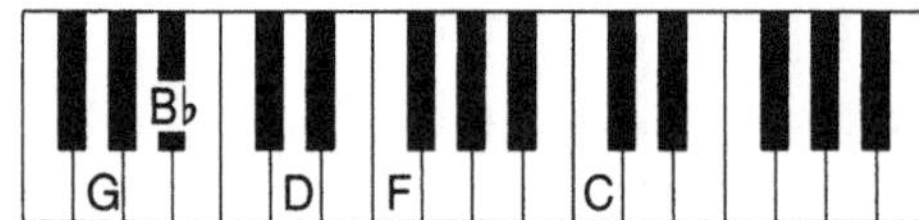

Gm7♭5(♭9)

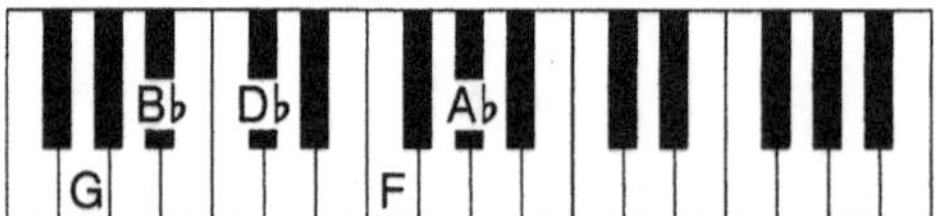

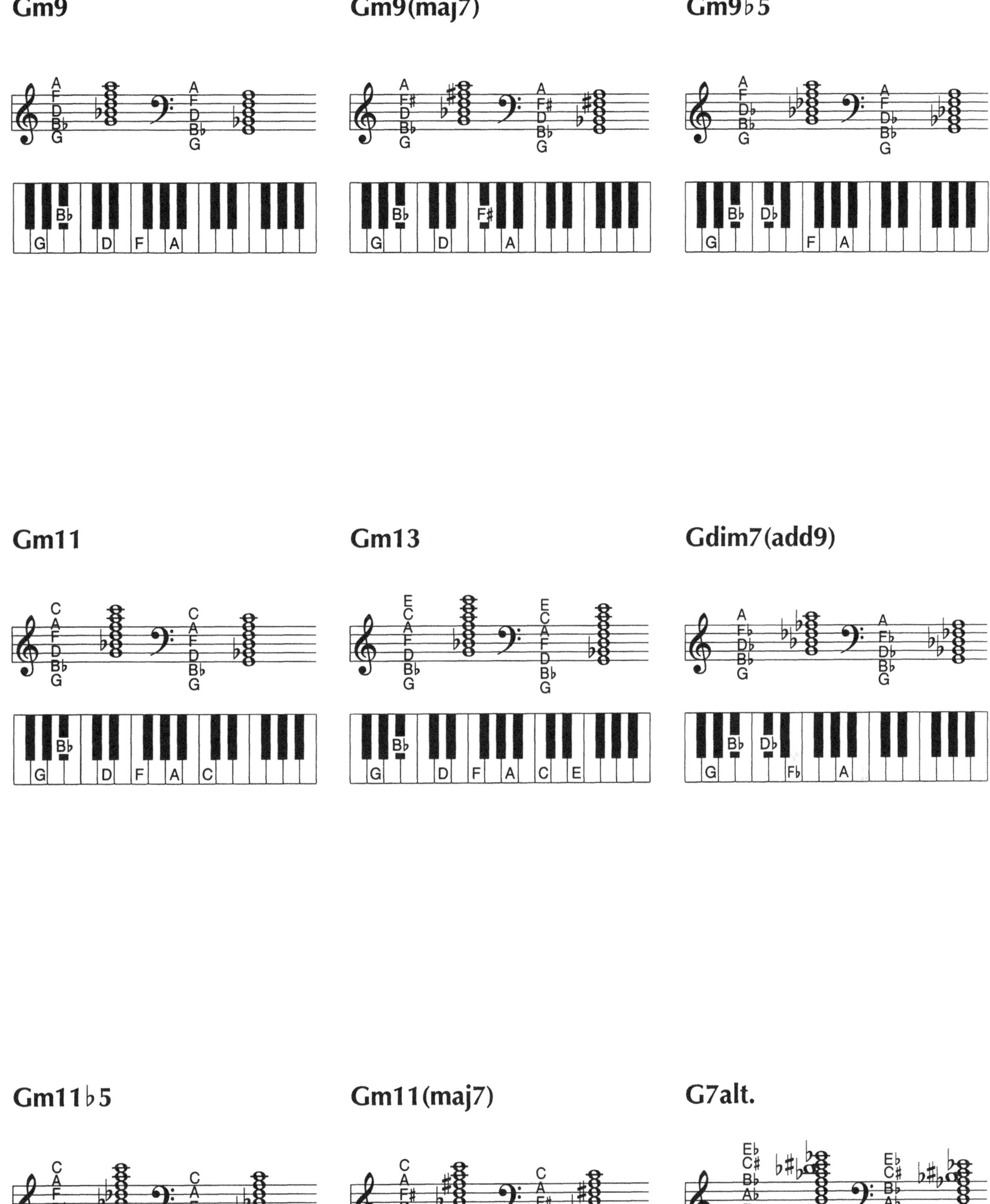
Gm9
A F D B♭ G
A F D B♭ G
B♭
G D F A
Gm9(maj7)
A F♯ D B♭ G
A F♯ D B♭ G
B♭ F♯
G D A
Gm9♭5
A F D♭ B♭ G
A F D♭ B♭ G
B♭ D♭
G F A
Gm11
C A F D B♭ G
C A F D B♭ G
B♭
G D F A C
Gm13
E C A F D B♭ G
E C A F D B♭ G
B♭
G D F A C E
Gdim7(add9)
A F♭ D♭ B♭ G
A F♭ D♭ B♭ G
B♭ D♭
G F♭ A
Gm11♭5
C A F D♭ B♭ G
C A F D♭ B♭ G
B♭ D♭
G F A C
Gm11(maj7)
C A F♯ D B♭ G
C A F♯ D B♭ G
B♭ F♯
G D A C
G7alt.
E♭ C♯ B♭ A♭ F D B G
E♭ C♯ B♭ A♭ F D B G
A♭ B♭ C♯ E♭
G B D F

A♭ CHORDS

A♭

Root Position

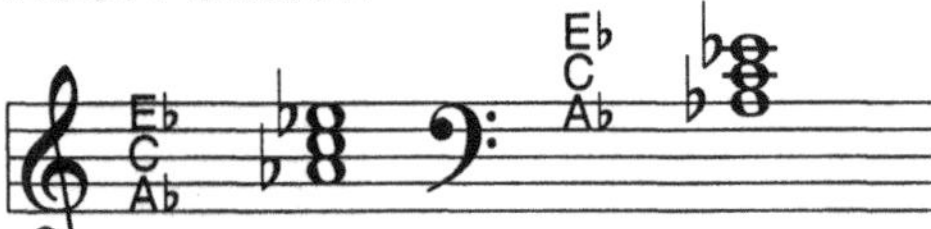

1st Inversion

2nd Inversion

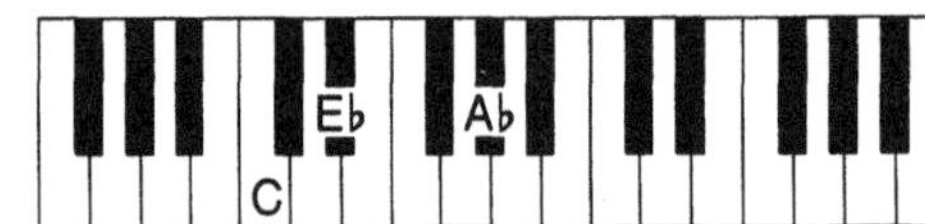

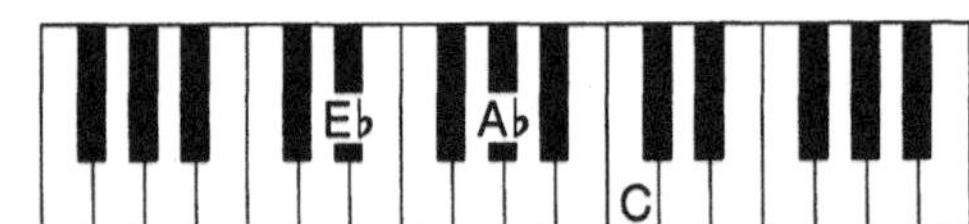

A♭m

Root Position

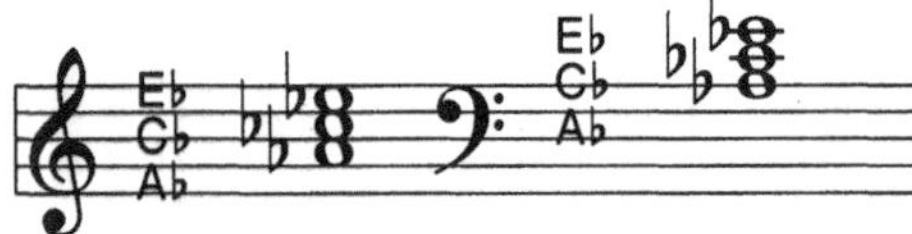

1st Inversion

2nd Inversion

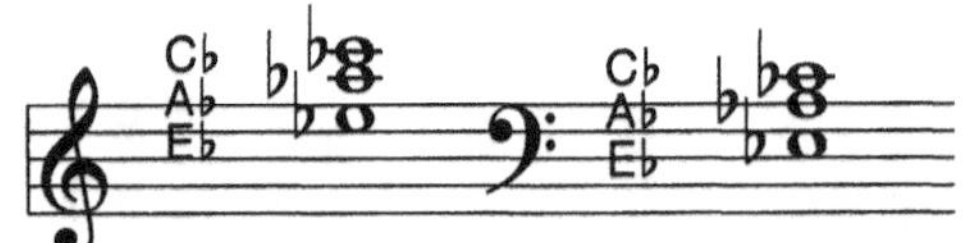

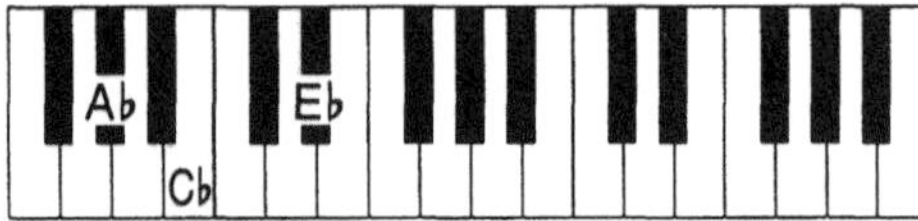

A♭+

Root Position

1st Inversion

2nd Inversion

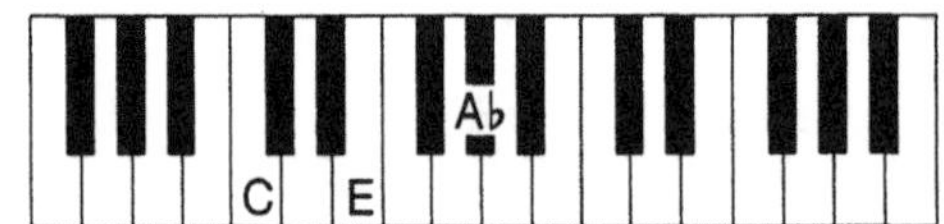

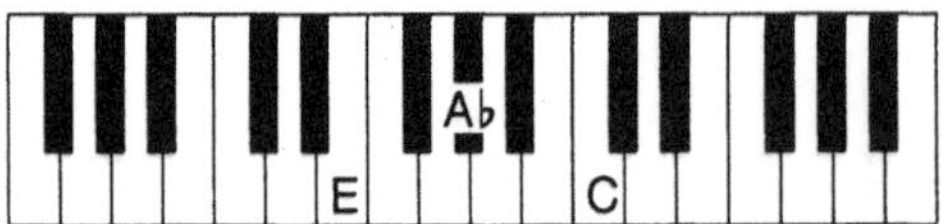

A♭dim

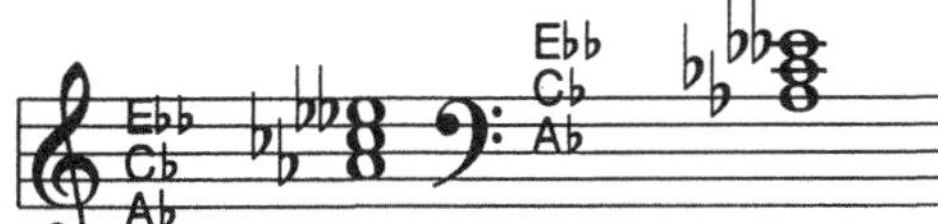

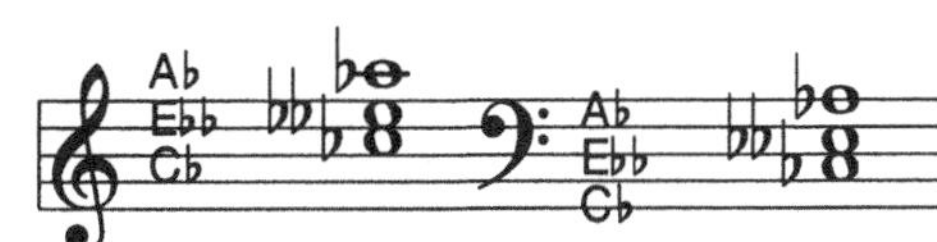

2nd Inversion

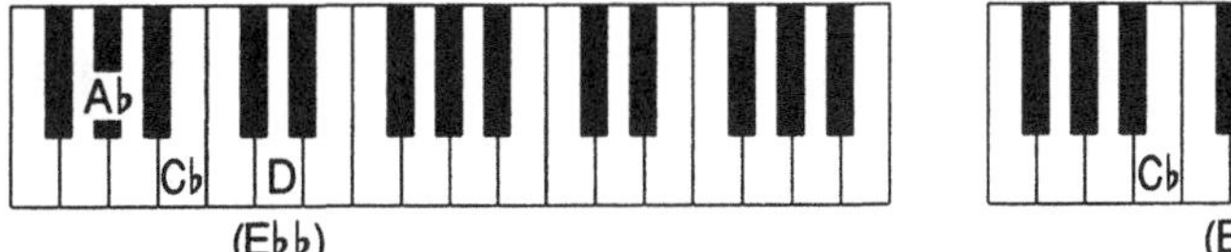

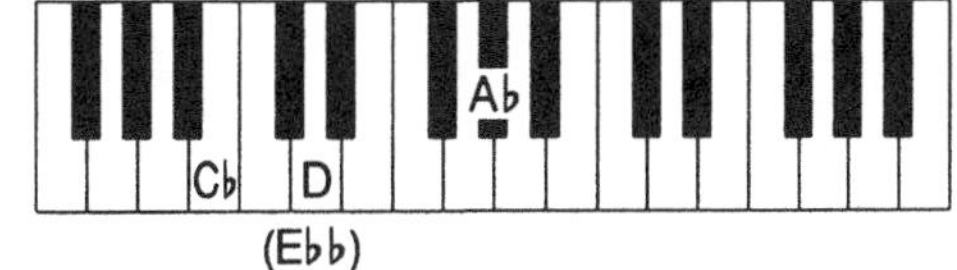

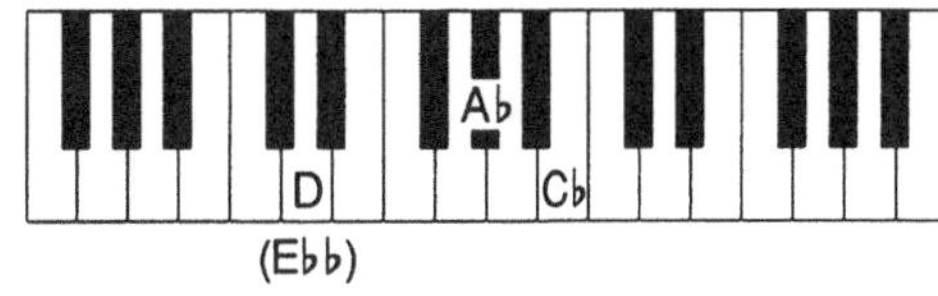

A♭sus

Root Position

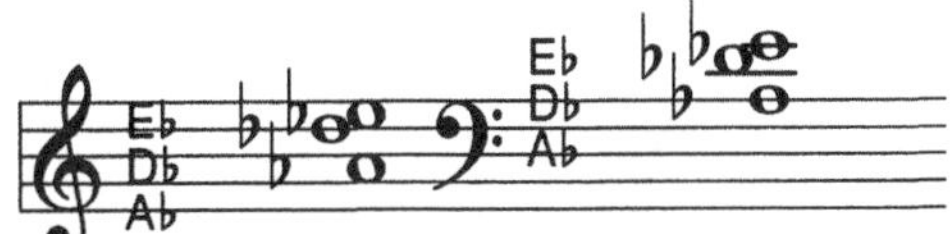

1st Inversion

2nd Inversion

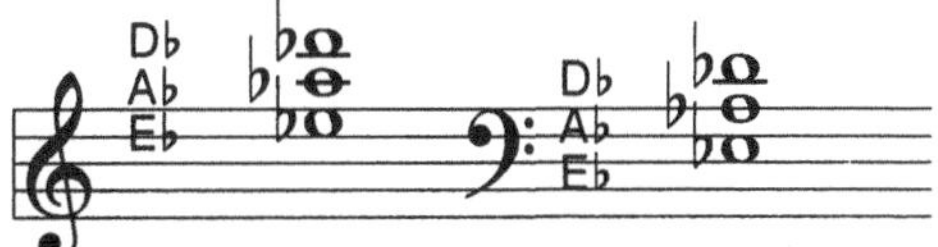

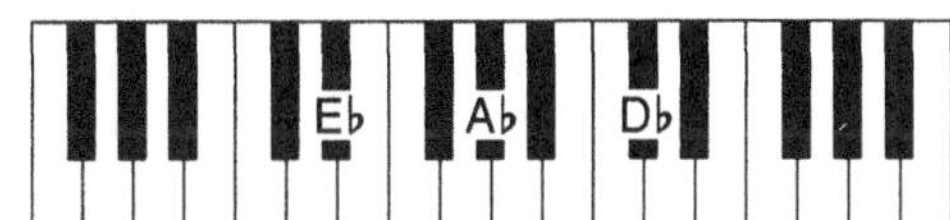

A♭(♭5)

Root Position

1st Inversion

2nd Inversion

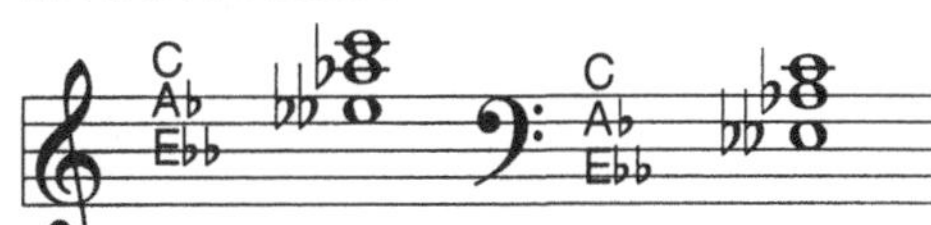

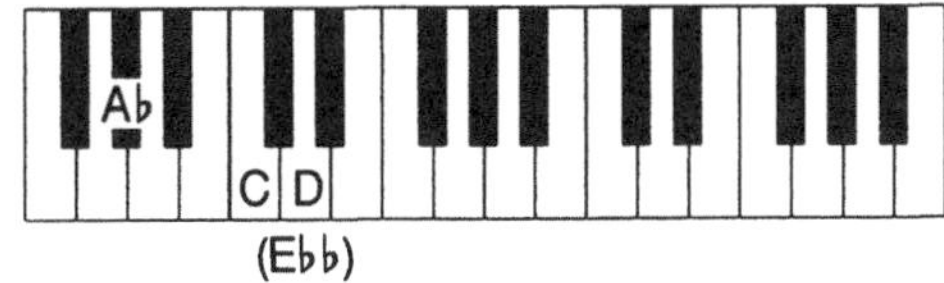

A♭ C D (E♭♭)

A♭ D C (E♭♭)

A♭sus2

Root Position

1st Inversion

2nd Inversion

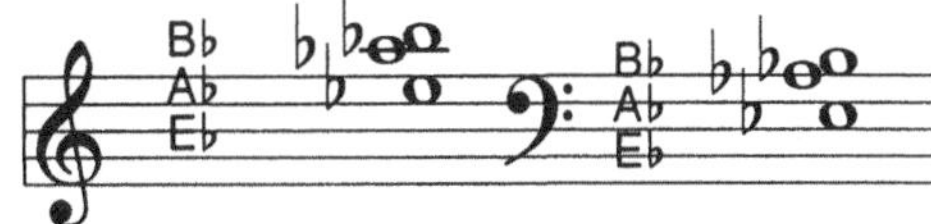

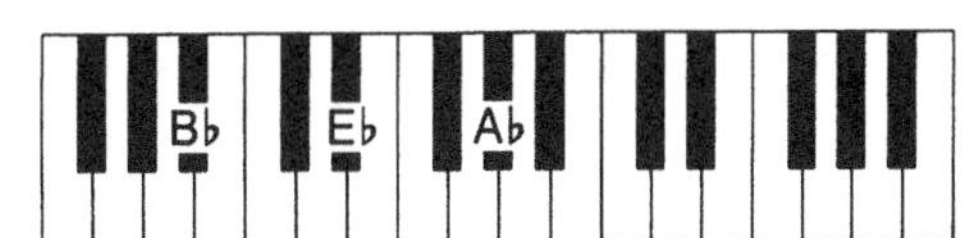

A♭6

Root Position

1st Inversion

2nd Inversion

3rd Inversion

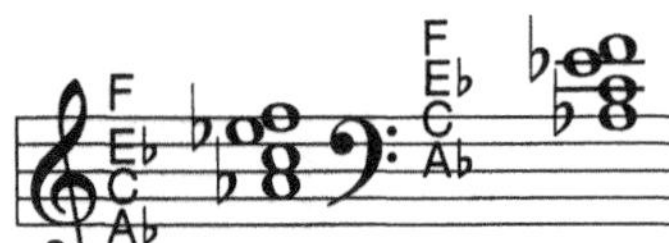

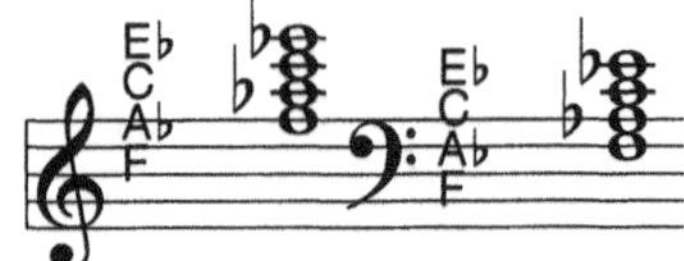

E♭ A♭ F C

A♭(add2), A♭(add9)

Root Position

1st Inversion

2nd Inversion

3rd Inversion

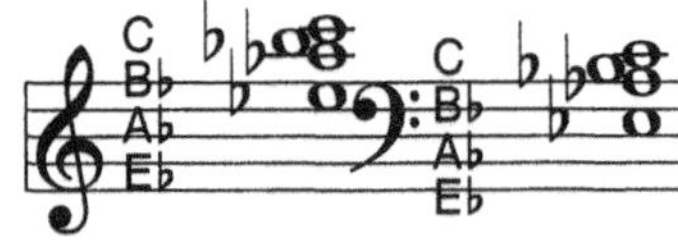

E♭ A♭B♭ C

A♭maj7

Root Position

1st Inversion

2nd Inversion

3rd Inversion

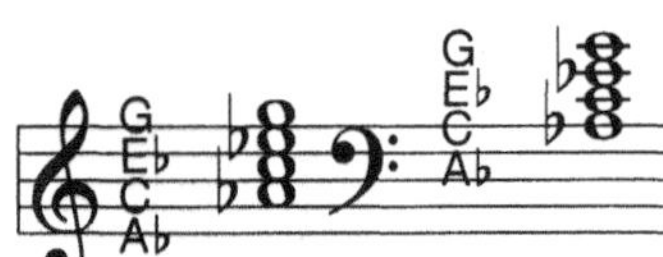

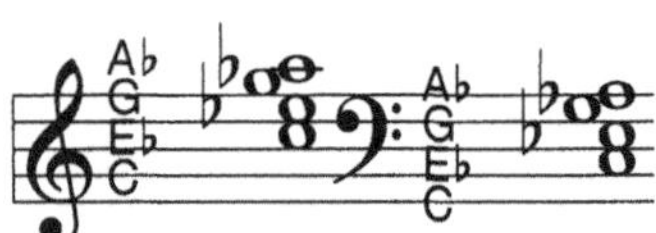

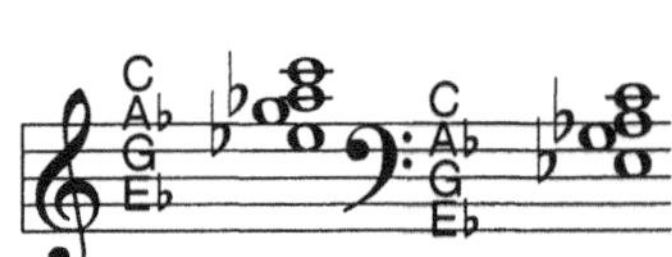

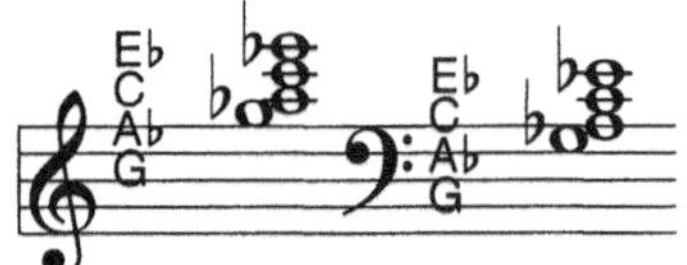

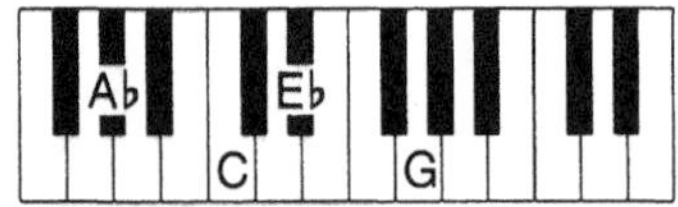

E♭ A♭ C G

E♭ A♭ G C

A♭ E♭ G C

A♭maj7♭5

Root Position

1st Inversion

2nd Inversion

3rd Inversion

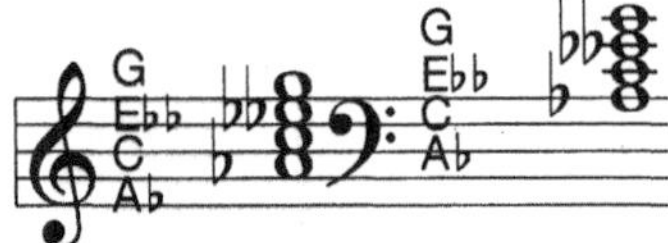

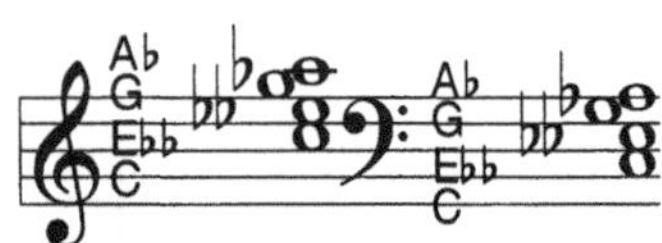

E♭♭ C A♭ G E♭♭ C A♭ G

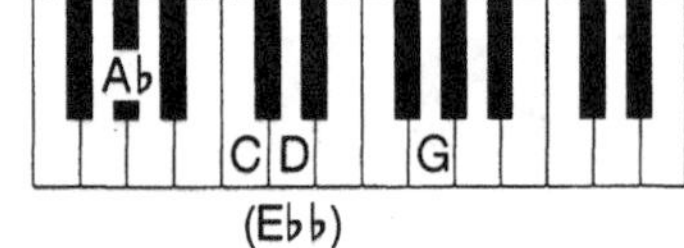

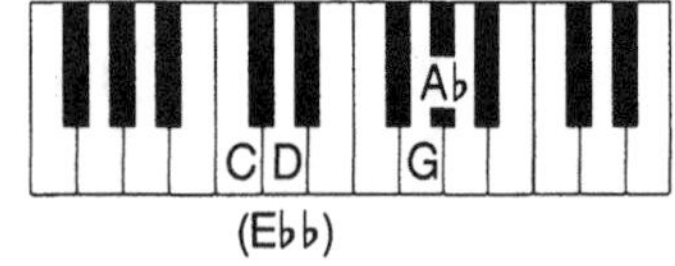

A♭ D G C (E♭♭)

A♭ G C D (E♭♭)

A♭maj7♯5

Root Position

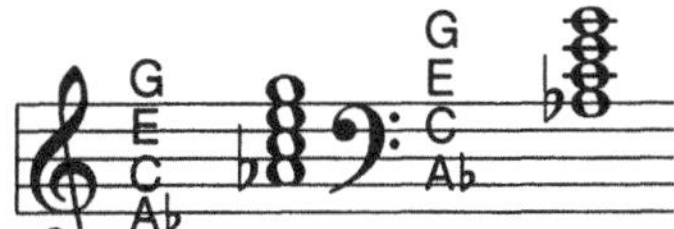

1st Inversion

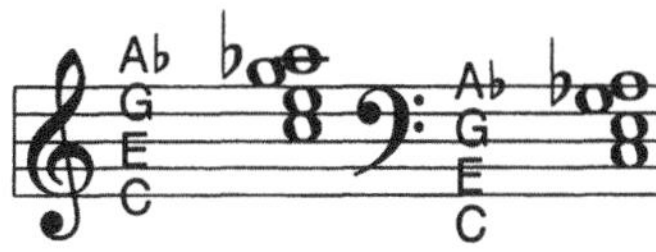

2nd Inversion

3rd Inversion

A♭7

Root Position

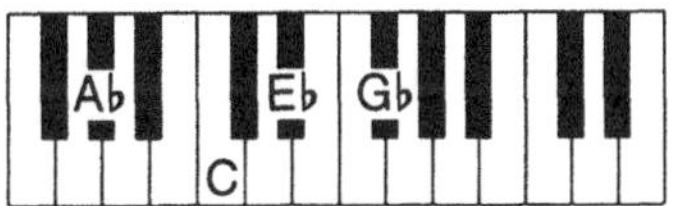

1st Inversion

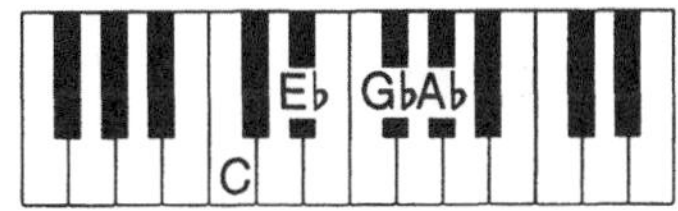

2nd Inversion

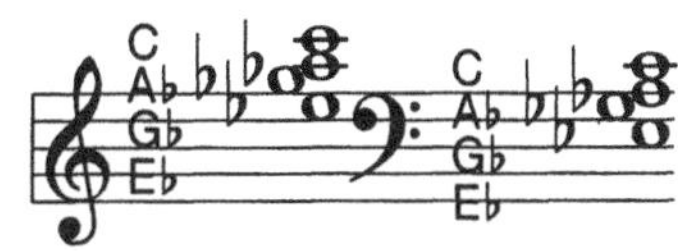

3rd Inversion

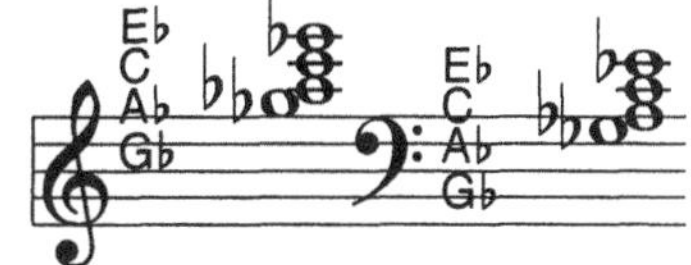

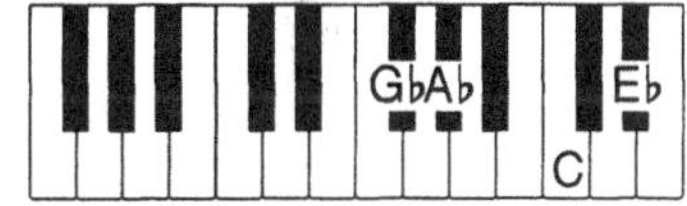

A♭7♭5

Root Position

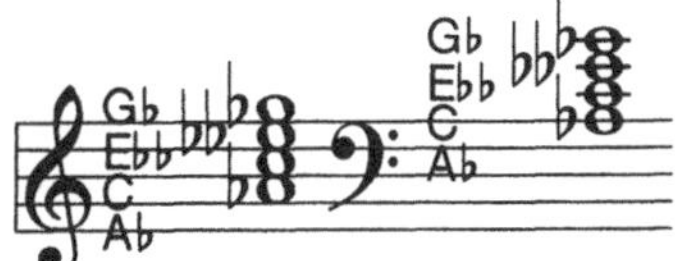

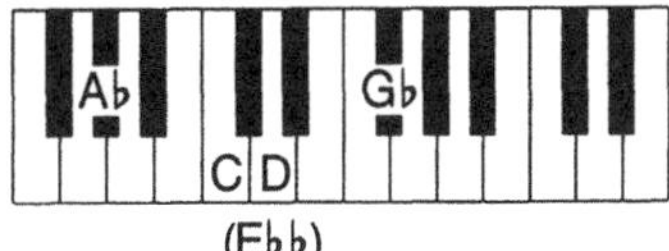

1st Inversion

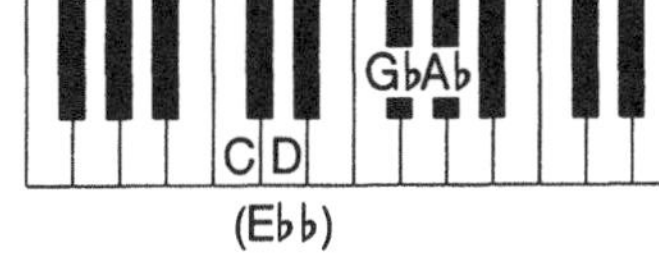

2nd Inversion

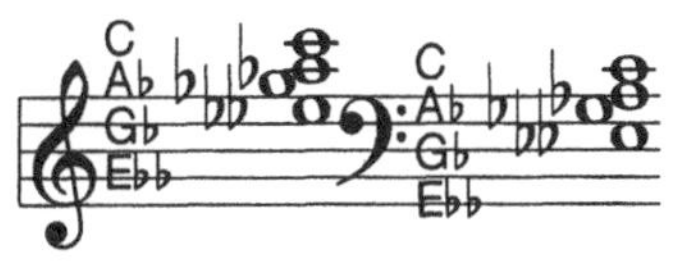

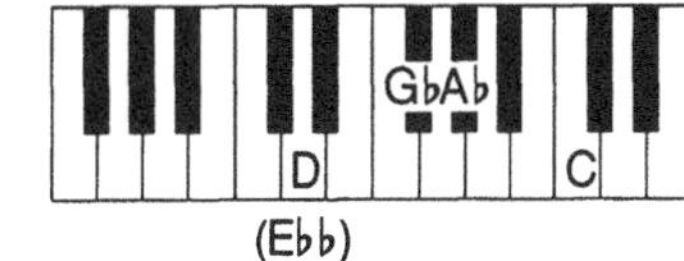

3rd Inversion

A♭7♯5

Root Position

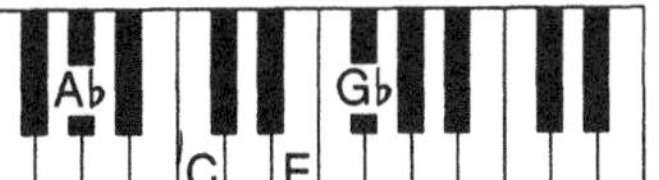

1st Inversion

2nd Inversion

3rd Inversion

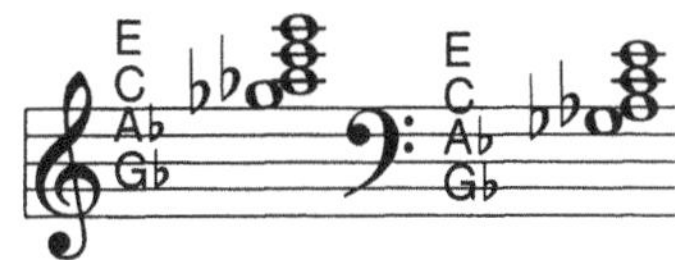

A♭7sus

Root Position

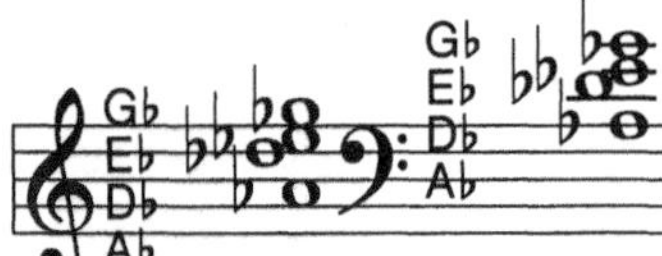

1st Inversion

2nd Inversion

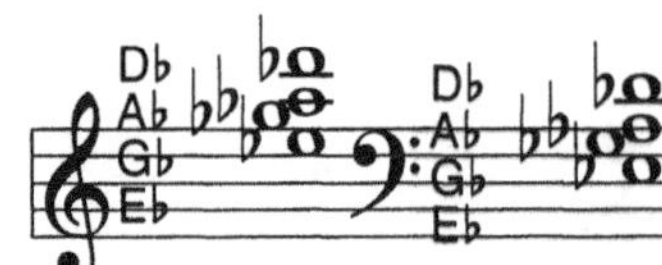

3rd Inversion

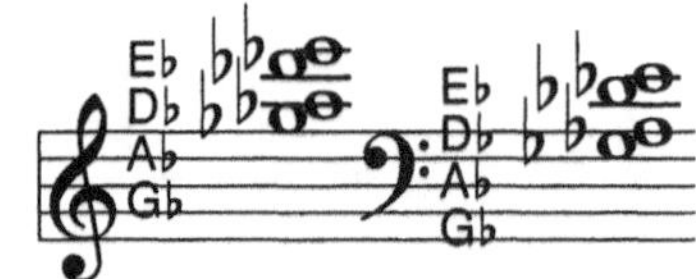

A♭m(add2), A♭m(add9)

Root Position

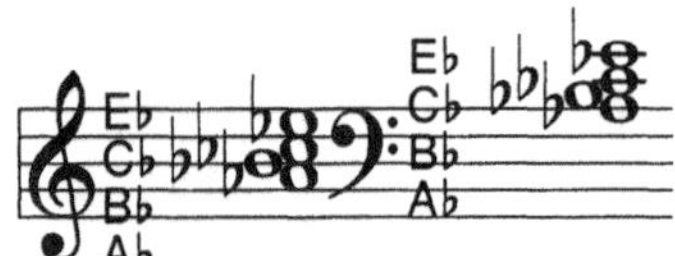

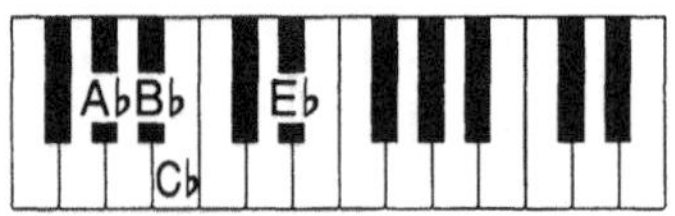

1st Inversion

2nd Inversion

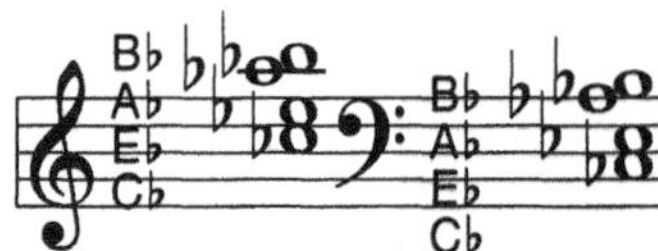

3rd Inversion

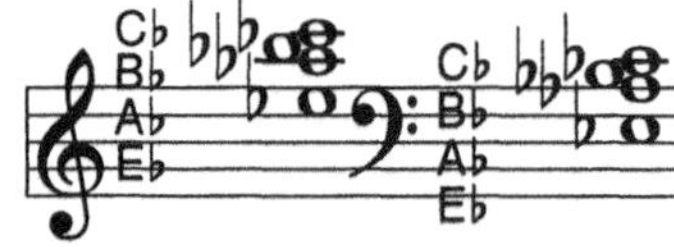

A♭m6

Root Position

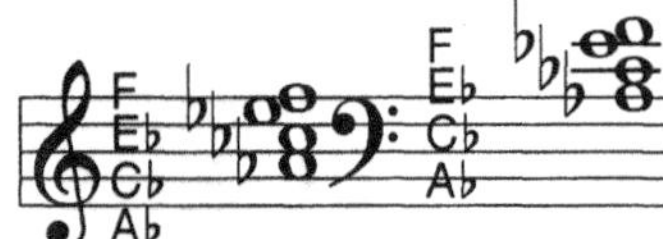

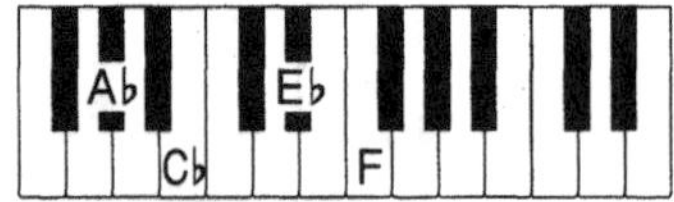

1st Inversion

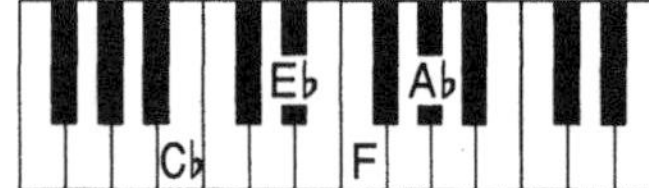

2nd Inversion

3rd Inversion

A♭m7

Root Position

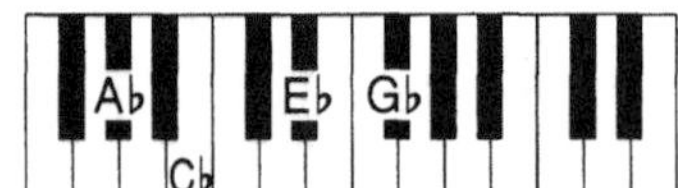

1st Inversion

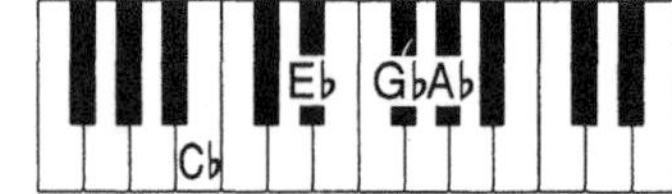

2nd Inversion

3rd Inversion

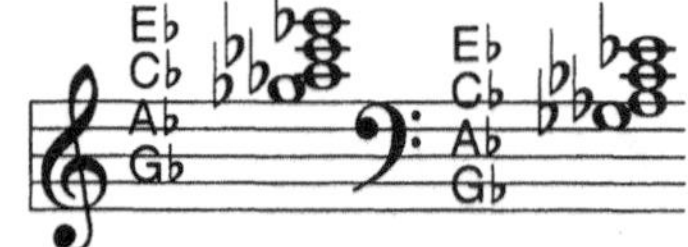

A♭m(maj7)

Root Position

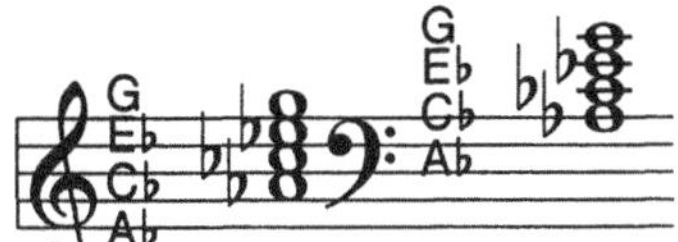

1st Inversion

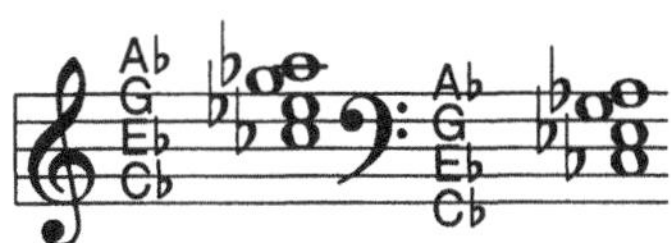

2nd Inversion

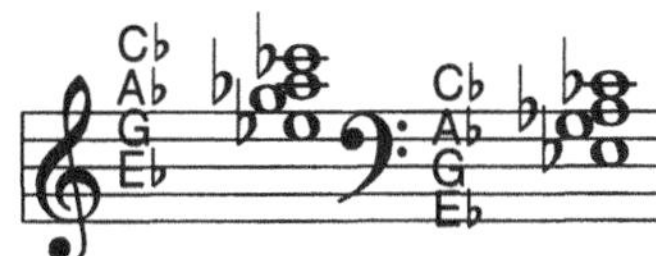

Eb Ab G Cb

3rd Inversion

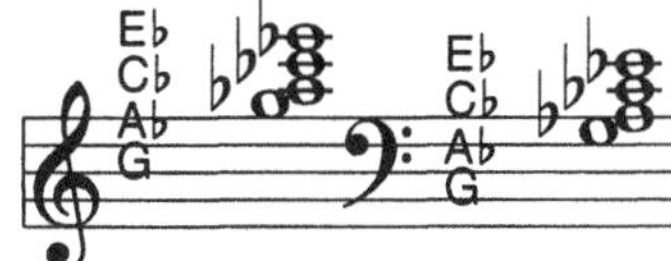

Ab Eb G Cb

A♭m7♭5

Root Position

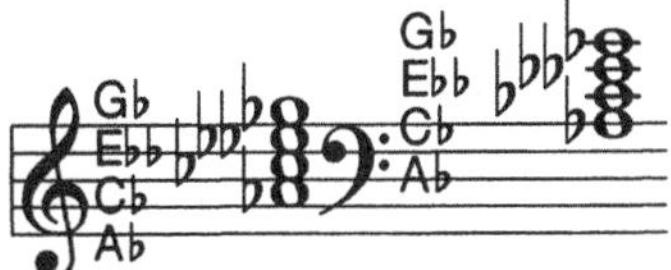

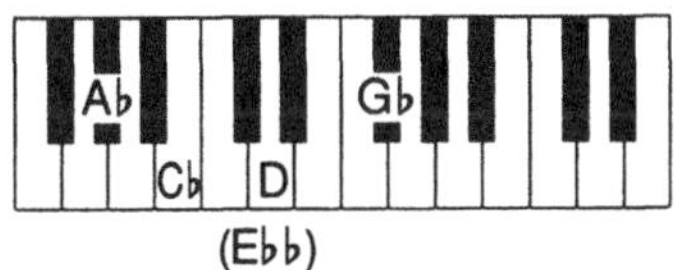

1st Inversion

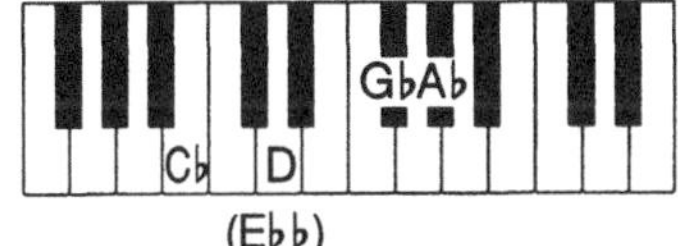

2nd Inversion

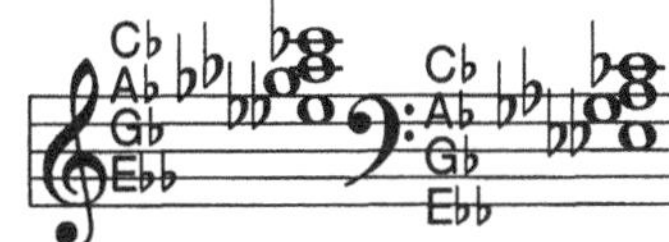

GbAb D Cb (Ebb)

3rd Inversion

GbAb Cb D (Ebb)

A♭dim7

Root Position

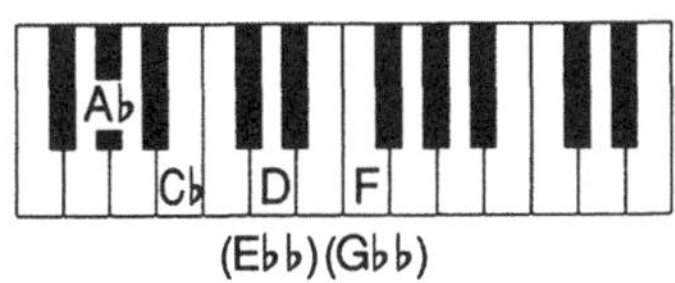

1st Inversion

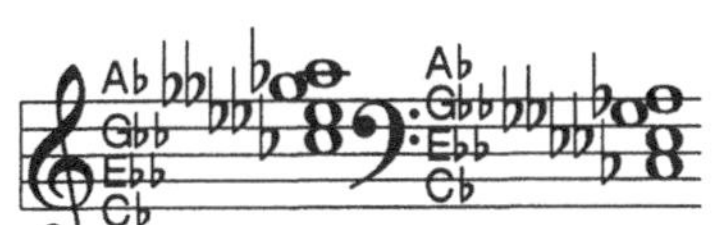

Ab Cb D F (Ebb)(Gbb)

2nd Inversion

Ab D F Cb (Ebb)(Gbb)

3rd Inversion

Ab F Cb D (Gbb) (Ebb)

A♭dim(maj7)

Root Position

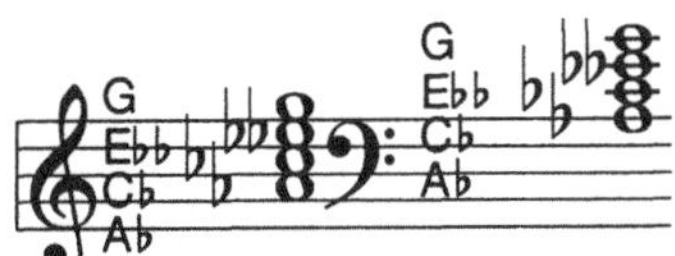

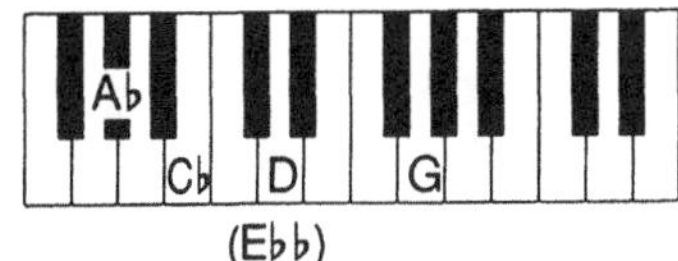

1st Inversion

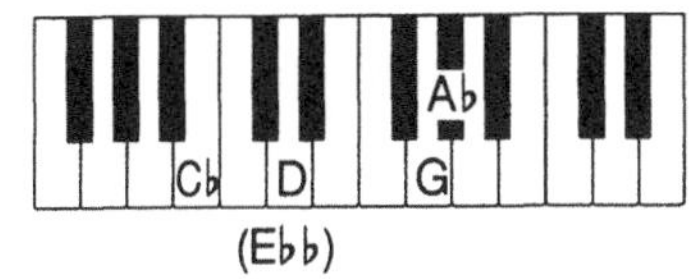

2nd Inversion

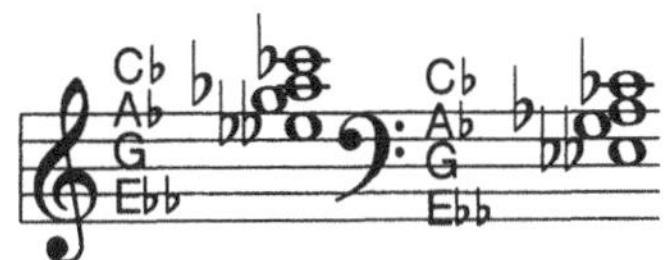

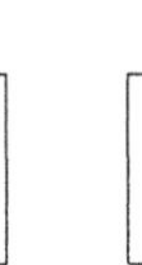

Ab D G Cb (Ebb)

3rd Inversion

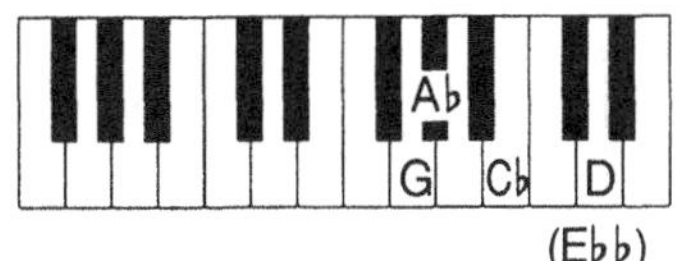

ADDITIONAL A♭ CHORDS

A♭5

A♭6/9

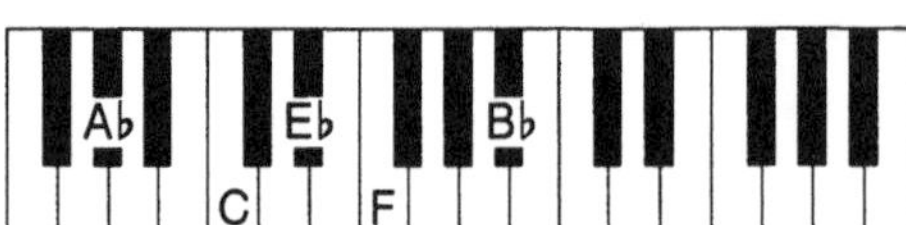

A♭maj6/9

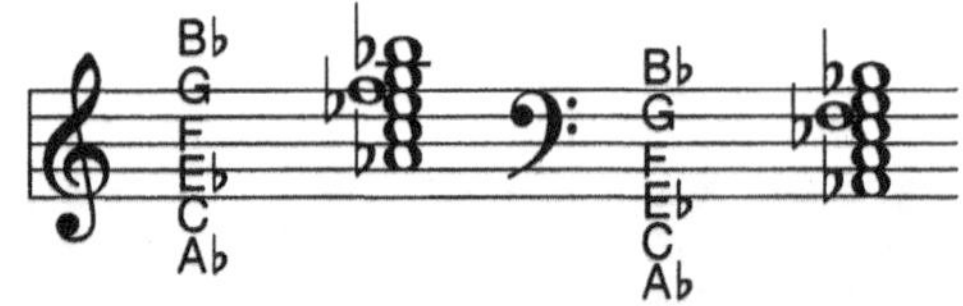

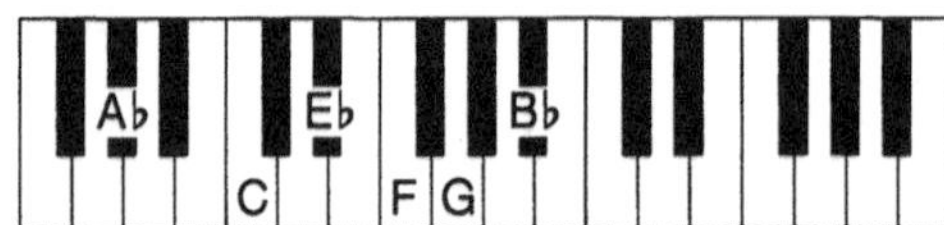

A♭maj7♯11

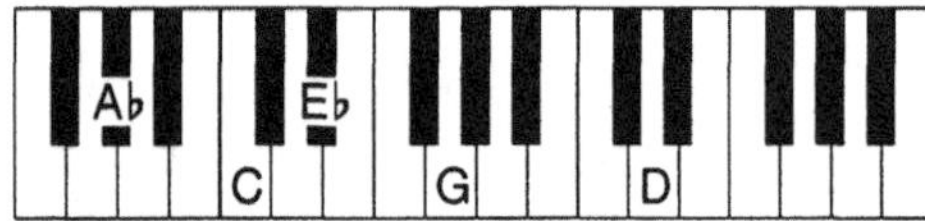

A♭maj9

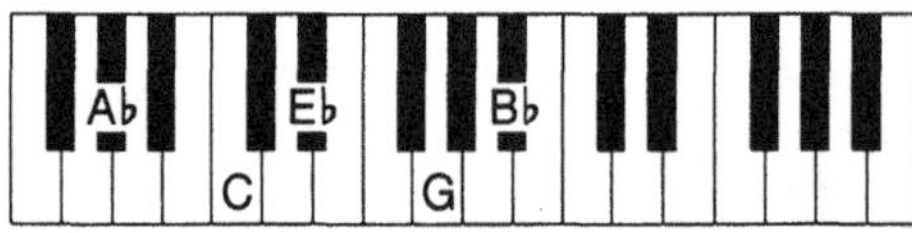

A♭maj9♭5

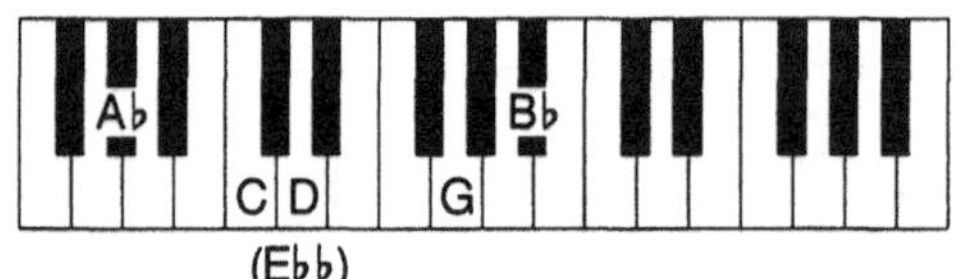

A♭maj9♯5

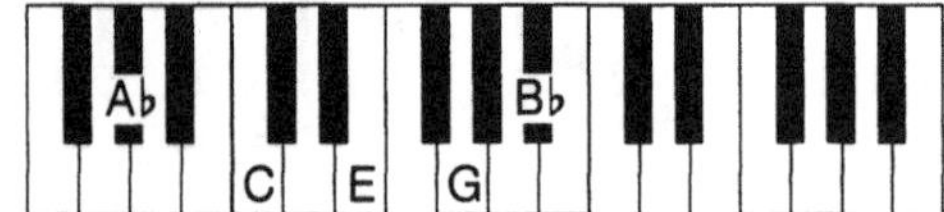

A♭maj9♯11

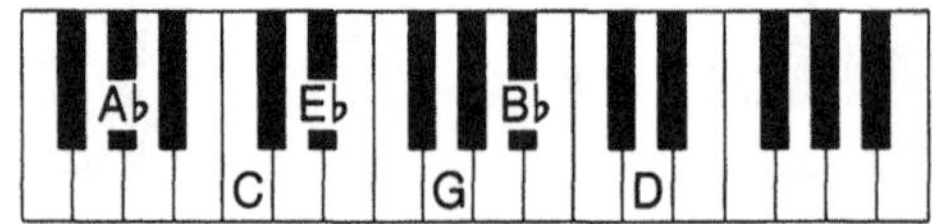

A♭maj13

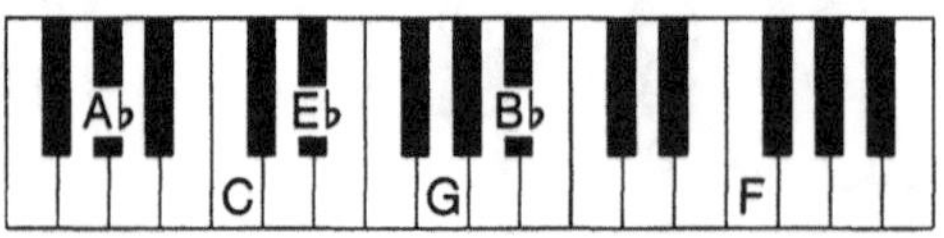

A♭maj13♭5

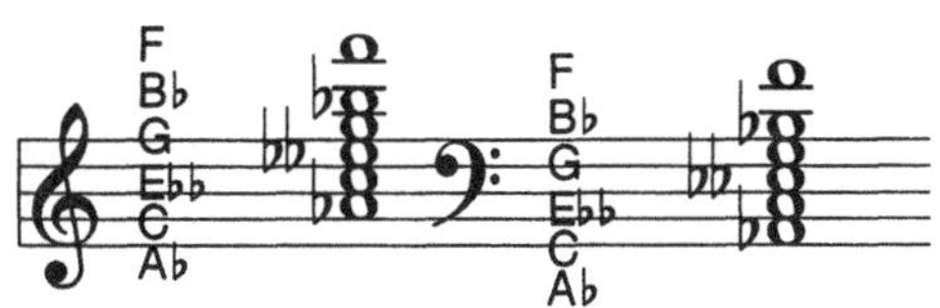

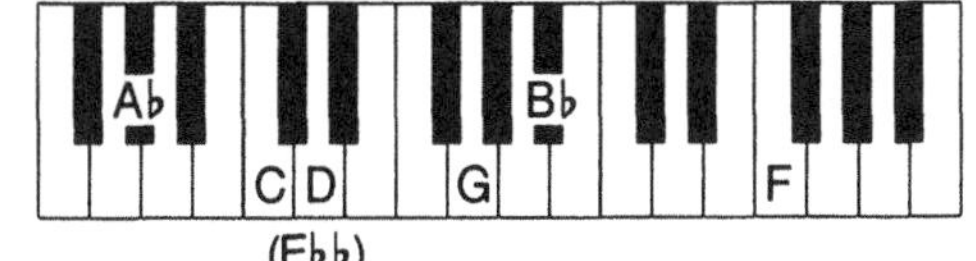

A♭maj13♯11

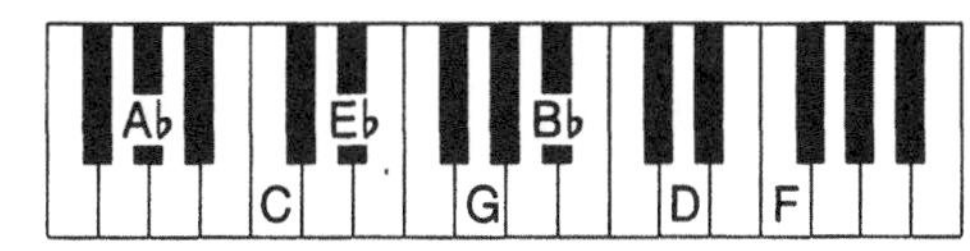

A♭7♭9

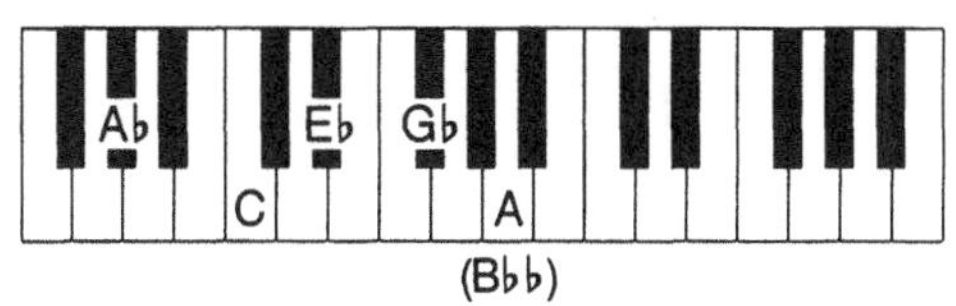

A♭7♯9

A♭7♯11

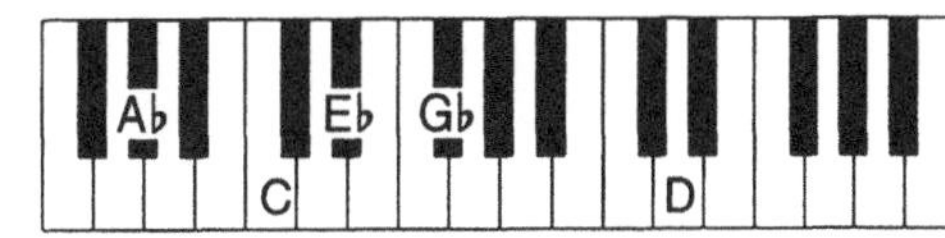

A♭7♭5(♭9)

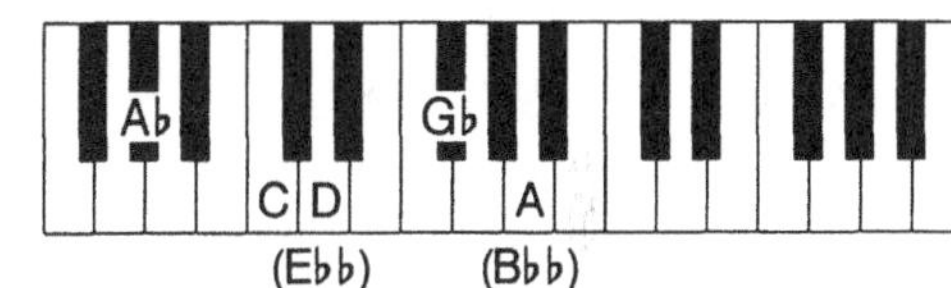

A♭7♭5(♯9)

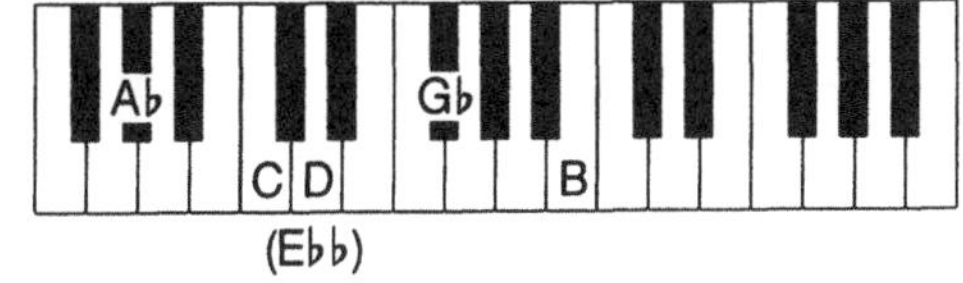

A♭7♯5(♭9)

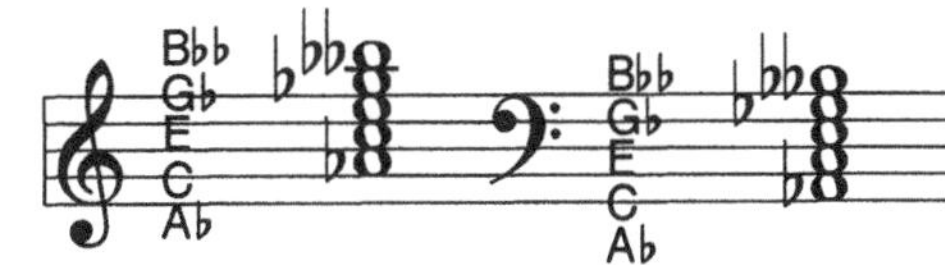

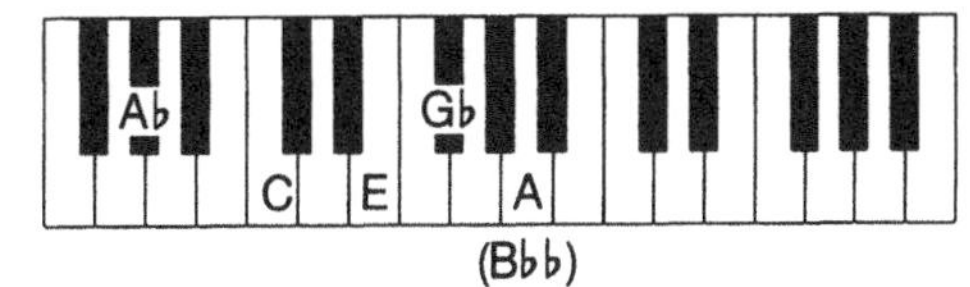

A♭7♯5(♯9)

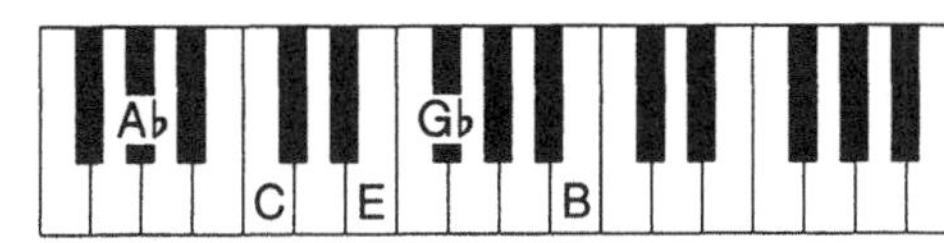

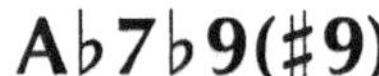

A♭7♭9(♯9)

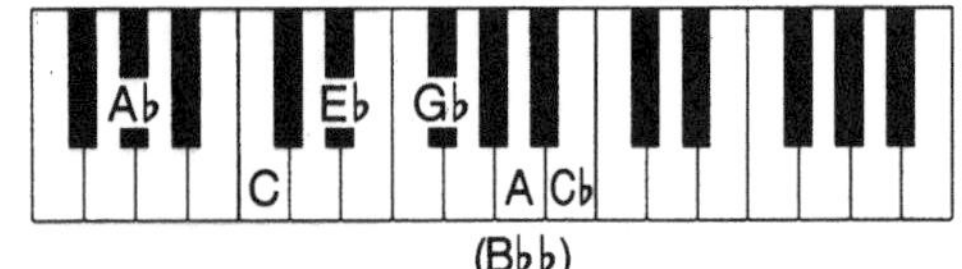

A♭7(add13)

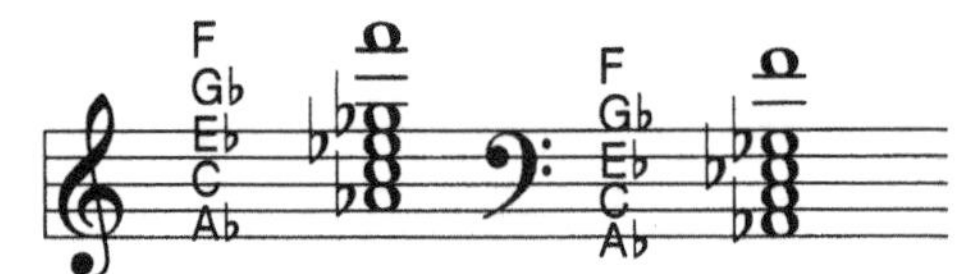

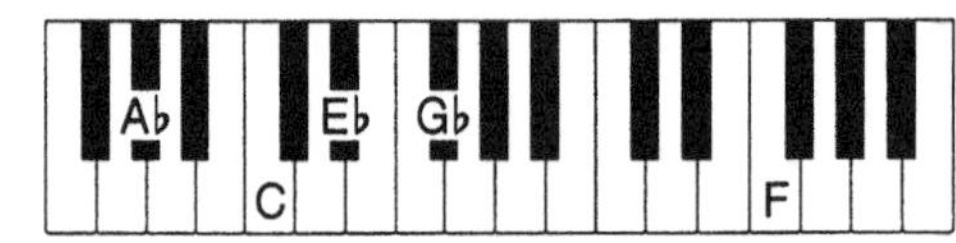

A♭7♭13

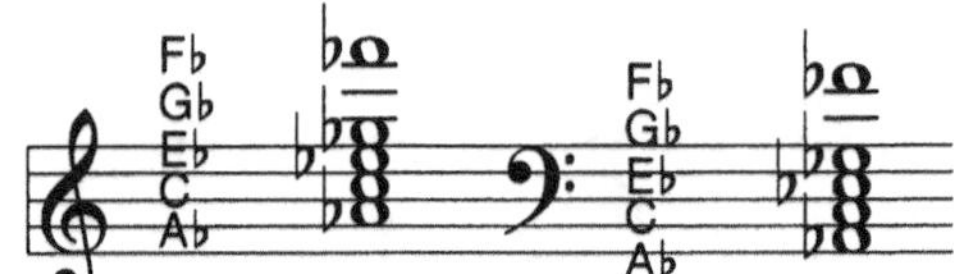

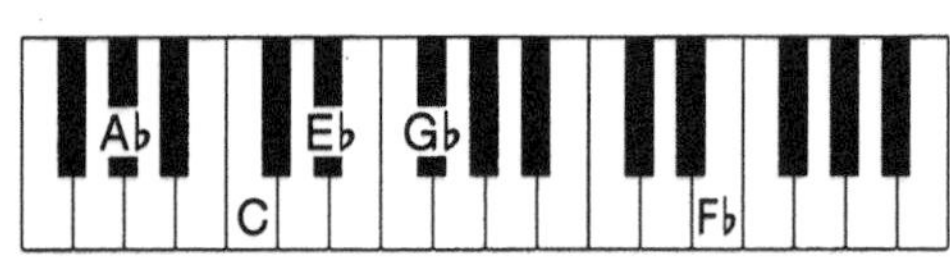

A♭7♭9(♯11)

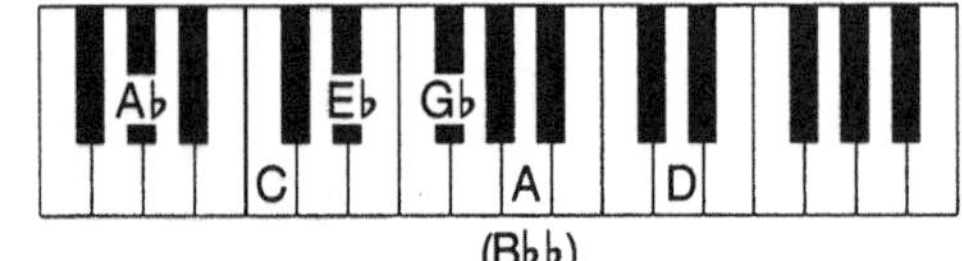

A♭7♯9(♯11)

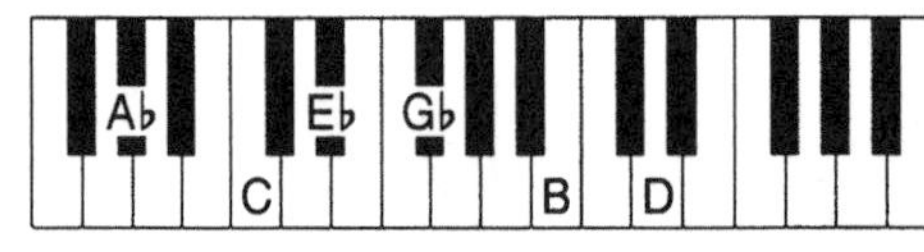

A♭7♭9(♭13)

Ab Eb Gb C A Fb

(Bbb)

A♭7♯9(♭13)

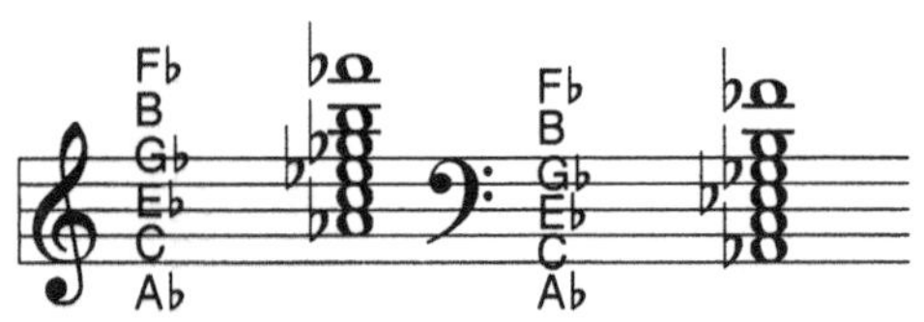

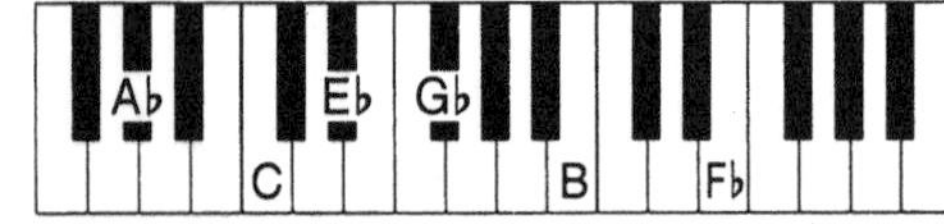

A♭7♯11(♭13)

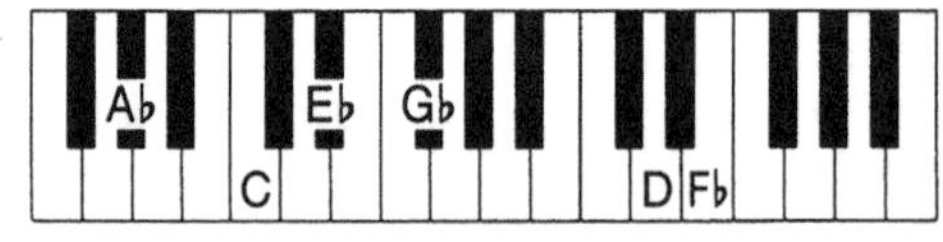

A♭7♭9(♯9,♯11)

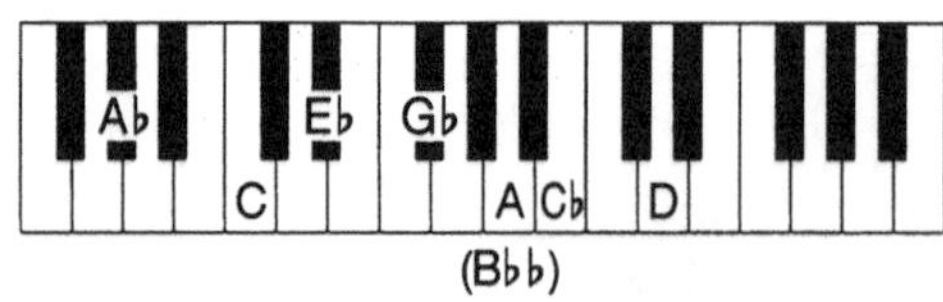

A♭9

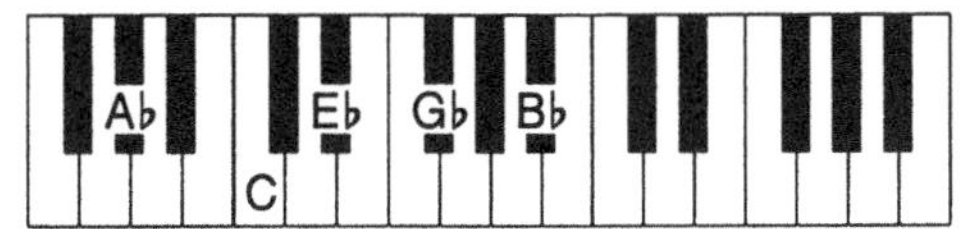

A♭9(♭5)

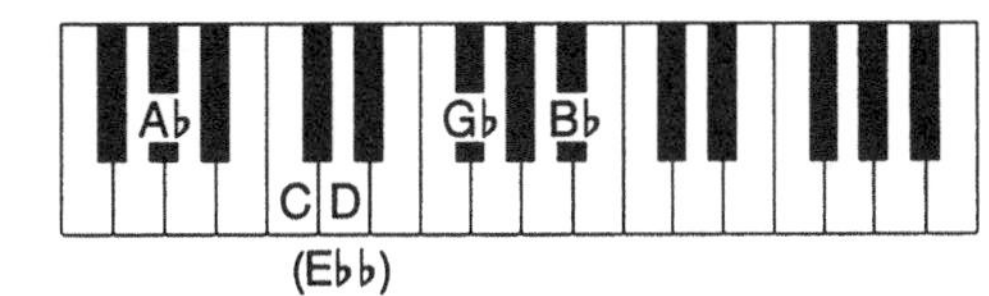

A♭9♯5

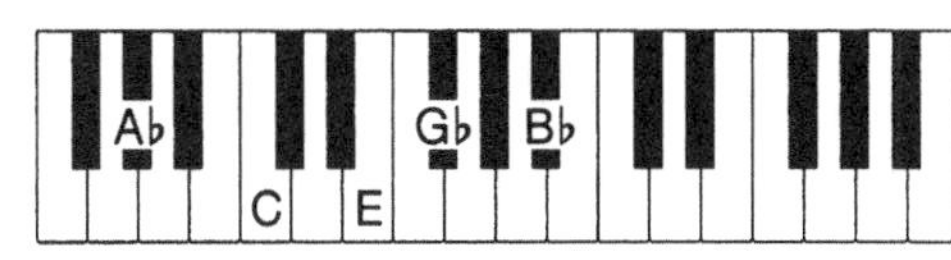

A♭9♯11

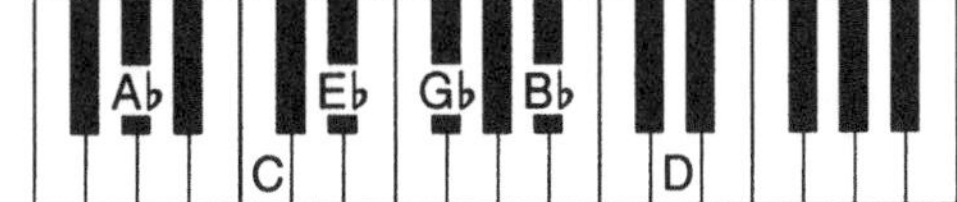

A♭9♭13

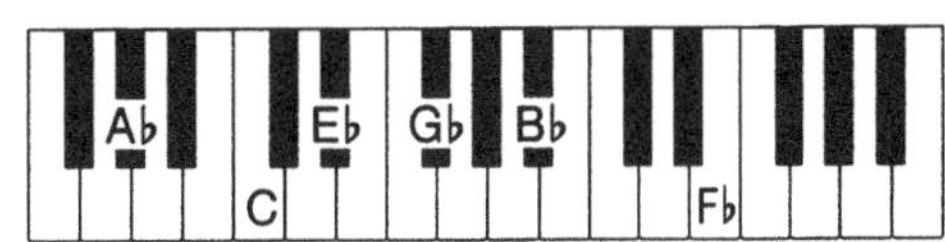

A♭9♯11(♭13)

A♭ E♭ G♭ B♭
C D F♭

A♭11, A♭9sus4

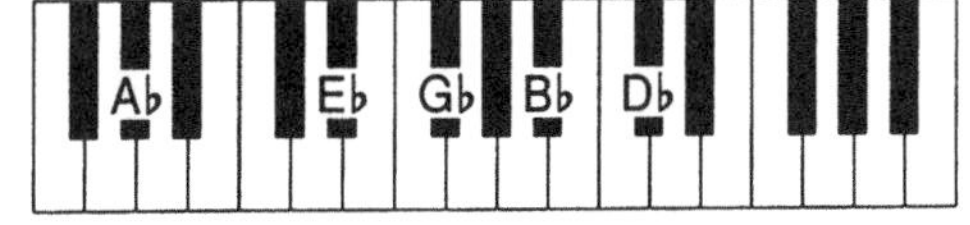

A♭13

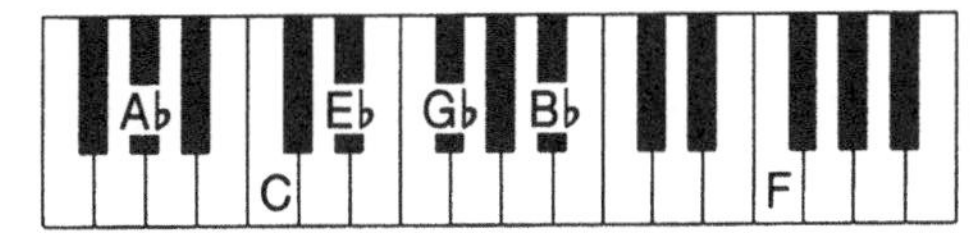

A♭13♭5

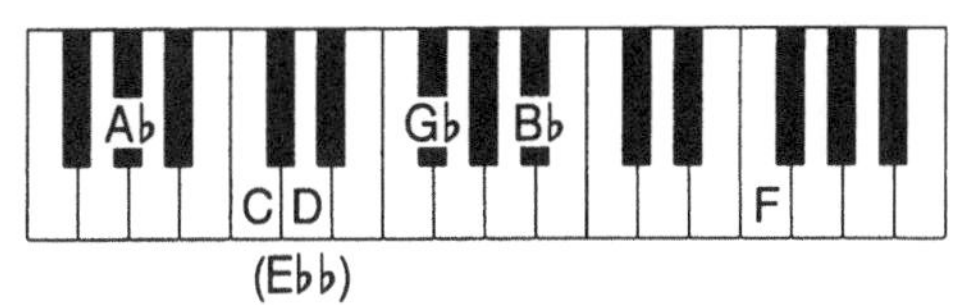

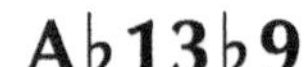

A♭13♭9

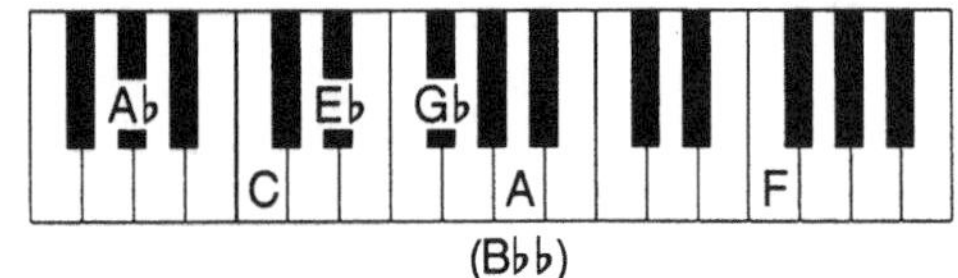

A♭13♯9

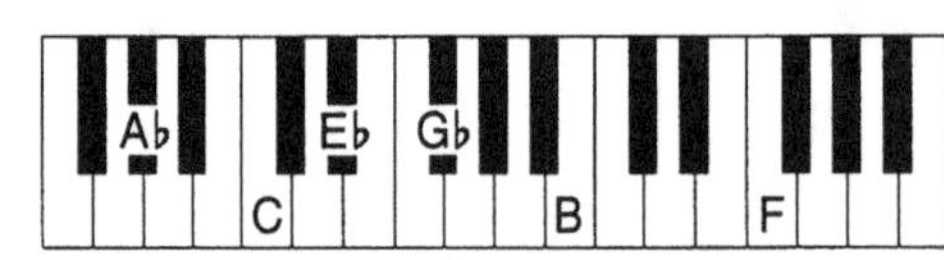

A♭13♯11

A♭ E♭ G♭ B♭ C D F

A♭13(sus4)

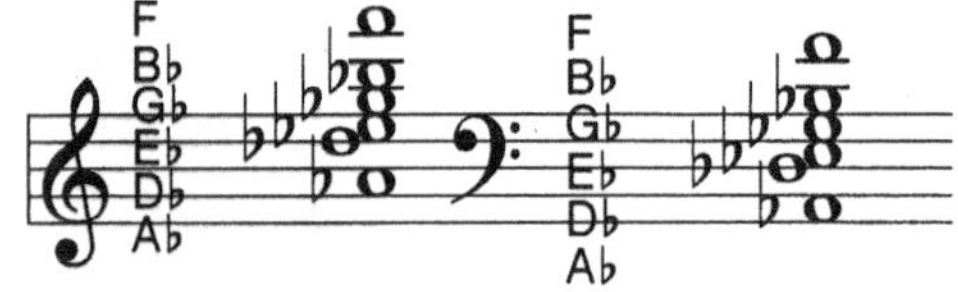

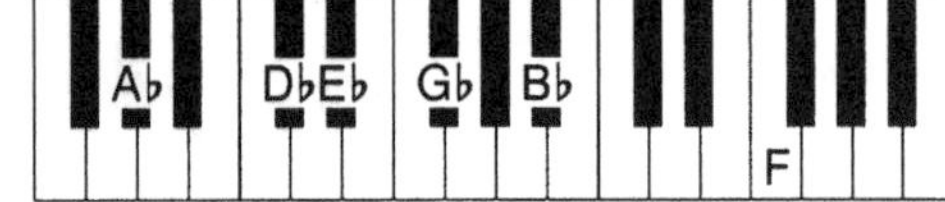

A♭m(♯5)

A♭m$^{6}_{9}$

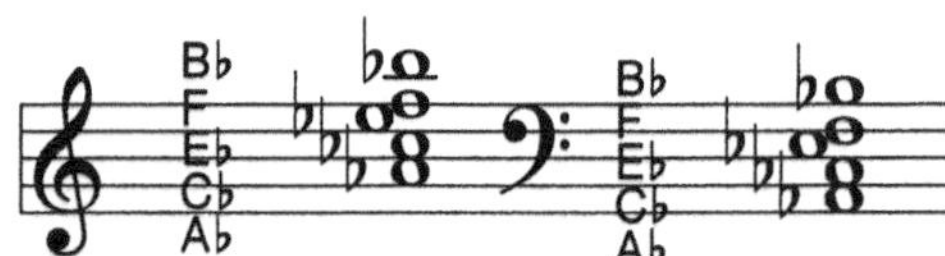

A♭ E♭ B♭ C♭ F

A♭m7(add4)

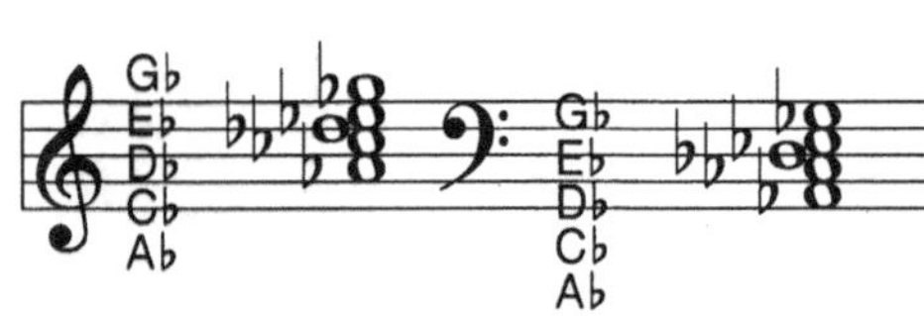

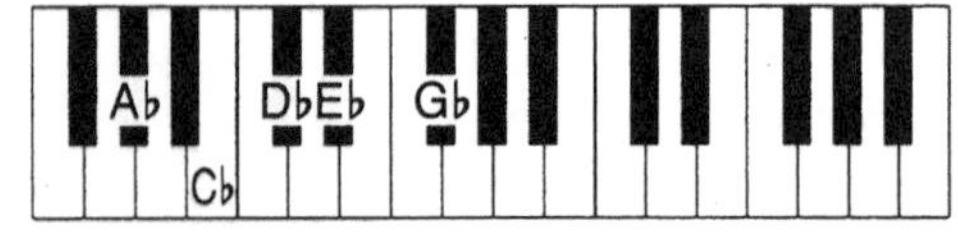

A♭m7(add11)

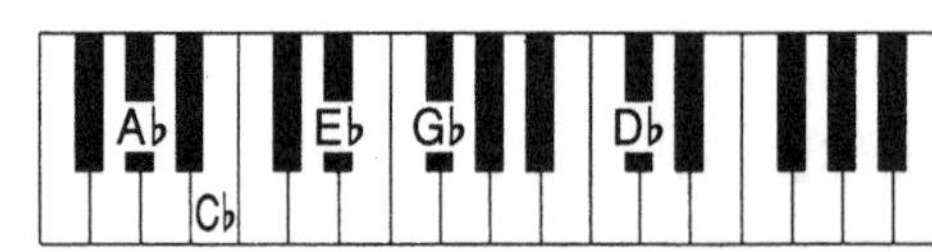

A♭m7♭5(♭9)

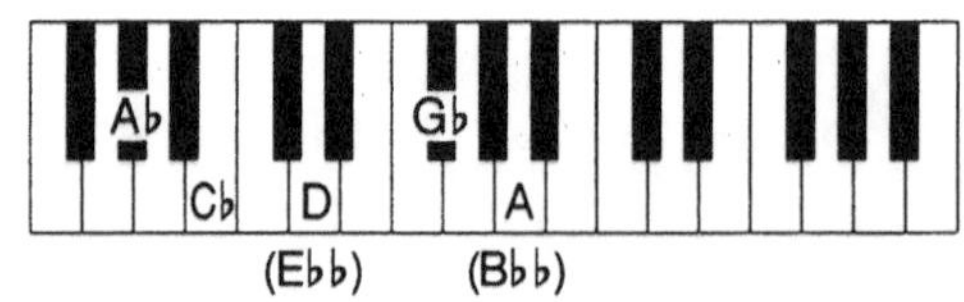

A♭m9

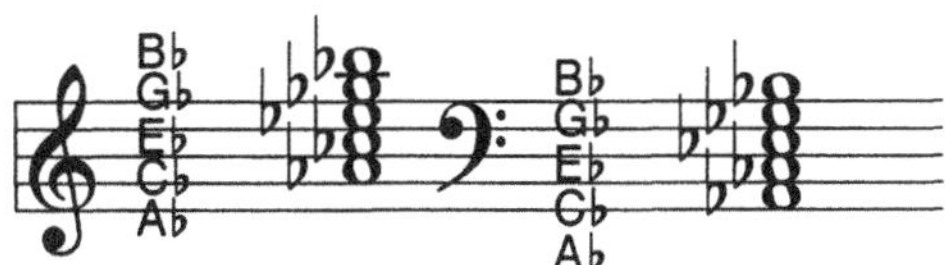

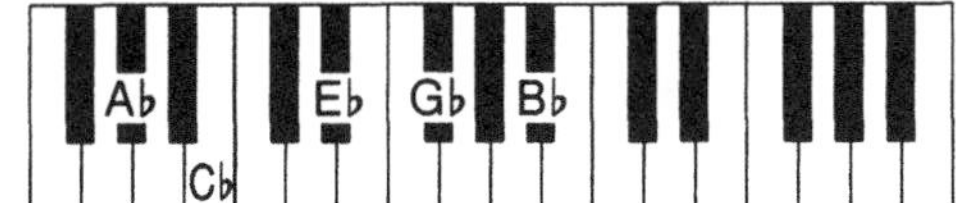

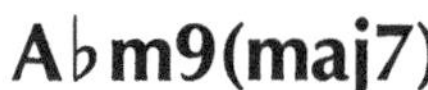

A♭m9(maj7)

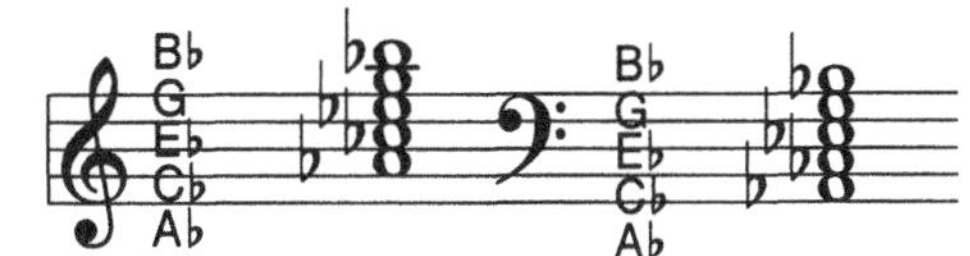

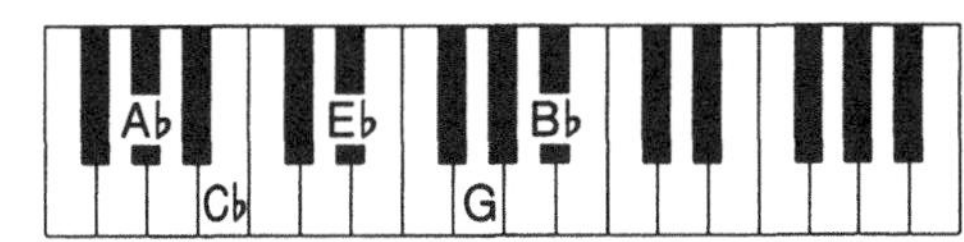

A♭m9♭5

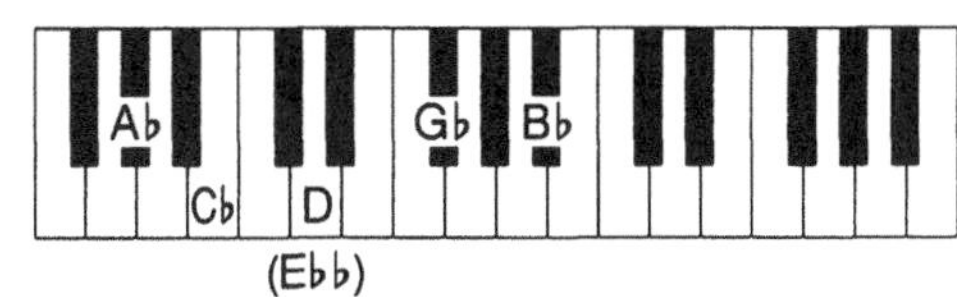

A♭m11

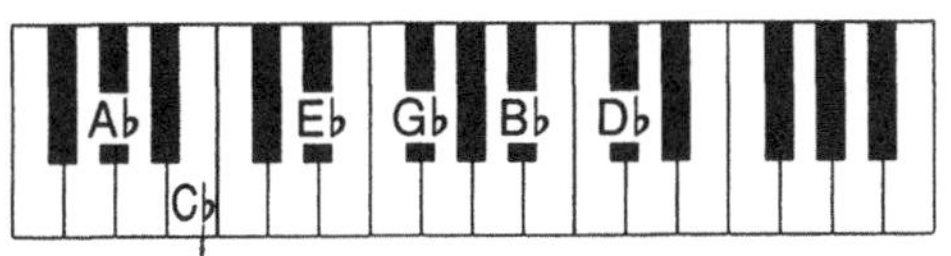

A♭m13

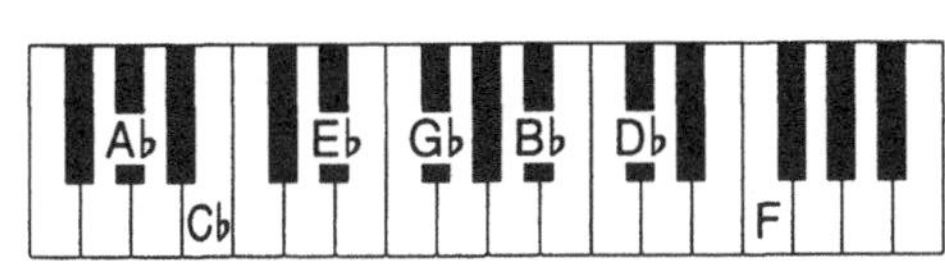

A♭dim7(add9)

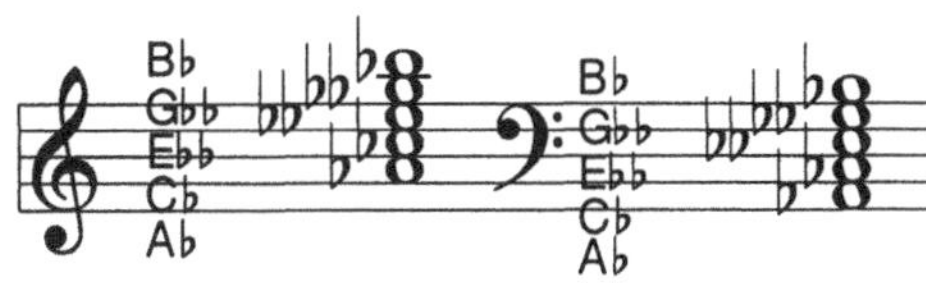

A♭ C♭ D F B♭

(E♭♭) (G♭♭)

A♭m11♭5

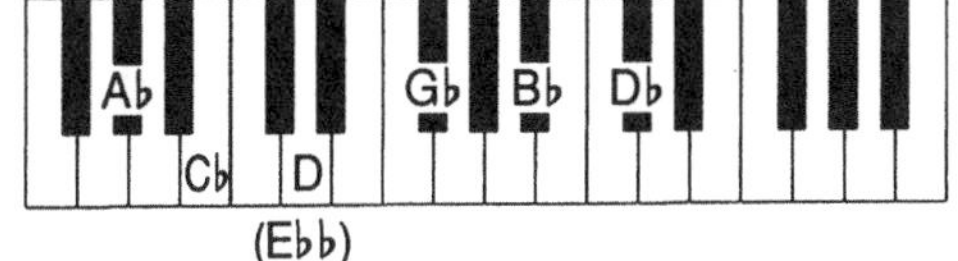

A♭m11(maj7)

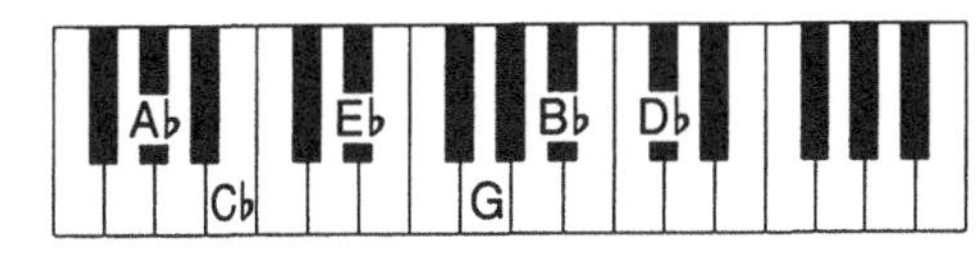

A♭7alt.

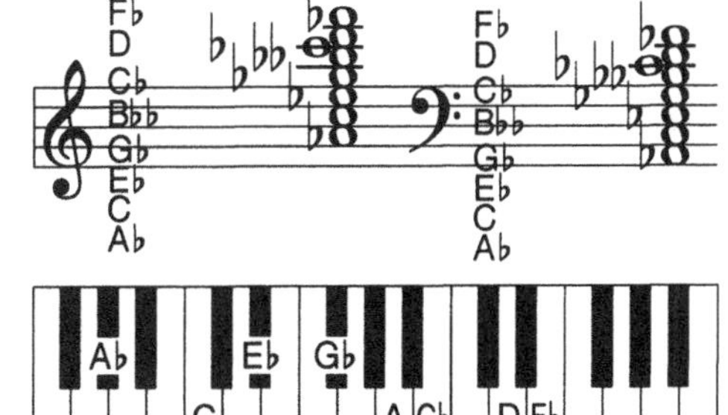

A CHORDS

A

Root Position

1st Inversion

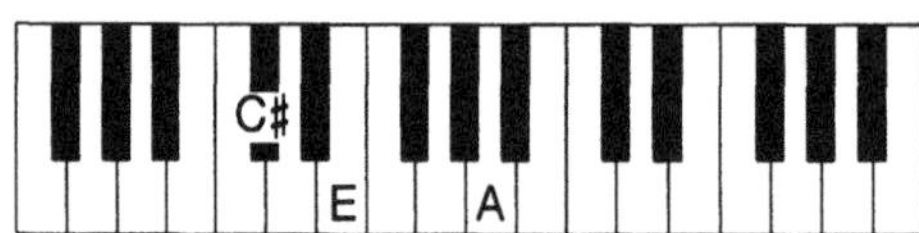

2nd Inversion

Am

Root Position

1st Inversion

2nd Inversion

A+

Root Position

1st Inversion

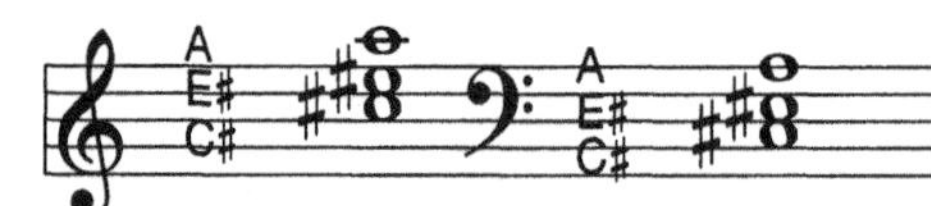

2nd Inversion

Adim

Root Position

1st Inversion

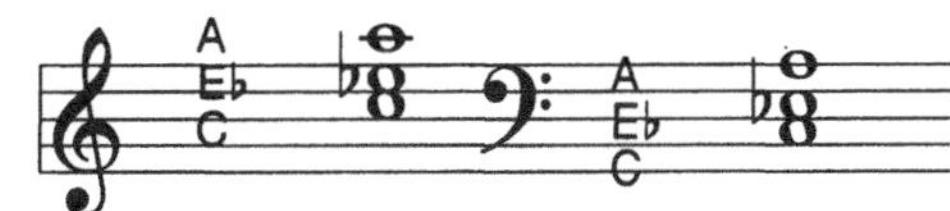

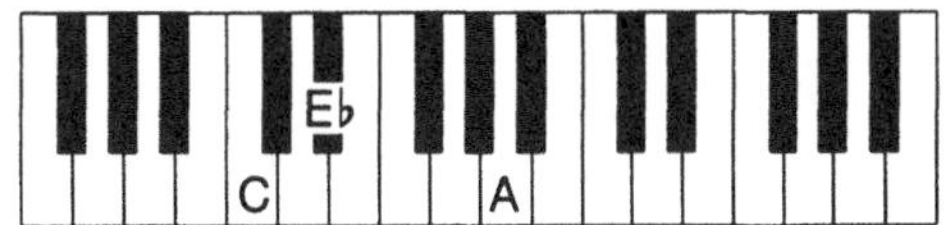

2nd Inversion

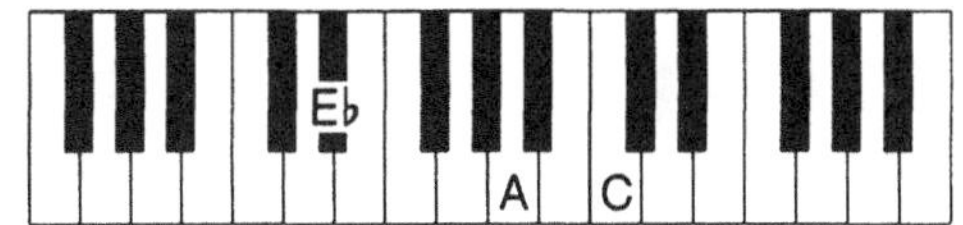

Asus

Root Position

1st Inversion

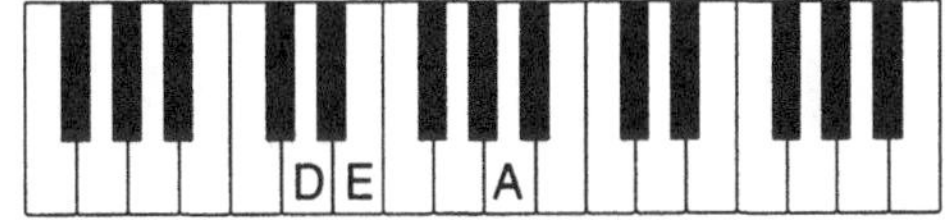

2nd Inversion

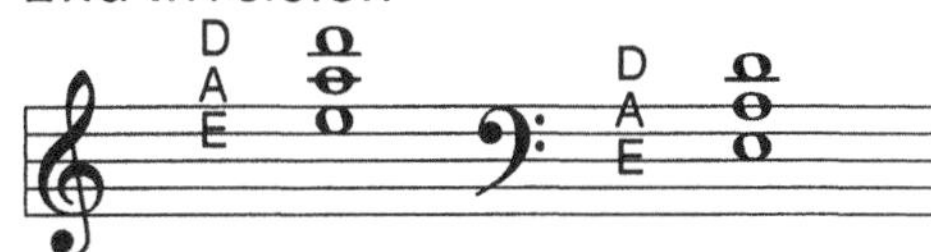

A(♭5)

Root Position

1st Inversion

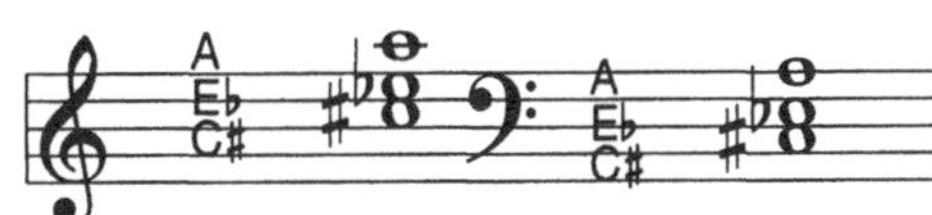

2nd Inversion

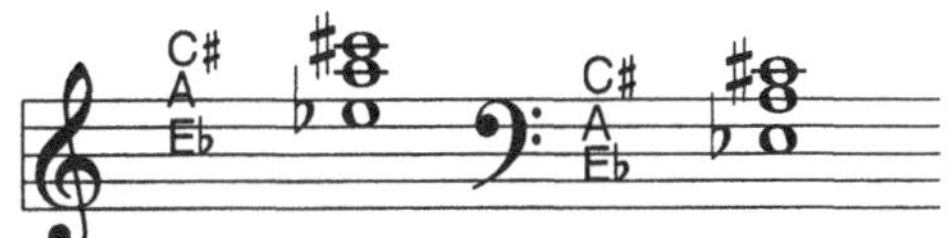

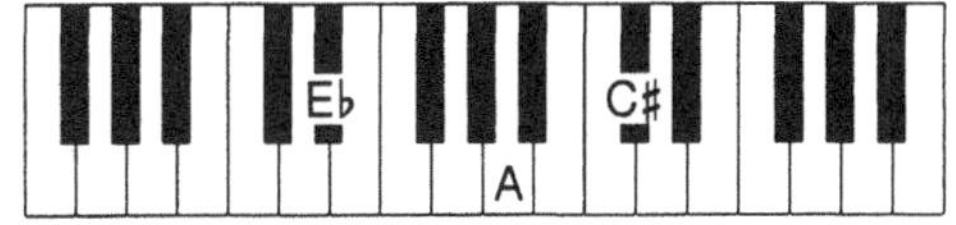

Asus2

Root Position

1st Inversion

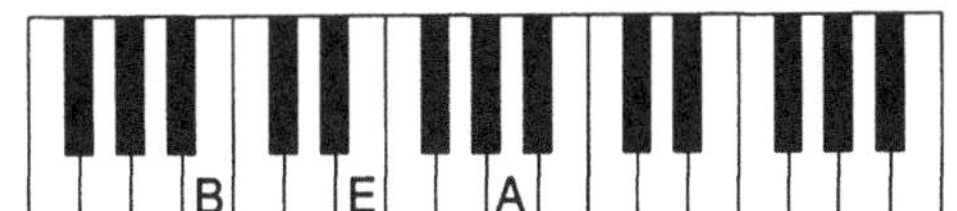

2nd Inversion

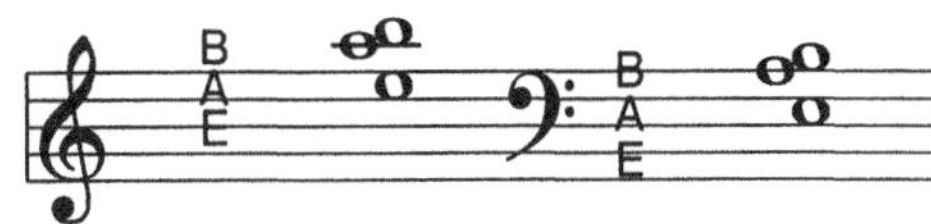

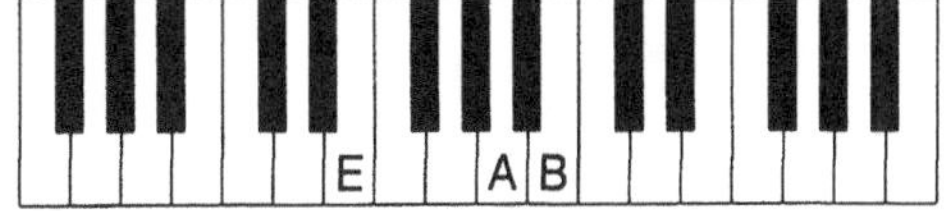

A6

Root Position

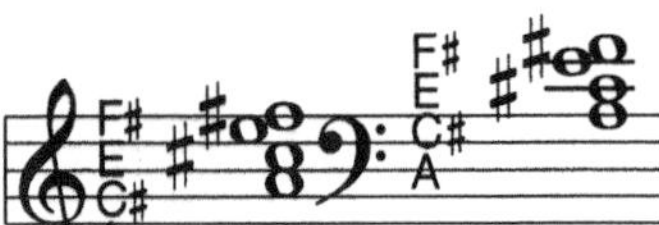

1st Inversion

2nd Inversion

3rd Inversion

A(add2), A(add9)

Root Position

1st Inversion

2nd Inversion

3rd Inversion

Amaj7

Root Position

1st Inversion

2nd Inversion

3rd Inversion

Amaj7♭5

Root Position

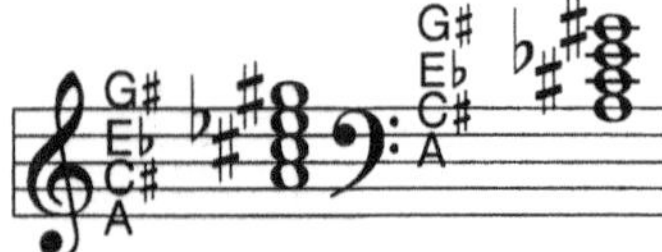

1st Inversion

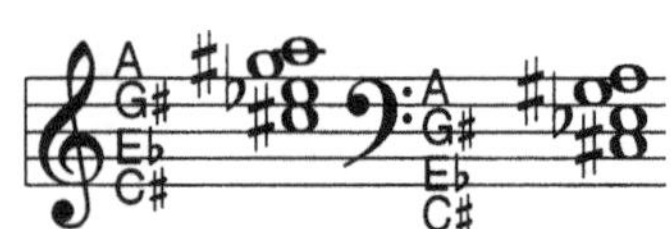

2nd Inversion

3rd Inversion

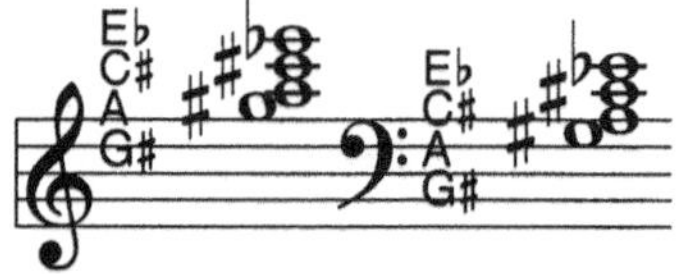

Amaj7♯5

Root Position

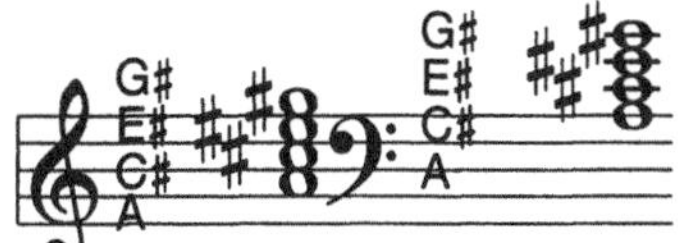

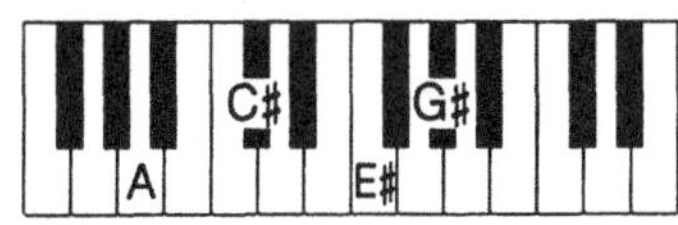

1st Inversion

2nd Inversion

3rd Inversion

A7

Root Position

1st Inversion

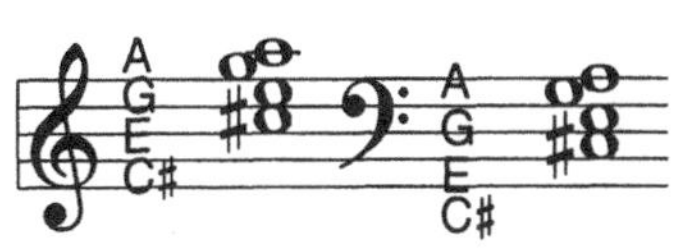

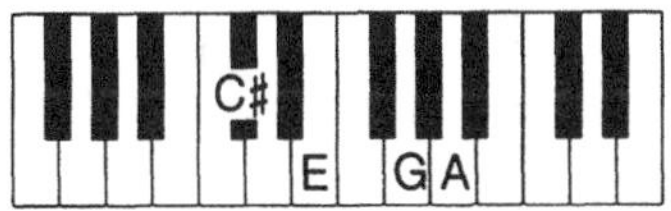

2nd Inversion

3rd Inversion

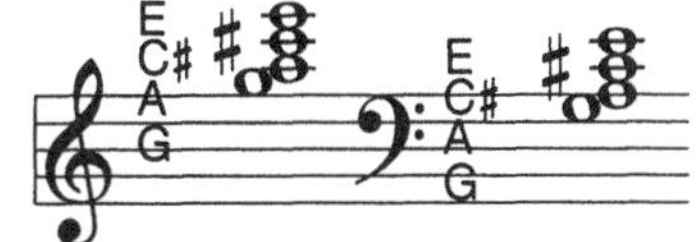

A7♭5

Root Position

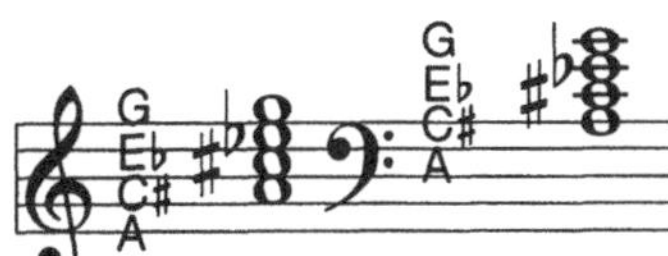

1st Inversion

2nd Inversion

3rd Inversion

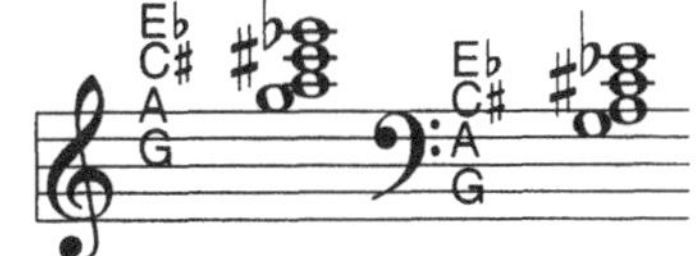

A7♯5

Root Position

1st Inversion

2nd Inversion

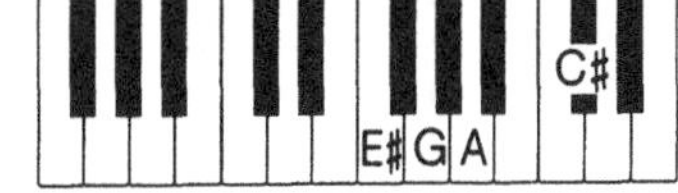

3rd Inversion

A7sus

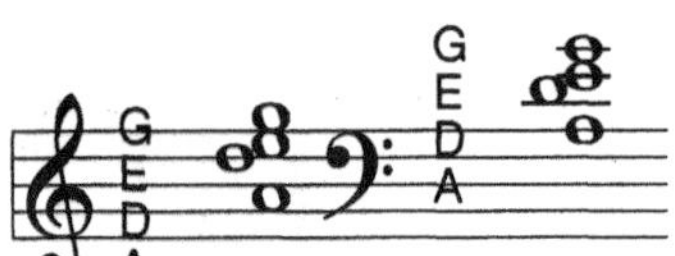

2nd Inversion

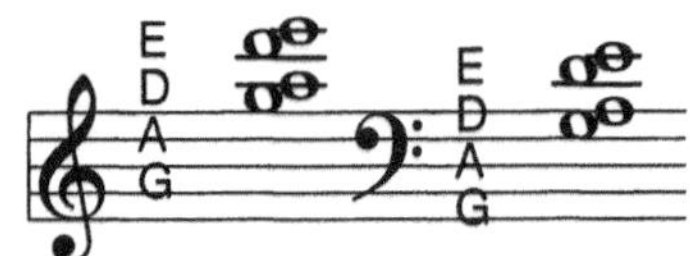

Am(add2), Am(add9)

Root Position

1st Inversion

2nd Inversion

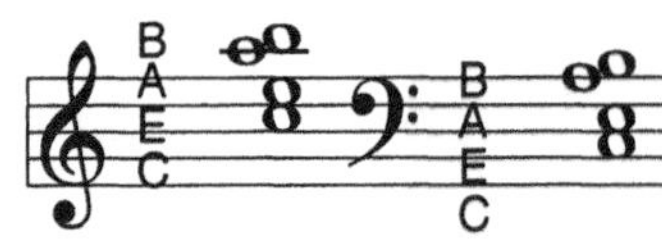

3rd Inversion

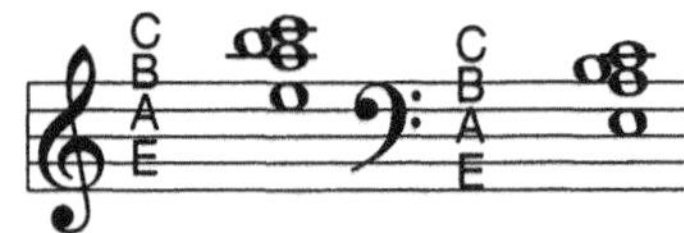

Am6

Root Position

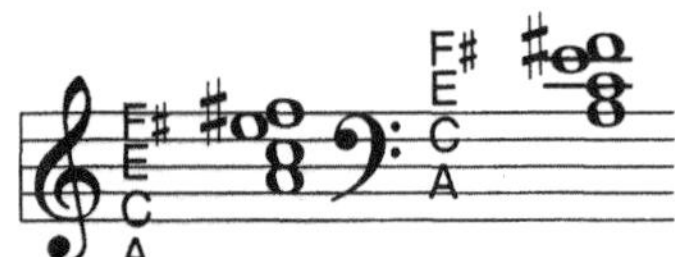

1st Inversion

2nd Inversion

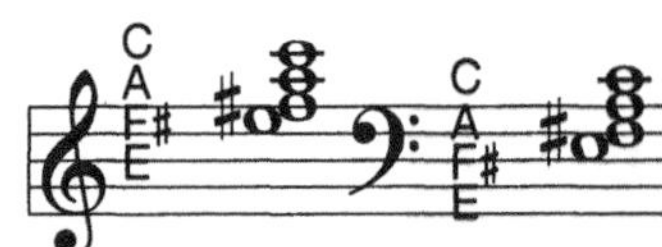

3rd Inversion

Am7

Root Position

1st Inversion

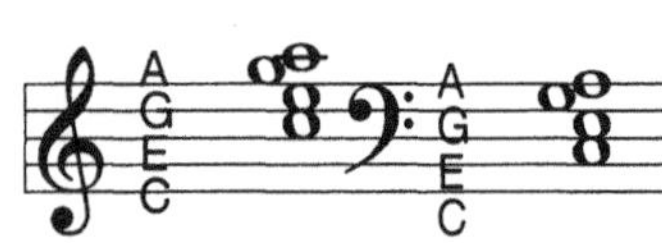

2nd Inversion

3rd Inversion

Am(maj7)

Root Position | 1st Inversion | 2nd Inversion | 3rd Inversion

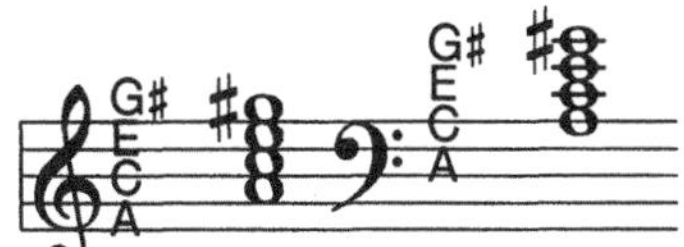

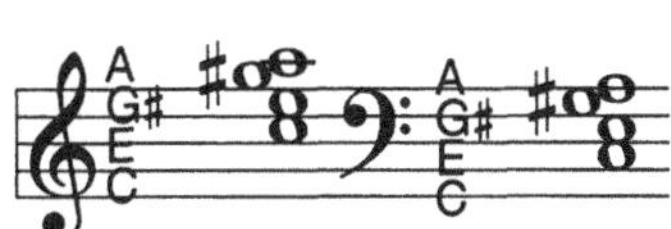

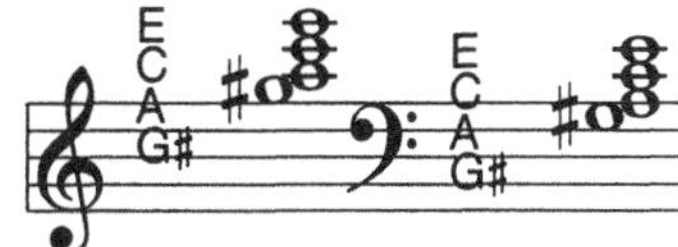

Am7♭5

Root Position | 1st Inversion | 2nd Inversion | 3rd Inversion

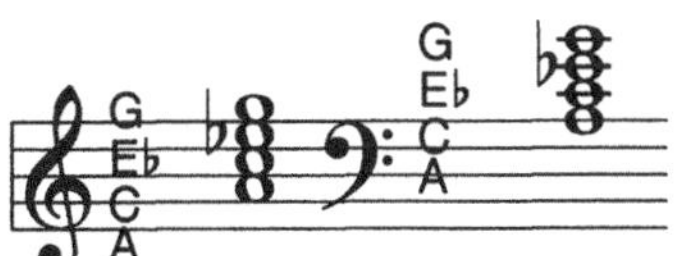

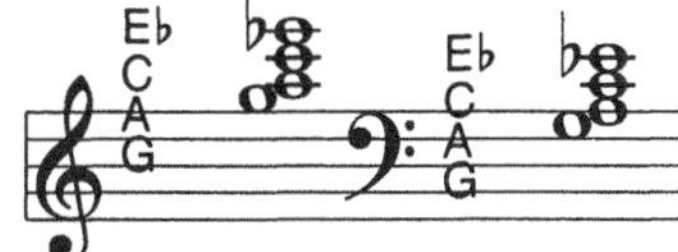

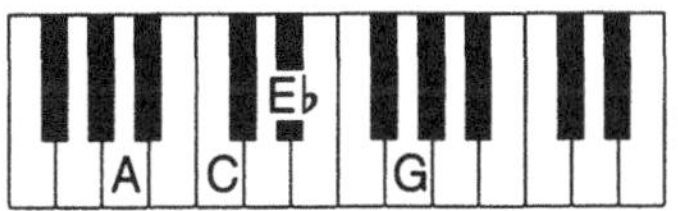

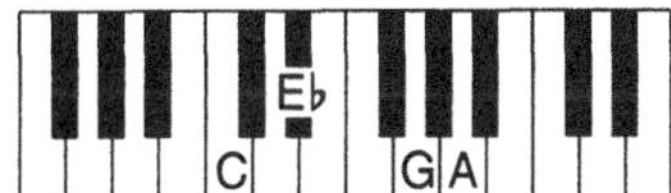

Adim7

Root Position | 1st Inversion | 2nd Inversion | 3rd Inversion

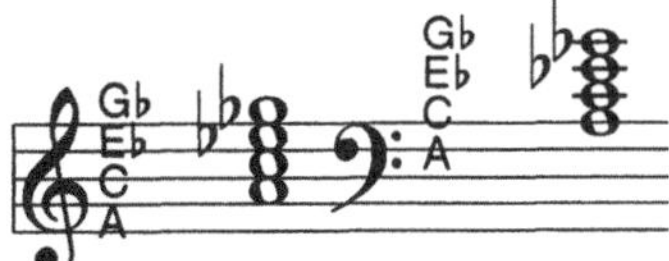

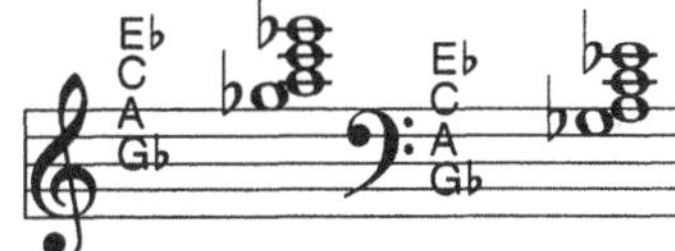

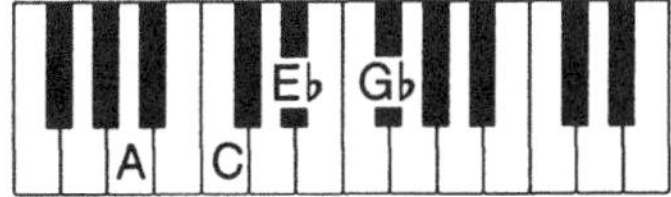

Adim(maj7)

Root Position | 1st Inversion | 2nd Inversion | 3rd Inversion

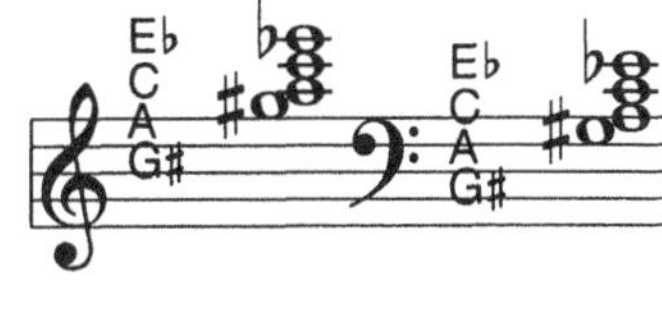

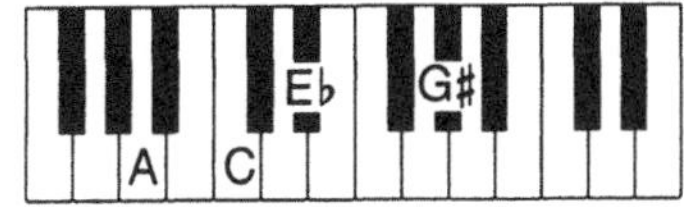

ADDITIONAL A CHORDS

A5

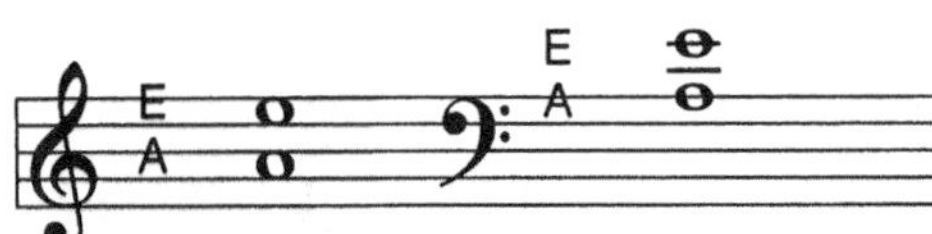

A$\frac{6}{9}$

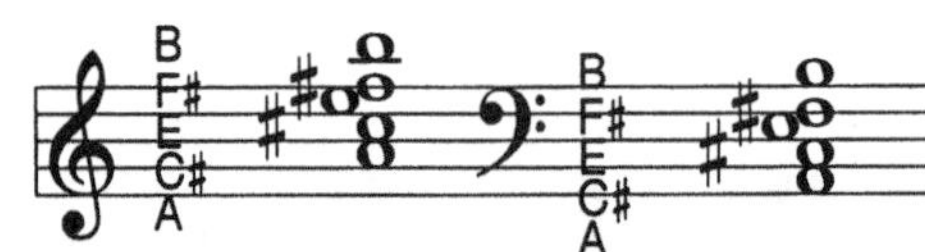

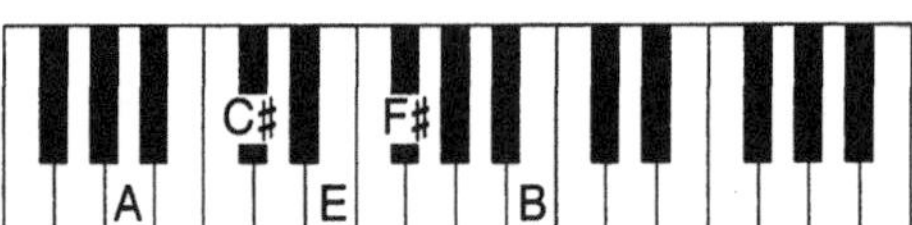

Amaj$\frac{6}{9}$

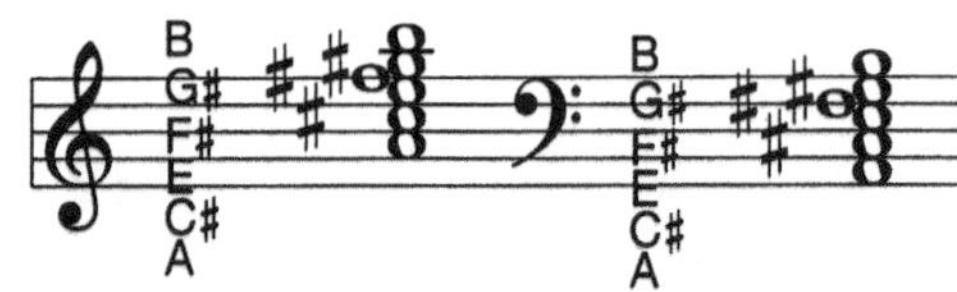

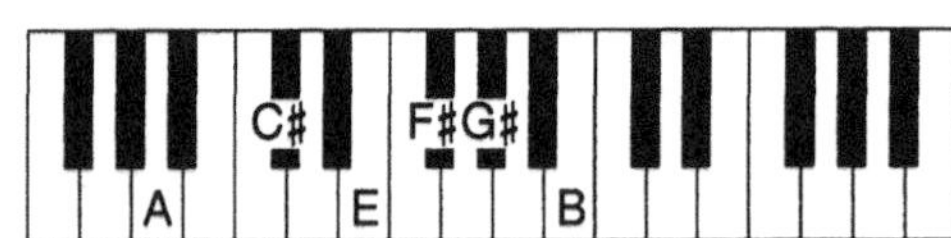

Amaj7♯11

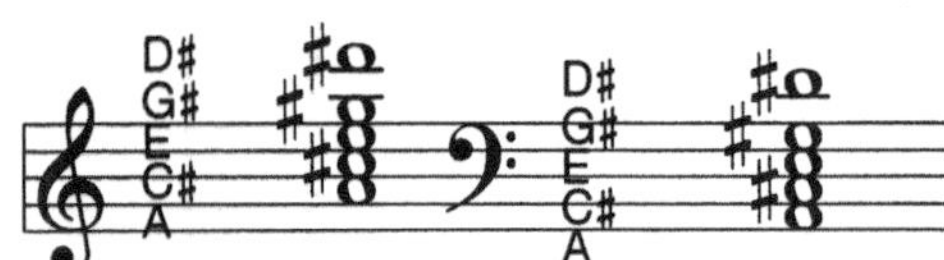

Amaj9

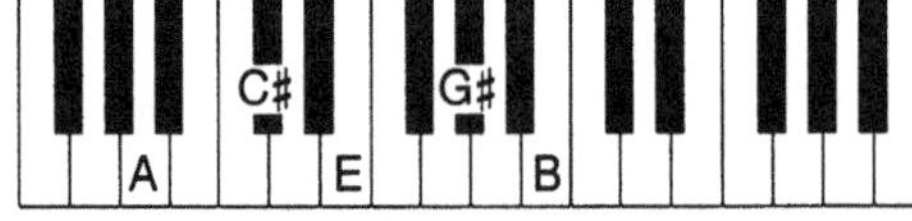

Amaj9♭5

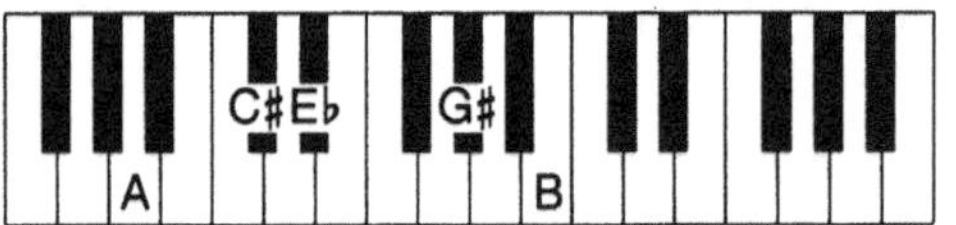

Amaj9♯5

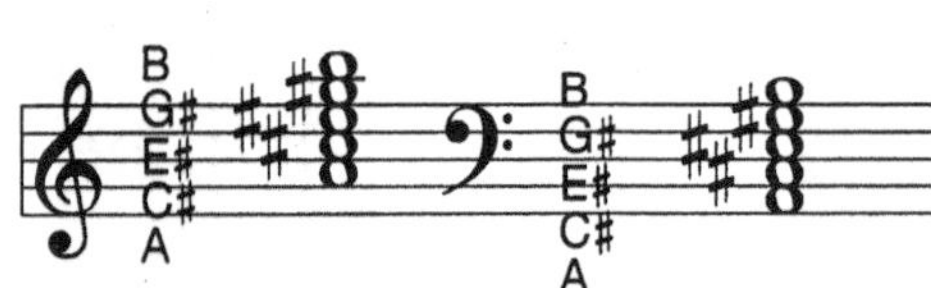

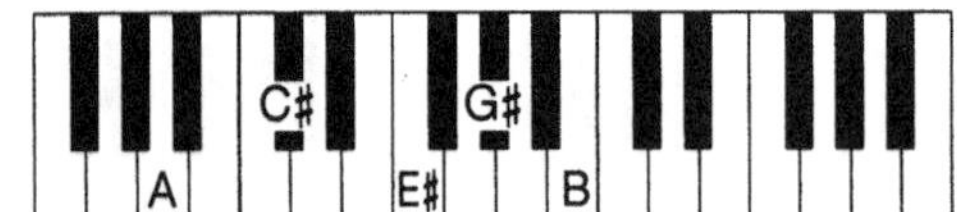

Amaj9♯11

Amaj13

Amaj13♭5

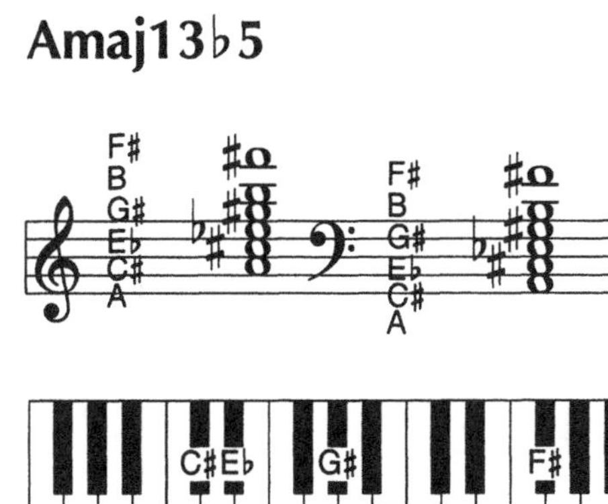

Amaj13♯11

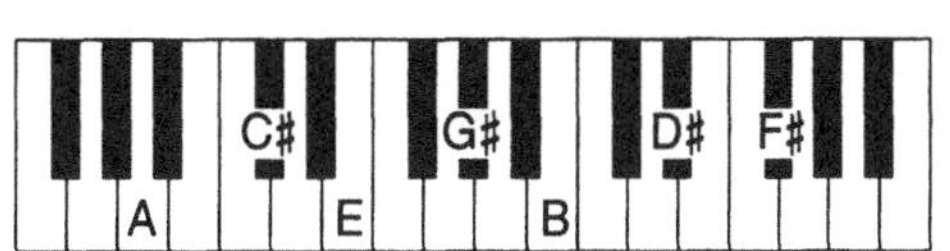

A7♭9

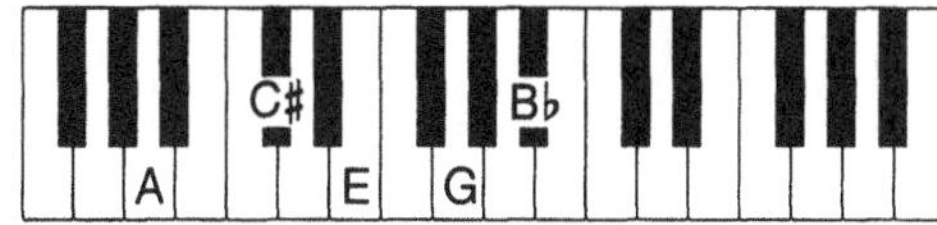

A7♯9

A7♯11

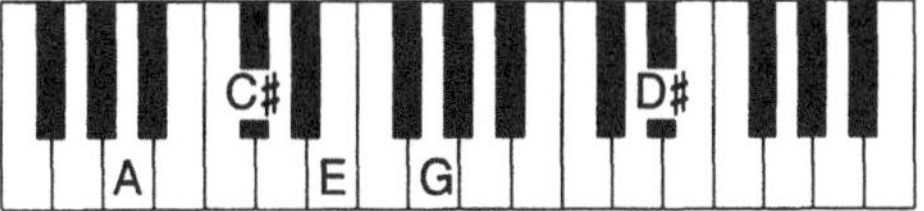

A7♭5(♭9)

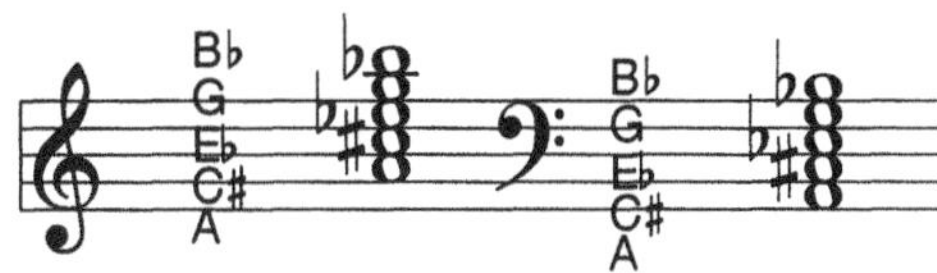

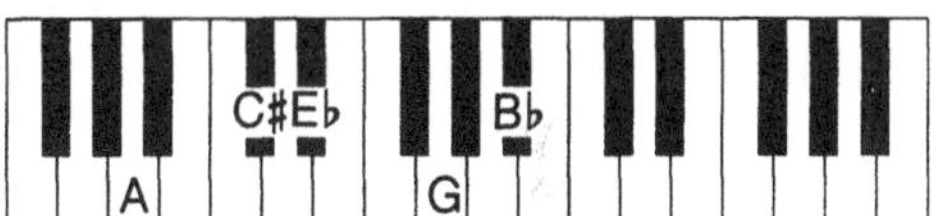

A7♭5(♯9)

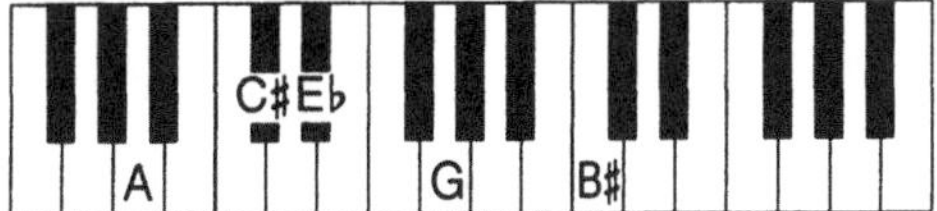

A7♯5(♭9)

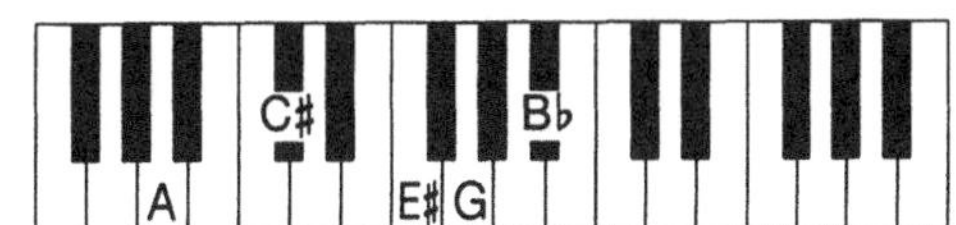

A7♯5(♯9)

A7♭9(♯9)

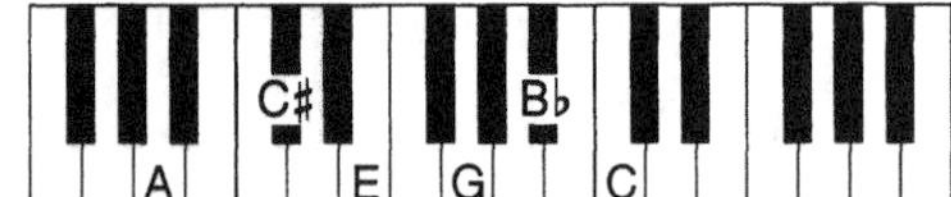

A7(add13)

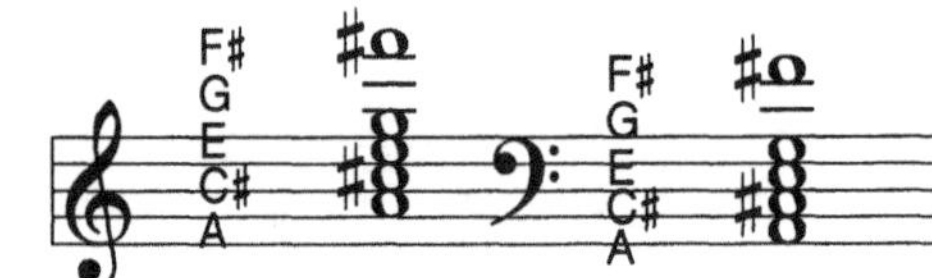

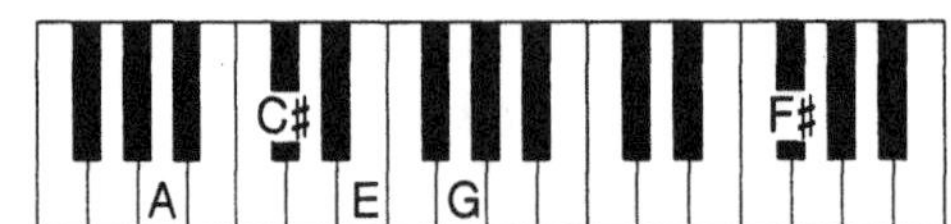

A7♭13

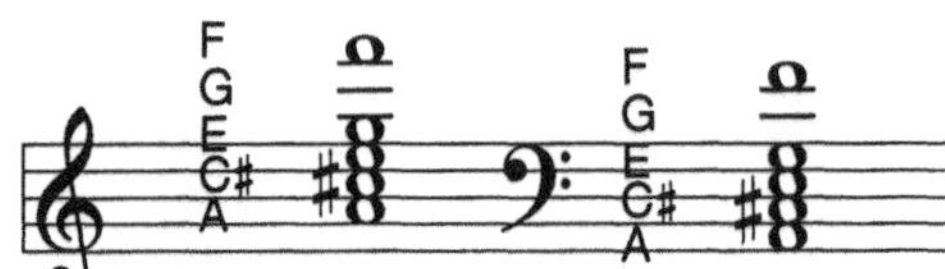

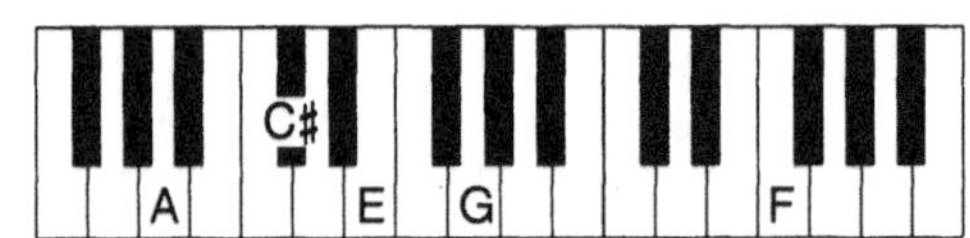

A7♭9(♯11)

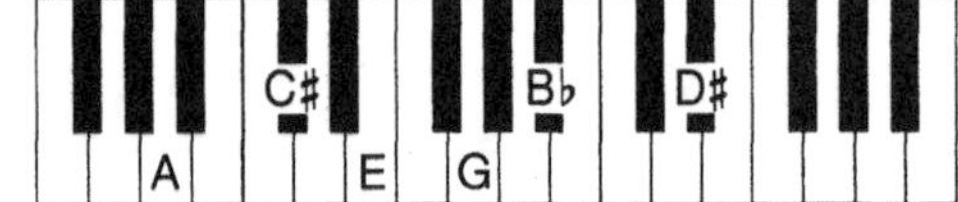

A7♯9(♯11)

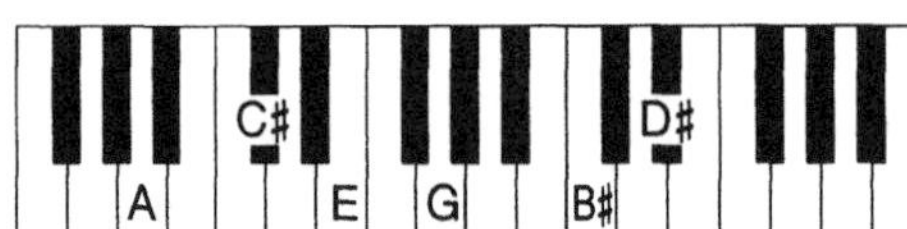

A7♭9(♭13)

C♯ B♭ A E G F

A7♯9(♭13)

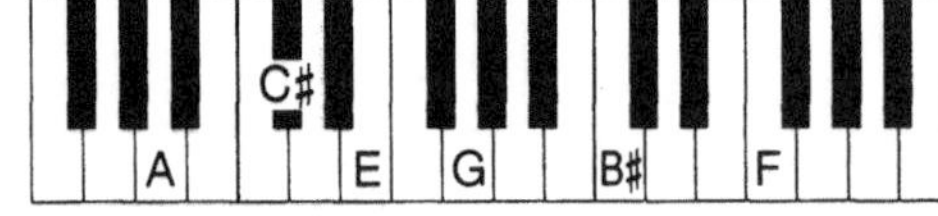

A7♯11(♭13)

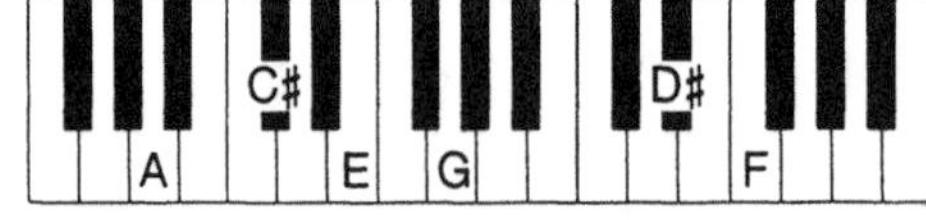

A7♭9(♯9,♯11)

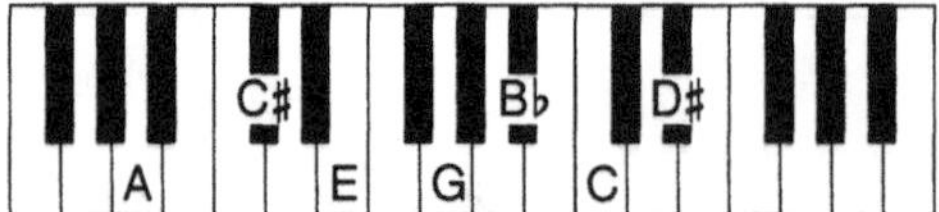

A9

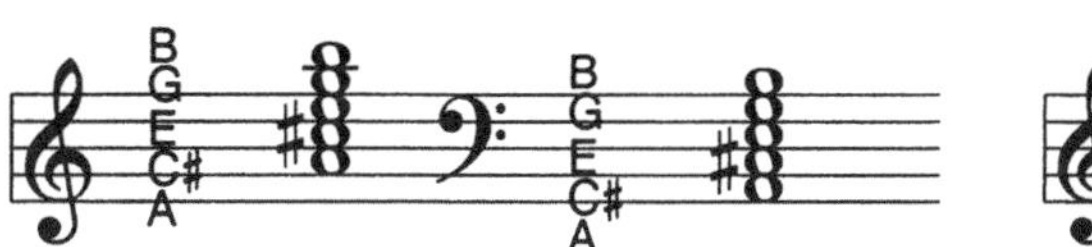

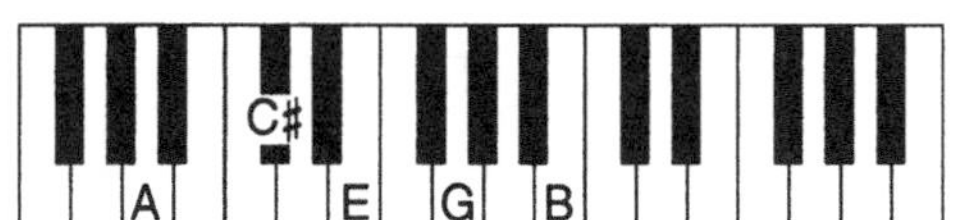

A9(♭5)

A9♯5

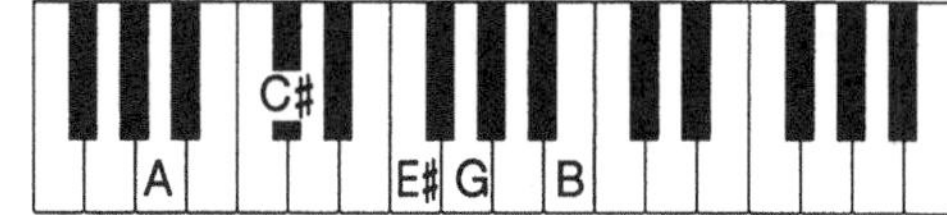

A9♯11

A9♭13

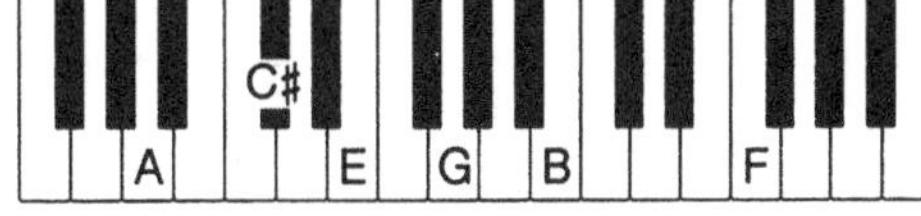

A9♯11(♭13)

A11, A9sus4

A13

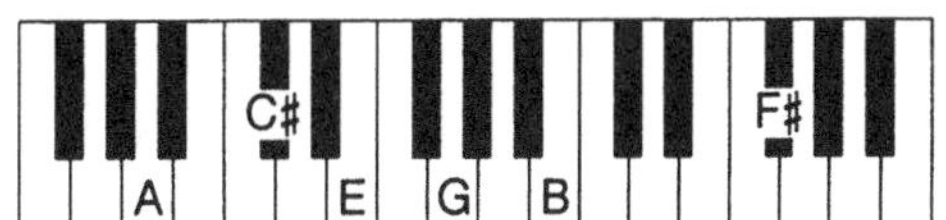

A13♭5

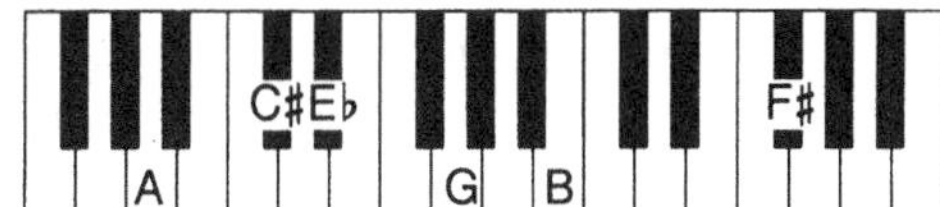

A13♭9

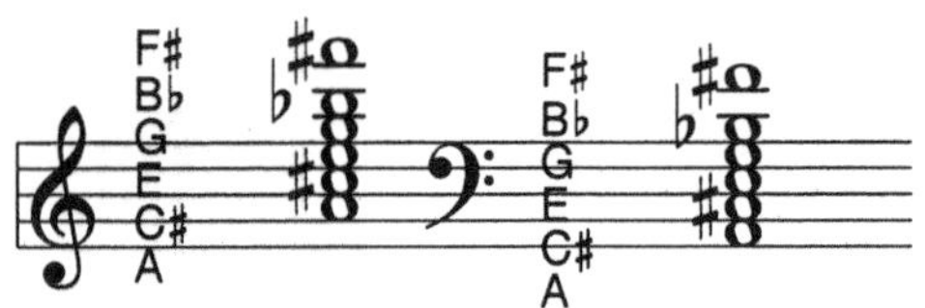

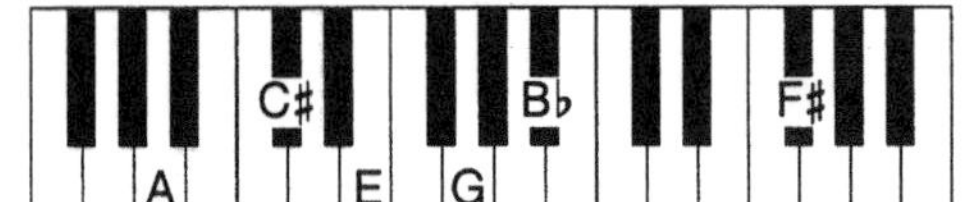

A13♯9

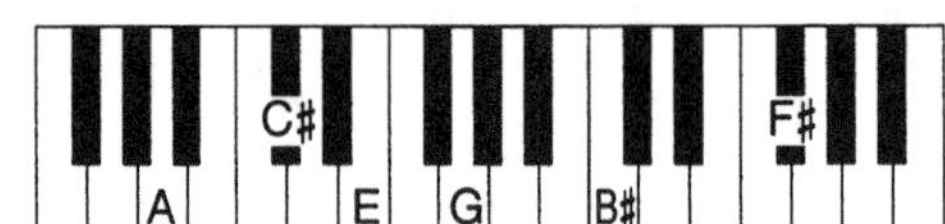

A13♯11

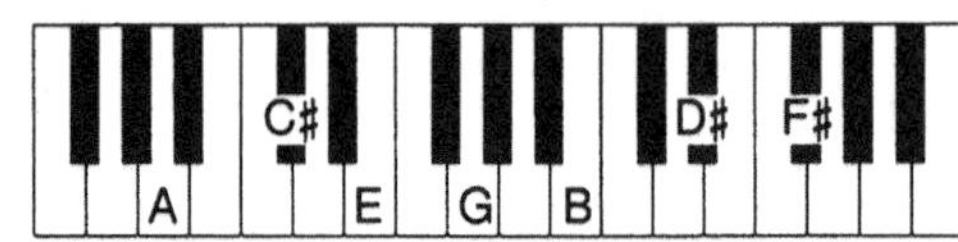

A13(sus4)

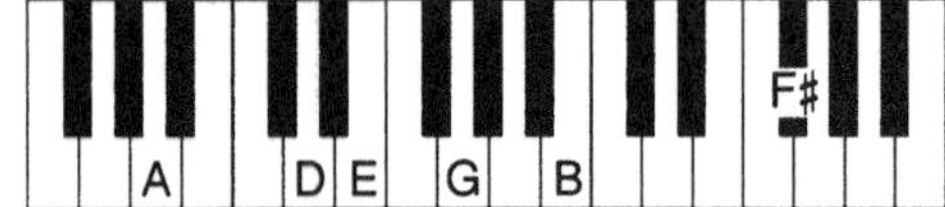

Am(♯5)

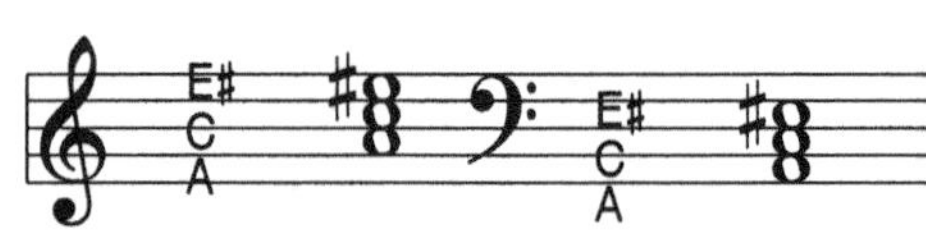

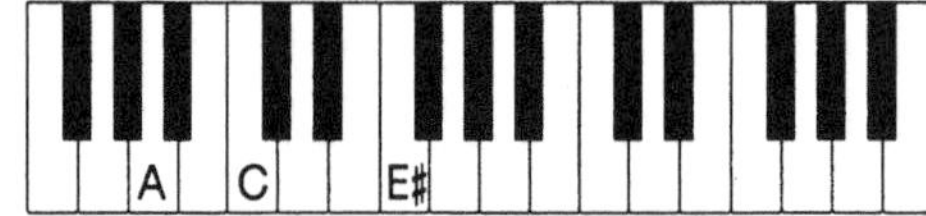

Am$^{6}_{9}$

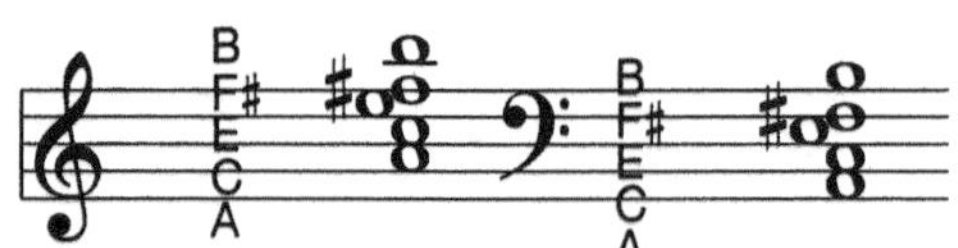

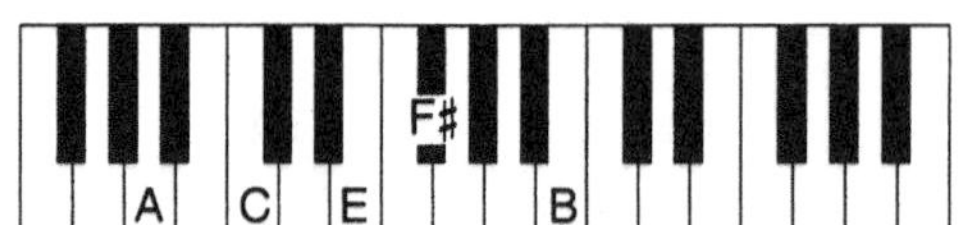

Am7(add4)

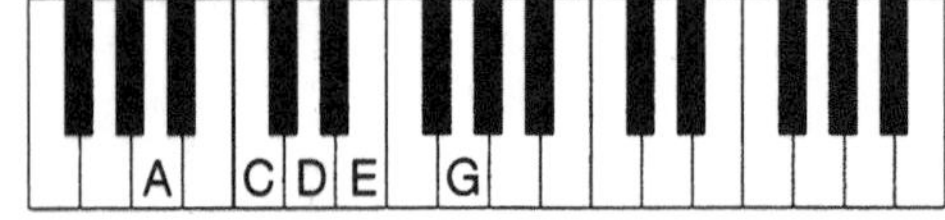

Am7(add11)

Am7♭5(♭9)

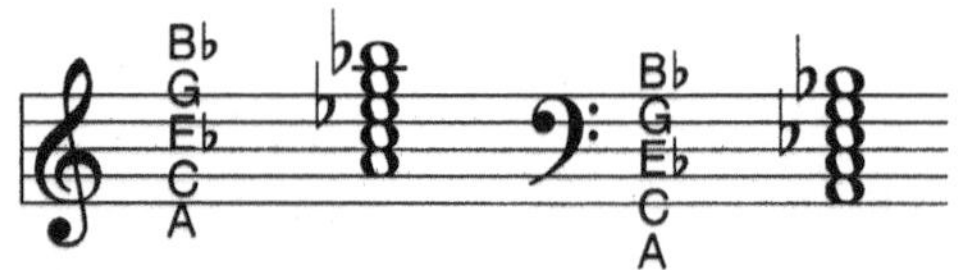

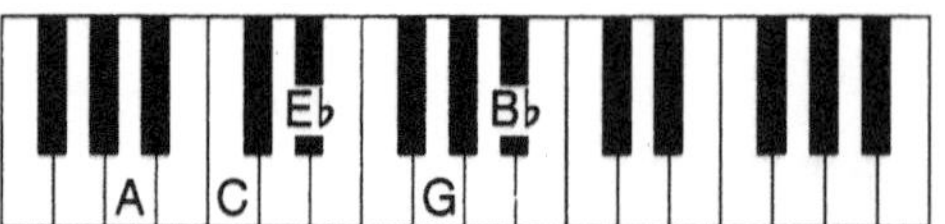

Am9

Am9(maj7)

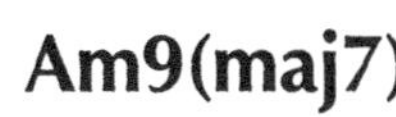

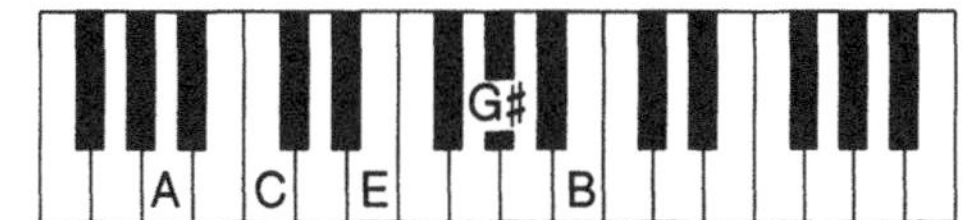

Am9♭5

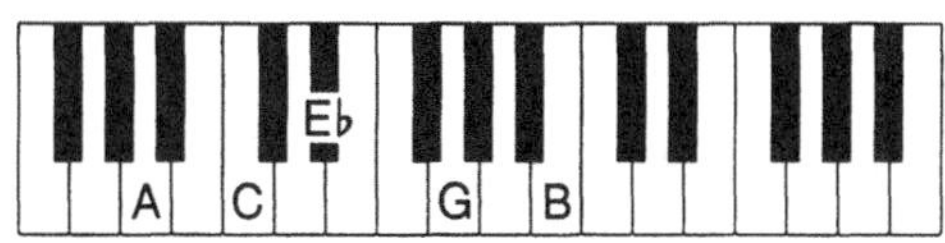

Am11

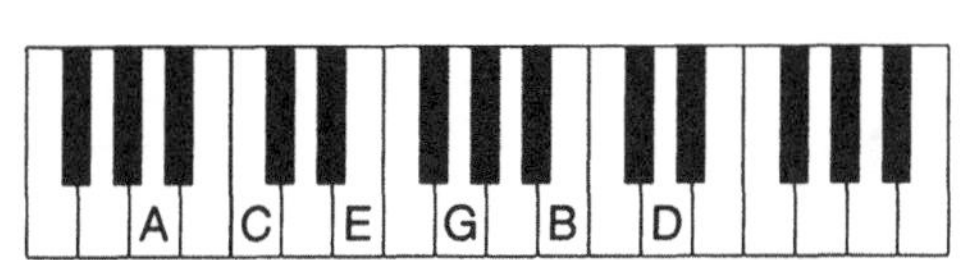

Am13

Adim7(add9)

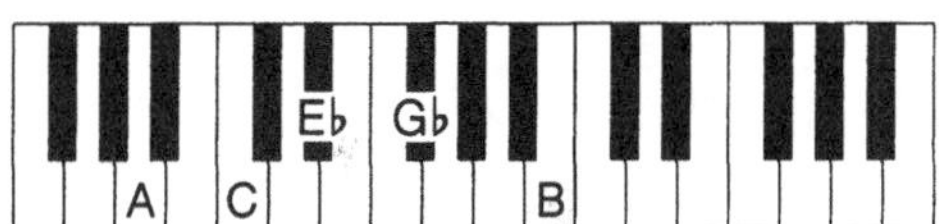

Am11♭5

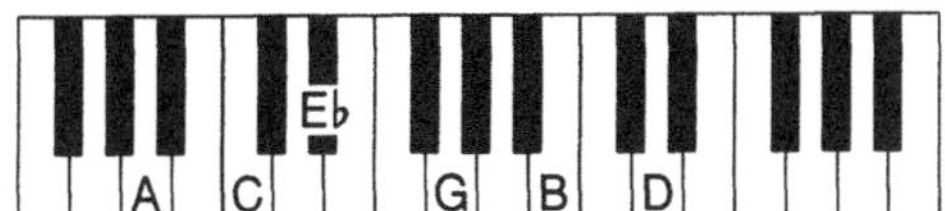

Am11(maj7)

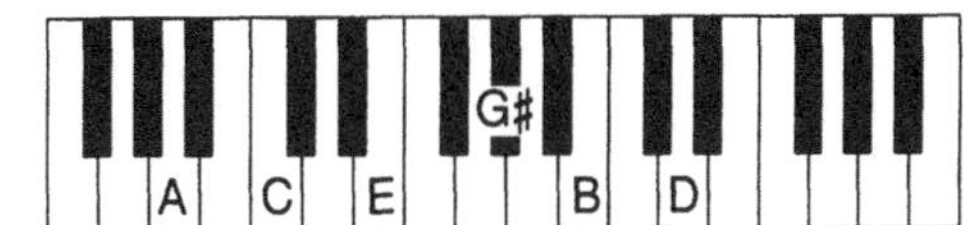

A7alt.

B♭ CHORDS

B♭

Root Position

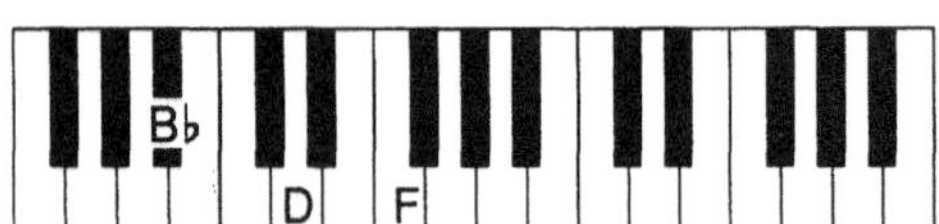

1st Inversion

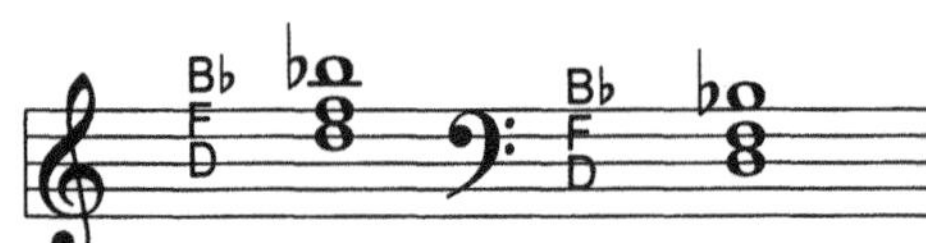

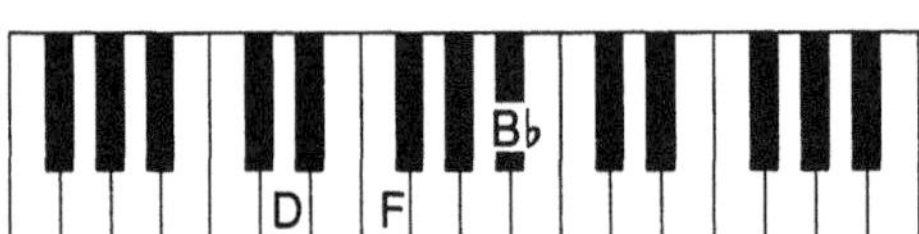

2nd Inversion

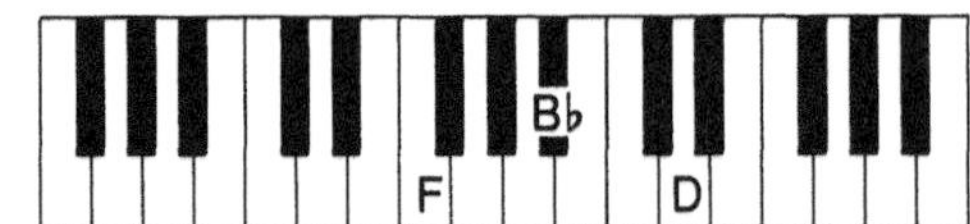

B♭m

Root Position

1st Inversion

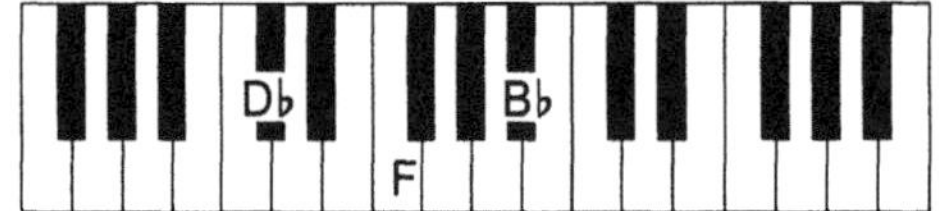

2nd Inversion

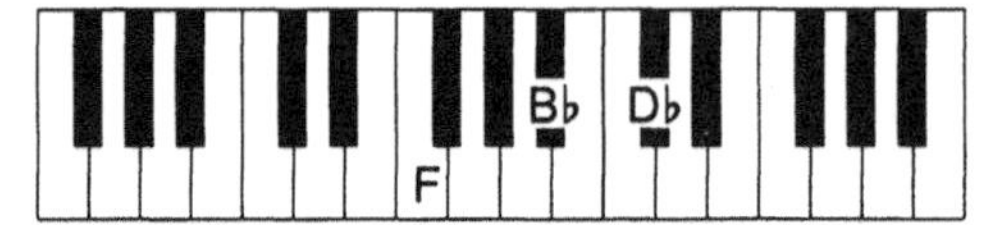

B♭+

Root Position

1st Inversion

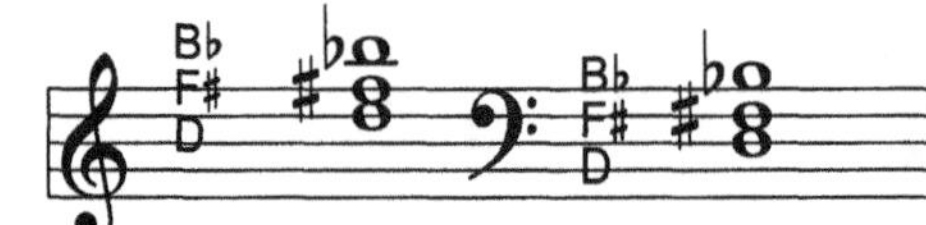

2nd Inversion

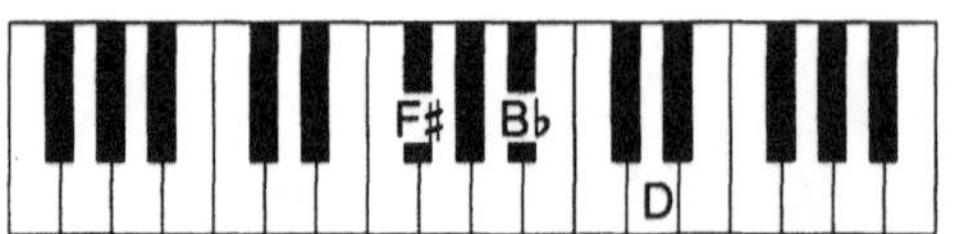

B♭dim

Root Position

1st Inversion

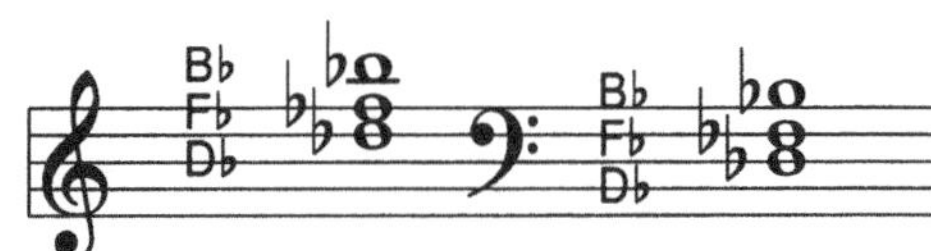

2nd Inversion

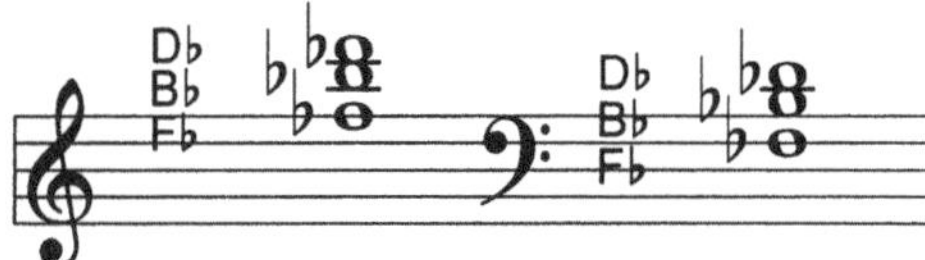

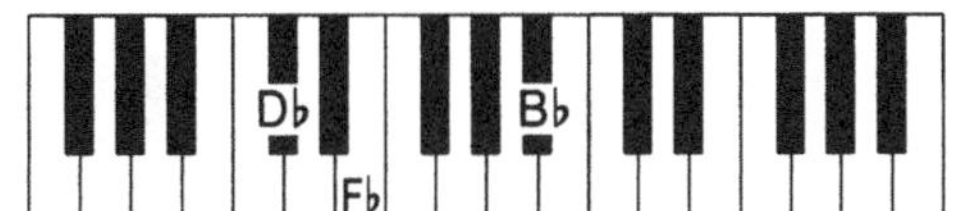

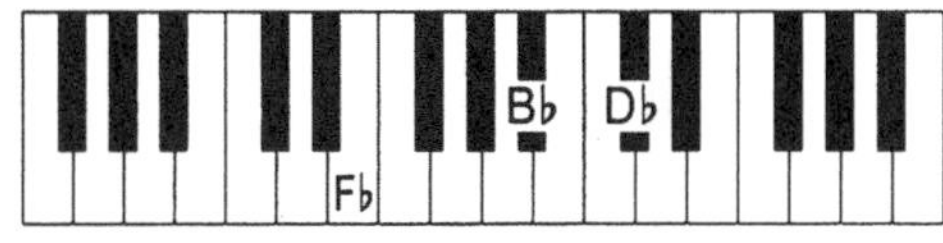

B♭sus

Root Position

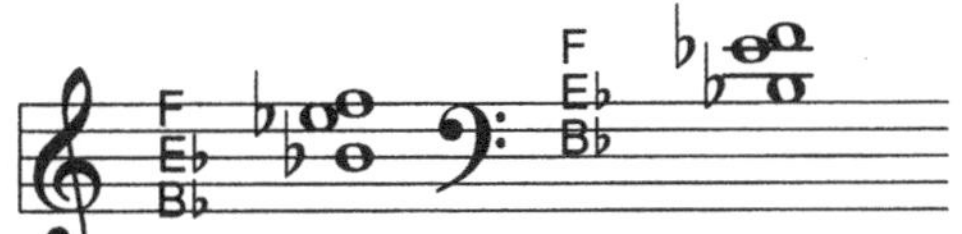

1st Inversion

2nd Inversion

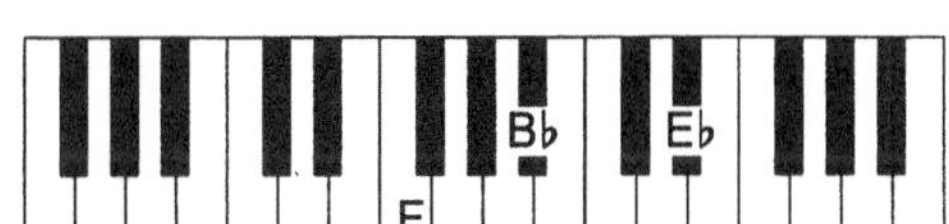

B♭(♭5)

Root Position

1st Inversion

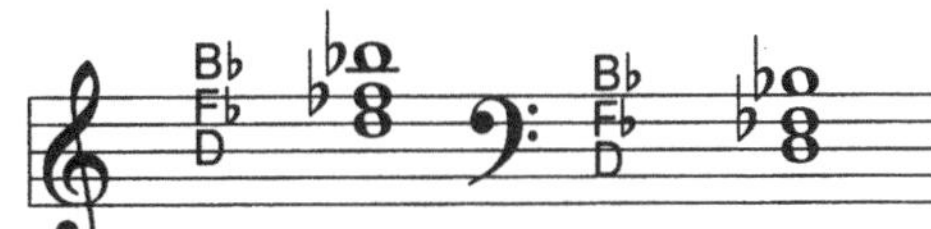

2nd Inversion

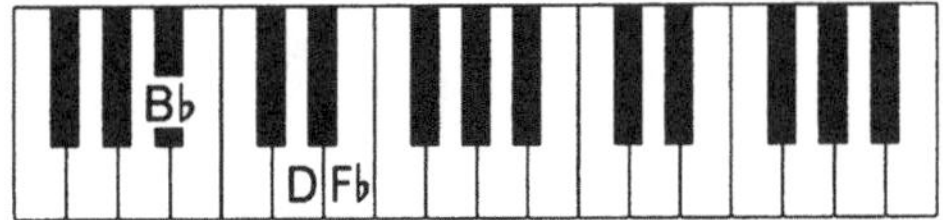

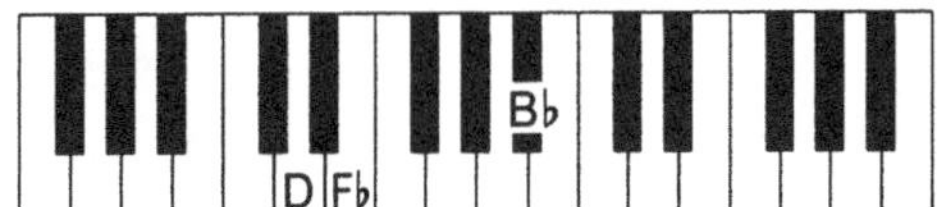

B♭sus2

Root Position

1st Inversion

2nd Inversion

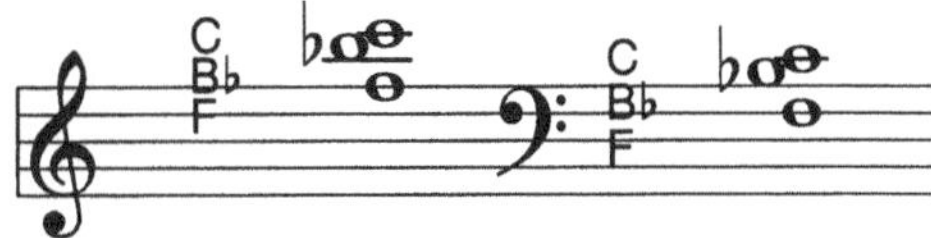

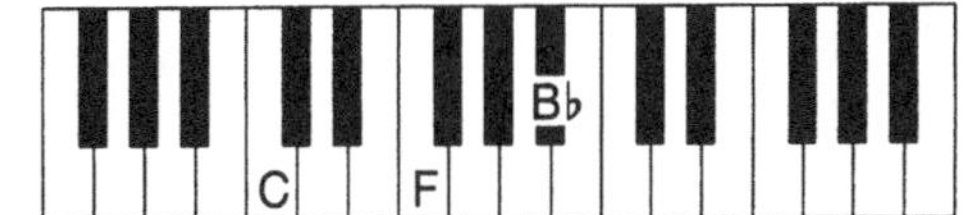

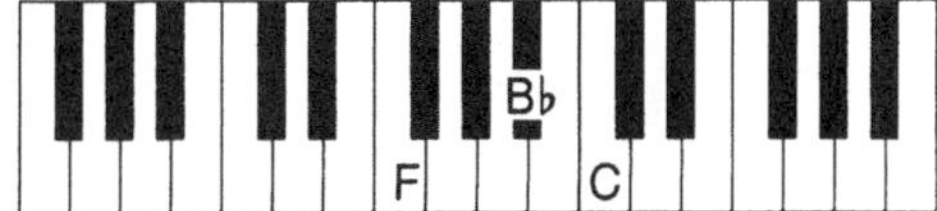

B♭6

Root Position

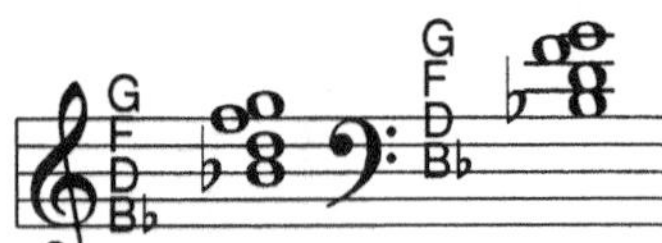

1st Inversion

2nd Inversion

3rd Inversion

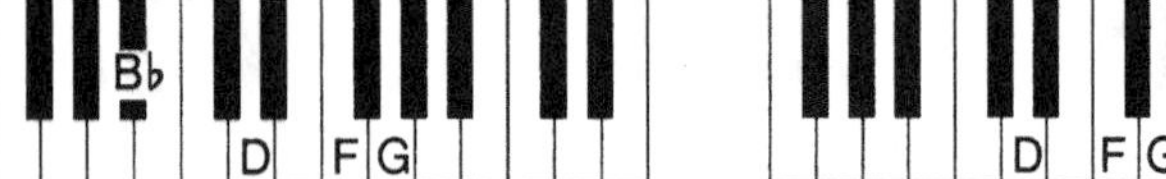

B♭(add2), B♭(add9)

Root Position

1st Inversion

2nd Inversion

3rd Inversion

B♭
D
F
C

B♭maj7

Root Position

1st Inversion

2nd Inversion

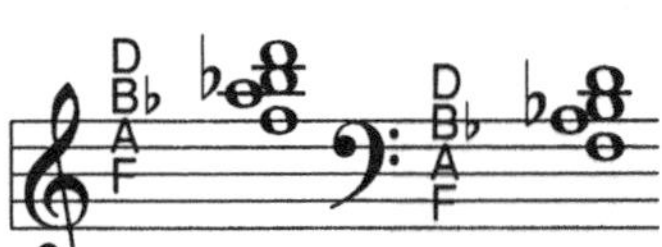

3rd Inversion

B♭
F
A
D

B♭
A
D
F

B♭maj7♭5

Root Position

1st Inversion

2nd Inversion

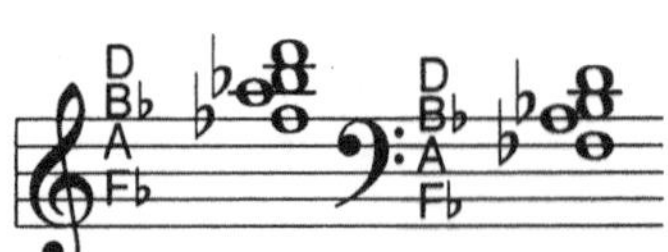

3rd Inversion

B♭
F♭
A
D

B♭
A
D
F♭

B♭maj7♯5

Root Position | 1st Inversion | 2nd Inversion | 3rd Inversion

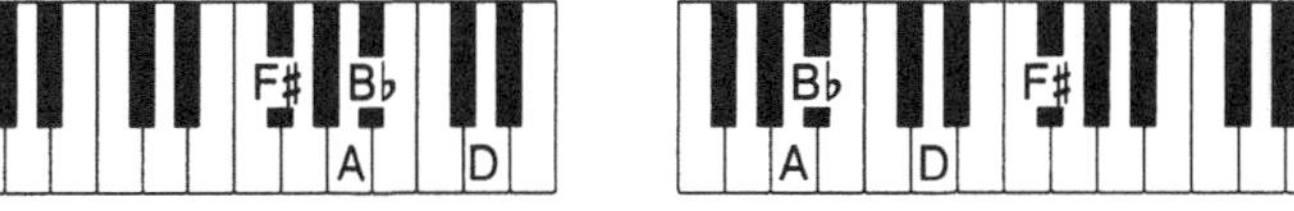

B♭7

Root Position | 1st Inversion | 2nd Inversion | 3rd Inversion

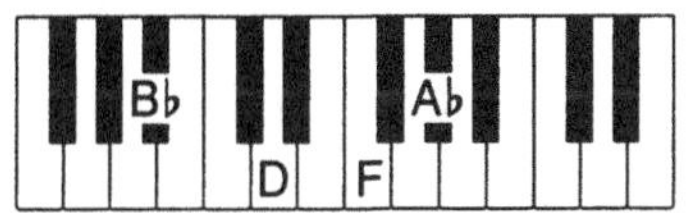

B♭7♭5

Root Position | 1st Inversion | 2nd Inversion | 3rd Inversion

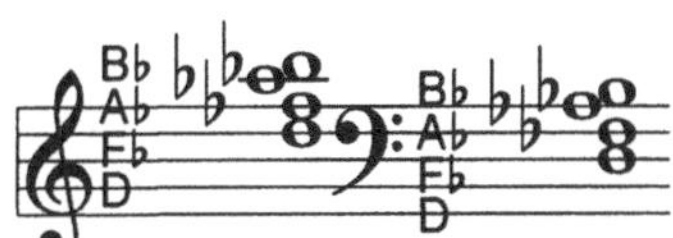

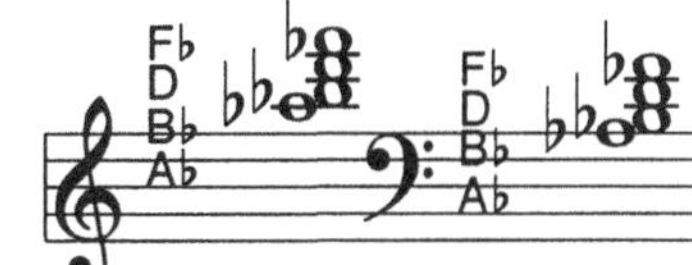

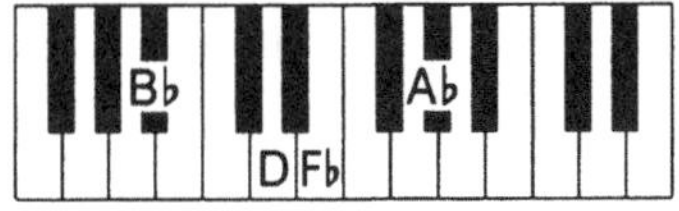

B♭7♯5

Root Position | 1st Inversion | 2nd Inversion | 3rd Inversion

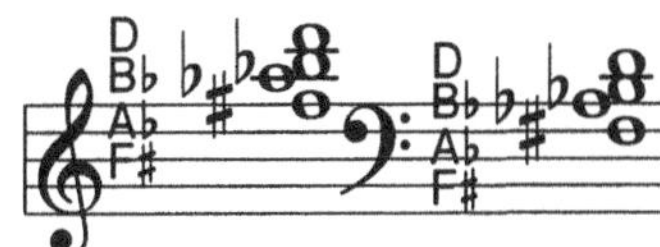

B♭7sus

Root Position | 1st Inversion | 2nd Inversion | 3rd Inversion

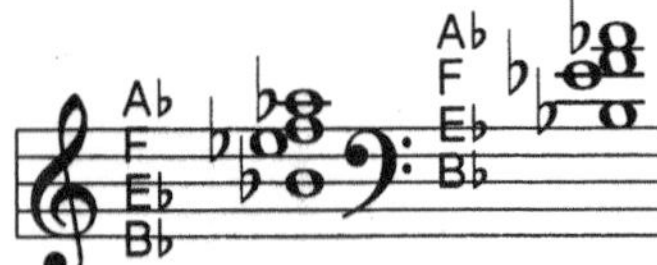

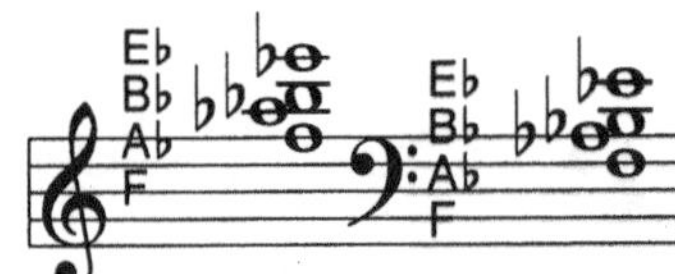

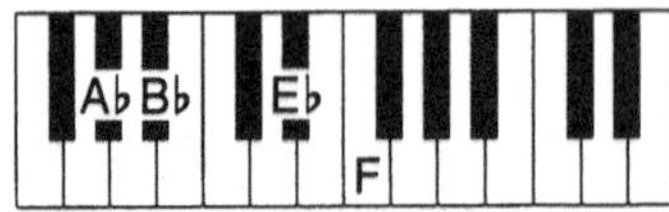

B♭m(add2), B♭m(add9)

Root Position | 1st Inversion | 2nd Inversion | 3rd Inversion

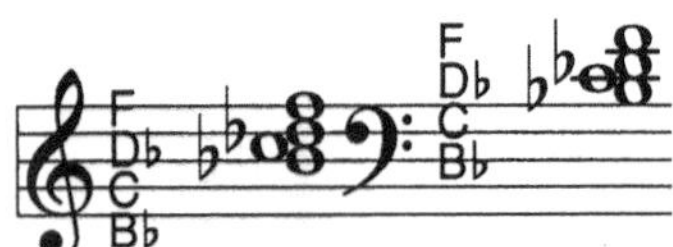

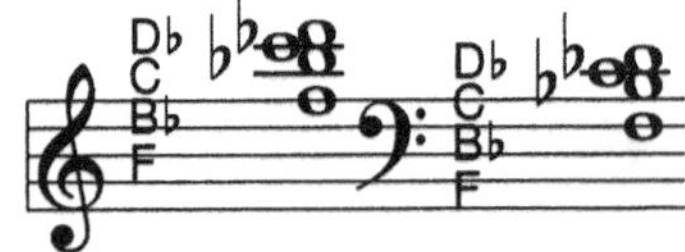

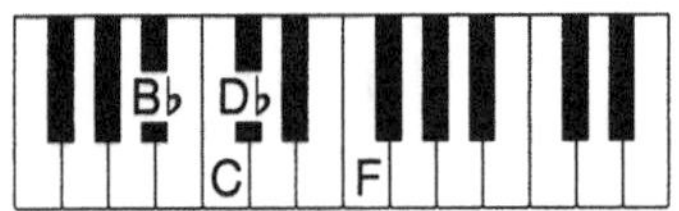

B♭m6

Root Position | 1st Inversion | 2nd Inversion | 3rd Inversion

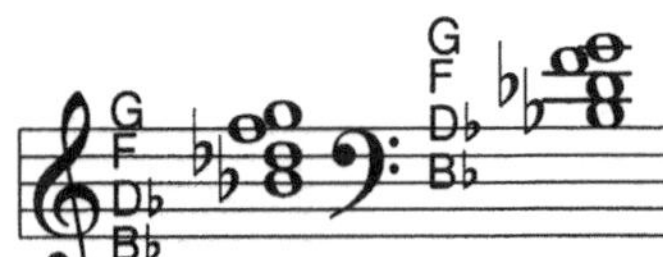

B♭m7

Root Position | 1st Inversion | 2nd Inversion | 3rd Inversion

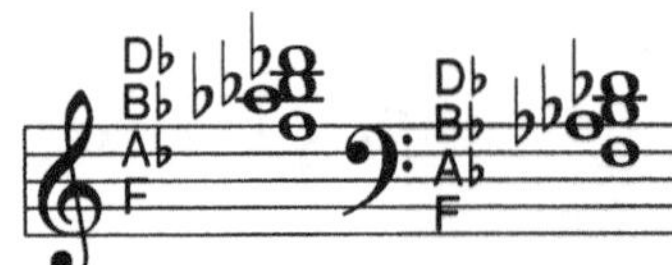

B♭m(maj7)

Root Position

1st Inversion

2nd Inversion

3rd Inversion

B♭ D♭ F A

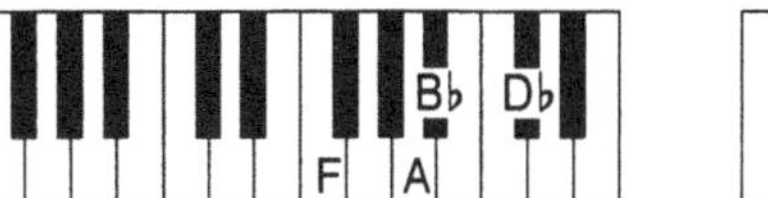

B♭m7♭5

Root Position

1st Inversion

2nd Inversion

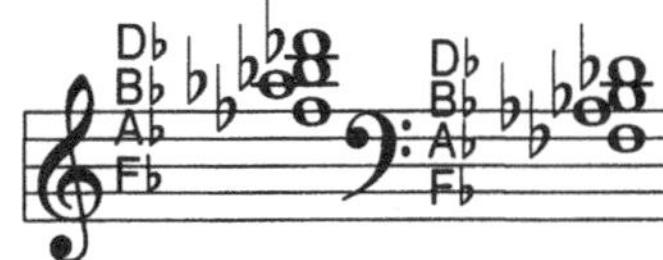

3rd Inversion

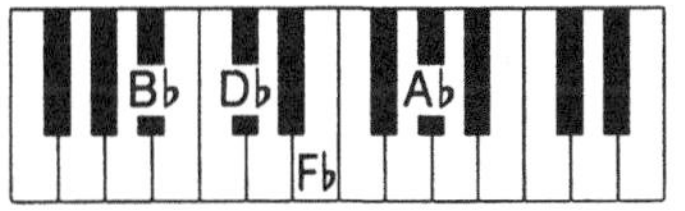

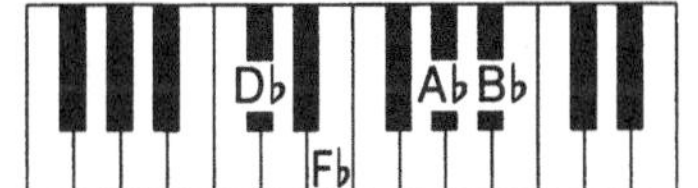

A♭ B♭ D♭ F♭

A♭ B♭ D♭ F♭

B♭dim7

Root Position

1st Inversion

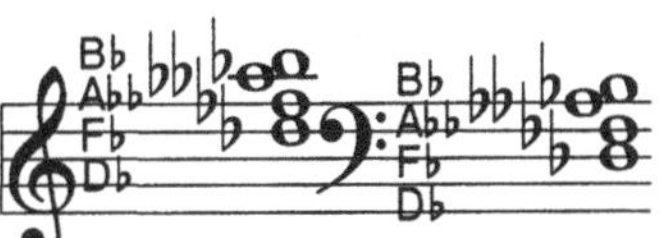

2nd Inversion

3rd Inversion

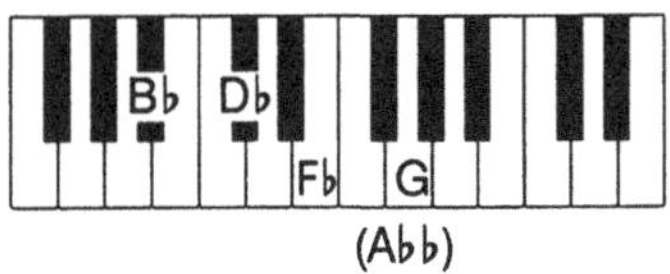

D♭ B♭ F♭ G (A♭♭)

B♭ D♭ F♭ G (A♭♭)

B♭ D♭ G F♭ (A♭♭)

B♭dim(maj7)

Root Position

1st Inversion

2nd Inversion

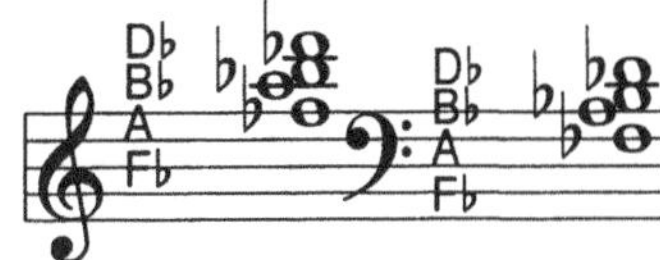

3rd Inversion

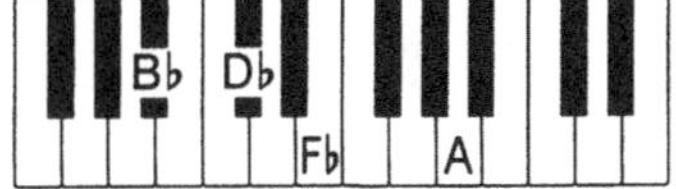

ADDITIONAL B♭ CHORDS

B♭5

B♭$^{6}_{9}$

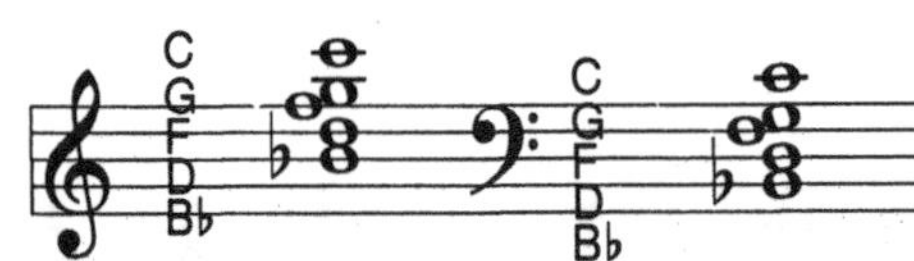

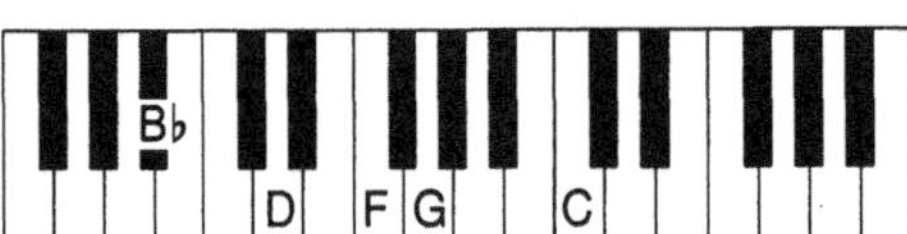

B♭maj$^{6}_{9}$

B♭maj7♯11

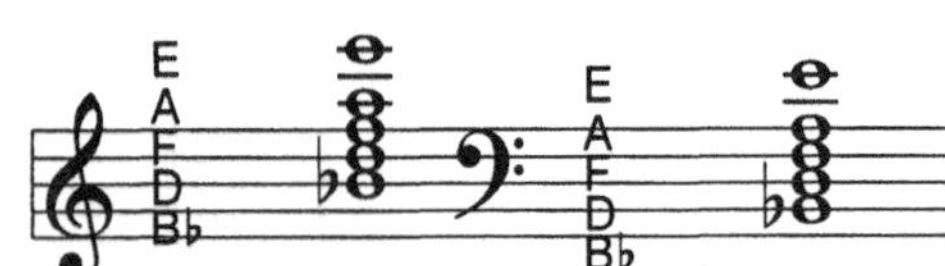

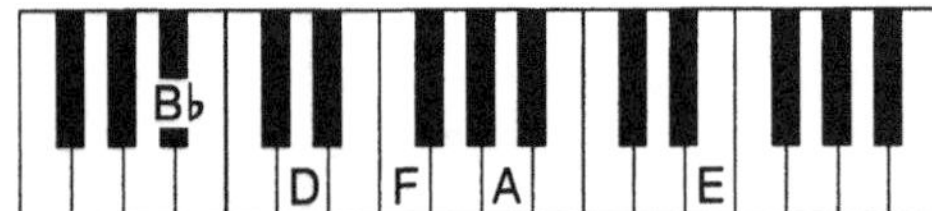

B♭maj9

B♭maj9♭5

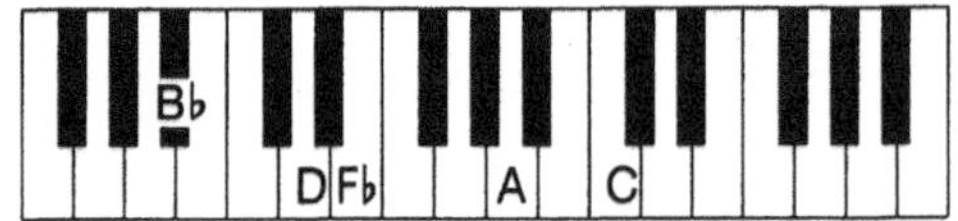

B♭maj9♯5

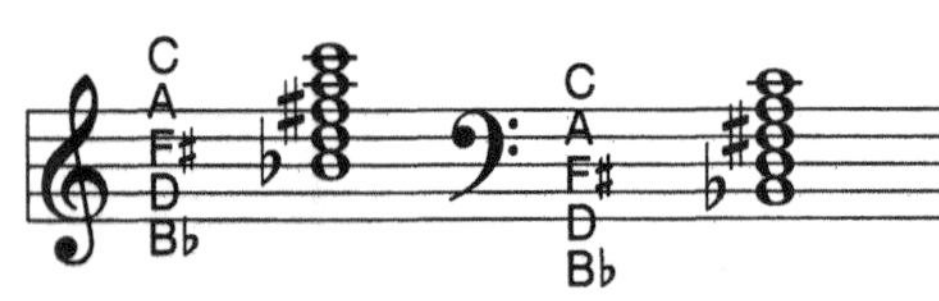

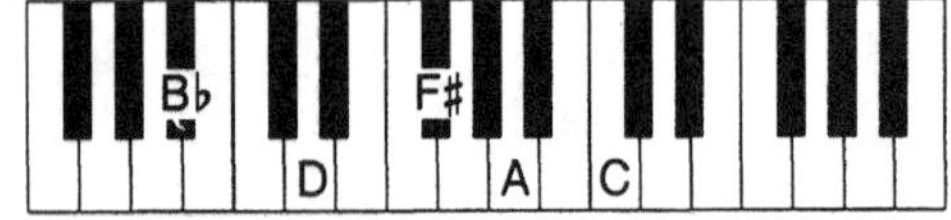

B♭maj9♯11

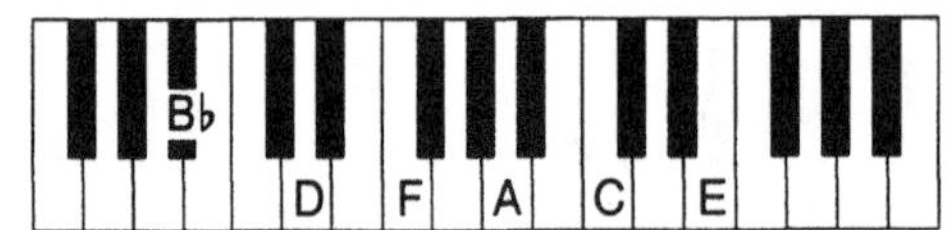

B♭maj13

B♭maj13♭5

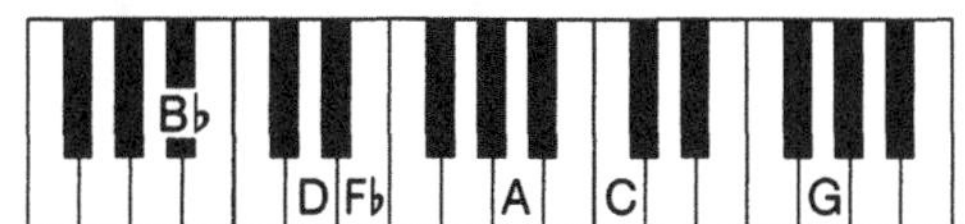

B♭maj13♯11

B♭7♭9

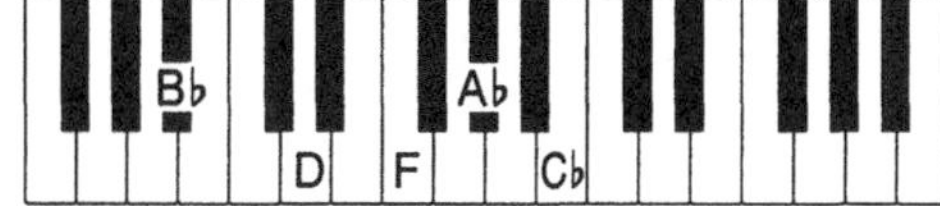

B♭7♯9

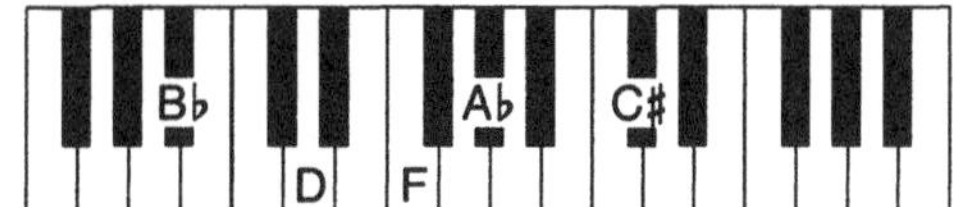

B♭7♯11

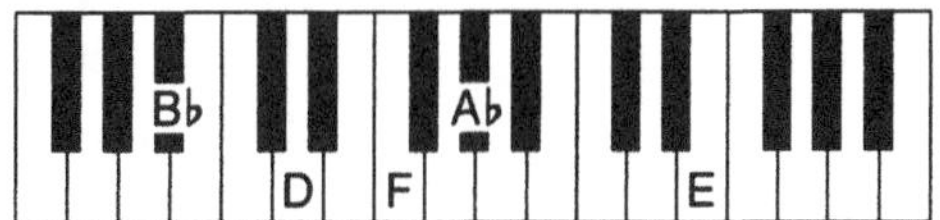

B♭7♭5(♭9)

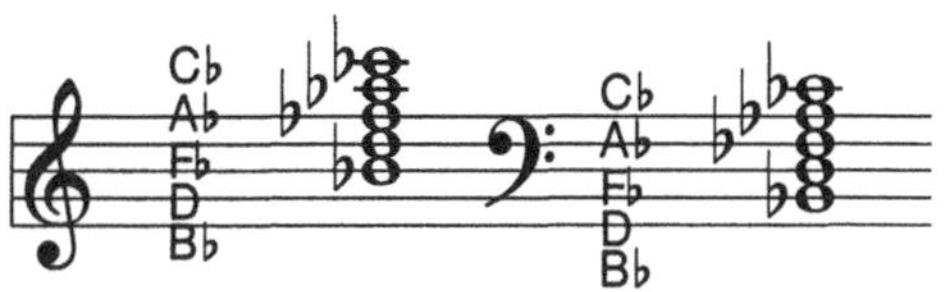

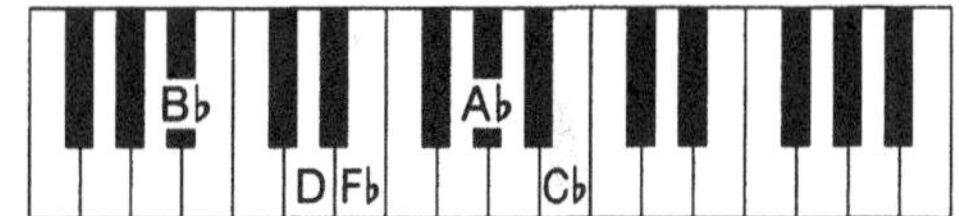

B♭7♭5(♯9)

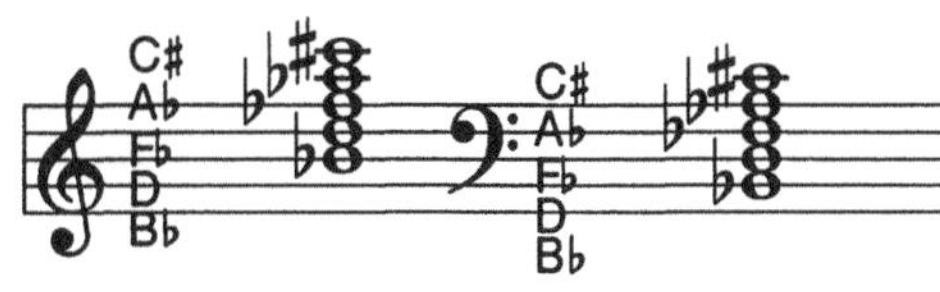

B♭7♯5(♭9)

B♭7♯5(♯9)

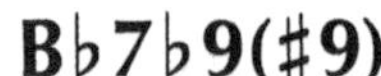

B♭7♭9(♯9)

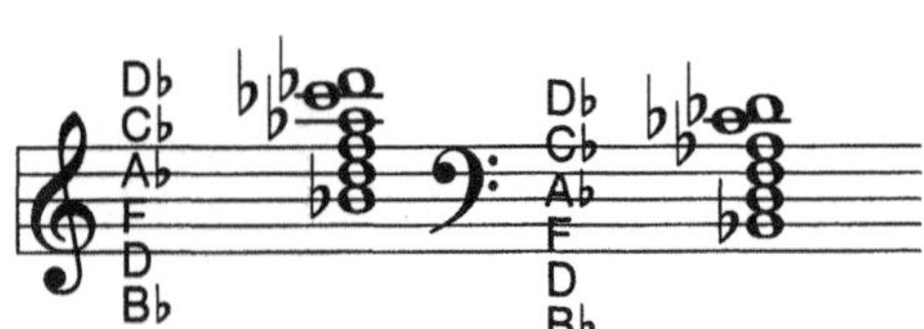

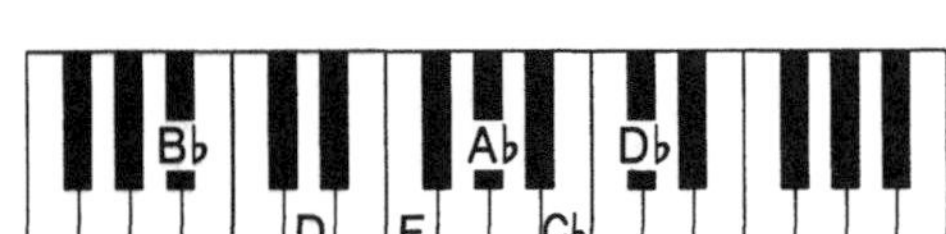

B♭7(add13)

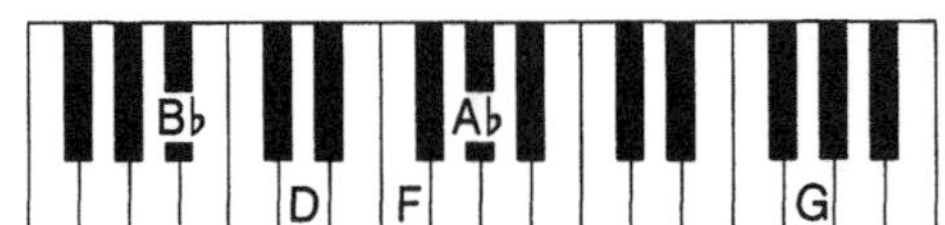

B♭7♭13

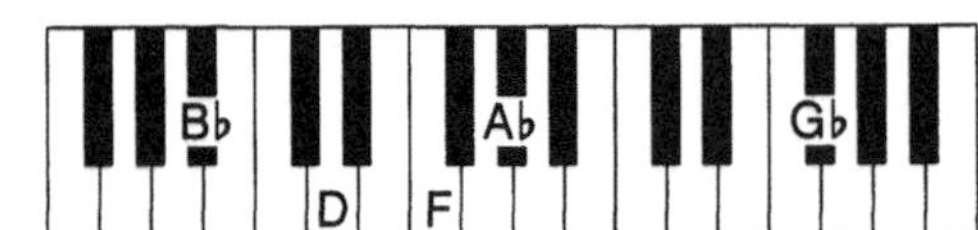

B♭7♭9(♯11)

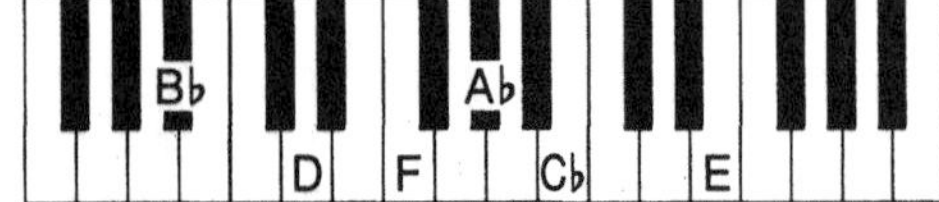

B♭7♯9(♯11)

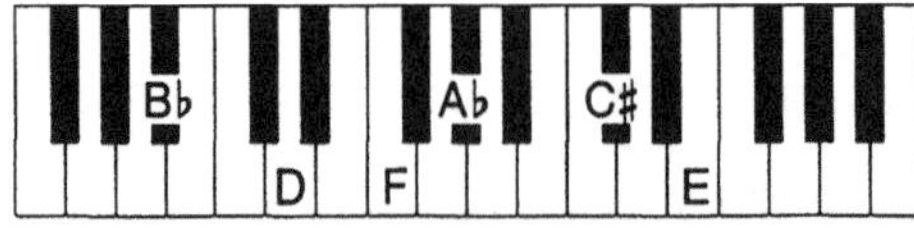

B♭7♭9(♭13)

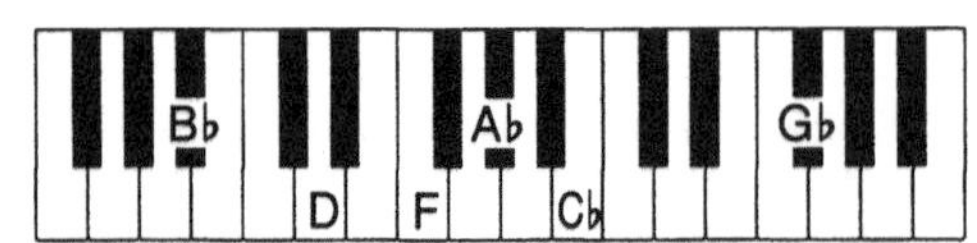

B♭7♯9(♭13)

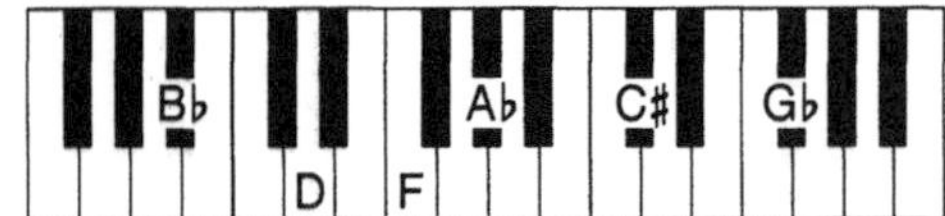

B♭7♯11(♭13)

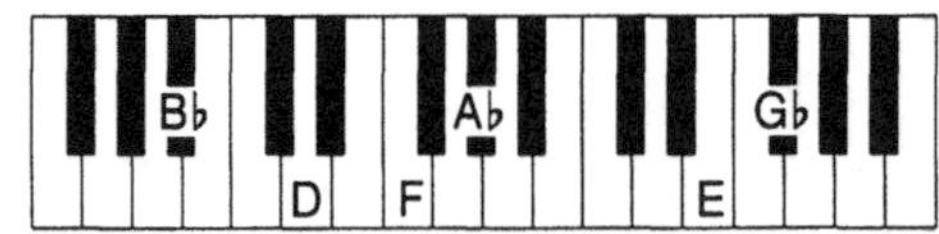

B♭7♭9(♯9,♯11)

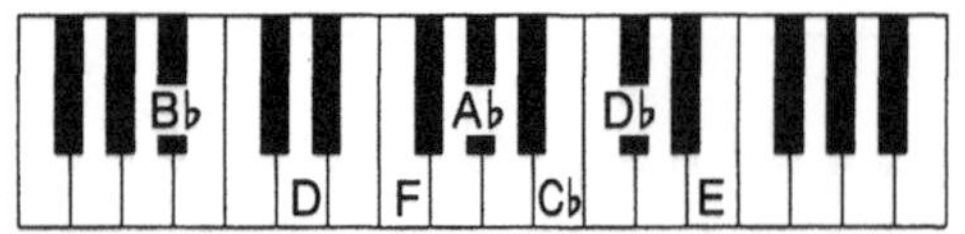

B♭9

B♭9(♭5)

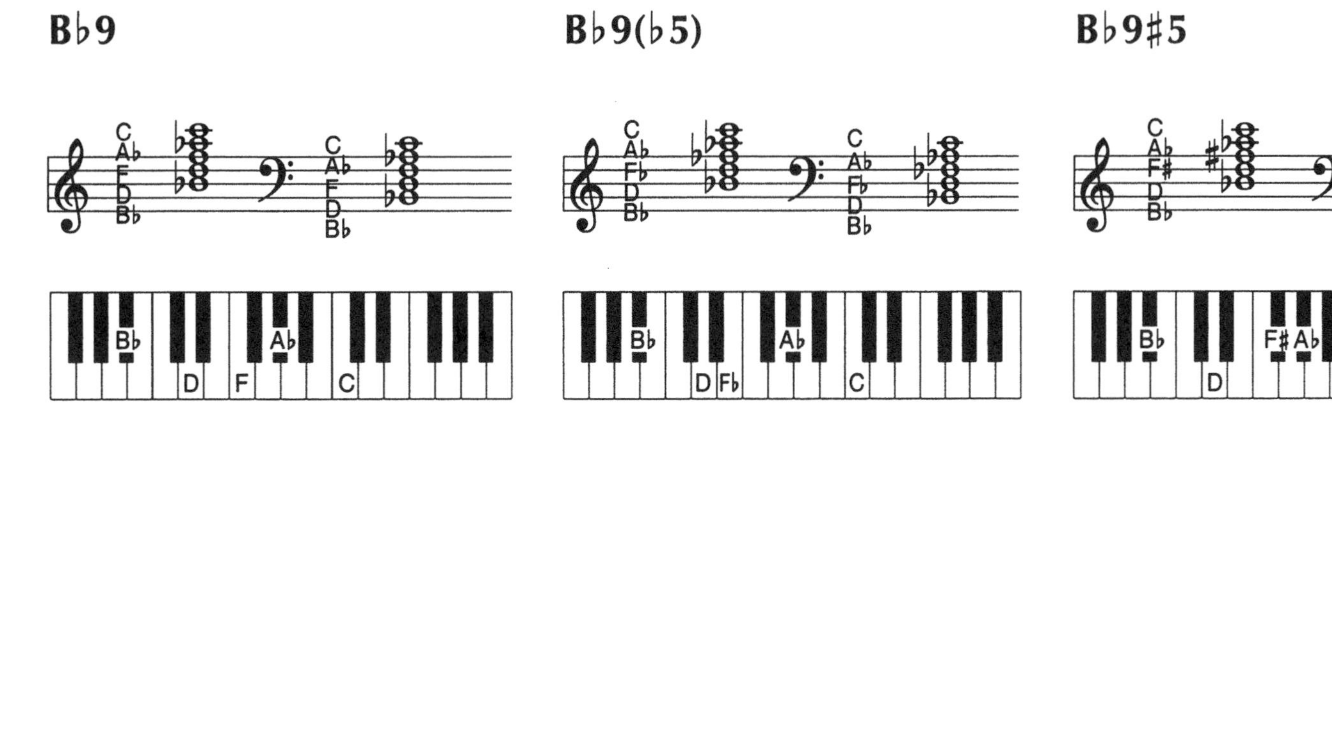

B♭9♯5

C
A♭
F♯
D
B♭
C
A♭
F♯
D
B♭
B♭
F♯ A♭
D
C

B♭9♯11

B♭9♭13

B♭9♯11(♭13)

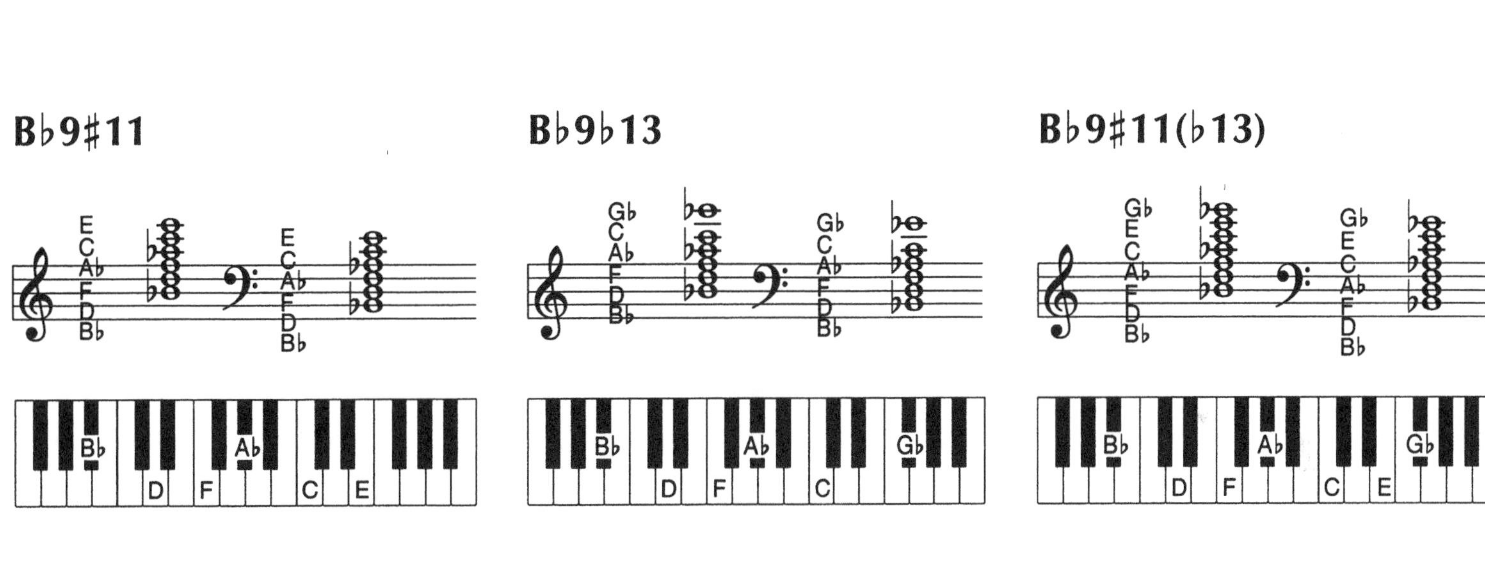

B♭11, B♭9sus4

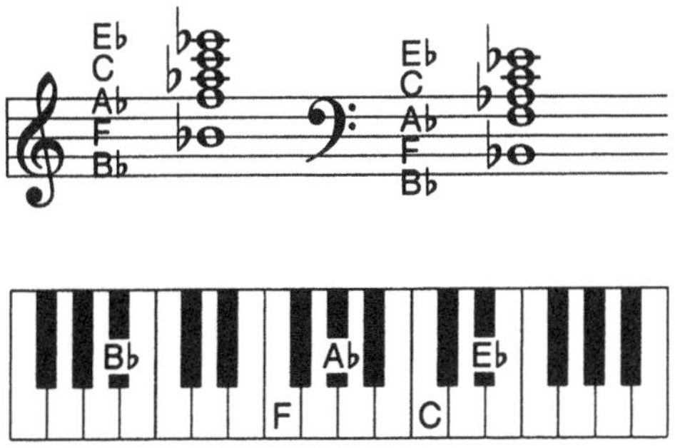

E♭
C
A♭
F
B♭
E♭
C
A♭
F
B♭
B♭
A♭
E♭
F
C

B♭13

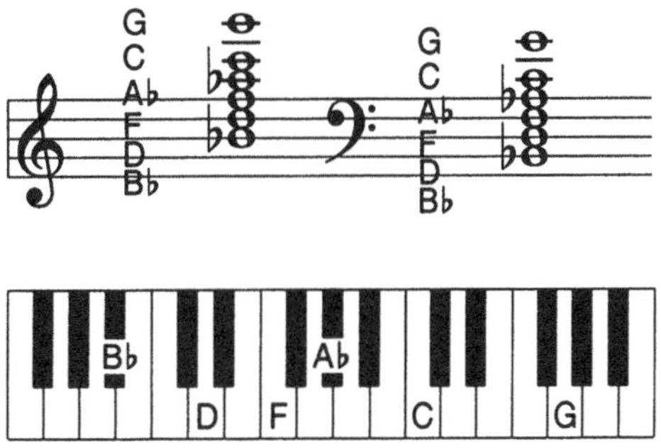

G
C
A♭
F
D
B♭
G
C
A♭
F
D
B♭
B♭
A♭
D
F
C
G

B♭13♭5

G
C
A♭
F♭
D
B♭
G
C
A♭
F♭
D
B♭
B♭
A♭
D F♭
C
G

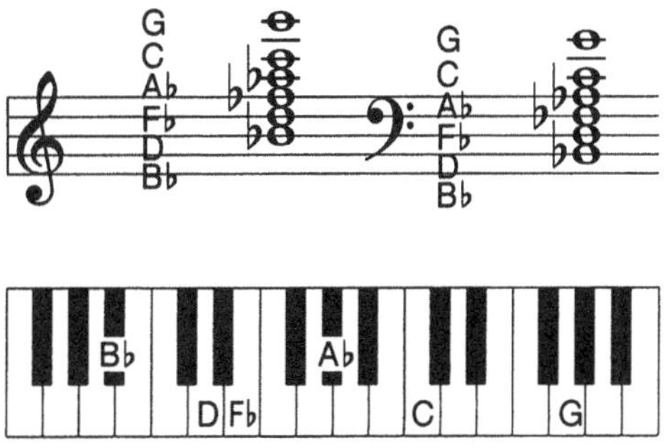

B♭13♯11

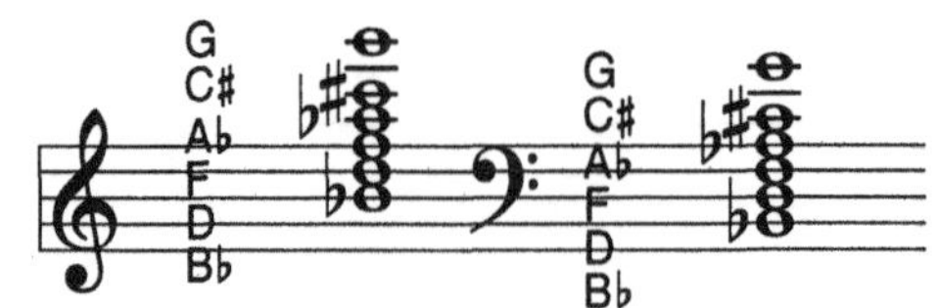

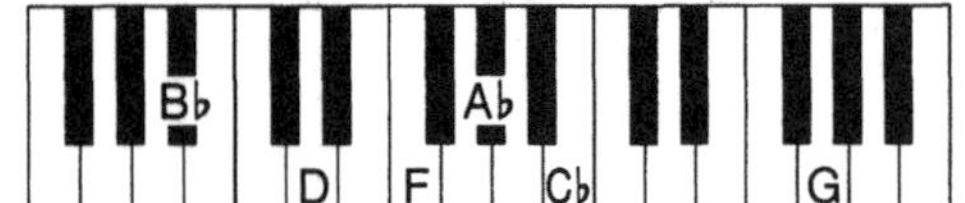

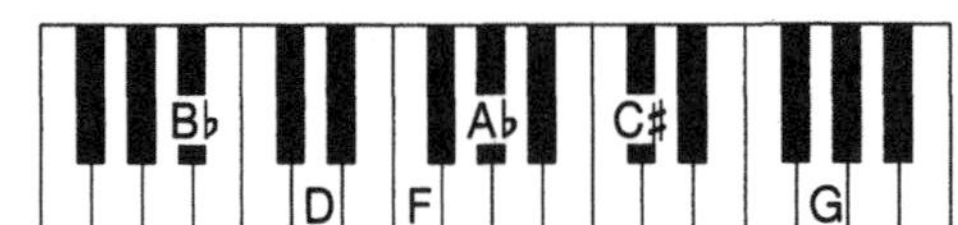

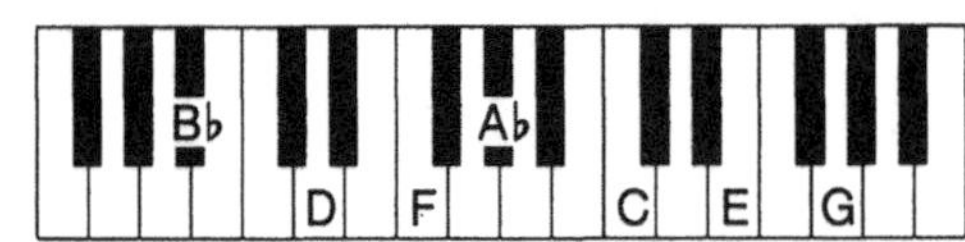

B♭13(sus4)

B♭m(♯5)

B♭m$^6_9$

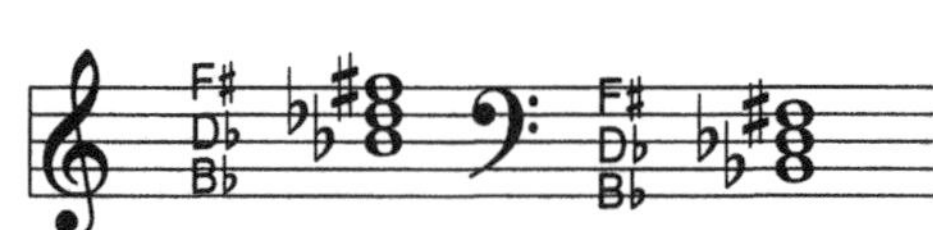

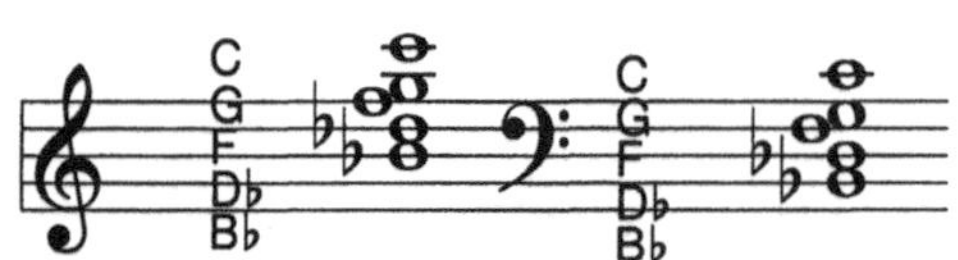

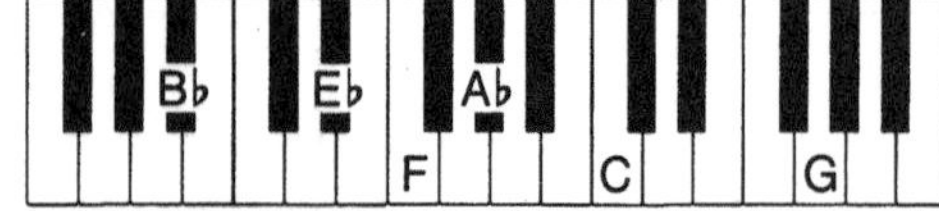

B♭ D♭ F G C

B♭m7(add4)

B♭m7(add11)

B♭m7♭5(♭9)

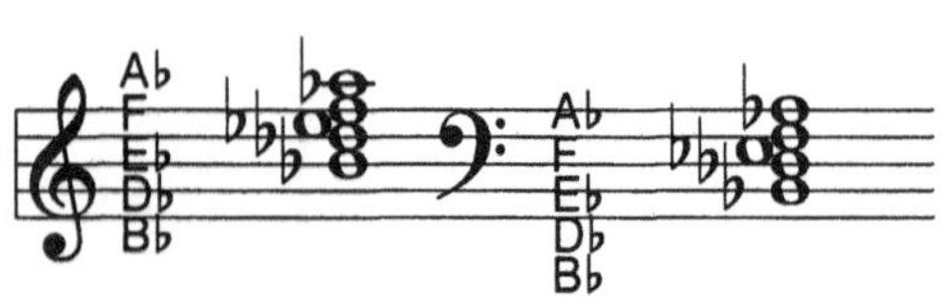

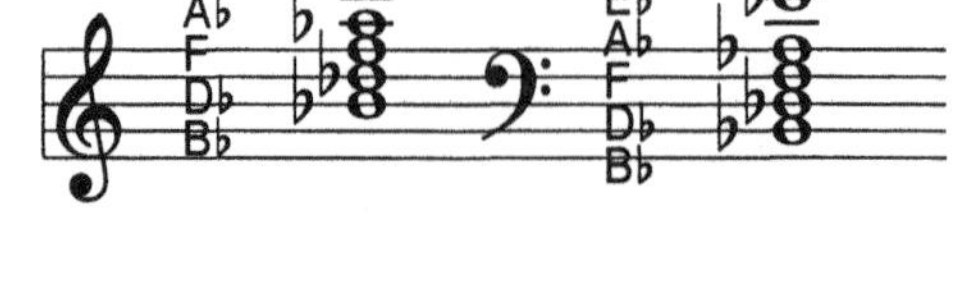

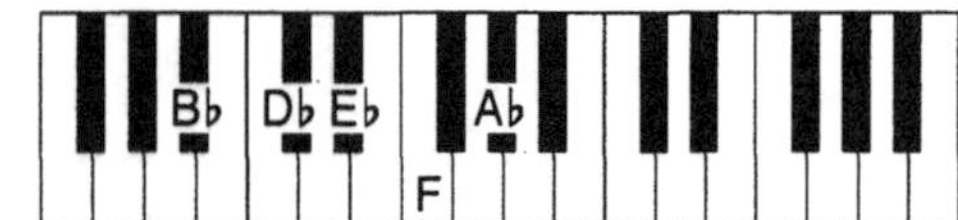

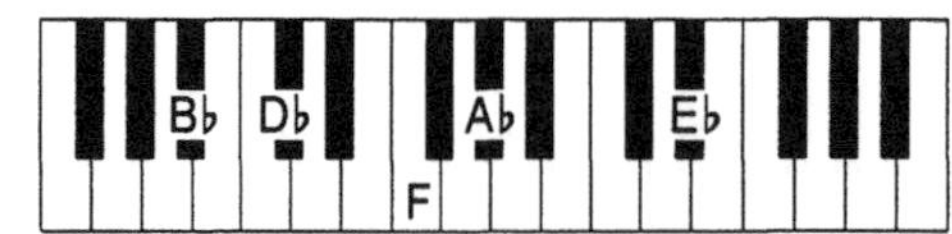

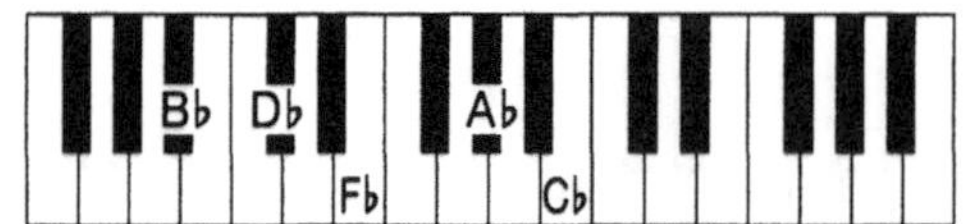

B♭m9

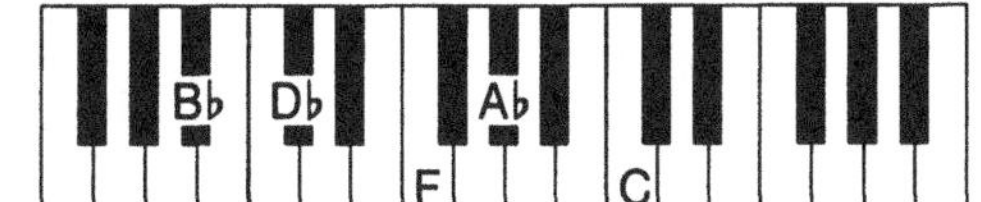

B♭m9(maj7)

B♭m9♭5

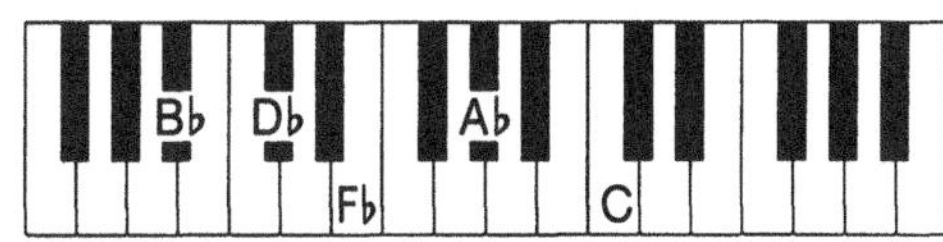

B♭m11

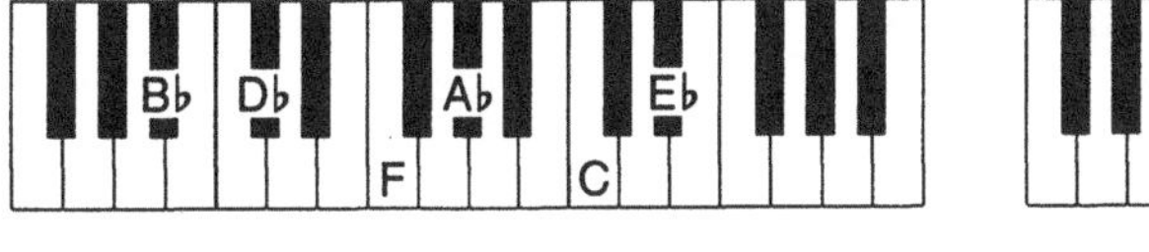

B♭m13

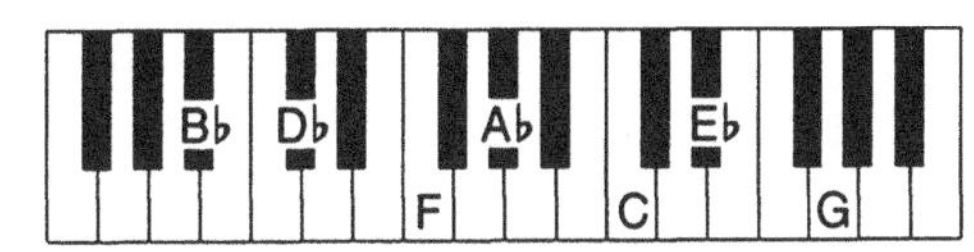

B♭dim7(add9)

B♭ D♭ F♭ G C

(A♭♭)

B♭m11♭5

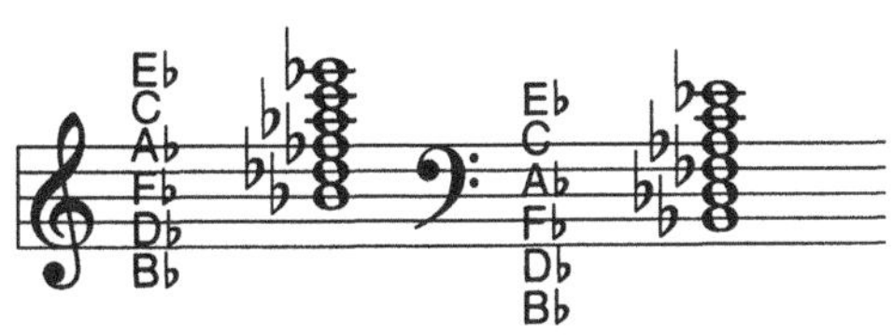

B♭ D♭ A♭ E♭ F♭ C

B♭m11(maj7)

B♭7alt.

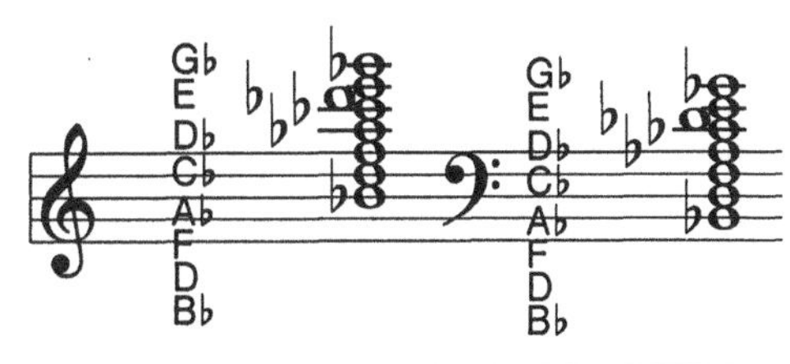

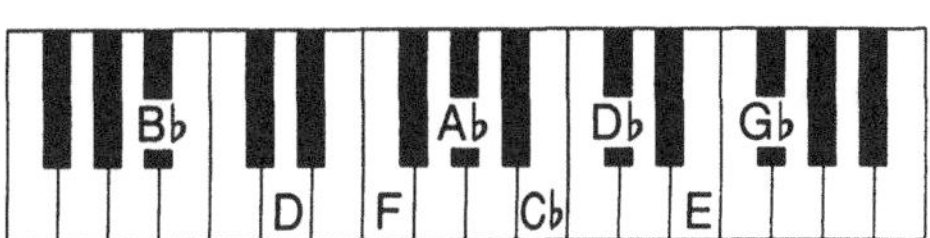

B/C♭ CHORDS

B

Root Position

1st Inversion

2nd Inversion

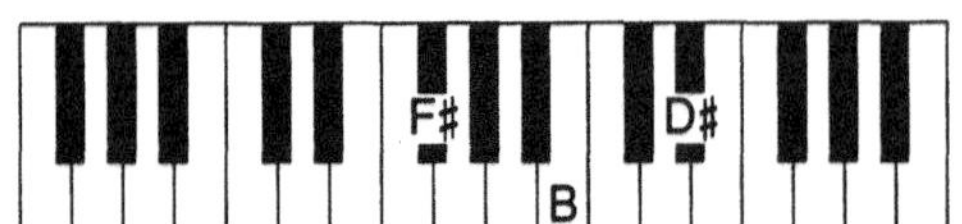

Bm

Root Position

1st Inversion

2nd Inversion

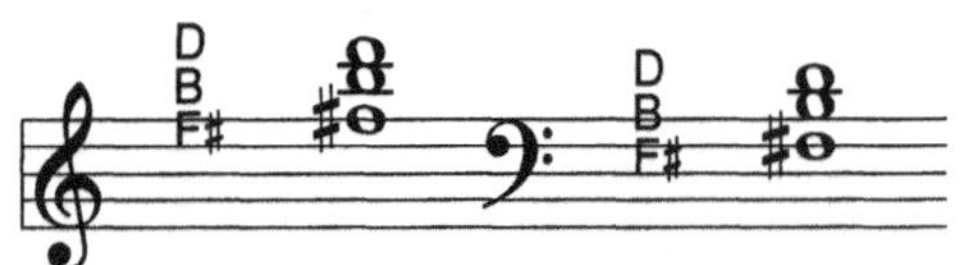

B+

Root Position

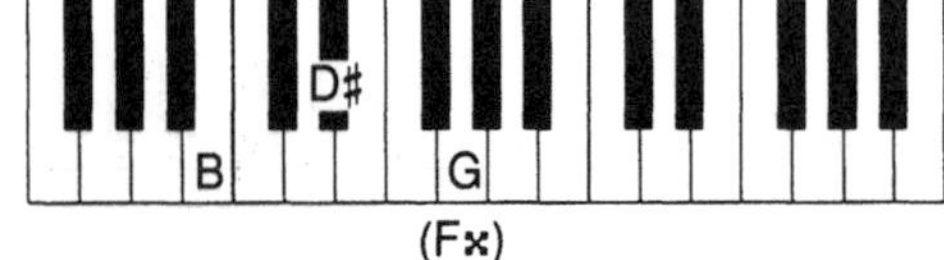

1st Inversion

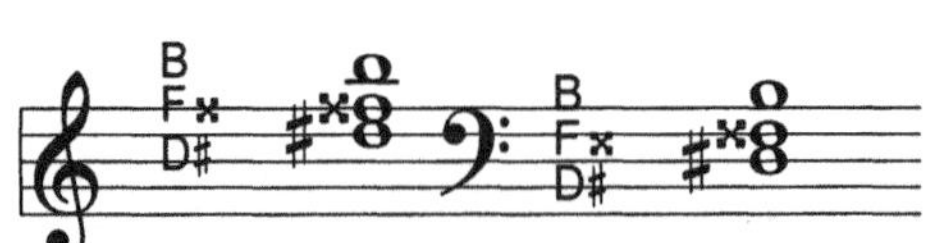

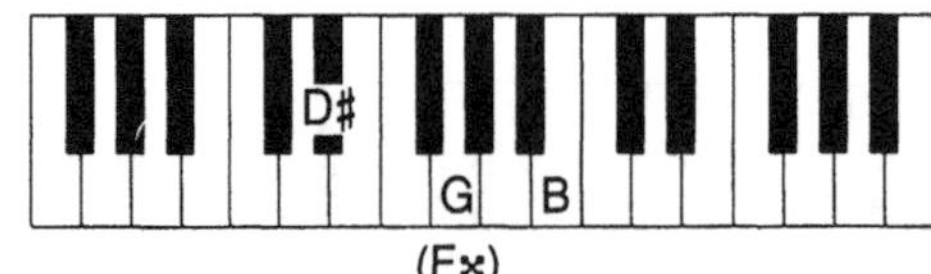

2nd Inversion

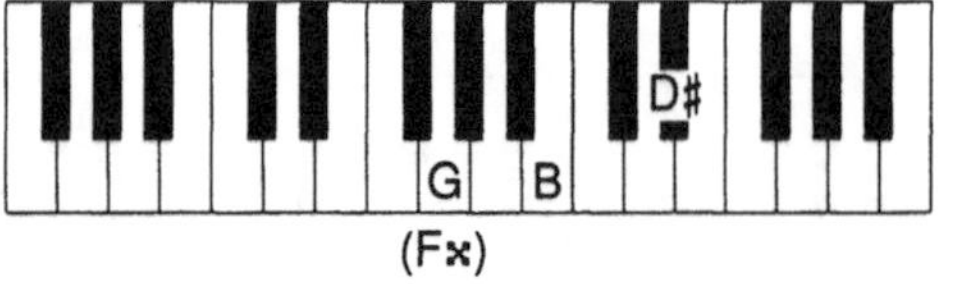

Bdim

Root Position

1st Inversion

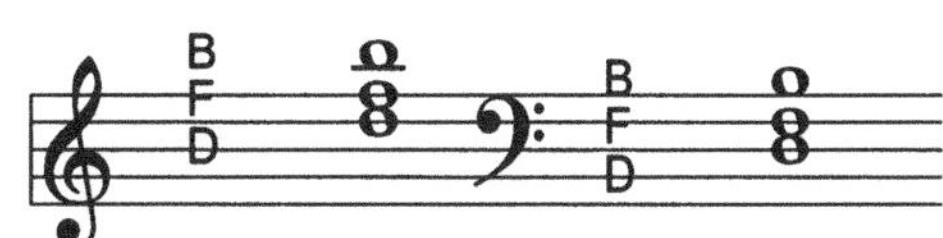

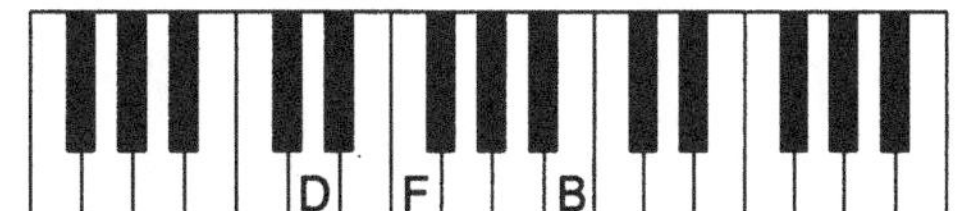

2nd Inversion

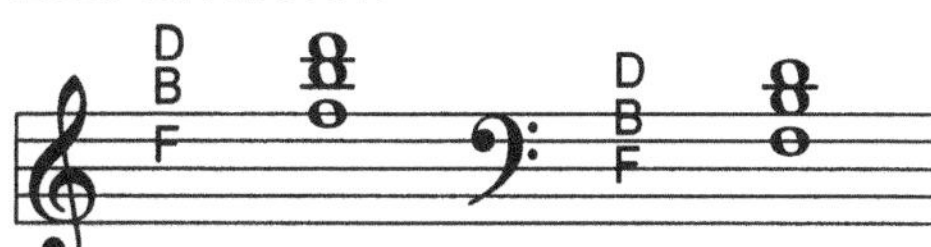

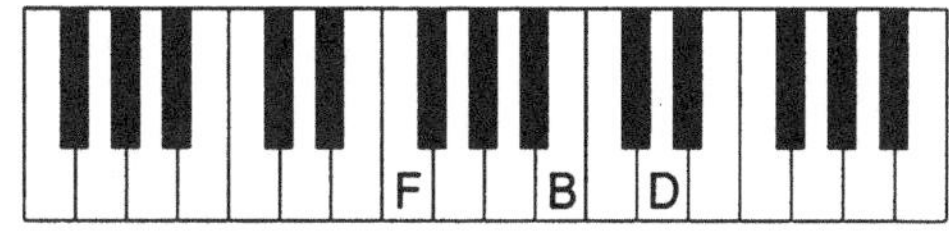

Bsus

Root Position

1st Inversion

2nd Inversion

B(♭5)

Root Position

1st Inversion

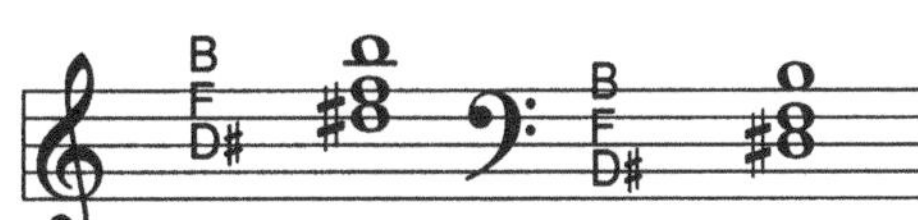

2nd Inversion

Bsus2

Root Position

1st Inversion

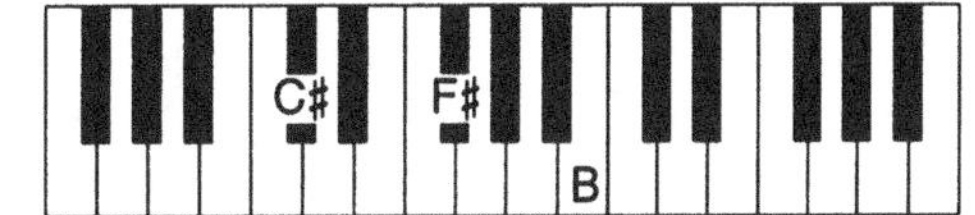

2nd Inversion

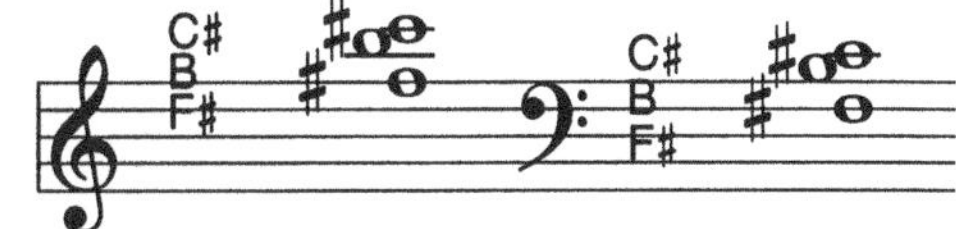

B6

Root Position

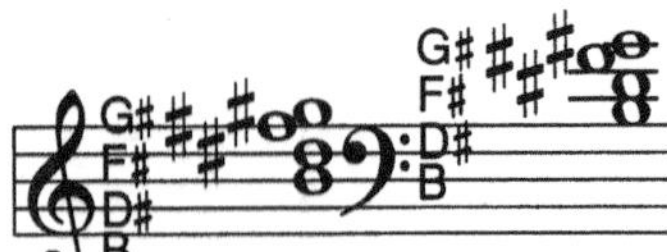

1st Inversion

2nd Inversion

3rd Inversion

B(add2), B(add9)

Root Position

1st Inversion

2nd Inversion

3rd Inversion

Bmaj7

Root Position

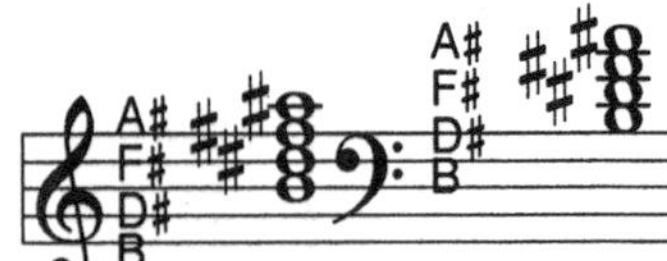

1st Inversion

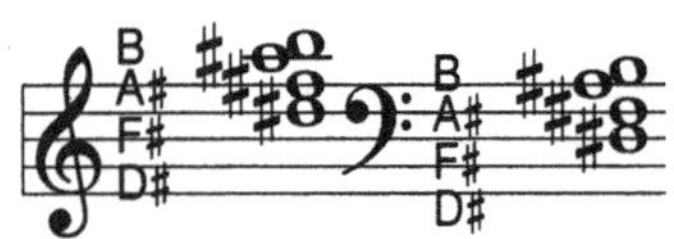

2nd Inversion

3rd Inversion

Bmaj7♭5

Root Position

1st Inversion

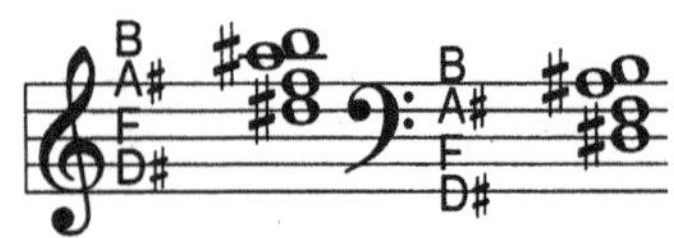

2nd Inversion

3rd Inversion

Bmaj7♯5

Root Position

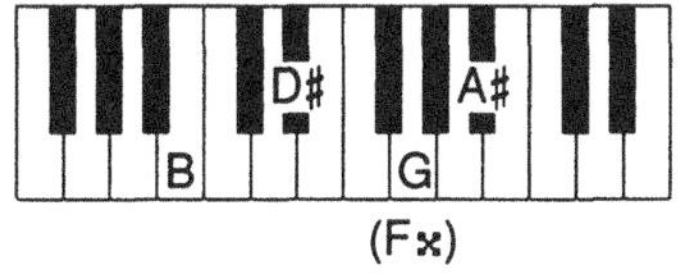

1st Inversion

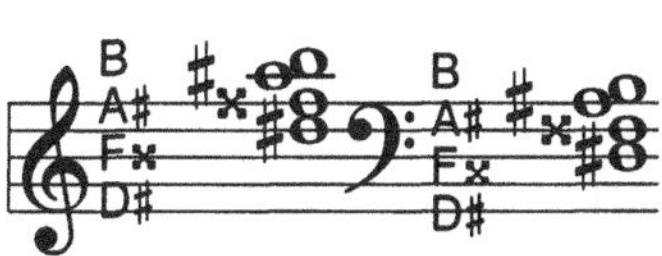

2nd Inversion

3rd Inversion

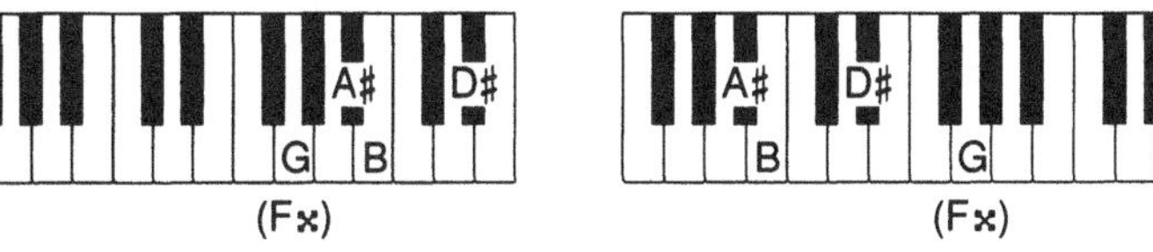

B7

Root Position

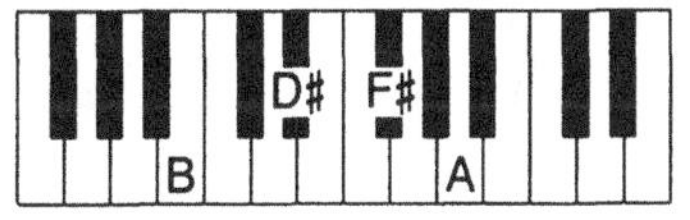

1st Inversion

2nd Inversion

3rd Inversion

B7♭5

Root Position

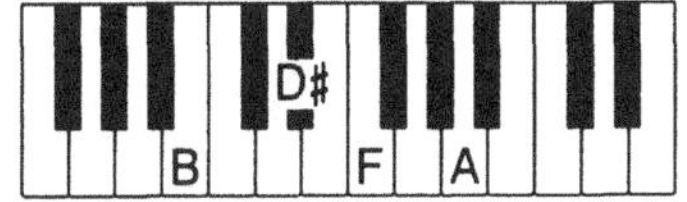

1st Inversion

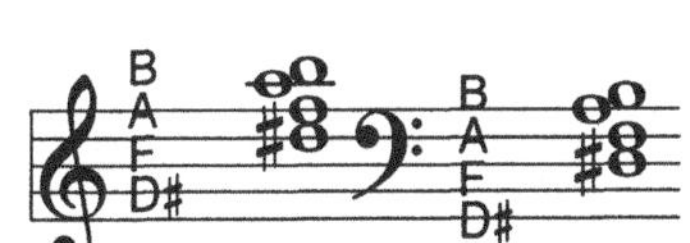

2nd Inversion

3rd Inversion

B7♯5

Root Position

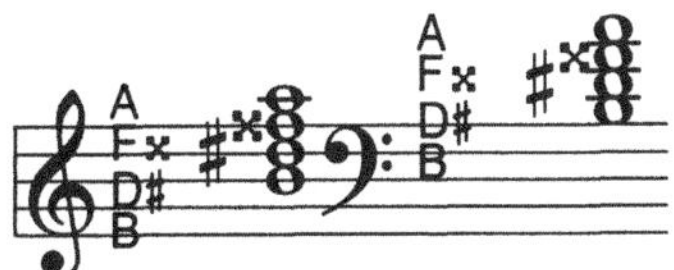

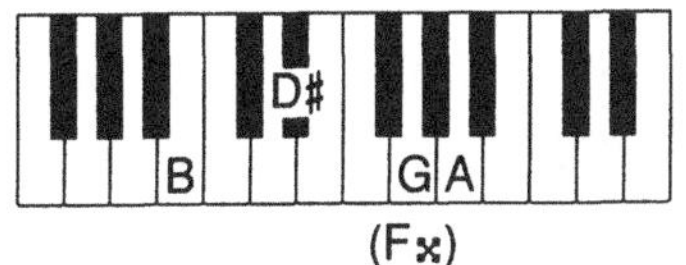

1st Inversion

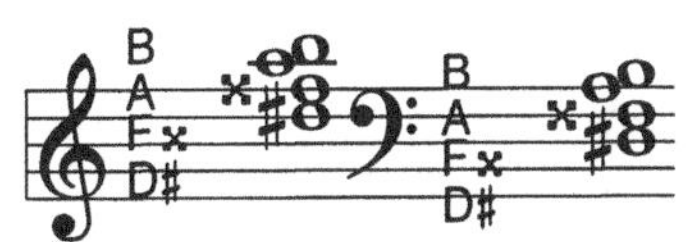

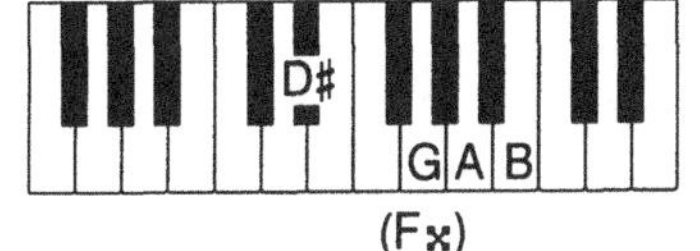

2nd Inversion

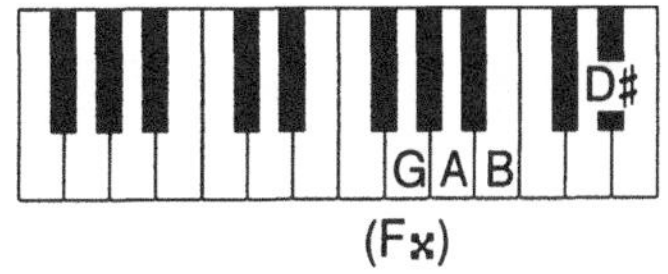

3rd Inversion

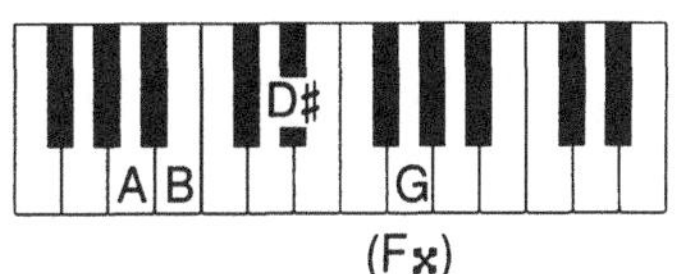

B7sus

Root Position

1st Inversion

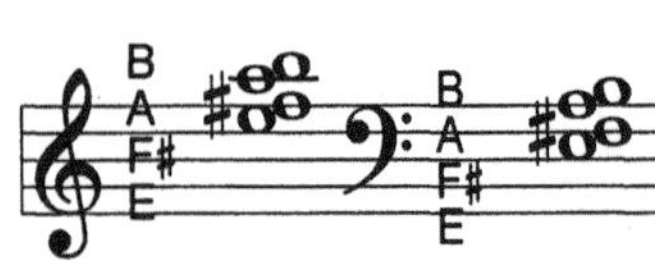

2nd Inversion

3rd Inversion

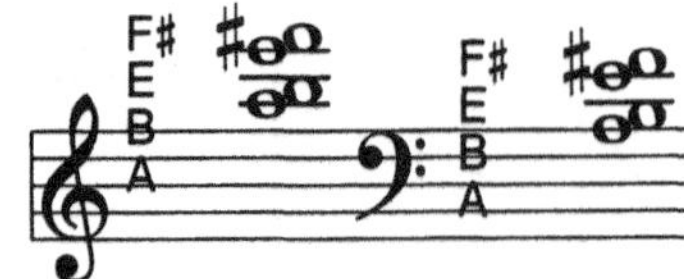

Bm(add2), Bm(add9)

Root Position

1st Inversion

2nd Inversion

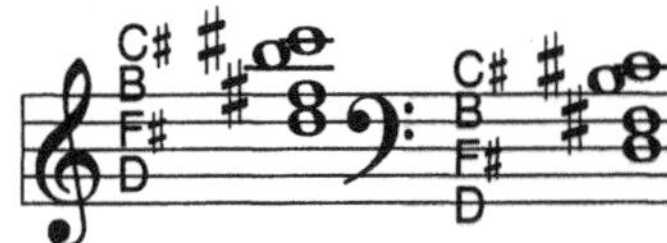

3rd Inversion

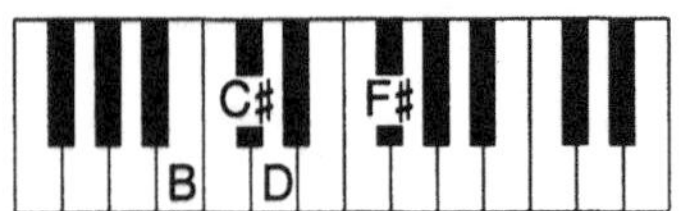

Bm6

Root Position

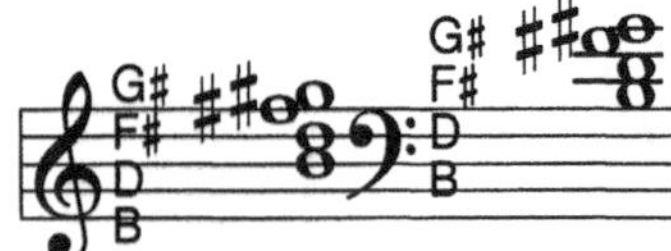

1st Inversion

2nd Inversion

3rd Inversion

Bm7

Root Position

1st Inversion

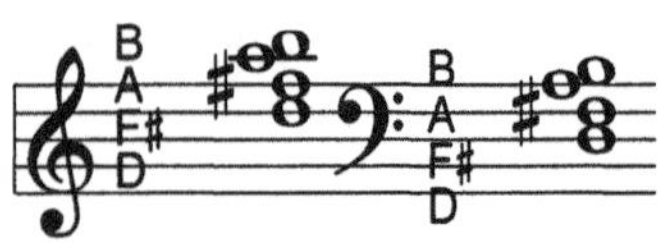

2nd Inversion

3rd Inversion

Bm(maj7)

3rd Inversion

Bm7♭5

Root Position

1st Inversion

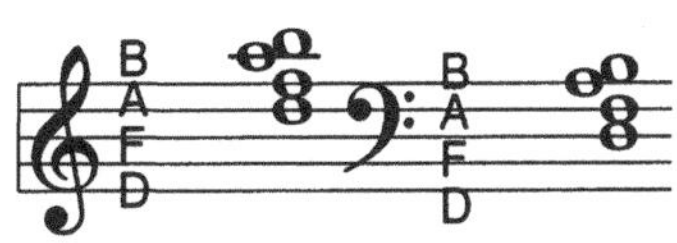

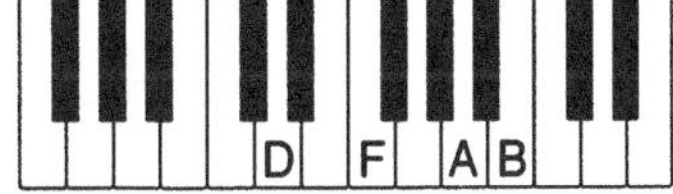

2nd Inversion

3rd Inversion

Bdim7

Root Position

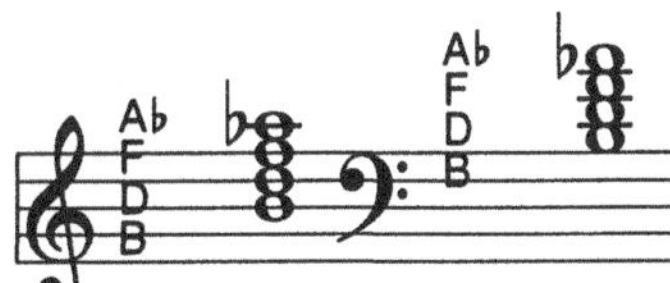

1st Inversion

2nd Inversion

3rd Inversion

Bdim(maj7)

Root Position

1st Inversion

2nd Inversion

3rd Inversion

ADDITIONAL B/C♭ CHORDS

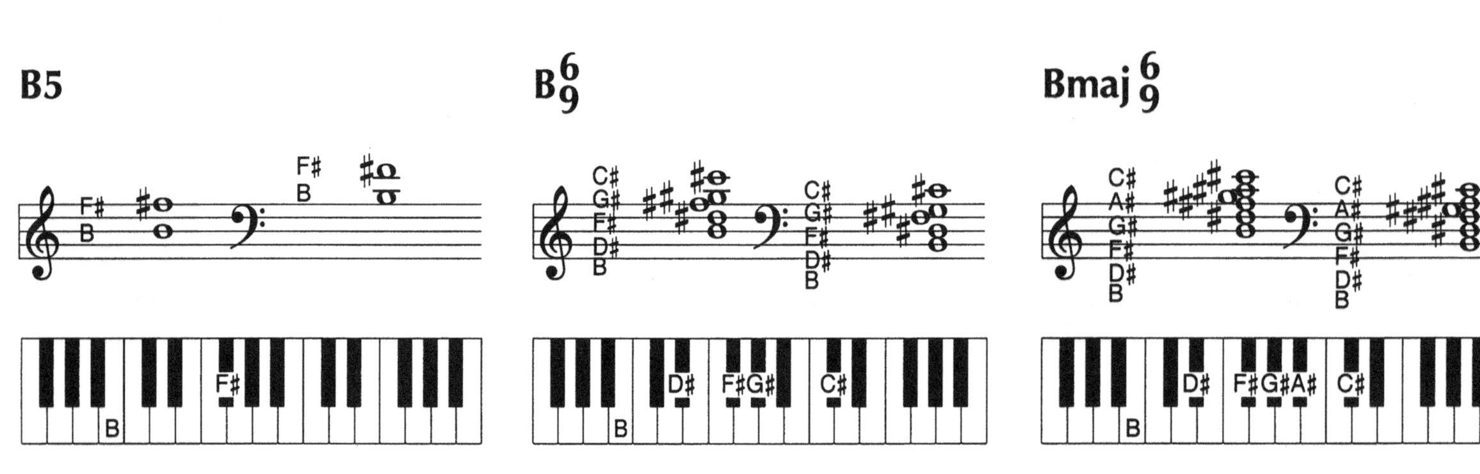

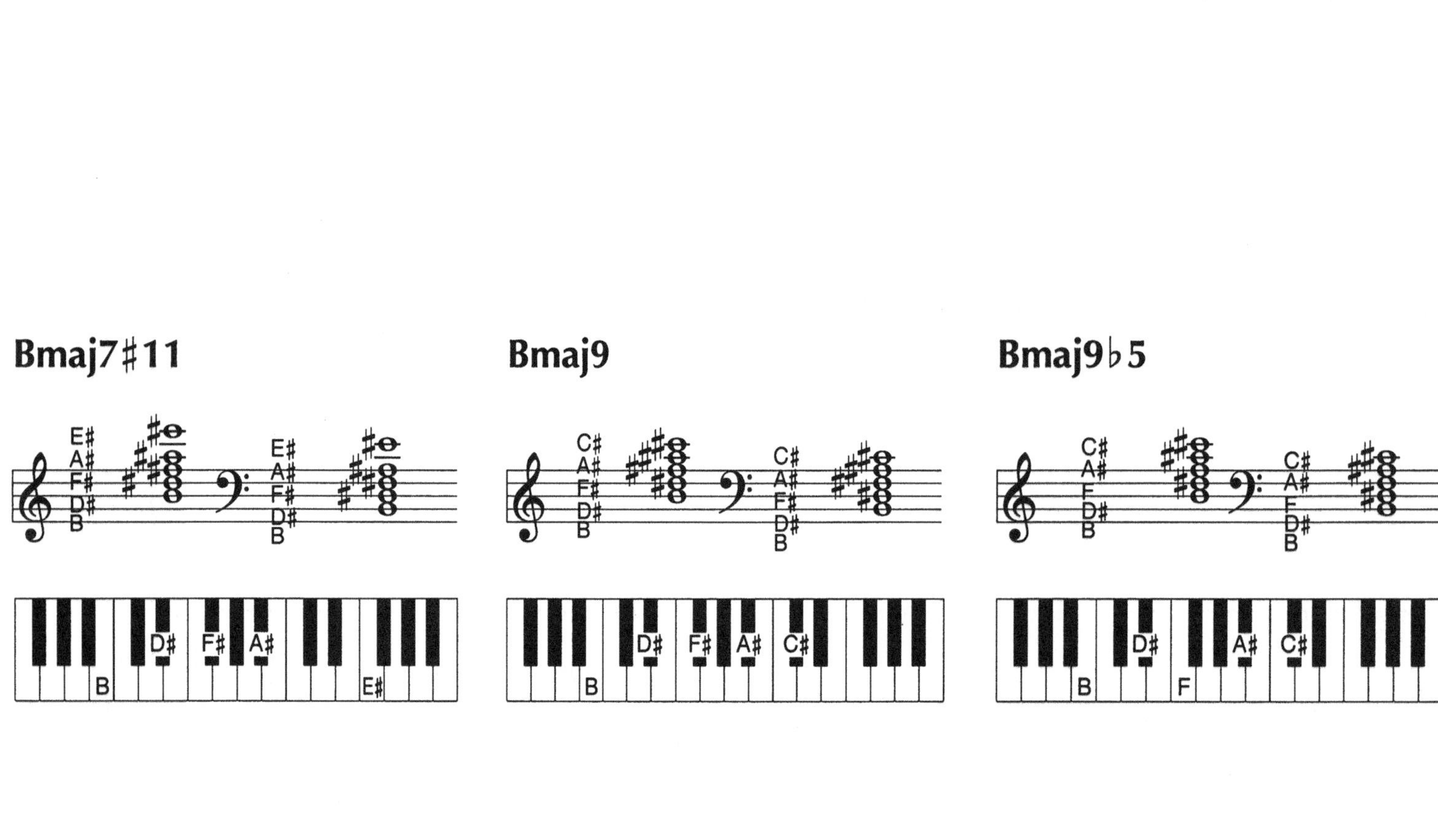

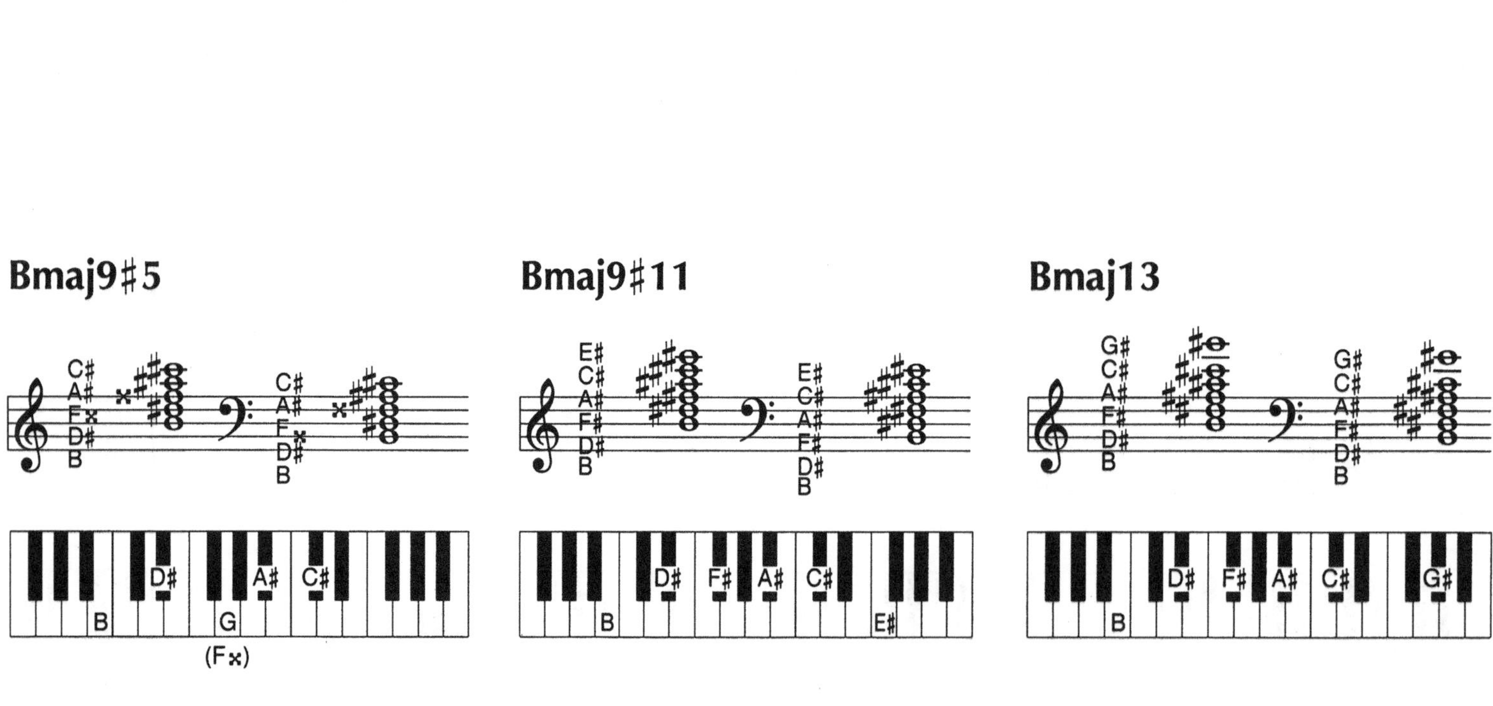

Bmaj13♭5

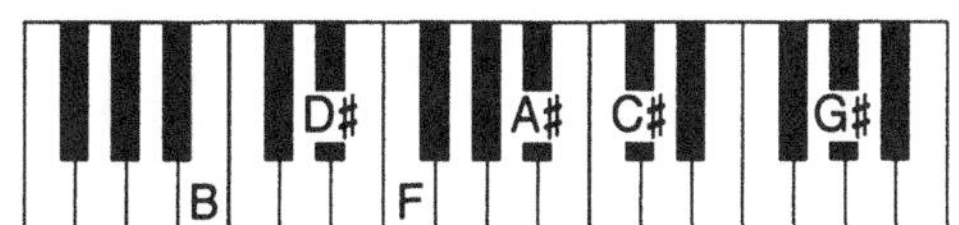

Bmaj13♯11

B7♭9

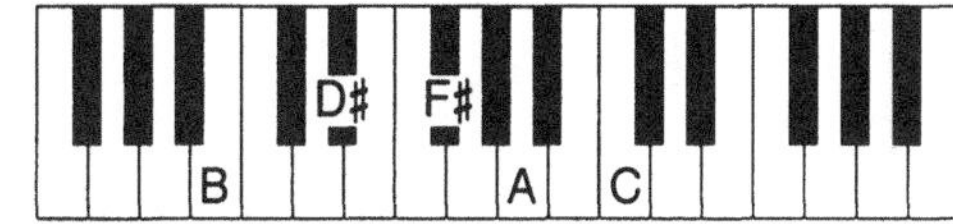

B7♯9

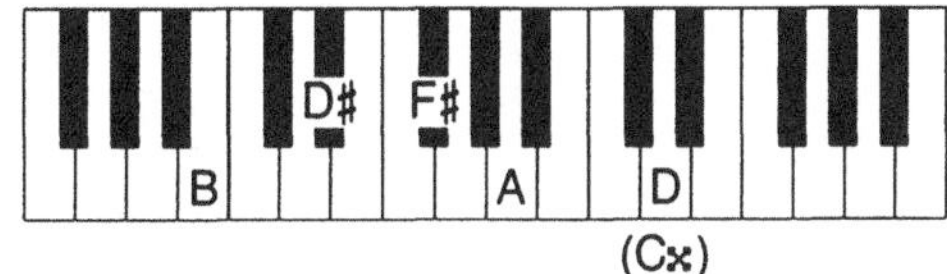

B7♯11

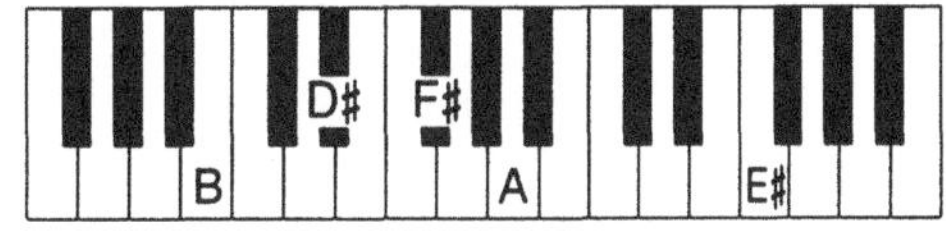

B7♭5(♭9)

B7♭5(♯9)

B7♯5(♭9)

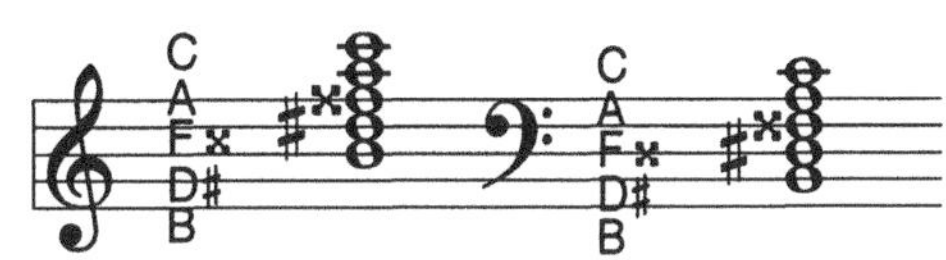

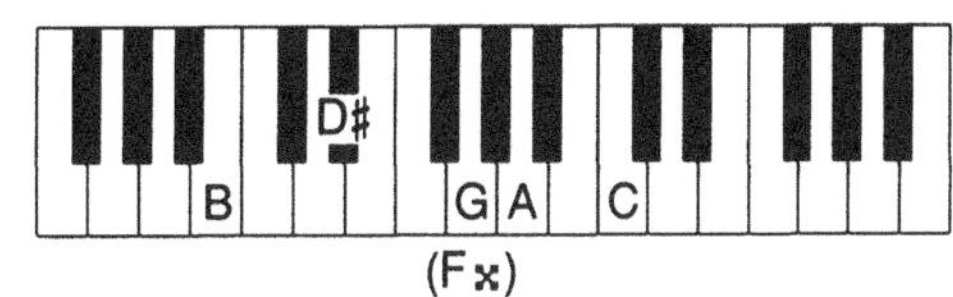

B7♯5(♯9)

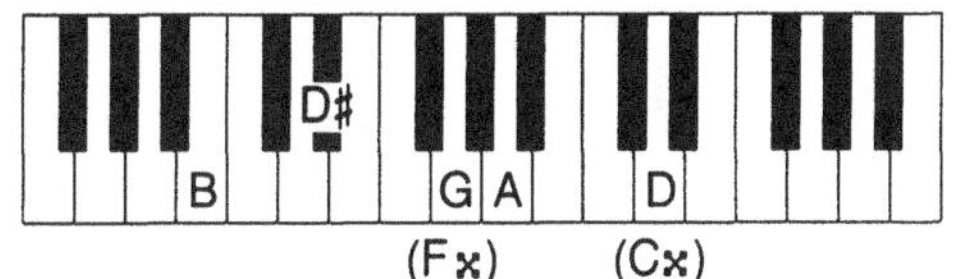

B7♭9(♯9)

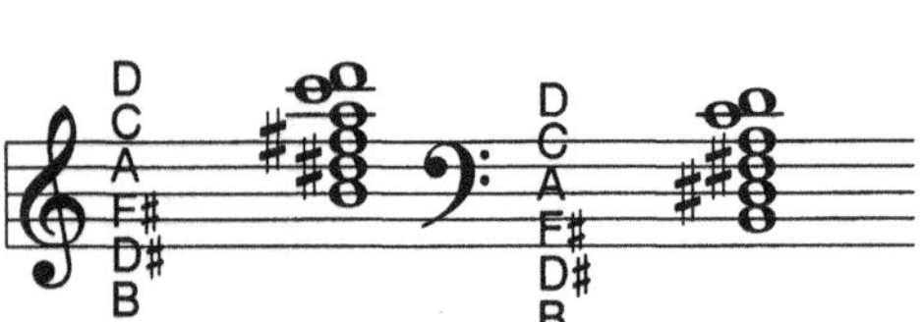

B7(add13)

B7♭13

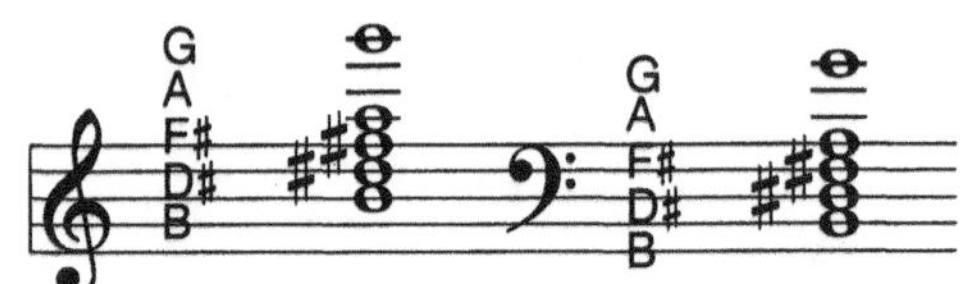

B7♭9(♯11)

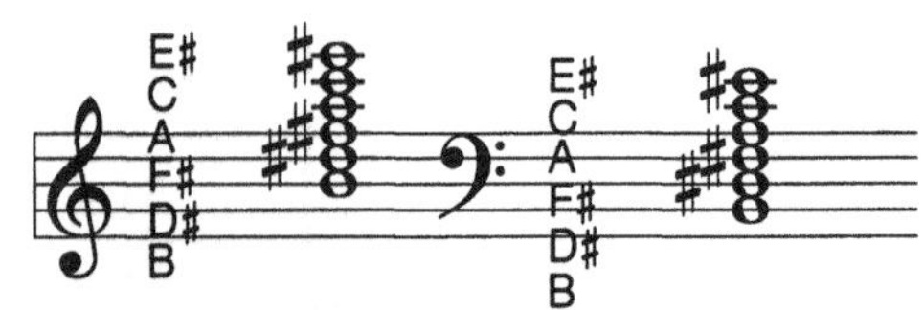

B7♯9(♯11)

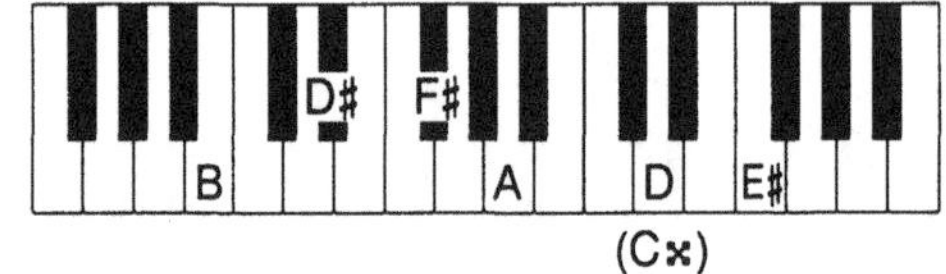

B7♭9(♭13)

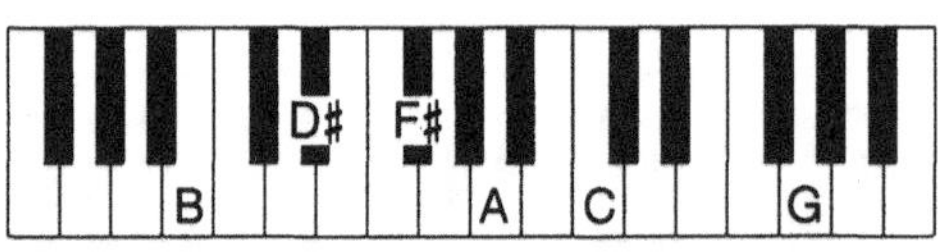

B7♯9(♭13)

B7♯11(♭13)

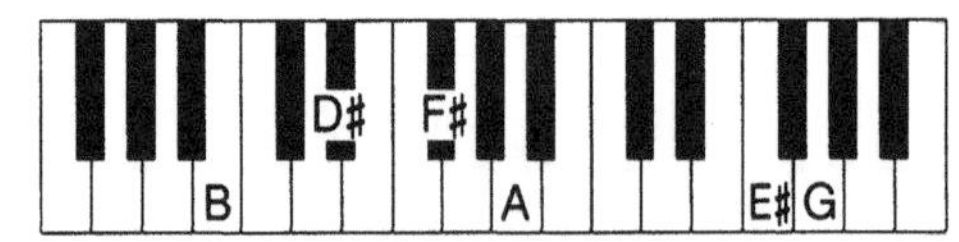

B7♭9(♯9,♯11)

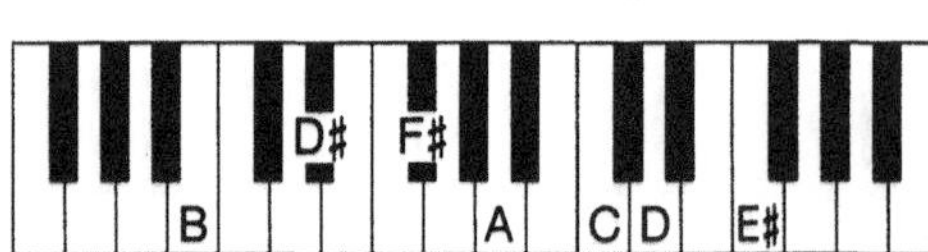

B9

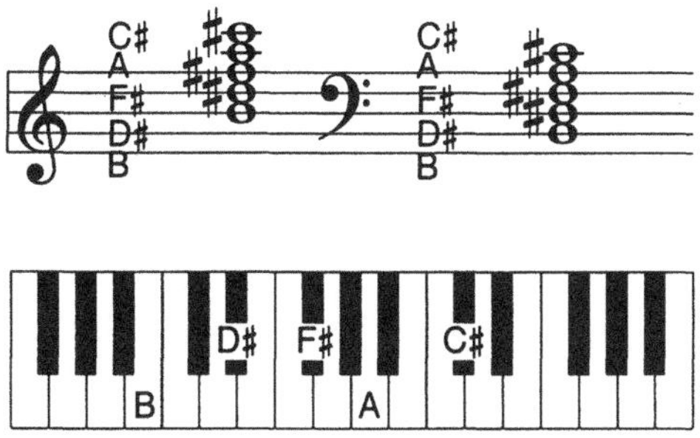

C♯ A F♯ D♯ B
C♯ A F♯ D♯ B
D♯ F♯ C♯
B A

B9(♭5)

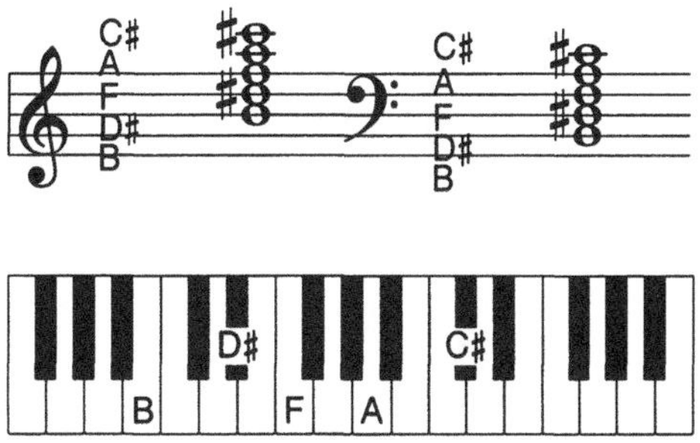

C♯ A F D♯ B
C♯ A F D♯ B
D♯ C♯
B F A

B9♯5

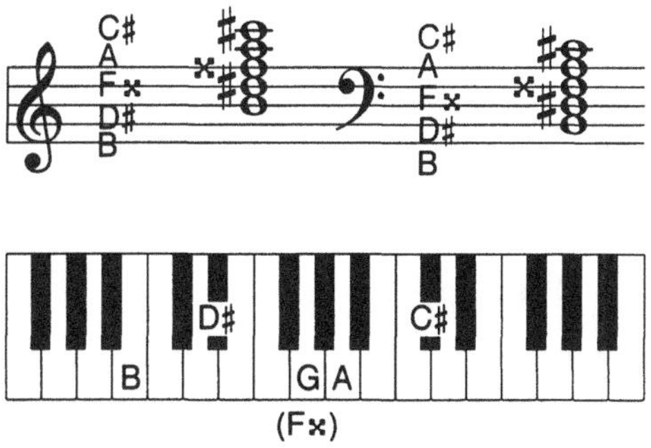

C♯ A F× D♯ B
C♯ A F× D♯ B
D♯ C♯
B G A
(F×)

B9♯11

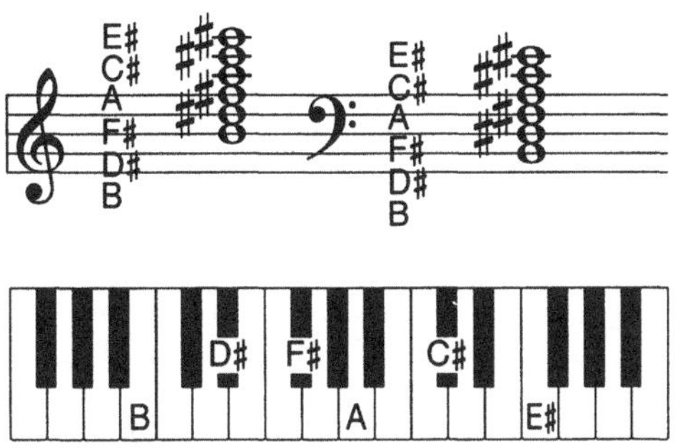

E♯ C♯ A F♯ D♯ B
E♯ C♯ A F♯ D♯ B
D♯ F♯ C♯
B A E♯

B9♭13

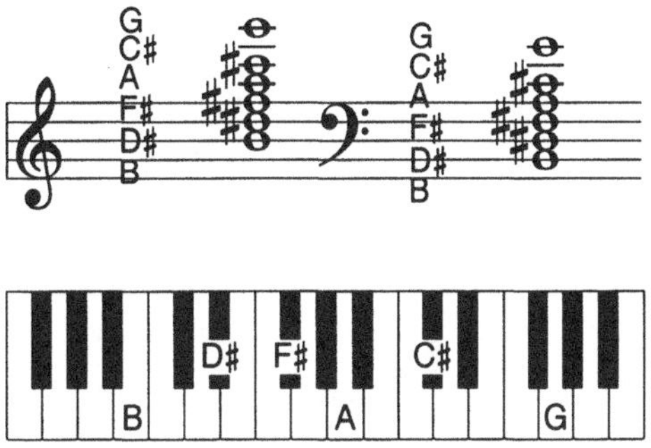

G C♯ A F♯ D♯ B
G C♯ A F♯ D♯ B
D♯ F♯ C♯
B A G

B9♯11(♭13)

G E♯ C♯ A F♯ D♯ B
G E♯ C♯ A F♯ D♯ B
D♯ F♯ C♯
B A E♯ G

B11, B9sus4

E C♯ A F♯ B
E C♯ A F♯ B
F♯ C♯
B A E

B13

G♯ C♯ A F♯ D♯ B
G♯ C♯ A F♯ D♯ B
D♯ F♯ C♯ G♯
B A

B13♭5

G♯ C♯ A F D♯ B
G♯ C♯ A F D♯ B
D♯ C♯ G♯
B F A

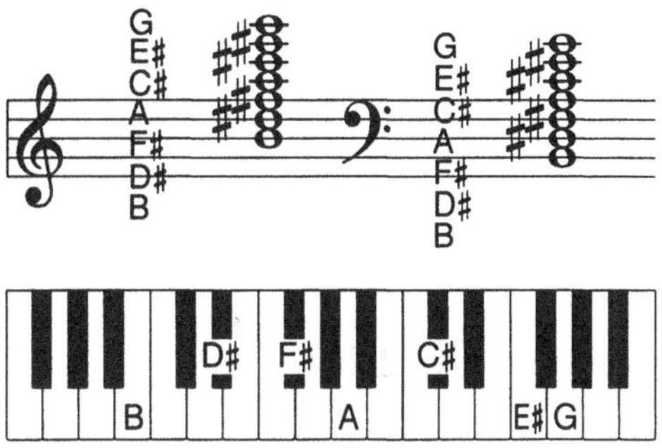

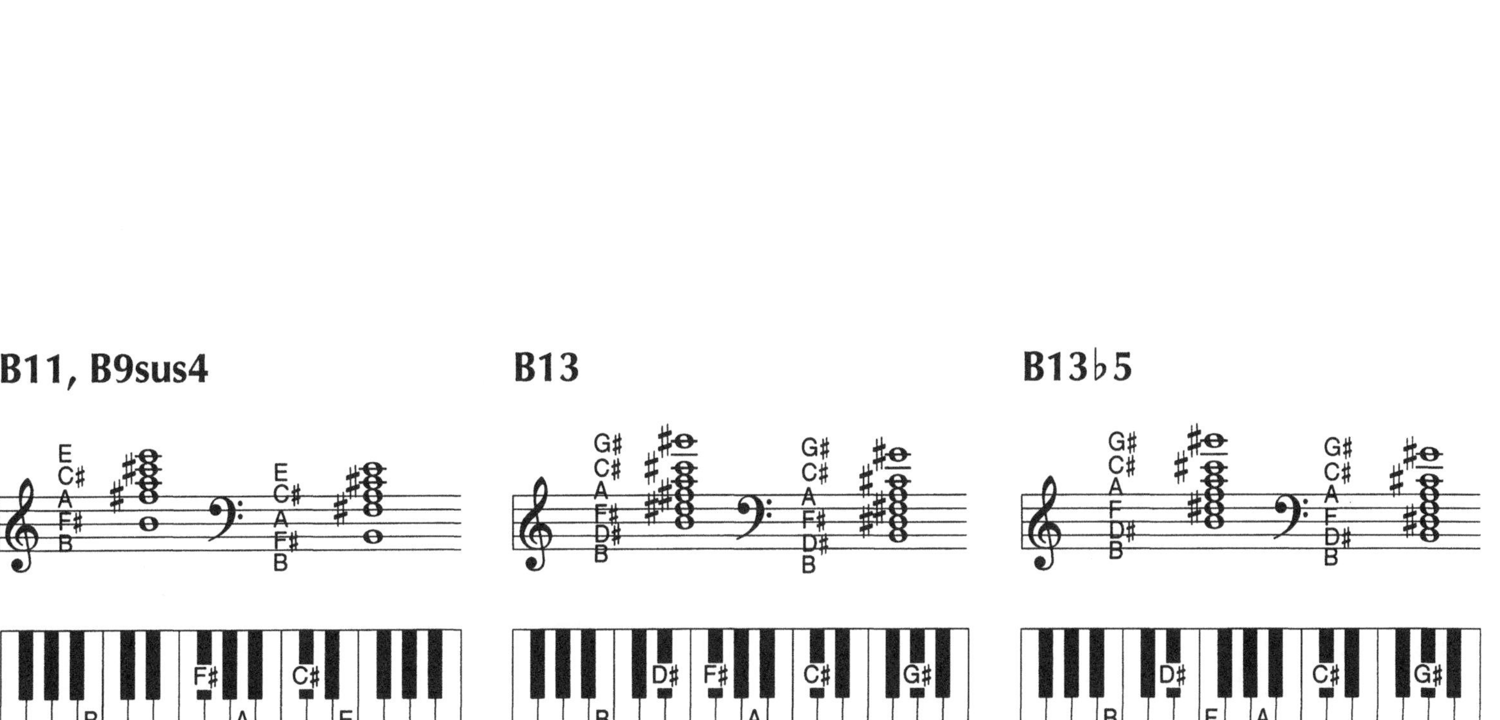

B13♭9

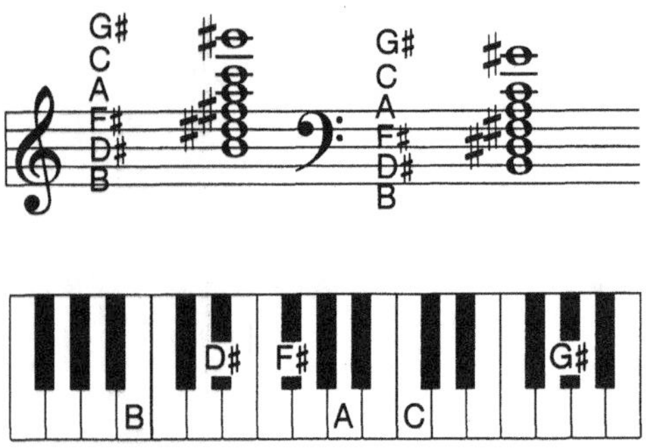

B13♯9

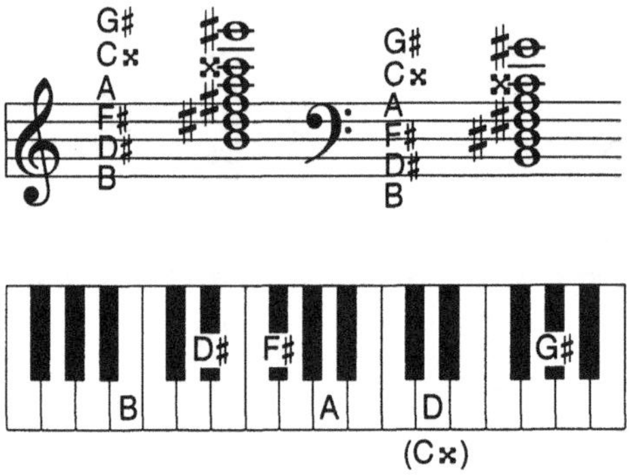

B13♯11

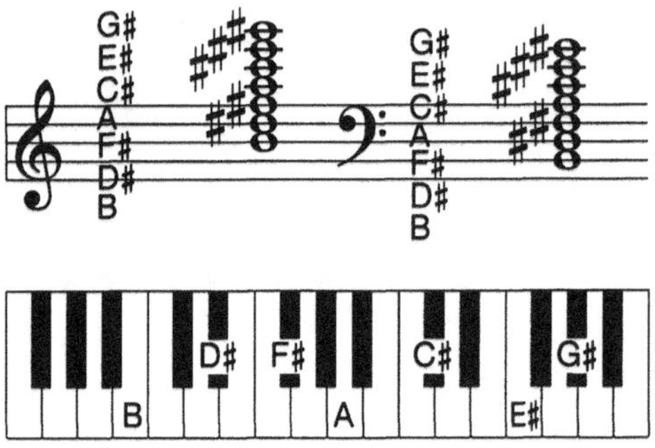

B13(sus4)

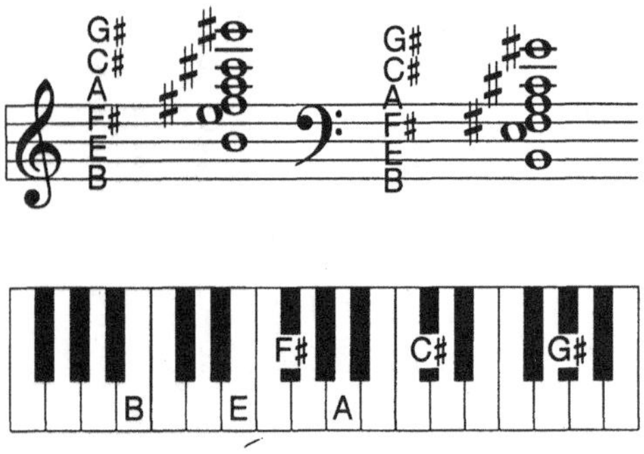

Bm(♯5)

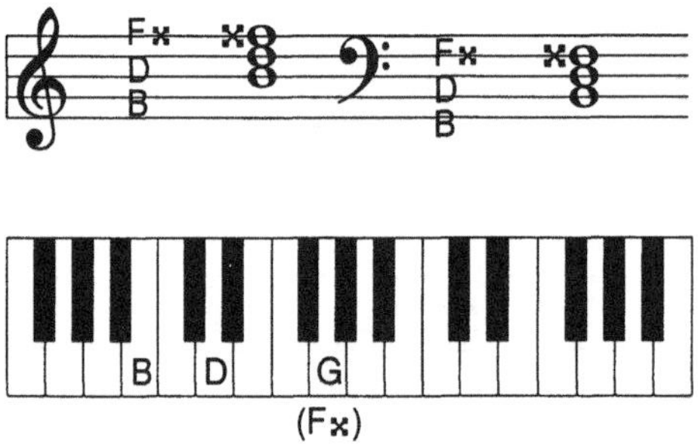

Bm$^{6}_{9}$

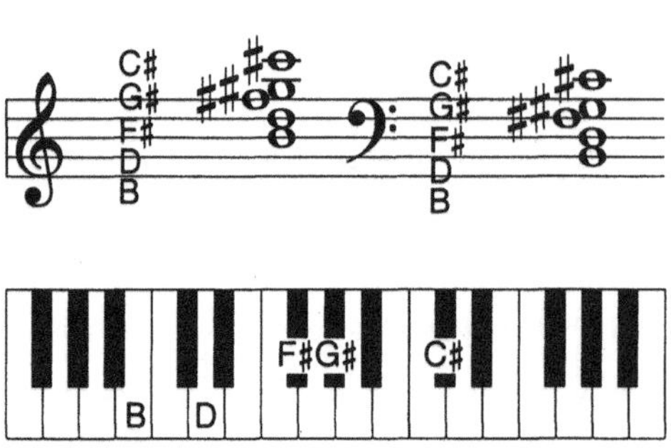

Bm7(add4)

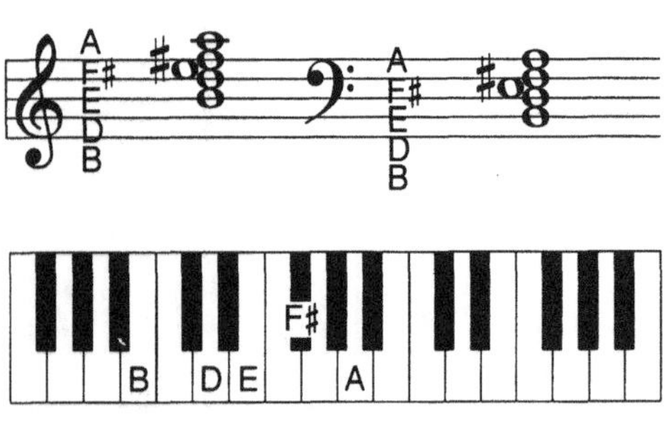

Bm7(add11)

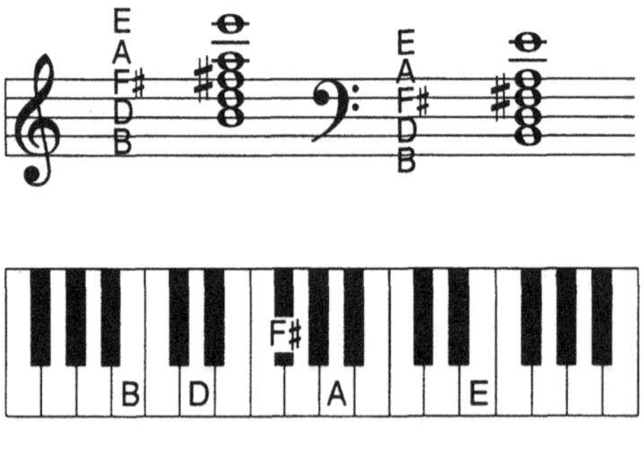

Bm7♭5(♭9)

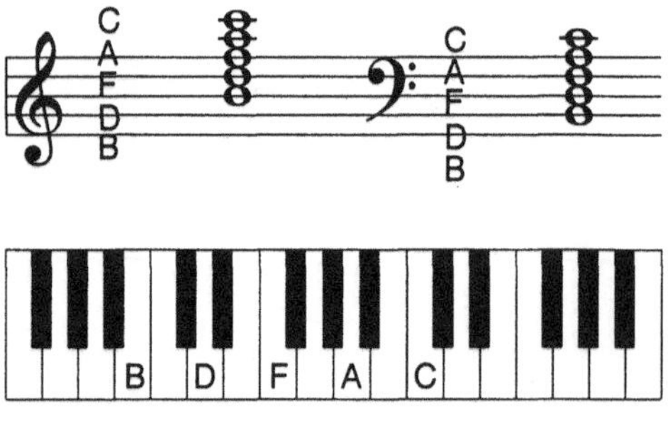

Bm9

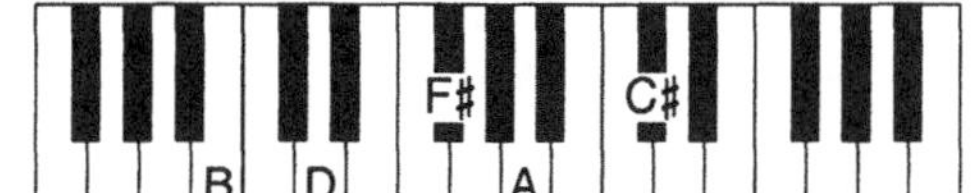

Bm9(maj7)

Bm9♭5

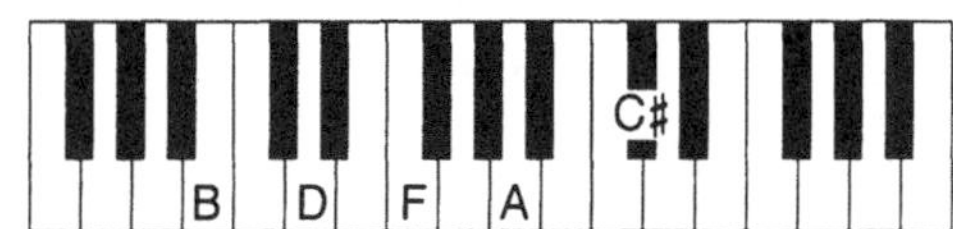

Bm11

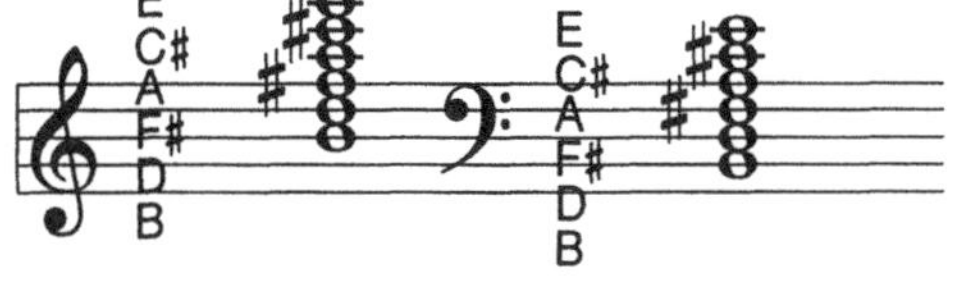

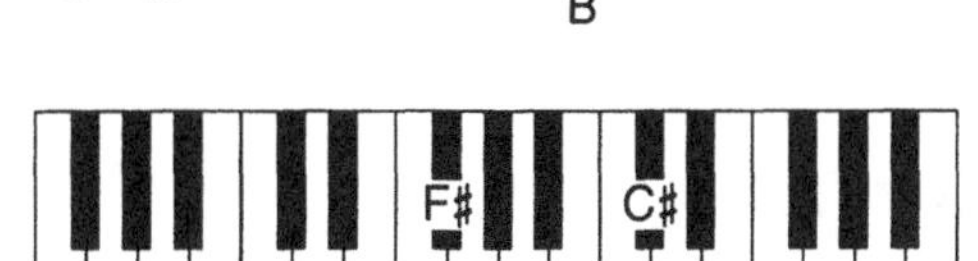

Bm13

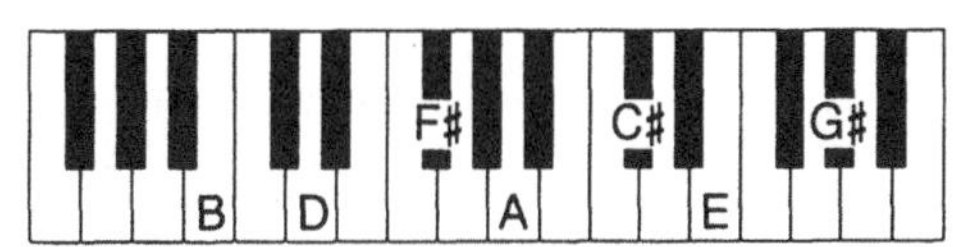

Bdim7(add9)

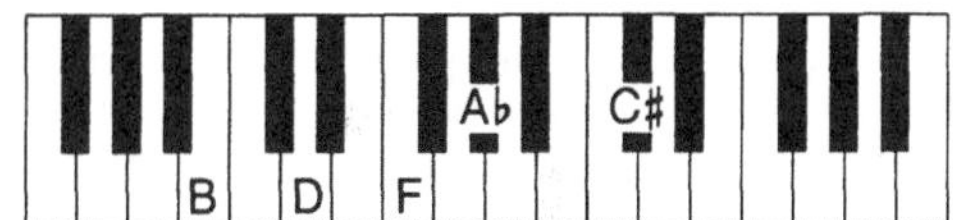

Bm11♭5

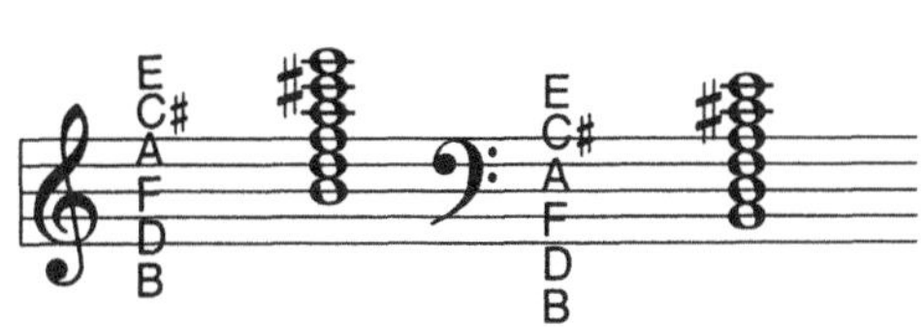

Bm11(maj7)

B7alt.

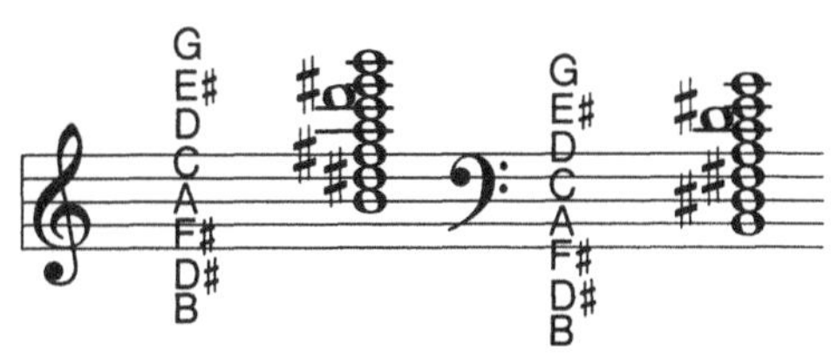

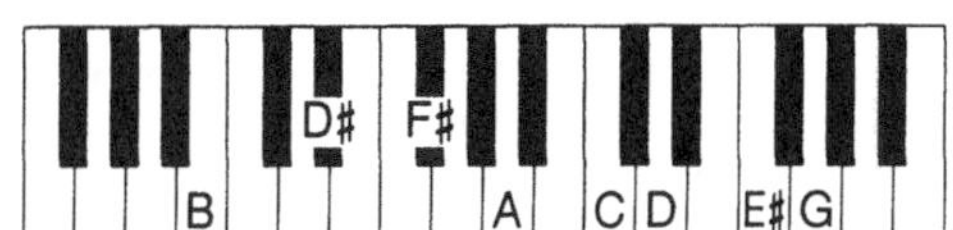

KEYBOARD STYLE SERIES

THE COMPLETE GUIDE!

These book/audio packs provide focused lessons that contain valuable how-to insight, essential playing tips, and beneficial information for all players. From comping to soloing, comprehensive treatment is given to each subject. The companion audio features many of the examples in the book performed either solo or with a full band.

BEBOP JAZZ PIANO
by John Valerio
This book provides detailed information for bebop and jazz keyboardists on: chords and voicings, harmony and chord progressions, scales and tonality, common melodic figures and patterns, comping, characteristic tunes, the styles of Bud Powell and Thelonious Monk, and more.
00290535 Book/Online Audio $21.99

BEGINNING ROCK KEYBOARD
by Mark Harrison
This comprehensive book/audio package will teach you the basic skills needed to play beginning rock keyboard. From comping to soloing, you'll learn the theory, the tools, and the techniques used by the pros. The accompanying audio demonstrates most of the music examples in the book.
00311922 Book/Online Audio $16.99

BLUES PIANO
by Mark Harrison
With this book/audio pack, you'll learn the theory, the tools, and even the tricks that the pros use to play the blues. Covers: scales and chords; left-hand patterns; walking bass; endings and turnarounds; right-hand techniques; how to solo with blues scales; crossover licks; and more.
00311007 Book/Online Audio $22.99

BOOGIE-WOOGIE PIANO
by Todd Lowry
From learning the basic chord progressions to inventing your own melodic riffs, you'll learn the theory, tools and techniques used by the genre's best practicioners.
00117067 Book/Online Audio $17.99

BRAZILIAN PIANO
by Robert Willey and Alfredo Cardim
Brazilian Piano teaches elements of some of the most appealing Brazilian musical styles: choro, samba, and bossa nova. It starts with rhythmic training to develop the fundamental groove of Brazilian music.
00311469 Book/Online Audio $19.99

CONTEMPORARY JAZZ PIANO
by Mark Harrison
From comping to soloing, you'll learn the theory, the tools, and the techniques used by the pros. The full band tracks on the audio feature the rhythm section on the left channel and the piano on the right channel, so that you can play along with the band.
00311848 Book/Online Audio $19.99

COUNTRY PIANO
by Mark Harrison
Learn the theory, the tools, and the tricks used by the pros to get that authentic country sound. This book/audio pack covers: scales and chords, walkup and walkdown patterns, comping in traditional and modern country, Nashville "fretted piano" techniques and more.
00311052 Book/Online Audio $19.99

GOSPEL PIANO
by Kurt Cowling
Discover the tools you need to play in a variety of authentic gospel styles, through a study of rhythmic devices, grooves, melodic and harmonic techniques, and formal design. The accompanying audio features over 90 tracks, including piano examples as well as the full gospel band.
00311327 Book/Online Adio $19.99

INTRO TO JAZZ PIANO
by Mark Harrison
From comping to soloing, you'll learn the theory, the tools, and the techniques used by the pros. The accompanying audio demonstrates most of the music examples in the book. The full band tracks feature the rhythm section on the left channel and the piano on the right channel, so that you can play along with the band.
00312088 Book/Online Audio $19.99

JAZZ-BLUES PIANO
by Mark Harrison
This comprehensive book will teach you the basic skills needed to play jazz-blues piano. Topics covered include: scales and chords • harmony and voicings • progressions and comping • melodies and soloing • characteristic stylings.
00311243 Book/Online Audio $19.99

JAZZ-ROCK KEYBOARD
by T. Lavitz
Learn what goes into mixing the power and drive of rock music with the artistic elements of jazz improvisation in this comprehensive book and CD package. This instructional tool delves into scales and modes, and how they can be used with various chord progressions to develop the best in soloing chops.
00290536 Book/CD Pack..........$17.95

LATIN JAZZ PIANO
by John Valerio
This book is divided into three sections. The first covers Afro-Cuban (Afro-Caribbean) jazz, the second section deals with Brazilian influenced jazz – Bossa Nova and Samba, and the third contains lead sheets of the tunes and instructions for the play-along audio.
00311345 Book/Online Audio $19.99

MODERN POP KEYBOARD
by Mark Harrison
From chordal comping to arpeggios and ostinatos, from grand piano to synth pads, you'll learn the theory, the tools, and the techniques used by the pros. The online audio demonstrates most of the music examples in the book.
00146596 Book/Online Audio $19.99

NEW AGE PIANO
by Todd Lowry
From melodic development to chord progressions to left-hand accompaniment patterns, you'll learn the theory, the tools and the techniques used by the pros. The accompanying 96-track CD demonstrates most of the music examples in the book.
00117322 Book/CD Pack..........$16.99

HAL•LEONARD®

Prices, contents, and availability subject to change without notice.

www.halleonard.com

POST-BOP JAZZ PIANO
by John Valerio
This book/audio pack will teach you the basic skills needed to play post-bop jazz piano. Learn the theory, the tools, and the tricks used by the pros to play in the style of Bill Evans, Thelonious Monk, Herbie Hancock, McCoy Tyner, Chick Corea and others. Topics covered include: chord voicings, scales and tonality, modality, and more.
00311005 Book/Online Audio $19.99

PROGRESSIVE ROCK KEYBOARD
by Dan Maske
You'll learn how soloing techniques, form, rhythmic and metrical devices, harmony, and counterpoint all come together to make this style of rock the unique and exciting genre it is.
00311307 Book/Online Audio $19.99

R&B KEYBOARD
by Mark Harrison
From soul to funk to disco to pop, you'll learn the theory, the tools, and the tricks used by the pros with this book/audio pack. Topics covered include: scales and chords, harmony and voicings, progressions and comping, rhythmic concepts, characteristic stylings, the development of R&B, and more! Includes seven songs.
00310881 Book/Online Audio $22.99

ROCK KEYBOARD
by Scott Miller
Learn to comp or solo in any of your favorite rock styles. Listen to the audio to hear your parts fit in with the total groove of the band. Includes 99 tracks! Covers: classic rock, pop/rock, blues rock, Southern rock, hard rock, progressive rock, alternative rock and heavy metal.
00310823 Book/Online Audio $17.99

ROCK 'N' ROLL PIANO
by Andy Vinter
Take your place alongside Fats Domino, Jerry Lee Lewis, Little Richard, and other legendary players of the '50s and '60s! This book/audio pack covers: left-hand patterns; basic rock 'n' roll progressions; right-hand techniques; straight eighths vs. swing eighths; glisses, crushed notes, rolls, note clusters and more. Includes six complete tunes.
00310912 Book/Online Audio $19.99

SALSA PIANO
by Hector Martignon
From traditional Cuban music to the more modern Puerto Rican and New York styles, you'll learn the all-important rhythmic patterns of salsa and how to apply them to the piano. The book provides historical, geographical and cultural background info, and the 50+-tracks includes piano examples and a full salsa band percussion section.
00311049 Book/Online Audio $19.99

SMOOTH JAZZ PIANO
by Mark Harrison
Learn the skills you need to play smooth jazz piano – the theory, the tools, and the tricks used by the pros. Topics covered include: scales and chords; harmony and voicings; progressions and comping; rhythmic concepts; melodies and soloing; characteristic stylings; discussions on jazz evolution.
00311095 Book/Online Audio $19.99

STRIDE & SWING PIANO
by John Valerio
Learn the styles of the stride and swing piano masters, such as Scott Joplin, Jimmy Yancey, Pete Johnson, Jelly Roll Morton, James P. Johnson, Fats Waller, Teddy Wilson, and Art Tatum. This book/audio pack covers classic ragtime, early blues and boogie woogie, New Orleans jazz and more. Includes 14 songs.
00310882 Book/Online Audio $22.99

WORSHIP PIANO
by Bob Kauflin
From chord inversions to color tones, from rhythmic patterns to the Nashville Numbering System, you'll learn the tools and techniques needed to play piano or keyboard in a modern worship setting.
00311425 Book/Online Audio $19.99